Key Thinkers of the Radical Right

Key Thinkers of the Radical Right

Behind the New Threat to Liberal Democracy

Edited by
MARK SEDGWICK

OXFORD
UNIVERSITY PRESS

Oxford University Press is a department of the University of Oxford. It furthers
the University's objective of excellence in research, scholarship, and education
by publishing worldwide. Oxford is a registered trade mark of Oxford University
Press in the UK and certain other countries.

Published in the United States of America by Oxford University Press
198 Madison Avenue, New York, NY 10016, United States of America.

© Oxford University Press 2019

All rights reserved. No part of this publication may be reproduced, stored in
a retrieval system, or transmitted, in any form or by any means, without the
prior permission in writing of Oxford University Press, or as expressly permitted
by law, by license, or under terms agreed with the appropriate reproduction
rights organization. Inquiries concerning reproduction outside the scope of the
above should be sent to the Rights Department, Oxford University Press, at the
address above.

You must not circulate this work in any other form
and you must impose this same condition on any acquirer.

Library of Congress Cataloging-in-Publication Data
Names: Sedgwick, Mark J., editor.
Title: Key thinkers of the radical right : behind the new threat to liberal democracy /
edited by Mark Sedgwick.
Description: New York, NY : Oxford University Press, 2019. |
Includes bibliographical references and index.
Identifiers: LCCN 2018040312 (print) | LCCN 2018050950 (ebook) |
ISBN 9780190877606 (updf) | ISBN 9780190877613 (epub) |
ISBN 9780190877583 (hardback) | ISBN 9780190877590 (paperback) |
ISBN 9780190926793 (online content)
Subjects: LCSH: Conservatism—Philosophy. | Political science—
Philosophy—History. | BISAC: POLITICAL SCIENCE / Government /
Comparative. | POLITICAL SCIENCE / History & Theory.
Classification: LCC JC573 (ebook) | LCC JC573 .K38 2019 (print) |
DDC 320.52—dc23
LC record available at https://lccn.loc.gov/2018040312

9 8 7 6 5 4 3 2 1

Paperback printed by Webcom, Inc., Canada
Hardback printed by Bridgeport National Bindery, Inc., United States of America

Contents

List of Contributors   vii

Introduction—MARK SEDGWICK   xiii

PART I: *Classic Thinkers*

1. Oswald Spengler and the Decline of the West—DAVID ENGELS   3
2. Ernst Jünger and Storms of Steel—ELLIOT Y. NEAMAN   22
3. Carl Schmitt and the Politics of Identity—REINHARD MEHRING   36
4. Julius Evola and Tradition—H. THOMAS HAKL   54

PART II: *Modern Thinkers*

5. Alain de Benoist and the New Right—JEAN-YVES CAMUS   73
6. Guillaume Faye and Archeofuturism—STÉPHANE FRANÇOIS   91
7. Paul Gottfried and Paleoconservatism—SETH BARTEE   102
8. Patrick J. Buchanan and the Death of the West—EDWARD ASHBEE   121
9. Jared Taylor and White Identity—RUSSELL NIELI   137

10. Alexander Dugin and Eurasianism—MARLENE LARUELLE   155

11. Bat Ye'or and Eurabia—SINDRE BANGSTAD   170

PART III: *Emergent Thinkers*

12. Mencius Moldbug and Neoreaction—JOSHUA TAIT   187

13. Greg Johnson and Counter-Currents—GRAHAM MACKLIN   204

14. Richard B. Spencer and the Alt Right—TAMIR BAR-ON   224

15. Jack Donovan and Male Tribalism—MATTHEW N. LYONS   242

16. Daniel Friberg and Metapolitics in Action—BENJAMIN TEITELBAUM   259

Select Bibliographies   277

Index   293

Contributors

Edward Ashbee is director of the International Business and Politics BSc and MSc programs at Copenhagen Business School, Denmark. He has had articles published in journals such as *Political Quarterly, Parliamentary Affairs, Global Discourse, Society, Journal of Political Power,* and *Journal of American Studies*. His recent work includes *The Right and the Recession* (2015) and *The Trump Revolt* (2017). He also coedited *The Obama Presidency and the Politics of Change* (2017).

Sindre Bangstad is a Norwegian social anthropologist with a background in ethnographic studies of Muslims in South Africa and Norway, and a researcher at KIFO (the Institute for Church, Religion, and Worldview Research) in Oslo. Bangstad, who has published extensively on secularism, racism, Islamophobia, right-wing extremism, hate speech, and right-wing populism in Norway, holds a cand. polit. degree from the University of Bergen in Norway and a PhD from Radboud University in Nijmegen in the Netherlands. He is a columnist at *Anthropology News* and has published in popular outlets such as *Boston Review, The Guardian* (UK), *Open Democracy,* the SSRC's *The Immanent Frame,* and in leading anthropological journals such as *American Ethnologist, American Anthropologist, Anthropological Theory, Anthropology Today,* and *Social Anthropology*. Among his books are *Anders Breivik and the Rise of Islamophobia* (2014), *The Politics of Mediated Presence: Exploring the Voices of Muslims in Norway's Contemporary Mediated Public Spheres* (2015), and *Anthropology of Our Times: An Edited Volume in Public Anthropology* (2017).

Tamir Bar-On received his PhD from McGill University. He is a professor-researcher in the School of Social Sciences and Government, *Tec de Monterrey* (Mexico). A member of Mexico's National System for Researchers since 2015, Bar-On is the author of *Where Have All The Fascists Gone?* (2007), *Rethinking the French New Right: Alternatives to*

Modernity (2013), *The World through Soccer: The Cultural Impact of a Global Sport* (2014), and *Beyond Soccer: International Relations and Politics as Seen through the Beautiful Game* (2017).

Seth Bartee is an Assistant Professor of History at Guilford Technical Community College in Jamestown, North Carolina. Currently, Prof. Bartee is serving as a New City Fellow in Raleigh, North Carolina and a Visiting Scholar at The Kirk Center in Mecosta, Michigan. Bartee is an intellectual historian and an active member of The Society for US Intellectual History.

Jean-Yves Camus is director of the Observatoire des radicalités politiques (ORAP) at the Jean Jaurès Foundation (Paris) and a Research Fellow at the Institut de relations internationales et stratégiques (IRIS). His last book (with Nicolas Lebourg), *Far Right Politics in Europe*, was published by Harvard University Press in 2017. He has also written extensively on the European New Right and the links between Russia and the European Far Right. On those topics, he contributed to Marlene Laruelle's *Eurasianism and the European Far Right: Reshaping the Europe-Russia Relationship* (2015) and to *Les Faux-semblants du Front national: Sociologie d'un parti politique* (2015), edited by Sylvain Crépon, Alexandre Dézé, and Nonna Mayer.

David Engels is professor of Roman history at the Université libre de Bruxelles, Belgium. He has published numerous articles and books on Roman Religion, Hellenistic Statecraft, the Reception of Antiquity, and the Philosophy of History. Among his best-known works is *Le déclin: La crise de l'Union européenne et la chute de la République romaine: Analogies historiques* (2013), translated since then into numerous languages. He also edited a survey of cyclical theories in the Philosophy of History titled *Von Platon bis Fukuyama* (2015).

Stéphane François has a PhD in political science and is an associated member of Groupe Sociétés Religions Laïcités (CNRS/Ecole Pratique des hautes Etudes). He is a specialist on the French extreme Right. His most recent books include *Histoire de la haine identitaire: Mutations et diffusions de l'altérophobie* (with Nicolas Lebourg, 2016), *L'Extrême droite et l'ésotérisme: Retour sur un couple toxique* (2016), *Le Retour de Pan:. Panthéisme, néo-paganisme et antichristianisme dans l'écologie radicale* (2016), *Les Mystères du nazisme:. Aux sources d'un fantasme contemporain* (2015), and *Au-delà des vents du Nord: L'extrême droite française, le Pôle nord et les Indo-Européens* (2014).

Hans Thomas Hakl is the founder of *Gnostika*, a German academic-esoteric magazine where he serves as coeditor. He has edited works by Julius Evola, Eliphas Lévi, Gérard Encausse ("Papus"), Maria De Naglowska, Hans Freimark, and others. He is a contributor to the *Dictionary of Gnosis and Western Esotericism* (2003) and to the new edition of the *Encyclopedia of Religions* (2005). His main work, *Eranos: An Alternative Intellectual History of the Twentieth Century*, was published by McGill-Queen's University Press in 2013. Hakl has translated four books of Evola into German and written more than thirty articles (including introductions, reviews, and dictionary entries) on various aspects of Evola in German, Italian, English, and French. Hakl met Evola shortly before his death.

Marlene Laruelle is an associate director and research professor at the Institute for European, Russian, and Eurasian Studies (IERES), Elliott School of International Affairs, The George Washington University. Laruelle is also a codirector of PONARS (Program on New Approaches to Research and Security in Eurasia), director of the Central Asia Program at IERES and a researcher at EUCAM (Europe-Central Asia Monitoring), Brussels. Laruelle received her PhD in history at the National Institute of Oriental Languages and Cultures (INALCO) and her postdoctoral degree in political science at Sciences-Po in Paris.

Matthew N. Lyons has been writing about right-wing politics for more than twenty-five years. His work focuses on the interplay between social movements and systems of oppression. He is coauthor with Chip Berlet of *Right-Wing Populism in America* (2000) and lead author of *Ctrl-Alt-Delete: An Antifascist Report on the Alternative Right* (2017). His essays have appeared in many periodicals and on the radical antifascist blog *Three Way Fight*.

Graham Macklin is an Assistant Professor/Postdoctoral Fellow at the Center for Research on Extremism (C-Rex) in Oslo, Norway, and an Honorary Fellow, Parkes Institute for the Study of Jewish/Non-Jewish Relations, Southampton University, United Kingdom. He has published widely about extreme right-wing politics in Britain in both the interwar and postwar period including *"Very Deeply Dyed in Black": Oswald Mosley and the Resurrection of British fascism after 1945* (2007). His forthcoming monograph *White Racial Nationalism in Britain* in Britain will be published by Routledge in 2019 as will two coedited collections, *Transnational*

Extreme Right-wing Networks and *Researching the Far Right: Theory, Method and Practice*. His research has been funded by local and national government as well as the European Union (H2020). He is also coeditor of the Routledge Studies in Fascism and the Far Right book series.

Reinhard Mehring is professor of political science at the University of Education Heidelberg. He has a PhD in political science from the University of Freiburg and a *Habilitation* from the Humboldt University of Berlin. His books include *Carl Schmitt zur Einführung* (1992, 5th ed. 2017), *Carl Schmitt: Aufstieg und Fall: Eine Biographie* (2009, translated as *Carl Schmitt: A Biography*, 2014), *Kriegstechniker des Begriffs: Biographische Studien zu Carl Schmitt* (2014), and *Carl Schmitt: Denker im Widerstreit: Werk–Wirkung–Aktualität* (2017).

Elliot Neaman is professor of modern European intellectual history at the University of San Francisco, where he has taught since 1993. He specializes in European political thought, ideology, and theory. His first book, *A Dubious Past: The Politics of Literature after Nazism* (1999), was on the writer Ernst Jünger. His latest book features the West German student movement, *Free Radicals* (1999). Neaman has also written extensively about other major European thinkers, including Martin Heidegger, Carl Schmitt, Georges Sorel, and Jacques Derrida. He also publishes in European newspapers on contemporary issues, particularly geopolitics and economics. His current research project focuses on espionage in the Federal Republic. Neaman teaches courses in intellectual history, modern German history, world history after 1945, and in the USF Honors Program.

Russell Nieli received his PhD from Princeton University where he specialized in political philosophy and the interface between religion and politics. He is a lecturer in Princeton University's Politics Department, and is a senior preceptor in Princeton's James Madison Program in American Ideals and Institutions. Nieli is the author of *Wittgenstein: From Mysticism to Ordinary Language,* and in recent years has written extensively on race relations in the United States, which he approaches from the perspective of classical liberalism and what he calls "theocentric humanism." In his book *Wounds That Will Not Heal* (2012), he takes up the continuing controversy over racial preference policies in the United States with a special focus on American universities. He is currently working on a book that explains the forces that can hold America together despite its vast demographic diversity in terms of race, ethnicity, religion, and collective achievement.

Mark Sedgwick was born in England and studied history at Oxford University before emigrating to Egypt. He did a PhD at the University of Bergen in Norway, taught history at the American University in Cairo, and then moved to Denmark to teach in the Department of the Study of Religion at Aarhus University. He was secretary of the European Society of the Study of Western Esotericism, and first became aware of the connections between esotericism and radical politics while working on his PhD.

Joshua Tait is a doctoral candidate in history at the University of North Carolina. His dissertation explores the intellectual origins of conservatism and right-wing engagement with the "American Political Tradition." Originally from New Zealand, he lives in Chapel Hill, NC.

Benjamin R. Teitelbaum is assistant professor of ethnomusicology and affiliate in International Affairs at the University of Colorado. His commentary on Western ultraconservatism, culture, and politics has appeared in *Foreign Policy*, the *New York Times*, the *Wall Street Journal* as well as on Swedish Radio, and his academic essays have appear in *Ethnomusicology, Patterns of Prejudice, Scandinavian Studies, Arkiv*, and *Current Anthropology*. His first book, *Lions of the North: Sounds of the New Nordic Radical Nationalism*, was published in 2017 by Oxford University Press.

Introduction

Mark Sedgwick

THE RADICAL RIGHT was once generally imagined in terms of skinheads, tattoo parlors, and hooligans. While all of these do play a role, there is much more to the contemporary radical Right than this. There is also an intellectual radical Right, little known to most, but increasingly important. The central purpose of *Key Thinkers of the Radical Right*: Behind the New Threat to Liberal Democracy is to explore it.

The existence of an intellectual radical Right is not a new phenomenon. Many prominent thinkers from the French Revolution to the Second World War could be put in this category. The horrors of the war and of the Nazi camps, however, contributed to a general reaction against the radical Right that led to its disappearance from mainstream politics and to its eclipse in intellectual life. For many decades, a new liberal orthodoxy ruled across the West, apparently unchallenged.

Since the start of the twenty-first century, the mainstream has been shifting. In Europe, "populist" political parties have pulled the mainstream in their direction, and the liberal orthodoxy of the postwar period is ever less hegemonic. In the US, a series of challenges to the Republican mainstream culminated in the 2016 election of Donald Trump, and America's liberal orthodoxy is also challenged. The reasons for these developments are many and complex, and it is not the objective of this book to add to what has already been written about them. Rather, the objective is to contribute to the understanding of one of the consequences of the general shift toward the Right: the new importance of the thinkers of the radical Right.

There are many problems of definition and classification involved in writing about the radical Right. Terms such as "Far Right" and "Extreme Right" are widely used and are thus useful for denoting the phenomenon in question, but they are less useful for defining or delimiting it. There is no general agreement as to where the mainstream ends and the extreme starts, and if there ever had been agreement on this, the recent shift in the mainstream would challenge it. Terms such as "Fascism" and "neo-Nazism" are also widely used but refer to political parties that rose and fell in historical circumstances very different from today's, and so have limited value in a contemporary context. Nazi symbolism may sometimes be used for its countercultural shock value, but there is no serious movement to reestablish the Nazi Party, and it is hard to imagine what real neo-Nazism would look like. Among contemporary thinkers of the radical Right, only one of any importance (Greg Johnson) expresses any sympathy for Nazism.

The radical Right, too, has its own terminology. The term "New Right" is often used, and the term "Alt Right" has recently come into prominence. There are also nationalists, identitarians, libertarians, neoconservatives, paleoconservatives, counter-jihadists, and neoreactionaries. These differ in important ways, but all have something in common.

The approach taken by this book is to avoid questions of definition and classification by focusing on thinkers who are widely read in all these circles, in the US and in Europe. The thinkers who are discussed have been selected on a number of bases. The selection reflects the editor's own view of the significance of different thinkers, and also the views of American and European scholars working on the right who were consulted by the editor. Reference has also been made to authors promoted on important rightist websites such as Arktos, which has a European emphasis, and Counter-Currents, which has an American emphasis, both of which are discussed in the book, and to the views of selected participants in the radical right scene. The key question has been whether a thinker is widely read today, whatever the period in which he (or, occasionally, she) wrote. Only thinkers with a major current international audience have been included. Many interesting contemporary thinkers writing in French or German who have a primarily national audience have thus been excluded. Thinkers who are also widely read outside the radical Right, and who for that reason are already widely known, have also been excluded. In some ways this is unfortunate, as the exclusion of Nietzsche and Heidegger implies a greater divide between the radical Right and the more general intellectual scene than actually exists. But many excellent discussions of Nietzsche and Heidegger are already available elsewhere.

Like all such selections, this book's choice of key thinkers is somewhat arbitrary. In the end, it is representative rather than exhaustive. This is especially true when it comes to younger thinkers. It is easier to identify the now classic thinkers who wrote in the early and middle twentieth century than it is to identify more modern thinkers,[1] and harder still to identify the key thinkers who are emerging today, as there are many more of them, and it is impossible to predict which will remain important.

Despite these limitations, this book gives a good idea of the thought of the "radical" Right—a term that is used as it carries somewhat less baggage than most alternatives. The book deliberately avoids making political judgments or value judgments. Its contributors write as scholars, not activists, and its purpose is likewise scholarly. Attempts were made to contact all the living thinkers covered, who were offered the opportunity to suggest corrections of any errors they found. Not everyone responded to these attempts, and not everyone then agreed to read and comment, but the comments of those who did provide them were all taken into account. Each chapter, however, is the responsibility of the author concerned.

The book is divided into three sections. It starts with four "classic" thinkers: Oswald Spengler, Ernst Jünger, Carl Schmitt, and Julius Evola. These four are classic in the sense that, along with Nietzsche and Heidegger, they are required reading for today's intellectual radical Right. Three of them were German (as, of course, were Nietzsche and Heidegger), part of the informal group that was later identified as forming a "Conservative Revolution," a group to which the fourth classic thinker, Evola, an Italian, was close. All save Spengler were active in the period in which their countries were under Nazi or Fascist rule, but only one, Schmitt, was an active member of the Nazi Party. Jünger was courted by the Nazis, but neither he nor Spengler supported them, Evola at times supported both the Fascists and the Nazis, but he was never a member of the Fascist Party. It is important, then, to distinguish between this group of classic thinkers of the radical Right and the historical Nazism and Fascism with which they were contemporary. Only one of the classic thinkers of the radical Right (Schmitt) was ever really a Nazi or Fascist, though one other (Evola) did have a strong relationship with both Nazism and Fascism.

All of these classic thinkers save Spengler wrote their most important work during the interwar period, and were thus marked by the First World War, either directly or indirectly. Spengler wrote his most important work, *The Decline of the West* (*Der Untergang des Abendlandes*), during the war, when a German victory was still possible. Schmitt was also marked by the troubles of the Weimar Republic, in which, as a constitutional lawyer, he was personally involved. All save Spengler, who died in 1936, also wrote in the postwar period, but only Evola's postwar work equals his interwar work in importance. There were, of course, many other comparable thinkers in the same period, from the official ideologists of Nazism and

Fascism to individual thinkers such as the English writer Hilaire Belloc. These other thinkers, however, are generally no longer much read. Belloc, ironically, is now remembered primarily as the author of *Cautionary Tales for Children* and of other books of verse that remain popular in Britain and which might be compared to the works of Dr. Seuss in America.

Spengler is best known for *The Decline of the West*, which was only incidentally political. It aimed to develop a philosophy of history through a comparative analysis of past cultures and civilizations, and on this basis concluded that the West had reached the stage development where decline would inevitably set in from about 2000. *The Decline of the West* introduces two ideas that remain central to the radical Right: apocalyptic visions of decline, and a focus on cultures and civilizations rather than on nations and states.

Jünger, likewise, was also only incidentally political. He is best known for his *Storm of Steel* (*In Stahlgewittern*), a book more literary than political, presenting the experience of war in heroic style, in stark contrast to alternative works such as Erich Maria Remarque's *All Quiet on the Western Front* (*Im Westen nichts Neues*)—also a literary work with political significance. Jünger's work did, however, draw explicit political consequences from the *Storm of Steel*: that the liberal nineteenth century was dead. In this he effectively agreed with Spengler. Jünger stands in today's radical Right for the virile and the heroic, for struggle. He was also the earliest key thinker of the radical Right in whom we find concern about the rise of a global cosmopolitan elite lacking specific cultural roots, a concern that is of great importance today.

Schmitt, in contrast, was directly political, though his primary focus was law, especially constitutional law. Schmitt attacked many of the assumptions of the political liberalism of his time, and especially the liberal parliamentary state. He was a distinguished academic scholar, and his arguments were complex in a way that the arguments of Spengler and Jünger were not. They have since been developed by the Left as well as the Right. Most significant for the radical Right, perhaps, is his distinction between friend and enemy—his argument that what ultimately underpins politics is the fundamental distinction between us and them, friend and enemy, and that any state must ultimately reflect this fundamental basis of the community. Schmitt's concept of the political emphasized the individual political community against liberal universalism, which he saw as a cover for economic interests and as doomed to failure, given that it denied the most important basis of the political community, the distinction between friend and enemy. Schmitt thus continues and develops the suspicion of the global universal elite that we find in Jünger.

Schmitt also developed the distinction between the "State of Normality" (*Normalzustand*) and the quasi-apocalyptic "State of Emergency" or "State of Exception" (*Ausnahmezustand*) to argue that any community had or needed a sovereign, and that under certain circumstances this sovereign could best represent the political community in a dictatorial state governed not by law but by decree. The ultimate objective, however, was the State of Normality, the stabilization of political forms as legal relationships. The antidemocratic potential of such arguments is obvious, and Schmitt used them to support the Third Reich. Schmitt also participated in the persecution of the Jews under Nazism, somewhat ironically, given that he also had close intellectual and personal relationships with individual Jews, both before and after the Third Reich.

Evola also addressed the political directly, though his own point of departure was not political but philosophical and spiritual. For Evola, the concept of "tradition" derived from the French esotericist René Guénon, leads directly to political consequences, both for political authority (which must be connected to the transcendent) and for society (which must be hierarchical). It also leads to an apocalyptic vision of inevitable decline. The tradition that Evola himself preferred was the pagan tradition, an anti-Christian position also found elsewhere in the radical Right. The concept of tradition was the basis of his engagement with Fascism and Nazism, and is why this strain of the radical Right is termed "Traditionalism." The concept of tradition also underlay Evola's postwar work, some of which developed a theory of *apoliteia*, especially in his *Ride the Tiger* (*Cavalcare la tigre*), his most important postwar book. The tiger that must be ridden until it collapses from exhaustion is modernity. *Apoliteia* is either a complete retreat from politics or an engagement in politics that does not allow one to be inwardly affected. Quite which Evola meant, and quite what the relationship is between *apoliteia* and political violence, remains controversial. *Apoliteia*, however, has been important to the radical Right, as has the idea of riding the tiger, an idea that fits with Jünger's heroic vision and also with Spengler's apocalypticism and Schmitt's State of Exception.

The book's second section covers seven "modern" thinkers: Alain de Benoist, Guillaume Faye, Paul Gottfried, Patrick J. Buchanan, Jared Taylor, Alexander Dugin, and "Bat Ye'or" (a pen name). All of these are still alive and form the generation succeeding the "classic" thinkers, writing under very different circumstances, and addressing not the interwar but the postwar world. All are explicitly political.

Two of the book's modern thinkers—de Benoist and Faye—are French, major figures in the so-called New Right (*Nouvelle Droite*) that emerged in the 1960s in parallel to the better-known New Left of the same period, and responding to similar stimuli. Antonio Gramsci, the Italian neo-Marxist of the interwar period whose thought was so important for postwar neo-Marxism and the New Left, was also of great importance for the French New Right, which embraced his view that political revolution starts with intellectual revolution: once the way people think about certain issues changes, political and social change inevitably follows. This idea, known as "Metapolitics," became central to the French New Right and then to other parts of the radical Right. The French New Right became a reference point for the radical Right elsewhere in the West, and especially for the single Russian thinker covered in the book, Dugin.

De Benoist drew on Nietzsche and Heidegger and on the classic thinkers of the radical Right, especially Jünger (whom he knew, and whose concept of the Anarch inspired him), Schmitt (whose distinction between friend and enemy he used), and Spengler. Like Evola, de Benoist is a self-declared pagan. He echoes Spengler's understanding of cultures, though he is interested in smaller communities than Spengler was. Like Jünger, he is alarmed by what he saw as a homogenizing "ideology of sameness" promoted by egalitarianism.[2] Against this he pitches the "right to be different," which he developed into "ethnopluralism," the idea of communities based on ethnicity rather than territory, called "ethnospheres" by Faye.[3] De Benoist and Faye were concerned about threats to European traditions and culture during the Cold War, and initially saw both the Soviet Union and the United States as a threat. Faye, but not de Benoist, then came to see Muslim immigration and Islam as the threat, and the pairing of Muslim immigration and ethnopluralism became characteristic of radical-Right thought, one of the main bases of identitarianism, which stresses the importance of protecting ethnic identities. Muslim immigration was not the only threat that Faye saw in an apocalyptic "convergence of catastrophes,"[4] which in effect constituted Schmitt's State of Exception and required a dictatorial response, but it was one of the most urgent.

Three other "modern" thinkers in this section of the book—Gottfried, Buchanan, and Taylor—are American, men who in different ways established intellectually sophisticated positions to the right of mainstream Republicanism, the space that had previously been occupied by the

"Straussians," conservatives who claimed the mantle of Leo Strauss, and neoconservatives. Gottfried and Buchanan are both "paleoconservatives," an important strain in the American radical Right. Gottfried, who was fluent in German and thus could continue interwar European debates in the postwar American context, argued against Strauss for reference to history and tradition as a weapon against liberalism and progressivism. Gottfried also echoed Schmitt in suspicion of global liberal elites, which he saw as perpetually adrift, the basis of what he called the "managerial state," working against the traditional bases of society.[5] Gottfried was thus also a traditionalist, though in a very different way from Evola. This alternative form of Traditionalism became especially important for the American radical Right, and also the "Alt Right," a term that Gottfried may have helped to invent.

Buchanan was an experienced political actor and TV journalist who could translate intellectual arguments into something that could be used as a basis for political mobilization. Like Gottfried, he believed that American society was based not on abstract universal principles (as many mainstream Republicans held) but on its history, on its white European (and not just its WASP) heritage. He saw this heritage as threatened by mass immigration, not of Muslims (as was the case with Faye) but of Mexicans. He also feared an apocalyptic *Death of the West* (the title of one of his most important books) through demographic collapse, at the root of which he saw the influence of Gramsci and the Frankfurt School. As Gottfried echoed Schmitt in suspicion of global liberal elites and the "managerial state," Buchanan took aim at the "placeless" managerial class. He ultimately brought together three powerful ingredients: an emphasis on the white European community, a hostility to globalist elites, and concern with immigration. This combination would later—during Trump's 2016 presidential campaign—prove to be a winner.

Taylor, in contrast to Gottfried and Buchanan, wrote especially about race, an issue that has concerned parts of the postwar American Right much more than it concerned the postwar European Right. This reflects the specificities of American history, and the continuing influence of such interwar American writers on race and eugenics as Madison Grant and Lothrop Stoddard, thinkers who are little known outside the United States. The approach taken to race by Taylor and many other American thinkers of the radical Right contrasts with that of the classic thinkers of the interwar period, notably Spengler, who criticized the idea of an Aryan race and preferred to think in terms of independent "cultures," and Evola, who likewise criticized the biological base of Nazi racial dogma. Taylor, though recognizing the importance of culture and of the historical basis of any nation, also stresses genetics. Despite the difference between this view of race and French New Right views on ethnicity Taylor identifies as an identitarian, formed links with the European radical Right, and is especially appreciative of Faye's work. Like Buchanan, he stands against mass immigration.

As Taylor drew on a distinctively American tradition, Dugin also drew on the distinctively Russian tradition of Eurasianism, as well as on Heidegger and the classic radical thinkers of the Conservative Revolution and Traditionalism, and on the French New Right, especially de Benoist, from whom he borrowed an emphasis on ethnopluralism. He adjusted both classic and modern French thinking for Russian conditions, which include a multiethnic state rather than a homogeneous nation, and for contemporary international relations. His neo-Eurasianism also appeals outside Russia in countries that are not comfortable with an American-led unipolar world. He is now perhaps more influential abroad than in Russia itself, due to the effectiveness of his activism as much as to his thought.

Faye was not the only modern thinker to focus on Islam and immigration. There was also Bat Ye'or, a thinker whose intellectual roots are very different from those of the other key thinkers of the radical Right, and who is also different in being female. All the other key thinkers discussed in the book are male, which is not a coincidence, as will become clear below. Bat Ye'or developed the ideas of "Eurabia" and "dhimmification," powerful representations of the threat thought to be posed to Europe by Muslim states and immigration, a threat that for some took on apocalyptic tones and is central for many parts of today's radical Right. The threat comes in part from Arab Muslims but most importantly from the "faceless networks of a huge administration,"[6] Bat Ye'or's version of the global liberal elites that had concerned Schmitt, Gottfried, and Buchanan. The idea that while the distant threat comes from Islam, the immediate threat that comes from one's own liberal elites has become very important to some sections of the radical Right. Bat Ye'or drew on other anti-Islamic writers such as the Italian journalist Oriana Fallaci, but what was most important for her work was probably her part in Israel's struggles and her position in Israeli politics. Her work was a major inspiration for the Norwegian terrorist Anders Behring Breivik. The extent to which fear of "Islamization," a form of Bat Ye'or's dhimmification, has become widespread among the general population of the West, and the consequences of this for mainstream politics, is an excellent example of metapolitics at work.

The book's final section looks at five "emergent" thinkers. It is of course impossible to say which of these five will actually definitively emerge and achieve status and significance comparable to that which the thinkers covered in the book's first two sections have already achieved. They are all of a younger generation, addressing today's audience, mostly on the internet, and have been chosen because they represent some of the directions in which the thought of the radical Right is now developing. They are "Mencius Moldbug" (a pen name), Greg Johnson, Richard B. Spencer, Jack Donovan, and Daniel Friberg. All are American save Friberg, who is Swedish. To some extent, this American emphasis reflects the way in which the European radical Right is still dominated by thinkers of an earlier generation, especially the French New Right and Dugin. It also reflects the way that it takes time before an author who writes in a language other than English is translated into English and can achieve the sort of international readership that has been one of the criteria for inclusion in this book. Friberg, like many Swedes, is as proficient in English as in Swedish and has increasingly been writing in English.

Moldbug and Johnson are both former libertarians. Moldbug draws on Gramsci's analysis of hegemonic intellectual elites, and Johnson draws directly on the French New Right and on the idea of metapolitics (as well as on Heidegger and Traditionalism). Moldbug, like many other key thinkers, warns against progressive elites and their universalism, the egalitarian rhetoric that conceals their rule, and the "feedback loop" of which they are part, which he labels "the Cathedral."[7] He goes farther than most on the radical Right in directly and explicitly condemning democracy as a mask for the Cathedral, preferring hierarchy (like Evola) to democracy. Johnson, who runs the important website Counter-Currents, is perhaps the most radical of the contemporary thinkers of the radical Right, certainly in ethnic and racial terms. He is unusual in being distinctly anti-Semitic, a position held otherwise only by Schmitt, and then really only during the Third Reich. As well as subscribing to the Traditionalist narrative of inevitable decline, Johnson sees an apocalyptic risk of "demographic Armageddon,"[8] and calls explicitly for forced population transfer and the nonlethal ethnic cleansing of both Jewish and black Americans to allow a white "ethnostate," with blacks getting their own ethnostate in the American South, and Jews moving to Israel. It is Johnson who, alone among modern and contemporary key thinkers of the radical right, expresses sympathy for Nazism. In a typical month in 2017, his Counter-Currents website attracted two hundred thousand visitors who viewed 1.5 million pages of content.

Spencer, who like Gottfried claims to have invented the term "Alt Right" (and who did establish the website AlternativeRight.com), is probably America's best-known radical-Right figure, largely due to the scandal that followed the use of the Fascist salute in conjunction with calls of "Hail Trump" at an event he organized in late 2016. His positions closely resemble those of Johnson, down to the ethnic cleansing, and he too combines American and European influences, and has worked with both Gottfried and Taylor. He follows Buchanan in stressing white America's European heritage, and also claims to be inspired by Nietzsche, the Conservative Revolution, Evola, the French New Right, and Dugin. It is not clear, however, what he is really closer to—the New Right or classic American white racism. He has something of a portmanteau approach, which includes concerns about Muslim immigration, more appropriate for European than for American circumstances.

If Moldbug, Johnson, and Spencer in some ways all resemble familiar "white nationalist" figures, Donovan is distinctly unusual: a homosexual man, he prioritizes gender over race or ethnicity.[9] Questions of gender were, of course, also important for the radical Right before Donovan. The martial virtues that mattered to Jünger and Evola are associated with men, and gender was explicitly a major issue for Spengler, who saw the mature phase of any culture as "virile, austere, controlled, intense"[10] and identified the feminine with anarchy, and for Evola, who identified the male with the upwardly directed heroic, and the female with the earthward and downward. Evola also wrote about the metaphysics of sex as a means of access to the transcendent. Modern and contemporary thinkers also address feminism, which for Buchanan is one of the causes of the demographic collapse of Western Europe and the consequent risk of the death of the West, and which for Taylor has led to out-of-wedlock births and consequent social problems in America. Johnson also attacks feminism. For all these, however, gender is ultimately incidental, while for Donovan it is central.

For Donovan, the threat of apocalypse comes from feminism and "globalist civilization,"[11] and also from liberal elites motivated by their own economic interests. The key political community, based in the end on the same distinction between friend and enemy that Schmitt developed, is the all-male gang or the tribe. Donovan is, like Evola and de Benoist, a self-declared pagan, belonging to a neopagan group that draws on Evola.

He has sometimes written approvingly of the European New Right, but is perhaps more influenced by what he calls "Ur-fascism," the fascism found in various countries between the 1920s and 1940s.[12] He for some time cooperated closely with Johnson and Counter-Currents. Although in some ways Donovan's thought seems unusual—especially given that to be openly homosexual is not a stance that is generally welcomed on the Right—it is also in some ways the culmination of other trends noted in *Key Thinkers of the Radical Right*.

The last of the book's emergent thinkers, Friberg, is, as has been said, a Swede. Metapolitics is central to his thought, and most visible in action. His Nordiska förbundet (Nordic League) promoted Traditionalism in Sweden and the Nordic region, and operated an alternative to Wikipedia, called Metapedia, that soon had three hundred thousand articles in sixteen languages. His English-language *Arktos* then became the world's largest publisher of radical-Right and Traditionalist literature. In 2017, he formally joined forces with Spencer.

All these key thinkers of the radical Right have something in common. They are nowadays read by the same people, and they read each other and refer to each other. They also have major themes in common. The four key themes in their work are (1) apocalypticism, (2) fear of global liberal elites, (3) the consequences of Schmitt's friend-enemy distinction (which include ethnopluralism), and (4) the idea of metapolitics.

Apocalypticism starts with Spengler's *Decline of the West*. The war that Jünger wrote about was inherently apocalyptic, and there was also something of the apocalyptic about Schmitt's vision of the transformation of the State of Normality into the State of Exception. Evola's vision of postwar modernity was also apocalyptic, as were de Benoist's fears for the extinction of European civilization during the Cold War, and fears for the extinction of European (or perhaps Judeo-Christian) civilization as a result of the mass immigration of Muslims, found in Faye and Bat Ye'or. Similar apocalyptic visions of decline are found in Buchanan's *The Death of the West*, in the work of Dugin, who follows Evola, and in Moldbug, Johnson, and Donovan.

The apocalypse is often associated with liberal elites, concern about which starts with Jünger's fear of the rootless global cosmopolitan elite and continues in Schmitt's struggle against liberal universalism. In the postwar period, the same concern is found in de Benoist and in Buchanan's fear of the "managerial state," in Gottfried, and then in Moldbug's "the Cathedral," and subsequently throughout the Alt Right.

Schmitt's friend-enemy distinction gives rise to a conception of the political community that fits neither the classic conceptions of the state nor of the nation. In the postwar period this conception, whether or not taken directly from Schmitt, is one of the sources of the French New Right's concept of ethnopluralism, a concept shared in different ways with Buchanan, Gottfried, and Dugin, and which then becomes hegemonic in the Alt Right, which combines it with interwar American writing on race.

Most hegemonic of all, though, at least in the postwar and contemporary periods, is the French New Right's concept of metapolitics, developed from Gramsci by de Benoist and Faye and others, then used by Moldbug and especially Johnson, and finally the basis of Friberg's thoughts and activities.

In addition to these four major key themes, there are also a number of other, less prominent, recurring themes. One of them—the respect for heroic struggle that starts with Jünger—is found in Evola's individual riding the tiger of modernity, and is again found in Donovan's fighting gang. This is related to the views on gender of Spengler and Evola, and views on gender are in turn linked to the antifeminism of Buchanan, Taylor, Johnson, and Donovan. Another recurring theme is the concept of tradition that starts with Guénon and is developed by Evola and used by Dugin, Moldbug, and Donovan, which should not be confused with the Traditionalism of Gottfried and Buchanan. Evola's Traditionalism is linked with his paganism and in the paganism that is also found in de Benoist and Donovan.

Finally, there are the distinctively American recurring concerns with race, found in Taylor, Moldbug, Johnson, and Spencer, and echoed by Donovan, and the distinctively European concern with mass immigration and Islam, found in Faye, Bat Ye'or, and Friberg. These concerns, which are not found in the classic thinkers of the radical Right, combine with concerns about apocalyptic threats and liberal elites, and with the friend-enemy distinction.

Race, Islam, and elites are especially important issues today because, more than the other themes common to the key thinkers of the radical Right, they have easy resonance at the street level, and in electoral politics. Apocalyptic visions of decline certainly played a part in the US 2016 election but have less wide appeal. Concern with gender has some resonance, but little wide appeal, and respect for martial virtues and reference to transcendent tradition have no appeal for contemporary electorates. They may, however, still be important to the private views of political actors who themselves have wide appeal, and Evola has been recommended on the websites of two European political parties, Golden Dawn (Chrysí Avgí) in Greece and Jobbik (Right Choice) in Hungary. Golden Dawn has never won more than 7 percent of the Greek national vote, but Jobbik won 20 percent of the Hungarian national vote in 2014. Jobbik's leader Gábor Vona wrote the foreword to an Evola collection published by Friberg's *Arktos*. Almost none of Golden Dawn's or Jobbik's voters will have heard of Evola, and even fewer would share his views on gender, war, or paganism, but Evola's thought is still of indirect importance for Greek and Hungarian politics, as it undoubtedly is for the politics of other countries whose politicians are more cautious about what they put on their websites and which authors and publishers they write forewords for. In the US, for example, President Trump's former "chief strategist," Steve Bannon, has referred to Evola and Dugin only obliquely, and has only once mentioned his appreciation of Guénon, the French esotericist who inspired both Evola and Dugin.[13] These key thinkers of the radical Right, then, matter everywhere that the Right is resurgent, in America as much as in France, Greece, Russia, and Hungary.

Notes

1. One of the inspirations of this book has been Kurt Lenk, Günter Meuter, and Henrique Ricardo Otten, *Vordenker der Neuen Rechten* [Key Thinkers of the New Right] (Frankfurt: Campus Verlag, 1997). This work by three German scholars, which has been translated into French but not into English, discusses six key thinkers, three of whom are also discussed in this book. The three that are not discussed are Heidegger, for reasons given earlier, Georges Sorel, and Hans Freyer. None of these, though undoubtedly important, especially in a German context, is now widely read internationally.
2. Alain de Benoist, *Vu de droite* (Arpajon: Editions du Labyrinthe, 2001), xii.
3. Guillaume Faye, *Pourquoi nous combattons: manifeste de la résistance européenne* (Paris: L'Æncre, 2001), 119.
4. Guillaume Corvus, *La convergence des catastrophes* (Paris: Diffusion International Éditions, 2004).
5. Paul Gottfried, *After Liberalism: Mass Democracy in the Managerial State* (Princeton, NJ: Princeton University Press, 1999).
6. Bat Ye'or, *Eurabia: The Euro-Arab Axis* (Madison, NJ: Farleigh Dickinson Press, 2005), 20.
7. Mencius Moldbug, "OL9: How to Uninstall a Cathedral," *UR*, June 12, 2008, https://unqualified-reservations.blogspot.com/2008/06/ol9-how-to-uninstall-cathedral.html.

8. Greg Johnson, "November 9, 2016," accessed December 14, 2017, https://www.counter-currents.com/2016/11/november-9-2016/.
9. He rejects the label "gay."
10. Oswald Spengler, *Der Untergang des Abendlandes: Umrisse einer Morphologie der Weltgeschichte* (Munich: C. H. Beck, 1922), 1:107–108.
11. Jack Donovan, *The Way of Men* (Milwaukie, OR: Dissonant Hum, 2012), 139.
12. Donovan, "Anarcho-Fascism," Jack Donovan, March 3, 2013, archived March 3, 2017, https://web.archive.org/web/20170331060008/http://www.jack-donovan.com/axis/2013/03/anarcho-fascism/.
13. Jason Horowitz, "Steve Bannon Cited Italian Thinker Who Inspired Fascists," *New York Times*, February 10, 2017, https://www.nytimes.com/2017/02/10/world/europe/bannon-vatican-julius-evola-fascism.html; Joshua Green, *Devil's Bargain: Steve Bannon, Donald Trump, and the Nationalist Uprising* (New York: Penguin Press, 2017), 204–207.

PART I

Classic Thinkers

1

Oswald Spengler and the Decline of the West

David Engels

"IN THIS BOOK is attempted for the first time the venture of predetermining history, of following the still untraveled stages in the destiny of a culture, and specifically of the only culture of our time and on our planet which is actually in the phase of fulfillment—the West-European-American."[1] These are the bold first words of Oswald Spengler's *The Decline of the West* (*Der Untergang des Abendlandes*), the aim of which was to sketch the potential future of the West on the basis of the method of cultural comparison, and to provide the blueprint for each and every human high culture. Spengler often considered himself one of the last representatives of the bourgeois society of the eighteenth and nineteenth centuries, and felt deeply unhappy with the twentieth century, an impression of "untimeliness," which also characterized several of his contemporaries, such as Thomas Mann and Hermann Hesse. This explains the nostalgic overtones in Spengler's writings as well as his (unconvincing) attempts at overcoming his melancholy by posing as a dogged advocate of technology, imperialism, and mass civilization.

Oswald Spengler's fame is based on his *The Decline of the West*, a monumental historical study that endeavored to show that all human civilizations live through similar phases of evolution, roughly equivalent to the different ages of a biological entity. During the 1920s, Spengler's ideas were much debated not only in Germany but everywhere in Europe and America, and though the academic world remained generally skeptical, Spengler's prophecy of the impending decline and ultimate fall of

Western civilization influenced many writers and artists, then and now. Spengler also dabbled in politics and attempted, in a series of smaller essays such as *Prussianism and Socialism*, *Political Duties of German Youth*, and *Building the German Empire Anew*, to promote the idea of a conservative renaissance in Germany.[2]

The rise of National Socialism gradually put Spengler in a situation of ideological opposition, illustrated by his *The Hour of Decision*, which criticized Hitler's racial theory and made him persona non grata.[3] After the Second World War, Spengler's elitism and his expectation of the advent of a German-dominated Europe as a modern equivalent of the Roman Empire overshadowed the reception of his work until the 1990s. This somewhat masked the complexity of his thought, which prefigures such modern debates as the criticism of technology, ecological issues, interreligious questions, the rise of Asia, and prehistoric human evolution. However, since the end of the Cold War, Spengler's work has been gradually rediscovered and discussed, and gives an intriguing—if highly controversial—perspective on the numerous challenges the Western world has been confronted with since the beginning of the twenty-first century.

Life and context

Oswald Arnold Gottfried Spengler was born on May 29, 1880, at Blankenburg, Harz, in Germany, the son of Bernhard Spengler, a stern and anti-intellectual official in the post office, and Pauline Grantzow, the somewhat depressive descendant of an artistic family.[4] Oswald was the oldest surviving child of their union, which also brought forth three girls, Adele, Gertrud, and Hildegard, the youngest of whom later lived with her brother as his housekeeper. In 1891 the family moved to Halle an der Saale, where Spengler was educated as a pupil of the Francke Foundations, a religiously motivated educational institution strongly influenced by Protestant Pietism. The siblings later on remembered their childhood as difficult and sad, and Oswald, also suffering from severe headaches, tried to secure some form of inner autonomy by keeping away from his schoolmates, indulging in the most diverse autodidactic studies, describing, in great detail, imaginary world empires,[5] and writing, at seventeen, a drama titled *Montezuma*.[6]

Exempted from military service because of a severe heart problem, Spengler took courses in mathematics, natural sciences, and philosophy at the universities of Halle, Munich, and Berlin, and received, in 1904, his PhD with a thesis on Heraclitus, "The Fundamental Metaphysical Thought of the Heraclitean Philosophy."[7] In 1905 he also submitted the secondary dissertation (*Staatsexamensarbeit*) needed to become a high-school teacher, this time on the evolution of the eye, "The Development of the Organ of Sight in the Higher Realms of the Animal Kingdom."[8] Despite his loathing for teaching (he reportedly suffered a nervous breakdown merely from looking at his first school), Spengler seems to have been appreciated by his pupils, though not by his colleagues, and he successively worked as a teacher in Saarbrücken, Düsseldorf, and Hamburg until 1911, when the small inheritance he received on the death of his mother (his father had died in 1901) enabled him to retire from teaching and live as an independent writer.

Spengler moved to Munich and started to write, alongside numerous smaller contributions for various journals and several (abortive) novels, his major scholarly work, *The Decline of the West*. The composition of this work, taking almost seven years, was particularly difficult, as is shown by Spengler's diaries from this period, *Eis heauton* ("On himself"), which permit valuable insights into his tormented personality and his permanent self-doubts.[9] The first volume of the *Decline of the West* appeared in 1918, shortly before the end of the First World War, and instantly made him a celebrity. While writing the second volume (published in 1922, followed by a revised edition of the first, varying marginally in style but not in content), Spengler also began to reflect on the German defeat and to actively engage with contemporary political questions. The first result was the publication, in 1919, of *Prussianism and Socialism*, followed by numerous shorter texts, which only marginally added to the positions developed in *The Decline of the West*, such as *Political Duties of German Youth* and *Building the German Empire Anew*. A confirmed bachelor and a man permanently riddled with deep psychological issues, Spengler never started a family but lived with his sister Hildegard, who had moved to Munich after her husband's death and acted as Spengler's housekeeper.[10]

After becoming something of a celebrity and, given his growing interest not only in political but also in economic and financial politics,[11] Spengler endeavored to get involved in politics in a decidedly conservative and elitist way.[12] His attempts, including his support in 1924 for General Hans von Seeckt's unsuccessful run at power, only demonstrated his personal shortcomings when it came to understanding the intrigues of everyday politics and to dealing with opponents and rivals. Over the following decade, Spengler slowly dropped his political ambitions and concentrated instead on reassessing questions that *The Decline of the West* had left open, though he was severely hampered in his work by health issues, which included a cerebral hemorrhage in 1927. In 1931 he published *Man and Technics*, a visionary reflection on the history and environmental shortcomings of technology from earliest times to the predicted end of the West.[13]

Unfortunately, the major monograph Spengler had started to sketch after the publication of *The Decline of the West* never reached completion and remained a collection of shattered fragments and aphorisms. However, the material, edited posthumously,[14] is substantial enough to indicate the outlines and general content of the project.[15]

Spengler's last years were overshadowed by the rise of Hitler. While Spengler, on the basis of his comparative method, had considered the transformation of ultracapitalist mass democracies into dictatorial regimes as inevitable, and had expressed some sympathy for Mussolini's Fascist movement as a first symptom of this development (a sympathy returned by Mussolini, who favored the translation of Spengler's writings into Italian),[16] he took a much more critical view of National Socialism. As admirer of the spirit of the old Prussian aristocracy, he loathed what he saw as the proletarian and demagogic character of Hitler's party and, given his own assumption of a radical parallelism between all past and present civilizations, considered the Aryan racial doctrine to be nonsense.[17] Despite a personal and deeply unsatisfying meeting with Hitler himself and the regime's initial endeavor to win him over in order to benefit from his international standing, Spengler gradually expressed his open contempt for the alleged "national uprising," culminating in his publication of *The Hour of Decision* (*Jahre der Entscheidung*) in 1933, in which he openly criticized the new regime, though from the antiliberal perspective resulting from his belief in the inevitable trend of history.[18] In 1934 Spengler even pronounced the funeral oration for one of the victims of Hitler's crushing of the (alleged) Röhm Putsch and, in 1935, he retired from the board of the highly influential Nietzsche Archive because of its outspoken support for the new regime. After having predicted the end of the Third Reich within the next ten years,[19] Spengler died of a heart attack on May 8, 1936. The *Festschrift* devoted to him by some of his admirers was published quietly;[20] a contribution promised by Mussolini was retracted,[21] probably in order to avoid diplomatic frictions.

Inspirations

In the introduction to *The Decline of the West*, Spengler felt the urge "to name once more those to whom I owe practically everything: Goethe and Nietzsche. Goethe gave me method, Nietzsche the questioning faculty."[22] Although the influence of Goethe's vitalism—mostly his interest in botanic sciences and what he called the "primordial plant" as the blueprint for all other living entities—and of Nietzsche's cultural criticism can indeed be felt everywhere,[23] Goethe and Nietzsche (neither of whom was a proper historian) were not Spengler's only sources. Spengler himself, as like every self-declared genius, generally insisted on the absolute "novelty" of his theory:

> The system that is put forward in this work ... I regard as the Copernican discovery in the historical sphere, in that it admits no sort of privileged position to the Classical or the Western Culture as against the Cultures of India, Babylon, China, Egypt, the Arabs, Mexico—separate worlds of dynamic being which in point of mass count for just as much in the general picture of history as the Classical, while frequently surpassing it in point of spiritual greatness and soaring power.[24]

This assertion, however, is not unproblematic. The scholarly literature cited by Spengler in his footnotes shows the wide array of the works he consulted, many of which prefigured some key features of his theory, including the universal and cyclical approach of world history, which was taken from the distinguished German academic historian Eduard Meyer, whom Spengler greatly appreciated. It is also clear that large parts of Spengler's personal worldview were deeply influenced by contemporary concepts in the philosophy of vitalism,[25] the belief that all living organisms as well as their social creations are fundamentally different from inorganic entities and submitted to their own set of laws characterized not merely by the mechanics of action and reaction but by the fate of birth, blossom, decline, and death. Furthermore, the idea that civilizations broadly follow the evolutionary steps of a living being and can thus be compared with reference to this common pattern goes back to classical antiquity and even beyond, although we cannot be sure to what extent Spengler himself was aware of this.[26] Cato the Elder, Cicero, Seneca, Florus, and Ammianus Marcellinus had all compared the rise, maturity, and decline of the Roman state to the different ages of man, an approach which exerted a tremendous influence on many later historians including even Francis Bacon, who used the biological analogy in order to compare different empires with each other. To some extent, this pattern also underlay another, equally influential interpretation of history, that of the dialectic approach first formulated in the theologico-historical speculations of Joachim of Fiore, who compared the history of salvation to the three persons of the Holy Trinity, and the philosophy of history of Hegel, who compared not only the three dialectical phases of human evolution to the three ages of man but who also tried, rather like Giambattista Vico, to show how the spirit of every people (*Volksgeist*) in itself evolved in a dialectical and biological way.[27]

Nevertheless, Spengler is right in claiming that nobody in Western thought had pushed historical comparatism to such a degree as himself. Although he engaged for the most part with the classical, Arab, and European civilizations and barely sketched the broad outlines of the others, the effort and knowledge poured into *The Decline of the West* was unequaled until Toynbee's monumental *Study of History*, and Spengler's book made a thorough impression on his readers, even those who did not accept his hypothesis.

Key issues and key ideas

Spengler's historical philosophy was based on two basic assumptions. On the one hand, Spengler assumed the existence of social entities called "cultures" (*Kulturen*) as the largest possible actors in human history which, in itself, has no real philosophical aim or metaphysical sense:

> "Mankind" . . . has no aim, no idea, no plan, any more than the family of butterflies or orchids. "Mankind" is a zoological expression, or an empty word. . . . I see, in place of that empty figment of one linear history which can only be kept up by shutting one's eyes to the overwhelming multitude of the facts, the drama of a number of mighty Cultures, each springing with primitive strength from the soil of a mother region to which it remains firmly bound throughout its whole life-cycle; each stamping its material, its mankind, in its own image; each having its own idea, its own passions, its own life, will and feeling, its own death.[28]

These cultures—according to Spengler, nine (the Egyptian, the Babylonian, the Indian, the Chinese, the Greco-Roman, the "Magic" or "Arabic," which included early and Byzantine Christianity as well as Islam, the Mexican, the Western, and, finally, the Russian)—coexist in time and space and thus interact to some degree with each other, but have no real "internal" connection with one another. Their evolution thus only follows their own inner logic and cannot be influenced by outer factors, except for the "Mexican culture," literally "beheaded" by the conquistadores—a further and sad proof for the absence of any proper "sense" in history, if one is to believe Spengler.

Spengler's second major hypothesis is that the inner evolution of these cultures is essentially parallel and corresponds exactly to the evolutionary stages of a living being, an idea deeply rooted (as we saw) not only in the philosophy of vitalism as it developed during the nineteenth century but ultimately going back to antiquity:

> Cultures are organisms, and world-history is their collective biography. Morphologically, the immense history of the Chinese or of the Classical Culture is the exact equivalent of the petty history of the individual man, or of the animal, or the tree, or the flower.[29]

However, Spengler does not confine his analogies to botanical images. He also uses the paradigm of the different ages of man and even the rhythm of the four seasons as comparative foil, tying his analysis to a string of poignant metaphors all linked to the cycle of life, and differentiated enough to permit a subtle and suggestive description of the different evolutionary steps of each culture, as is also demonstrated through his use of these topoi in a series of synchronoptic comparative tables. Though somewhat long, the following quotation contains not only the blueprint of the evolution of each culture in a nutshell and brilliantly illustrates his play with historical references and allusions but also demonstrates the literary, nearly poetic quality Spengler tried to achieve:

> Every Culture passes through the age-phases of the individual man. Each has its childhood, youth, manhood and old age. It is a young and trembling soul, heavy with misgivings, that reveals itself in the morning of Romanesque and Gothic. It fills the Faustian landscape from the Provence of the troubadours to the Hildesheim cathedral of Bishop Bernward. The spring wind blows over it. . . . Childhood

speaks to us also—and in the same tones—out of early-Homeric Doric, out of early-Christian (which is really early-Arabian) art and out of the works of the Old Kingdom in Egypt that began with the Fourth Dynasty.... The more nearly a Culture approaches the noon culmination of its being, the more virile, austere, controlled, intense the form-language it has secured for itself, the more assured its sense of its own power, the clearer its lineaments. In the spring all this had still been dim and confused, tentative, filled with childish yearning and fears—witness the ornament of Romanesque Gothic church porches of Saxony and southern France, the early-Christian catacombs, the Dipylon vases. But there is now the full consciousness of ripened creative power that we see in the time of the early Middle Kingdom of Egypt, in the Athens of the Pisistratids, in the age of Justinian, in that of the Counter-Reformation, and we find every individual trait of expression deliberate, strict, measured, marvelous in its ease and self-confidence. And we find, too, that everywhere, at moments, the coming fulfilment suggested itself; in such moments were created the head of Amenemhet III (the so-called "Hyksos Sphinx" of Tanis), the domes of Hagia Sophia, the paintings of Titian. Still later, tender to the point of fragility, fragrant with the sweetness of late October days, come the Cnidian Aphrodite and the Hall of the Maidens in the Erechtheum, the arabesques on Saracen horseshoe-arches, the Zwinger of Dresden, Watteau, Mozart. At last, in the grey dawn of Civilization, the fire in the Soul dies down. The dwindling powers rise to one more, half-successful, effort of creation, and produce the Classicism that is common to all dying Cultures. The soul thinks once again, and in Romanticism looks back piteously to its childhood; then finally, weary, reluctant, cold, it loses its desire to be, and, as in Imperial Rome, wishes itself out of the overlong daylight and back in the darkness of protomysticism, in the womb of the mother, in the grave.[30]

This description clearly defines the actual situation and imminent future of the Western world, which has entered, since Napoleon (the rough equivalent of Alexander), the late stage of the petrification of a culture into a civilization (*Zivilisation*), characterized by technology, expansion, imperialism, and mass society, and is expected to fossilize and decline from the year 2000 on. This dichotomy between "culture" and "civilization," central to the understanding of Spengler's historical philosophy, is another concept deeply anchored in nineteenth-century German thought, for example in Schiller's 1795 treatise on naïve and sentimental poetry or in Thomas Mann's *Reflections of an Unpolitical Man*.[31] Accordingly, Spengler describes the current, "civilized" state of the West as follows:

> A century of purely extensive effectiveness, excluding big artistic and metaphysical production—let us say frankly an irreligious time which coincides exactly with the idea of the world-city—is a time of decline. True. But we have not chosen this time. We cannot help it if we are born as men of the early winter of full Civilization, instead of on the golden summit of a ripe Culture, in a Phidias or a Mozart time. Everything depends on our seeing our own position, our destiny, clearly, on our realizing that though we may lie to ourselves about it we cannot evade it. He who does not acknowledge this in his heart, ceases to be counted among the men of his generation, and remains either a simpleton, a charlatan, or a pedant.[32]

One of the consequence of Spengler's cultural monism is the debate about the extent to which cultures and civilizations are able to influence each other or even to merge. According to Spengler, who seems to be using the classic German concept of the *Volksgeist* (national character) first developed by Herder, each of these nine cultures is characterized by a specific, inimitable "soul image" (*Seelenbild*) or worldview, which is largely inaccessible to anyone from the outside. This also explains why any real intercultural dialog or fusion is considered as thoroughly impossible: the takeover of the spiritual or artistic creations of other cultures can be based only on their misinterpretation and must remain superficial, comparable to the use of architectural remnants of bygone societies through misplaced *spolia*.[33]

Whereas such a monolithic hypothesis is not difficult to uphold when it comes to describing the evolution of spatially rather isolated cultures such as the Chinese, Egyptian, or Indian, it becomes very difficult to argue the case for full cultural self-sufficiency for those overlapping each other, a fact most notable in Late Antiquity. This problem prompted Spengler to surmise that the whole first-millennium Near East was not, in fact, a mere "transition" between Classical Antiquity, Western Christianity, and Islam, but rather a wholly new and distinct culture (labeled "Arabian" or "Magic") merely borrowing its formal language partly from its Greco-Roman, partly from its Babylonian predecessor, but filling it with a totally new content, a feature Spengler calls, in analogy to "pseudomorphosis," a mineralogical phenomenon. Unsurprisingly, Spengler's endeavor to explain Messianic Judaism, Zoroastrianism, early Christianity, and Islam as different expressions of a unique cultural worldview distinct from that of other cultures has provoked many criticisms, even though it prefigured, at the same time, the attempts of recent research to focus less on the differences than rather on the intense interactions of the first millennium as a "supermarket of religions."[34]

Spengler's determinist view of history has prompted many to label him a "pessimist" and to consider his philosophy as ultimately promoting fatalism and inaction. Spengler always denied such an attitude and—influenced by Nietzsche's heroic "Amor fati"—invited his readers to adopt a "realistic" approach toward the limited possibilities of the aging Western culture, to accept the inevitable outcome of the history of the next generations, and to do their best within the limits of the possible instead of fighting a lost battle for ideals long dead, while fully realizing that "optimism is cowardice."[35] Thus, in the last lines of the *Decline of the West*, he refers the reader to the philosophy of Stoicism when quoting Seneca in order to demonstrate his own view of a "heroic" pessimism, based on the acceptance of the inevitable:

> For us, however, whom a Destiny has placed in this Culture and at this moment of its development—the moment when money is celebrating its last victories, and the Caesarism that is to succeed approaches with quiet, firm step—our direction, willed and obligatory at once, is set for us within narrow limits, and on any other terms life is not worth the living. We have not the freedom to reach to this or to that, but the freedom to do the necessary or to do nothing. And a task that historic necessity has set will be accomplished with the individual or against him. *Ducunt Fata volentem, nolentem trahunt* [fate guides the willing, but drags the unwilling].[36]

Reception

The reception of Spengler is essentially bipartite. During the 1920s, he was one of the most discussed intellectuals of the Western world, his theory considered either as a thorough revolutionizing of the writing of history or as the fruit of mere dilettantism. Even though the scholarly reception remained rather skeptical, the poetical qualities of Spengler's work and the suggestiveness of his pessimistic and tragic worldview made him very popular with many artists, not only in Europe but also in America. The Second World War proved an important hiatus: whereas the previous reception had focused on his achievements as a comparatist historian of past civilizations, his work was now reduced to its prophecy of the end of democracy and the rise of Caesarism, and accordingly considered as illiberal. Only since the end of the Cold War has Spengler's work triggered a new interest and led to a reevaluation, which is still in full course.

Prewar reception

The early reception of Spengler's *The Decline of the West* was a phenomenon of its own: everywhere in Europe, journalists and scholars discussed the interest, validity, and shortcomings of Spengler's "morphology of history." It would take us too long to discuss different positions in detail, even more so as the early reception has already been presented and analyzed in detail by Manfred Schröter in 1922.[37] Let us only stress that the discussion around Spengler rapidly became not only a German or even a European but an international phenomenon,[38] given the rapidity with which his work was translated into numerous other languages. Academic historians only reluctantly participated in this debate and, with a few notable exceptions such as Eduard Meyer or Ernst Kornemann, either ignored Spengler's work or drew attention only to selected inaccuracies related to their own fields. Very few historians or philosophers tried to discuss the validity of Spengler's theory in its entirety, an endeavor rendered even more complex by the intimate links between Spengler's analysis of the past and his claims concerning the advent of Caesarism and an inevitable impending showdown between the German and the Anglo-Saxon model of politics and society. This topic was mainly developed in *Prussianism and Socialism*, where the conflict is seen as a mere modern variation on the wars between Rome and Carthage, Spengler's personal sympathies lying, unsurprisingly, on the German rather than the Anglo-Saxon side, while he considered France as historically "finished."[39]

With some notable exceptions such as the Hispanic philosophy of history, where José Ortega y Gasset and Ernesto Quesada were deeply influenced by Spengler, and the juridical profession, where Spengler's theory on Roman and Germanic law was heavily discussed,[40] it was mainly in the domain of literature that Spengler's vision of a "declining"

West characterized by a dwindling creative impetus made the strongest impression. This is not altogether surprising, given that Spengler focused in large part on aesthetics[41] and tried to confer an inimitable literary quality to his own work, once characterized by the German novelist Thomas Mann as a "highly entertaining intellectual novel."[42] Outside Germany, where the book especially interested Thomas Mann and Hermann Hesse,[43] it seems to have been essentially the English-speaking world where Spengler's thought rapidly entered the literary creations of writers as different as Henry Miller, Francis Scott Fitzgerald, and H. P. Lovecraft,[44] and where even some historians such as Arnold Toynbee and Philip Bagby endeavored to develop Spengler's approaches further.

The rise of National Socialism in 1933 represented a hiatus in the reception of Oswald Spengler. While Spengler found himself persona non grata in Nazi Germany and was publicly attacked by the proponents of the new regime as a "reactionary,"[45] his patriotic hope (not uncommon at that period) that Germany might constitute the nucleus of a future European-style Roman Empire was erroneously amalgamated, abroad, with the reigning National Socialist ideology and seen as its direct forerunner.[46] This was only very partly justified. Admittedly, Spengler helped to discredit the Weimar Republic because of his criticism of contemporary democracy as a mere transition toward Caesarism, and the collapse of the Weimar Republic indeed enabled Hitler's takeover. However, from an ideological point of view, National Socialist racial theory and the optimistic hope of creating a thousand-year Reich were fundamentally opposed to Spengler's belief in the irremediable decline of the West, even if under German rule, and his conviction that all human cultures were radically equal.

Postwar reception

Contrary to the expectation of Spengler's family and of some close friends such as the French scholar André Fauconnet, who hoped that the demise of Nazi Germany would finally open up the path to a new, politically more unbiased study of Spengler, the year 1945 brought no change to the increasingly hostile attitude toward the "morphology of history."[47] On the contrary, the hegemonic optimism of an increasingly American-styled capitalism in the West and of Russian-dominated socialism in the East made Spengler's prophecy of the decline and end of the West seem overly pessimistic, perhaps even obsolete—an attitude even more pronounced after 1968 and its hostile stance toward bourgeois historiography and elite culture.

Despite some notable exceptions, such as Henry Kissinger and leading member of the Frankfurt School Theodor Adorno, who once stated that "forgotten, Spengler takes his revenge by threatening to be right. . . . Spengler found hardly an adversary who was his equal; his oblivion is the product of evasion,"[48] and the French scholar Gilbert Merlio, who devoted his influential PhD dissertation on the study of Spengler and his context,[49] Spengler and his philosophy of history were largely forgotten by academia and press alike.[50] When not forgotten, they were merely remembered in the narrower context of the German "Conservative Revolution," perhaps somewhat too simplistically, as Spengler, unlike many other thinkers of the Weimar Republic, had no illusions concerning the ultimate shortcomings of traditional conservatism; he was convinced that Western culture was doomed to decline and fossilize during coming generations, regardless of its political choices.

Only in the late twentieth and early twenty-first centuries has there been something of a renaissance of Spengler, exemplified by an ever-growing series of studies and conferences.[51] The end of the Cold War, the slow decline of Western political domination over the globe, the rise of China, the unification of Europe, the return of religious fundamentalism, the dominant place of Germany within the European Union and the increasing strength of populism have led to a rediscovery of *The Decline of the West*, not only in academia but also in the media. Spengler has again become a figure of interest, and there have even been attempts to reapply Spengler's thought to the political realities and historical knowledge of the twenty-first century.[52]

Conclusion

No consensus has yet been reached on the place Spengler might or should occupy in our endeavor to understand history, and although the current discussion on the *Decline of the West* is becoming more and more lively, it is also characterized by a series of still somewhat monolithic methodological approaches, unwilling to make contact and to soften their positions.[53] However, this conflict is surprisingly representative of the different facets of Spengler's complex thought, situated somewhere in between historiography, philosophy, politics, and prophecy, and should be quickly summarized in order to provide a conclusion and outlook to the present study.

First, there is what might be called an "orthodox" approach, essentially endeavoring to demonstrate the rightness of Spengler's philosophy of history, represented by an admittedly small group often battling with tendencies to make much of Spengler's occasional shortcomings as a historian and to define themselves in relation to Spengler's obvious elitism, a Nietzschean legacy that is unsurprisingly deeply unpopular and disturbing in a period of mass democracy and social inclusiveness.

Then there is what might be called the "moralizing" tendency, characteristic of most discussions of Spengler in the media, and reducing his morphology of history to the cliché of "yet another conservative philosopher" or even of a "precursor of National Socialism." This view exaggerates the limited place contemporary German politics played within Spengler's much larger oeuvre, and it is based on an insufficient distinction between Spengler's admittedly elitist view of social history, his disappointment with the Weimar Republic, and his (unenthusiastic) expectancy of Caesarism as the inevitable fate of every declining civilization.

Finally, we can refer to what may be called "antiquarian" scholarship, to which most of the current literature on Spengler belongs, and which is essentially interested in Spengler as a historical phenomenon while omitting any attempt to discuss or even consider the validity of his thought in itself. Of course, addressing this question is essential not only for the broader study of the intellectual evolution of the 1920s and 1930s but also for a deeper understanding of Spengler's life and work. However, there is an increasing tendency in the study of past philosophical and political thought to be more interested in form than in content, and in history rather than in "truth" (or even probability); most studies belonging to this school are able to propose fascinating enquiries into the psychological roots, sources, context, and reception of Spengler's historical analogies without even once referring to the question of their factual, logical, or metaphysical validity, leaving the general reader somewhat frustrated.

In view of this specific scholarly situation, given that Spengler not only described past events but also dared to forecast at length and with many details the future course of Western history for the next two hundred years, it should be one of the tasks of twenty-first-century scholarship to overcome and transcend the deficiencies of current research. Thus, one hopes that future studies will, on the one hand, finally discuss to what extent the present state of historical research factually confirms, alters, or even invalidates

Spengler's intercultural comparison of past events, and, on the other hand, objectively confront Spengler's prophecies to the actual history of the last decades in order to discuss to what extent his cultural morphology may be considered just another outdated piece of early twentieth-century scholarship or a reliable tool in our endeavor to understand past, present, and future.

Notes

1. Oswald Spengler, *The Decline of the West: Outlines of a Morphology of World History*, trans. Charles Francis Atkinson (New York: Alfred A. Knopf, 1927). Originally published as *Der Untergang des Abendlandes: Umrisse einer Morphologie der Weltgeschichte* (vol. 1, Vienna: Braumüller, 1918; rev. ed. Munich: Beck, 1923; vol. 2, Munich: C. H. Beck, 1922), 1:3.
2. Oswald Spengler, *Preußentum und Sozialismus* (Munich: C. H. Beck, 1919); *Neubau des deutschen Reiches* (Munich: C. H. Beck, 1924); *Politische Pflichten der deutschen Jugend* (Munich: C. H. Beck, 1924).
3. Oswald Spengler, *Jahre der Entscheidung* (Munich: C. H. Beck, 1933).
4. On Spengler's life and times, see in general Anton M. Koktanek, *Oswald Spengler in seiner Zeit* (Munich: C. H. Beck, 1968); Jürgen Naeher, *Oswald Spengler: In Selbstzeugnissen und Bilddokumenten* (Reinbek bei Hamburg: Rowohlt, 1984); Detlef Felken, *Oswald Spengler: Konservativer Denker zwischen Kaiserreich und Diktatur* (Munich: C. H. Beck, 1988); Angela Van der Goten, *Im gespaltenen Zauberland: Oswald Spengler und die Aneignung des Fremden* (Heidelberg: Heidelberger Abhandlungen, 2016).
5. For an analysis of these early fantasies, see Van der Goten, *Im gespaltenen Zauberland*.
6. Oswald Spengler, "Montezuma: Ein Trauerspiel (1897)," in Anke Birkenmaier, *Versionen Montezumas: Lateinamerika in der historischen Imagination des 19. Jahrhunderts* (Berlin: De Gruyter, 2011).
7. "Der metaphysische Grundgedanke der Heraklitischen Philosophie," in *Reden und Aufsätze*, ed. Hildegard Kornhardt (Munich: C. H. Beck, 1937).
8. *Die Entwicklung des Sehorgans bei den Hauptstufen des Tierreiches*, a text now unfortunately lost.
9. Cf. Oswald Spengler, *Ich beneide jeden, der lebt: Die Aufzeichnungen "Eis heauton" aus dem Nachlaß*, ed. Gilbert Merlio (Düsseldorf: Lilienfeld Verlag, 2007).
10. She and her daughter Hilde later tried to organize his literary fragments, and proved important intermediaries between early scholarly research on Spengler and the extant archival material.
11. Cf. Max Otte, "Oswald Spengler und der moderne Finanzkapitalismus," in *Oswald Spenglers Kulturmorphologie—eine multiperspektivische Annäherung*, ed. Sebastian Fink and Robert Rollinger (Berlin: Springer, 2018), 355–392.

12. Cf. Markus Henkel, *Nationalkonservative Politik und mediale Repräsentation: Oswald Spenglers politische Philosophie und Programmatik im Netzwerk der Oligarchen* (Baden-Baden: Nomos, 2012).
13. Oswald Spengler, *Der Mensch und die Technik* (Munich: C. H. Beck, 1931).
14. Oswald Spengler, *Urfragen; Fragmente aus dem Nachlaß*, ed. Anton Mirko Koktanek and Manfred Schröter (Munich: C. H. Beck, 1965); *Frühzeit der Weltgeschichte: Fragmente aus dem Nachlass*, ed. Anton Mirko Koktanek and Manfred Schröter (Munich: C. H. Beck, 1966).
15. Koktanek also published a selection of Spengler's letters permitting insights into the vast network of political and scholarly connections Spengler had managed to build up, and some selected fragments of his other correspondence have been published in other contexts. Oswald Spengler, *Briefe, 1913–1936*, ed. Anton Mirko Koktanek and Manfred Schröter (Munich: C. H. Beck, 1963); Oswald Spengler, *Der Briefwechsel zwischen Oswald Spengler und Wolfgang E. Groeger*, ed. Xenia Werner (Hamburg: Helmut Buske Verlag, 1987). Nevertheless, a substantial amount of material accessible in the Munich Staatsbibliothek library still remains unpublished, not least due to the extreme difficulty of deciphering Spengler's late handwriting, the near illegibility of which is due in part to not only the numerous abbreviations he used but also to the impact his 1927 cerebral hemorrhage had on his psychomotor capacities. See the "Spengler Nachlaß," Sign. Ana 533.
16. Cf. Michael Thöndl, *Oswald Spengler in Italien: Kulturexport politischer Ideen der "Konservativen Revolution"* (Leipzig: Leipziger Universitätsverlag, 2010).
17. Cf. Michael Thöndl, "Das Politikbild von Oswald Spengler (1880–1936) mit einer Ortsbestimmung seines politischen Urteils über Hitler und Mussolini," *Zeitschrift für Politik* 40 (1993): 418–443.
18. Spengler, *Jahre der Entscheidung*.
19. Hans Frank, *Im Angesicht des Galgens* (Neuhaus: Eigenverlag Brigitte Frank, 1955), 247.
20. Paul Reusch and Richard Korherr, eds., *Oswald Spengler zum Gedenken* (Nördlingen: C. H. Beck, 1937).
21. Cf. David Engels, "André Fauconnet und Oswald Spengler (mitsamt der bislang unveröffentlichten Korrespondenz Fauconnets mit August Albers, Hildegard und Hilde Kornhardt und Richard Korherr)," in *Oswald Spengler als europäisches Phänomen*, ed. Zaur Gasimov and Cornelius A. Lemke Duque (Göttingen: Vandenhoeck and Ruprecht, 2013), 105–156.
22. Spengler, *Decline*, vol. 1, xiv.
23. On Spengler, Goethe, and Nietzsche, cf. Uwe Janensch, *Goethe und Nietzsche bei Spengler: Eine Untersuchung der strukturellen und konzeptionellen Grundlagen des Spenglerschen Systems* (Berlin: Wissenschaftsverlag, 2006).
24. Spengler, *Decline*, vol. 1, 18.
25. Cf. in general Hans Joachim Schoeps, *Vorläufer Spenglers: Studien zum Geschichtspessimismus im 19. Jahrhundert* (Leiden: Brill, 1955).

26. David Engels, ed., *Von Platon bis Fukuyama. Biologistische und zyklische Konzepte in der Geschichtsphilosophie der Antike und des Abendlandes* (Brussels: Latomus, 2015).
27. On Hegel and Spengler cf. David Engels, "Ducunt fata volentem, nolentem trahunt. Spengler, Hegel und das Problem der Willensfreiheit im Geschichtsdeterminismus," *Saeculum* 59 (2009): 269–298.
28. Spengler, *Decline*, vol. 1, 21.
29. Ibid., 104.
30. Ibid., 107f.
31. Thomas Mann, *Betrachtungen eines Unpolitischen* (Berlin: Fischer, 1918).
32. Spengler, *Decline*, vol. 1, 44.
33. Ibid., 165.
34. On this problem, see David Engels, "Is There a 'Persian' Culture? Critical Reflections on the Place of Ancient Iran in Oswald Spengler's Philosophy of History," in *Persianism in Antiquity*, ed. Miguel J. Versluys and Rolf Strootman (Stuttgart: Steiner, 2017), 21–44.
35. Spengler, *Der Mensch und die Technik*.
36. Spengler, *Decline*, vol. 2, 507.
37. Manfred Schröter, *Der Streit um Spengler: Kritik seiner Kritiker* (Munich: C. H. Beck, 1922).
38. Cf. e.g., Gasimov and Lemke Duque, eds., *Oswald Spengler als europäisches Phänomen*.
39. This explains, for instance, the very hostile position of the French press, summarized in André Fauconnet, *Oswald Spengler, le prophète du déclin de l'occident* (Paris: Félix Alcan, 1925). See also Engels, "André Fauconnet und Oswald Spengler."
40. Cf. Lutz Keppeler, *Oswald Spengler und die Jurisprudenz* (Tübingen: Mohr Siebeck, 2014).
41. Cf. Marie-Elisabeth Parent, *Recherches sur les éléments d'une conception esthétique dans l'oeuvre d'Oswald Spengle* (Frankfurt/Bern: Peter Lang, 1982); Ingo Kaiserreiner, *Kunst und Weltgefühl: Die bildende Kunst in der Sicht Oswald Spenglers: Darstellung und Kritik* (Frankfurt a.M.: Peter Lang, 1994).
42. Thomas Mann, *Von deutscher Republik* (Berlin: Fischer, 1923).
43. Cf. Barbara Beßlich, *Faszination des Verfalls: Thomas Mann und Oswald Spengler* (Berlin: Akademie Verlag, 2002).
44. Cf. in general Hugh L. Trigg, "The Impact of a Pessimist. The Reception of Oswald Spengler in America 1919–1939" (PhD, Peabody College for Teachers of Vanderbilt University, 1968). See also the two following case studies: David Engels, "'Spengler Emerges Biggest and Best of All': Die Rezeption Oswald Spenglers bei Henry Miller," *Sprachkunst* 43 (2012): 113–130; David Engels, "'This Is an Extraordinary Thing You've Perhaps Heard of': Die Rezeption Oswald Spenglers bei Francis Scott Fitzgerald," in *Spengler ohne Ende*, ed. Gilbert Merlio and Daniel Meyer (Frankfurt a.M.: Peter Lang, 2014), 217–242.

45. For example, Arthur Zweiniger, *Spengler im Dritten Reich: Eine Antwort auf Oswald Spenglers "Jahre Der Entscheidung"* (Oldenburg: Stalling, 1933); Günther Gründel, *Jahre der Überwindung: Umfassende Abrechnung mit dem "Untergangs"-Magier* (Breslau: Korn, 1934).
46. Discussion in Alfred von Martin, *Geistige Wegbereiter des deutschen Zusammenbruchs, Hegel—Nietzsche—Spengler* (Recklinghausen: Bitter, 1948). It is noteworthy that Fauconnet gave a public lecture in France devoted to the question "Spengler a-t-il été national-socialiste?" in August 1945 and answered in the negative: André Fauconnet, "Spengler a-t-il été national-socialiste?" (public conference 1945), in *Mélanges littéraires de l'Université de Poitiers* (1946): 69–79.
47. Correspondence published in Engels, "André Fauconnet und Oswald Spengler"; see also Hildegard Kornhardt's 1941 attempt to launch a small volume with aphorisms, *Gedanken* (Munich: C. H. Beck, ca. 1941).
48. Theodor W. Adorno, "Spengler nach dem Untergang" (1950) in Adorno, *Prismen* (Berlin: Suhrkamp, 1955), 51–81.
49. Gilbert Merlio, *Oswald Spengler: Témoin de son temps* (Stuttgart: Akademischer Verlag Hans-Dieter Heinz, 1982).
50. Some noteworthy exceptions: Manfred Schröter, *Metaphysik des Untergangs: Eine kulturkritische Studie über Oswald Spengler* (Munich: Leibniz Verlag, 1949); Anton M. Koktanek, ed., *Spengler Studien: Festgabe für M. Schröter zum 85. Geburtstag* (Munich: C. H. Beck, 1965); Peter Chr. Ludz, ed., *Spengler heute: Sechs Essays mit einem Vorwort von Hermann Lübbe* (Munich: C. H. Beck, 1980).
51. Klaus P. Fischer, *History and Prophecy: Oswald Spengler and the Decline of the West* (New York: Peter Lang, 1989); Alexander Demandt and John Farrenkopf, eds., *Der Fall Spengler: Eine kritische Bilanz* (Köln: Böhlau, 1994); Karen Swassjan, *Der Untergang eines Abendländers: Oswald Spengler und sein Requiem auf Europa* (Berlin: Raphael Heinrich, 1998); Frits Boterman, *Oswald Spengler und sein "Untergang des Abendlandes"* (Cologne: SH-Verlag, 2000); John Farrenkopf, *Prophet of Decline: Spengler on World History and Politics* (Baton Rouge: Louisiana State University, 2001); Domenico Conte, *Oswald Spengler—Eine Einführung* (Leipzig: Leipziger Universitätsverlag, 2004); Maurizio Guerri and Markus Ophälders, eds., *Oswald Spengler: Tramonto e metamorfosi dell'Occidente* (Milan: Mimesis, 2004); Frank Lisson, *Oswald Spengler: Philosoph des Schicksals* (Schnellroda: Antaios, 2005); Samir Osmancevic, *Oswald Spengler und das Ende der Geschichte* (Vienna: Turia + Kant, 2007); Manfred Gangl, Gilbert Merlio, and Markus Ophälders, eds., *Spengler—Ein Denker der Zeitenwende* (Frankfurt a. M.: Peter Lang, 2009); Dezsö Csejtei and Aniko Juhász, *Oswald Spengler élete és filozófiája* (Máriabesnyő: Gödöllő, 2009); Gasimov and Lemke Duque, eds., *Oswald Spengler als europäisches Phänomen*; Merlio and Meyer, eds., *Spengler ohne Ende*; Arne De Winde et al., eds., *Tektonik der Systeme: Neulektüren von Oswald Spengler* (Heidelberg: Synchron, 2016); Alexander Demandt, *Untergänge des Abendlandes: Studien zu Oswald*

Spengler (Cologne: Böhlau, 2017); Fink and Rollinger, eds., *Oswald Spenglers Kulturmorphologie*; David Engels, Max Otte, and Michael Thöndl, eds., *Der lange Schatten Oswald Spenglers: 100 Jahre Untergang des Abendlandes* (Waltrop: Manuscriptum, 2018).

52. For example, David Engels, *Le Déclin: La crise de l'Union européenne et la chute de la république romaine—analogies historiques* (Paris: Toucan, 2013); David Engels, "Spengler im 21. Jahrhundert: Überlegungen und Perspektiven zu einer Überarbeit der Spengler'schen Kulturmorphologie," in Fink and Rollinger eds., *Oswald Spenglers Kulturmorphologie*, 451–486.

53. See also David Engels, "Déterminisme et morphologie culturelle: Quelques observations méthodologiques autour du 'Déclin de l'Occident' d'Oswald Spengler," forthcoming in *La philosophie allemande de l'histoire*, ed. Louis Carré and Quentin Landenne.

2

Ernst Jünger and Storms of Steel

Elliot Neaman

HALLEY'S COMET IS the only known, short-period, naked-eye comet that humans can possibly observe twice in a lifetime. Ernst Jünger witnessed this celestial wonder in 1910 and then in 1986. He marched off to war in 1914 and lived long enough to see Germany reunified, passing on in 1998, a celebrated centenarian. In this chapter I outline the main turning points in Jünger's long life and track his intellectual development. As a young man he was recognized as a leading figure of the nationalist Right in Germany on the basis of his war diaries and journalistic efforts, but his authorial talents were broader and more profound. His importance lies in the evolution from young radical to an acute observer of Germany's cataclysmic rise and fall under National Socialism, and then his role in the Federal Republic of Germany as a sophisticated voice of classical European conservatism, a sage, and critic of technological modernity.

Early life

Jünger was born 1895 in Heidelberg, the oldest of six children, two of whom did not survive infancy. Of his siblings, he was closest to his younger brother Friedrich-Georg, born in 1898. From his father, Ernst Georg, a chemist, he inherited the sharp analytical skills of a scientist, and from his mother, Karoline Lampl, artistic capacities and an eye for natural beauty.[1] He combined both these artistic and scientific capacities in his writing by developing a penchant for the stereoscopic gaze, whereby a third dimension is added to the normal vision of the left and right eye, a magical and synesthetic quality which he claims takes our understanding deeper into the observable phenomenon. A velvet carnation that emits the fragrance of cinnamon is stereoscopic, for example, because the nose both smells and tastes the qualities of spice simultaneously.[2] One sense organ has to take over the function of another. Jünger may have physically experienced synesthesia, or at least he was able to simulate the ability of having one sense organ take over the function of another in his literary opus.

In his youth Jünger's family moved from place to place, partly in search of a good school for Ernst, who daydreamed too much and got poor grades. In 1913, he struck out for his first genuine adventure. He diverted money given to him to pay for half a year's food at school, boarded a train to Verdun, then to Marseilles, where he lied about his age and joined the French Foreign Legion. His father arranged for his release through the German Foreign Office, instructing the boy to have a photograph taken before leaving.

The First World War

On his return, the young man was promised a trip to Kilimanjaro if he finished school. This plan was interrupted the following year by the guns of August. He finished an emergency high-school degree, volunteered for service, and arrived at the Western Front by December. He quickly earned a reputation as a daring storm trooper. After suffering fourteen battle wounds, he received the Pour le Mérite on September 22, 1918, the highest honor awarded by the Prussian military, rarely given to soldiers of his tender age, or to the infantry, for that matter.

The First World War was the single most defining experience of Jünger's life. He carried a slim notebook with him at all times in battle, sixteen of which he filled with impressions and observations. At the urging of his father, he assembled these notes into a war memoir, titled *In Stahlgewittern*, literally *In Storms of Steel* but better known in English as *Storm of Steel*. This was first self-published in 1920, and then in several heavily revised new editions over the next decade (he even made revisions as late as 1961). The book was influenced by school books of that era, above all Homer and Dante, but also by Nietzsche. Educated German soldiers more often carried *Thus Spake Zarathustra* than the Bible into battle during World War I.[3]

Storm of Steel provided a graphic yet accurate account of the experience of war, which Jünger presented in a heroic and masculine style. By contrast, other war memoirs of that era were often romantic and internally homoerotic, such as *The Wanderer in Two Worlds* by Walter Flex, or pacifist and humanist, like Remarque's best seller from the end of the 1920s, *All Quiet on the Western Front*. Jünger's book and a series of postwar essays such as the "Battle as Inner Experience" (1922) and "Fire and Blood" (1925) transformed the young soldier into a recognized leader of the "New Nationalists," veterans who were intent on bringing their war experiences to bear on the heady politics of the fledgling Weimar Republic. These writers inflated war memories into mythic proportions to justify the enormous loss of life on the battlefields and to create a nationalist and collectively utopian narrative as an alternative to the unpopular republic, which was founded on liberal-democratic principles. Jünger described the experience of battle with astounding clarity, but not without expressionist pathos. In his view, war brings men back into a natural, unchanging order, subject to elementary forces that reveal the primordial violent rhythms of life below the thin veneer of civilization. Some modern critics, such as Klaus Theweleit, have accused Jünger of thus legitimizing the embrace of death and destruction by means of a Fascist literary imagination.[4]

The interwar period

Jünger remained in the *Reichswehr* until 1923 when he left, disillusioned with the empty socializing and alcoholic excesses of his fraternizing officers. He enrolled in the natural sciences in Leipzig for the winter semester of 1923. There he joined the illegal paramilitary *Freikorps* and the legal Veterans' group *Stahlhelm* and began writing for various nationalist newspapers. The years from 1923 to 1927 mark the high point of Jünger's engagement with the young intellectuals whom Armin Mohler later identified as proponents of a "Conservative Revolution" in Germany.[5]

In his 1950 book *The Conservative Revolution in Germany 1918–1932*, Mohler attempted to establish a common identity between many different kinds of writers and thinkers, from fairly obscure and now-forgotten journalists of the Weimar era to highly original thinkers who did not necessarily act or think in concert with one another, such as Carl Schmitt, Martin Heidegger, Julius Evola, Oswald Spengler, Thomas Mann, and Hans Freyer. To add to the somewhat artificial nature of the "revolutionary" designation, Mohler included "father figures" from the nineteenth and early twentieth centuries.

For Mohler, a common theme that characterized the Conservative Revolution was to pit the "ideas of 1914" against the "ideas of 1789." For Jünger's circle, the "ideas" of the 1914–18 war meant an emancipation from liberal civilization and a return to the organic *Volk* (ethnic) community. The war had signaled the death knell for the nineteenth-century belief in progress. These young firebrands did not accept the old conservative desire to uphold the moral and judicial fundamentals of the state. They wanted instead to establish a charismatic base for politics outside democratic institutions and looked for a figure like Louis Napoleon, whose appeal went beyond warring factions, classes, and parties. A social Darwinian influence allowed them to view world politics as a fight for existence in which a national collective either triumphed or was destroyed.[6] Their critique of parliamentary political systems follows in many ways the path laid out by Carl Schmitt in his seminal 1923 essay "The Crisis of Parliamentary Democracy."[7]

Jünger married Gretha von Jeinsen in 1925 and moved to Berlin with their infant son in 1927. He continued to engage in political journalism but moved increasingly away from the fixation on war and nationalism of his Leipzig years. In the new editions of *Storm of Steel*, for example, he removed the opening epigraph "Germany Lives and Germany shall not Perish."[8] His artistic eye shifted to the bustling metropolis whose vitality and energy were on display around the clock. In Berlin he wrote *The Adventurous Heart*, notes written down by "day and night." The first edition, published in 1928, and the second, very different version of 1938 has been called "surrealist," but the approach was only loosely connected with André Breton's famous movement of the same period. Karl-Heinz Bohrer has memorably labeled Jünger's style an "aesthetics of shock," since this book contained a phantasmagoria of scientific and poetic vignettes, a collage of wild associations and ghostly images that recalled the war-inspired art of surrealist and expressionist painters.[9] The method was stereoscopic, a journey into magical sub-realms below everyday existence. A key term Jünger borrowed from the French was *désinvolture*, the casual and innocent observation of reality from a distance (as in Nietzsche's *Unschuld der Werdens*).[10]

As the National Socialists began their final ascent to power after winning 107 seats in the Reichstag in the elections of September 1930, Jünger distanced himself from the Nazi Party while advocating his own, in some ways more radical, version of the nationalist revolution: authoritarian and ruthless, but not racist. He rejected the Nazi fixation with blood and soil. In 1927 he refused to accept an offer from Hitler of a seat in the Reichstag. When the Nazis published excerpts from *Storm of Steel* without permission, he forbade any further use of his writings.[11] The one expressly anti-Semitic tirade that came from his pen during this period was phrased in cultural terms: the *Gestalt* (form or contours) of Germans and Jews were as separate as "oil and water."[12]

During his last two years in Berlin he published two "proto-Fascist" works, *The Total Mobilization* (*Die totale Mobilmachung*) and *The Worker* (*Der Arbeiter*), both odd mixtures of social analysis, political polemic, and cultural pessimism. These books are often taken as evidence of Jünger's role as a "pathbreaker" for National Socialism, but in fact, the Nazis used the title of the former solely as a powerful slogan, disregarding its contents, and rejected the esoteric metaphysics of the latter. Jünger's vision of a brave new world, set forth in steel-cold prose in *The Worker*, was uncompromising but also too global to be of use to the racially obsessed Nazi ideologues. Even worse, the Nazi ideologues took his ideas as heretical. Thilo von Trotha, a personal assistant to the Nazi chief ideologue Alfred Rosenberg, wrote in the party newspaper, just after *The Worker* appeared in print, that Jünger was "entering the zone of the head shot" since his work lacked any sense of racial biology and sacrificed the nationalist for a planetary perspective.[13]

The Third Reich

The threat from Trotha was not idle. The Gestapo searched Jünger's apartment in early 1933, and Jünger began burning papers and letters from the previous decade. He now entered a period of "inner emigration," remaining in Germany and continuing to publish, but studiously avoiding the language that characterized writers who ingratiated themselves with the new regime. In November 1933 he rejected membership in the Nazi-aligned Prussian Academy of the Arts. In 1934 he published *Leaves and Stones* (*Blätter und Steine*), a collection of his essays on language, travel, and philosophical topics that offered a stark contrast to the daily reality of the Third Reich as Hitler's popularity soared to unprecedented heights.

In 1939 he published *The Marble Cliffs* (*Die Marmorklippen*), which has gone down in the history of the Third Reich as a subtle novel of opposition, but the fact that it received the official imprimatur of the regime shows how successfully the writer was able to camouflage the tale, wrapped in an allegory. On the surface the fable tells of a peaceful agricultural people living contentedly on the shores of a large bay; they are increasingly threatened by primitive nomads from the hinterland and by the followers of an unscrupulous tyrant named the Head Ranger, whose thugs torture their enemies in a spooky camp called Köppelsbleek. The site is surrounded by the skulls and flayed skins of the victims. At the end of the novel, the Head Ranger conquers and destroys the entire lake area, while the two protagonists, modeled after Ernst himself and his father, Friedrich-Georg Jünger, are forced to flee. Jünger resisted the tendency to view the novel as an allegory about concentration camps and totalitarianism (the Head Ranger had similarities to Goering, who was in fact the "Imperial Forest Ranger" of Nazi Germany), since the fictional tyrant could have represented Stalin, Franco, Hitler, or any dictator of that era. Despite the framing of the story in the gothic horror style, many readers in the 1940s, both in and outside of Germany, interpreted the novel as an aristocratic and conservative critique of National Socialism.

Soon after the war broke out in 1939, Jünger enlisted as a lieutenant and was promoted to captain. His troops were stationed first at the West Wall by the Maginot Line. Then came a lucky break—in April 1941 his regiment was ordered to occupied Paris. The Germans allowed the French to administer the metropolis, under supervision, so Jünger found himself in the enviable position of enjoying the charms of the City of Light in a position of near casual authority. He was even permitted to stroll through the streets and markets in civilian clothing. His official job was to censor the mail, but he was also surreptitiously to write reports for his superiors about internal conflicts between the German Army and the Nazi Party, in particular the SS, the SD, the embassy, and the Gestapo, all of which operated their own surveillance systems in Paris. He found an admirer in the aristocratic General Otto von Stülpnagel, and then a distant cousin of the general, Carl Heinrich von Stülpnagel, who succeeded Otto in February 1942. Through the latter, Jünger came into contact with officers involved in a conspiracy to overthrow Hitler, centered around the legendary General Erwin Rommel.[14] After the failed Stauffenberg plot of July 20, 1944, the SS made a sweep of the military command in Paris, but Jünger had kept enough distance from the plotters to avoid arrest. As Jean Cocteau (who socialized with Jünger in Paris) once wittily observed, under the occupation "some people had dirty hands, some people had clean hands, but Jünger had no hands."[15]

Jünger's eldest son, his namesake Ernst, was killed in November 1944 in the marble cliffs of Cararra, Italy. Ernst Jr. had expressed sentiments hostile to the regime and was denounced and arrested in January 1944. Jünger Sr. received permission to leave Paris in February and met with the authorities in Berlin, displaying his Pour le Mérite insignia ostentatiously across his chest. His son was allowed to return to military service but given a dangerous assignment in the Italian mountains. Jünger was never sure if his son had been shot by the enemy or murdered by the SS.[16] His war diaries of the Second World War are written with cold, emotionless precision, except for the entries about his son's death, which reflected the deep and enduring pain he felt all his life at the loss of his eldest son.

In France, Jünger secretly kept notes that formed the basis for his later published war memoirs *Emanations (Strahlungen)*. These war diaries offer a unique perspective from "inside the Belly of the Leviathan," as Jünger described his role in the Third Reich. Some critics have accused the writer of posing as a *flâneur* and dandy while others suffered. In one infamous scene, Jünger climbed up to the roof of the Hotel Raphael and, holding a glass of burgundy, observed a night bombing raid on Paris, as "its red towers and spires lay in stupendous beauty, like petals blown over in an act of deadly fertilization."[17] Whatever moral judgment one wishes to make about these aesthetics of violence, the diaries are indispensable as first-hand accounts of Paris under the German occupation and provide sharply observed portraits of Jünger's contemporaries as they struggled with the apocalyptic destruction of Germany and during the first years of its own, later, occupation.

The postwar period

The Paris Diaries from 1941 to early 1944 read like entries in the log of a sinking ship. The sections written after the summer of 1944 project the stark mood of a shipwreck. Messages in a bottle washed up on his shore as he gradually received news about friends, acquaintances, and relatives. Some alive, others barely alive after brutal treatment by the Russians in the eastern zone, others dead by fate or their own hand.

On July 21, 1945, Jünger wrote in his diary, "The Conservative mind aims to conserve, even conserve his enemy, that is part of his natural inclination."[18] This observation, written with bitterness, sums up the attitude of a writer entering a kind of second inner emigration. The British, he notes, share a fundamental misunderstanding of the German situation since 1918. "Unconditional surrender is the flip side of total war," he notes, by inference comparing Churchill, Stalin and Roosevelt to Goebbels.[19] He compares anti-German sentiments to anti-Semitism."[20]

Jünger travels through different dream worlds in these pages, actual dreams, images, and ideas from books, and mental journeys into the past. The trauma of the immediate past preoccupied him. In a series of arresting reflections on Hitler, he observed that he himself, like many in Germany, underestimated the demonic power that lifted the little nationalist drummer to the heights of power and then self-destruction. Hitler was a "moon character," who could reflect back to the German people their fears and desires in a way that the other Weimar politicians were incapable of.[21] It is striking that he goes to great lengths to dissect the personalities of some leading Nazis, in particular Heinrich Himmler and Josef Goebbels, but says relatively little about the Holocaust. When he does, relativizing comparisons are offered, for example between the treatment of German Sudeten refugees to the tragic fate of the Jews in Germany,[22] or examples of persecution from the Old Testament.[23] On the other hand, he develops, around a decade and half before Hannah Arendt made the idea famous, the notion that some leading Nazis were extraordinarily mundane. Himmler was characterized by "penetrating bourgeois characteristics," he observes, and "evil in the modern world shows up in the ordinary actions of a bureaucrat behind a desk."[24]

Politics make up only a fraction of these postwar diaries. Jünger often describes long walks in the moorlands around Kirchhorst, noting the changing seasons, discussing philosophy, quoting passages from esoteric books. He dwells on the daily hardships of the Germans under occupation, the cold winters, the scavenging for food and basic necessities. In the end these are the reflections of a solitary man living in a world from which he feels both alienated and simultaneously deeply attached.

Jünger hoped to make a comeback in the postwar period, despite having been placed on a literary blacklist, and despite his physical remoteness from German cultural life. He had to face a number of obstacles. The reading public, especially youth, hungered for authors who were banned under National Socialism, especially American authors like Hemingway and Thomas Wolfe. Sartre and the French Existentialists were starting their conquest of intellectual life across Western Europe. Jünger had kept another work in his secret vault during the war: a long essay which he hoped would provide a vision for a peaceful postwar Europe that would put him back on the cultural map. He titled it simply *The Peace* (*Der Friede*).

Jünger viewed his own nationalist writings from the 1920s as his "Old Testament," and works like *The Peace* as part of his new evangelical spirit.[25] They fit together: *The Total Mobilization* was just the flip side of *The Peace*, he wrote to Armin Mohler in 1947.[26] He argued that in the wake of the two disastrous world wars, Europe's future lay in overcoming nationalism through organic unity and integration. These ideas were fairly common after 1945, but Jünger's conservative contribution was first to appeal to a return to Christianity as a solution to Europe's problems, and second, quite contentiously, to relativize the question of war guilt, a topic widely discussed in public in this period by eminent figures such as the philosopher Karl Jaspers, the theologian Martin Niemöller, and the psychologist Carl Jung. Jünger objected to laying blame on any one side or nation. This was an outlier position in the debates about German guilt, and *The Peace* did not play a major role in the public discourse. In the larger context, Jünger's theological turn after 1945 was an outsider position as well, or it could have been viewed as part of the deradicalization of European conservatism,[27] since the radical Right in Europe after the war was trending in an anti-Christian direction.

Jünger held high hopes for a major novel he had been working on in those years. *Heliopolis* is a dystopian work about a power struggle between plebeians and an old aristocracy. In many ways it was a roman à clef about the period of National Socialism as seen from occupied Paris by using obscure designations to refer to historical figures and events. The novel contains many theological diversions, a result of an intense reading of the Bible that Jünger had begun in occupied Paris. The reception of *Heliopolis* was disappointing. Even his friend Carl Schmitt, writing in his diary in 1950, displayed irritation with Jünger's apparent religiosity and his proclivity to mask history with "pseudo-mythological" descriptions.[28]

In 1950 Jünger moved one last time. He was offered an eighteenth-century baroque villa by Freiherr Schenk zu Stauffenberg, a distant relative of the coup plotter against Hitler. The new home was in the small village of Wilflingen in Upper Swabia, a few kilometers from the nearest train station and post office. Jünger became the famous recluse of Wilflingen, where he would live out the many years left in his long life.

In hindsight, Jünger's turn to theology in the late 1940s misled his readers. He could best be described in religious terms as a neopagan, who considered Christianity just one interesting variant of Neoplatonism (though at the end of his life he did convert from Protestantism, his religion at birth, to Catholicism). A little-read novel from 1953, *Visit to Godenholm* (*Besuch auf Godenholm*), signaled his interest in mind-expanding drugs, esoterica, and mystery religions, which would remained a lifelong passion and made him a cult author in the psychedelic 1960s. The novel was written under the influence of LSD, which Jünger had imbibed under medical supervision with the drug's inventor, Albert Hoffman, in a visit to Bottmingen, Switzerland, in February 1951.[29] Jünger's project was to recover the truths embedded in both past religions and metaphysics, which amounted to a rebuke of the positivist and materialist spirit of the postwar rebuilding period.

The early 1950s saw a series of works from Jünger's pen that expanded on this antimodernist tendency. In 1950 he published an essay called "Over the Line" ("Über die Linie"), dedicated to Martin Heidegger on his sixtieth birthday, in which he echoes Heidegger's concerns about technology. As the economic boom was taking off in Germany, Jünger viewed feverish production by despiritualized workers and the increasing specialization of the human and natural sciences as signs of an ever-diminishing ability to grasp the totality of life as proof of the growing nihilism of the age.[30] In 1951 he published *The Forest Passage* (*Der Waldgang*), which amounts to instructions for passive resistance to the modern condition. The individual walks in a metaphorical forest, taking her own path, to escape domination by the forces of technology, the omnipresent Leviathan state, and the banality of modern culture. Religion, counter-Enlightenment thought, and myth are all put in the service of subverting the corrosive effects of instrumental rationality, which, he claims, undergirds all modern totalitarian forms of government.[31]

Although Jünger could appear as a conservative defender of the West— for example in *The Gordian Knot* (*Der gordische Knoten*) from 1953, which pits the freedom of the West against the despotism of the East,[32] and even supporting a "World State" (the title of another essay from 1960)—his political writing always contained a consistent strain of antidemocratic suspicion. A good example is a little-known essay he wrote in 1956 about the eighteenth-century French writer Rivarol, a defender of the monarchy and a fervent critic of the French Revolution.[33] Jünger identified with Rivarol's rebellion against French society and viewed himself in a similar position of revolt against the imposed laws of the occupying posers in postwar Germany.

On March 29, 1965, Jünger turned seventy. He began a new set of diaries, which he maintained until the last days of his life. He observed the world from a distance, as a naturalist would view insects (he was a respected amateur entomologist). The day after the Berlin Wall fell he casually remarks that he expected Germany to reunify, just not in his lifetime. Nothing more is said about European politics in his diary for the rest of the autumn of 1989, a revolutionary period during which the world held its breath as communism fell in state after state.[34]

In his old age Jünger saw his time increasingly through a posthistorical lens. For the European Right after World War II, thinkers such as Martin Heidegger, Arnold Gehlen, Carl Schmitt, and others, in various versions of the same idea, postulated that the postwar world would be characterized by the decline of Europe as a world power and the rise to dominance of technological systems that would expand to the entire globe.[35] The "end of history" implied that after the demise of European culture, intellectuals could only take stock of what had been handed down.

Jünger captured this mood in his 1949 introduction to the war journals, in which he postulated that the Copernican quest for ordering the cosmos, and the diary as a modern literary form, fall together chronologically. They have in common "the bifurcation of mind from object, the author from the world."[36] The First World War marked the end of history, because it represented the demise of heroic action in a pretechnological sense. The end of history, he once said, can be equated with the end of the aristocratic order.[37]

In his own science fiction novel, *Eumeswil* from 1977, posthistorical themes are omnipresent. The protagonist is a young historian, Michael Venator, who operates computers with databanks full of sources on the history of past civilizations, and through a kind of virtual reality can transport himself back in time. The protagonist projects medieval aristocratic values and Faustian personal perseverance in the face of defeat.

Later reception

In October 1982 the conservative Christian Democratic Party came to power under Chancellor Helmut Kohl. The end of the social democratic era was viewed as a turn (*Wende*) toward soft patriotism and an attempt to gradually emerge from the shadows of the Fascist past, thus replacing the politics of reparation and shame with a larger view of German history and of Germany's place in the world that was not reducible to the twelve years of Nazi rule. Kohl famously said he had been born with the clemency of a late birth (he was born in 1930). Kohl turned to Jünger as an apposite symbol of this fundamental shift in Germany's view of itself from a conservative perspective.

In that same month of 1982, Jünger was awarded the Goethe Prize, the most prestigious literary award in Germany, by the conservative city administration of Frankfurt am Main. The bestowal of the prize was greeted by howls of protest not just from hostile commentators across Germany but also by street demonstrations in the city of Frankfurt on the day of the ceremony. According to the critics, this award in the name of Germany's most hallowed humanist should not be bestowed on a writer who had "paved the way" for the rise of Fascism in Germany.

A decade later, as Jünger approached his hundredth birthday, this unsympathetic sentiment had shifted toward a more favorable appreciation of an Olympian figure in whom many Germans could take pride. He was also honored with a visit in Wilflingen by Chancellor Kohl and French president François Mitterand on July 20, 1993, the anniversary of the failed Stauffenberg plot against Hitler.[38] Jünger still had many critics, but the German public was prepared, some grudgingly, others enthusiastically, to accept that Ernst Jünger's lifework was pan-European, a century long, and that his talents could be seen as on par, or at least approaching, the likes of the almost universally adored Goethe.

Conclusion

As Jünger's lifework has become historicized, it is clear that his influence on European thought and letters has been considerable. He has come to be regarded as an important contributor to aesthetics with a sharp eye for the disfiguring effects of modern forms of violence in everyday life. He has influenced the thinkers of the New Right in Europe, but in a broader sense, along with Carl Schmitt and Martin Heidegger, his work offers a challenge to technological modernity and Enlightenment belief in progress in general.

Jünger's place in the conservative European pantheon is hard to determine. As a young man he undoubtedly belonged to the generation of radicals who rejected the bourgeois state and welcomed the overthrow of the European order that had been tenuously reestablished after 1918. He both foresaw and welcomed some combination of nationalism and socialism as a revolutionary solution in the 1920s and early 1930s, but just as clearly he rejected the actual party that carried out the coup in Germany after 1933. In the wake of two disastrous world wars, he predicted that modern technology and the growth of the power of the state would lead to planetary integration on a scale never before seen in human affairs (a phenomenon we today call globalization). In his late posthistorical analysis, he predicted the decline and eventual eclipse of temporal and geographical particularity as European culture melted away to be replaced by a sterile planetary culture and a new cosmopolitan elite lacking specific cultural roots. The result, he feared, would be the rise of demagogues and tyrants who knew how to manipulate modern technology to play to the anxieties of the masses. The only answer for the individual would be to retreat to the security of an autonomous self, to become a forest wanderer, an Anarch, a concept taken up by later thinkers of the radical Right. His life work offers a model for those who accept his cultural pessimism. But considering the decline in faith in politics in our own age, particularly among the young, the rise of petty tyrants and demagogues, and the current revolt against elites across the globe, his vision may also have been prophetic.

Notes

1. A list of important biographies of Jünger is included in the bibliography at the end of this book. I point, in particular to Amos, Kiesel, Nevin, Noack, Martus, Meyer, Mitchell, and Schwilk.
2. Eliah Bures and Elliot Neaman, introduction to *The Adventurous Heart*, by Ernst Jünger (Candor, NY: Telos Press, 2012), xix.
3. Stephen E. Aschheim, *The Nietzsche Legacy in Germany 1890–1990* (Berkeley: University of California Press, 1994), 135.
4. Klaus Theweleit, *Männerphantasien*, 2 vols. (Frankfurt: Roter Stern, 1977). See in particular vol. 1:57–59. and vol. 2, chap. 3.
5. Armin Mohler and Karlheinz Weissmann, *Die Konservative Revolution in Deutschland 1918–1923* (Graz: Ares Verlag, 2005), 115–117.
6. Elliot Neaman, *A Dubious Past: Ernst Jünger and the Politics of Literature after Nazism* (Berkeley: University of California Press, 1999), 32–33.
7. Carl Schmitt, *The Crisis of Parliamentary Democracy*, trans. Ellen Kennedy, (Cambridge, MA: MIT Press, 1985).
8. Helmuth Kiesel, ed., *Stahlgewittern: Historish-kritische Ausgabe* (Stuttgart: Klett-Cotta, 2014).
9. Karl Heinz Bohrer, *Ästhetik des Schreckens: die pessimistische Romantik und Ernst Jüngers Frühwerk* (Hamburg: Ullstein, 1983).

10. "The Innocence of Becoming" was a title given by the Nazi philosopher Alfred Baumler to a collection of Nietzsche's unpublished works in 1931.
11. Letter to the *Völksicher Beobachter*, June 14, 1934, cited in Heimo Schwilk, *Ernst Jünger: Leben und Werk*, 142.
12. Ernst Jünger, "Über Nationalismus und Judenfrage," *Süddeutsche Monatshefte* 12 (September 1930): 843–845.
13. Thilo von Throta, "Das endlose dialektische Gespräch," *Völkischer Beobachter* (October 22, 1932).
14. Neaman, *Dubious Past*, 122–126.
15. Nevin, *Ernst Jünger and Germany*, 169.
16. Helmut Kiesel, *Ernst Junger: Die Biographie* (Munich: Siedler, 2007), 529.
17. Ernst Jünger, *Sämmtliche Werke* 3:270 (May 27, 1944).
18. Jünger, *Sämmtliche Werke* 1:3, 494.
19. Ibid., 493.
20. Ibid., 582.
21. Ibid., 609.
22. Ibid., 563.
23. Ibid., 415.
24. Ibid., 455.
25. Both Jünger's Collected Works, ten volumes in 1964 and eighteen in 1978, omitted the nationalist writings from the 1920s and 1930s.
26. Ernst Jünger to Armin Mohler, unpublished letter, February 17, 1947.
27. Jerry Z. Muller, *The Other God That Failed: Hans Freyer and the Deradicalization of German Conservatism* (Princeton, NJ: Princeton University Press, 1988).
28. Gerd Giesler and Martin Tielke, eds., *Glossarium: Aufzeichnungen der Jahre 1947–1951* (Berlin: Duncker and Humblot), 280.
29. Elliot Neaman, introduction to *Visit to Godenholm*, by Ernst Jünger, trans. Annabel Moynihan (Stockholm: Edda, 2015), 5–7.
30. Jünger, *Sämmtliche Werke* 7:257–259.
31. Russell A. Berman, introduction to *The Forest Passage*, by Ernst Jünger, trans. Thomas Friese (Candor, NY: Telos, 2013), xiii–xxii.
32. Jünger, *Sämmtliche Werke* 7:375–480.
33. On Jünger and Rivarol, see Neaman, *Dubious Past*, 197–199.
34. Ernst Jünger, *Siebzig Verweht* 4 (Stuttgart: Klett-Cotta, 1995), 382.
35. On the history of *posthistoire* in European thought, see Lutz Niethammer, *Posthistoire: ist die Geschichte zu Ende?* (Hamburg: Rowohlt, 1989).
36. Jünger, *Sämmtliche Werke* 2:10.
37. Jacques le Rider, "Le réalisme magique d'Ernst Jünger," *Le Monde*, August 29, 1982.
38. Rudolf von Thadden, "Schiefe Allianzen: Warum trafen sich Mitterrand und Kohl gerade am 20. Juli mit Ernst Jünger?" *Die Zeit* 6, August 1993. http://www.zeit.de/1993/32/schiefe-allianzen.

3

Carl Schmitt and the Politics of Identity

Reinhard Mehring (Translated by Daniel Steuer)

CARL SCHMITT WAS born in 1888 in Plettenberg, Westphalia, Germany, and died there in 1985, at the age of ninety-six.[1] He was a jurist and professor of public law specializing in constitutional law and international law. His career stretched over seven decades, from 1910 to 1982. In the 1920s he developed a constitutional theory which declared that the liberal parliamentary state under the rule of law was outdated, and which he later used to justify rule by presidential decree at the end of the Weimar Republic; he then went on to provide a justification of National Socialism. Schmitt was not only an insightful thinker but also an actor who intervened in politics. While as a jurist he avoided strong theological or philosophical commitments, in political terms he mobilized the distinction between friend and enemy in order to argue for the nationalism and statism of the interwar years and to defend counterrevolutionary, apocalyptic, and anti-Semitic positions. Today, his texts are the subject of debate as the work of both a brilliant and a Mephistophelian author. In terms of Germany's twentieth-century academic exports, Schmitt's work is on a par with that of Max Weber, Martin Heidegger, or Jürgen Habermas.

Life and context

Schmitt studied jurisprudence in Berlin, Munich, and Strasbourg, and completed his doctorate "On Guilt and Types of Guilt" (Über Schuld und Schuldarten) by 1910. In the same year, he began legal training at the

Upper Regional Court in Düsseldorf, becoming familiar with the practical aspects of the work of lawyers and courts. In 1915, a few months after the outbreak of the First World War, he passed his second state examination. He married Carita Dorotič, who not only pretended to be of aristocratic descent but also five years younger than she actually was. This passionate relationship continued to trouble Schmitt, particularly when it came to his academic life, even after the annulment of their marriage in 1924. His second marriage was also marked by various crises.

In his legal work, Schmitt distinguished between the "State of Normality" (*Normalzustand*) and the "State of Emergency" or "State of Exception" (*Ausnahmezustand*). The State of Exception might also be seen as the model for long phases of his personal life. Schmitt did not lead his life as a staid bourgeois scholar but looked at it through the lens of the State of Exception, perceiving all kinds of crises: economic hardship, social dependence, relationship and marital crises, political worries, and intellectual challenges. One might even speak of a harmony between life and work, of a translation of a chaotic life into a theory of the State of Exception. In his programmatic 1922 treatise *Political Theology* (*Politische Theologie*), Schmitt developed a theory of sovereignty that called for the overcoming of the State of Exception and the establishment of a State of Normality. In his private life, however, it seems that he still often sought the State of Exception.

The thinker of the State of Exception

The 1910s was a formative decade for Schmitt. Although he often called himself a Catholic, he always rejected mainstream Catholicism, with its ecclesiastical practices, scholastic belief in a "natural law," and political commitment to the party of the center (*Zentrumspartei*). Instead, Schmitt held an apocalyptic religious belief that set him apart from the church and the morality of the majority. He was keenly aware of the aesthetic revolution of modern art. During his early years in Düsseldorf and Munich, he socialized with literary bohemians and established a friendly relationship with the renowned expressionist poet Theodor Däubler. At the time, expressionism took on the religious and apocalyptic pathos of early Christianity. Schmitt was not an enthusiastic follower of the nationalist and militarist "ideas of 1914," and in fact condemned "militarism" in an apocalyptic tone. A key experience that led to his rejection of the Great War was the death of his closest friend, Fritz Eisler, to whom he dedicated not only his 1916 book

Theodor Däubler's Northern Lights (*Theodor Däublers Nordlicht*) but also his magnum opus, *Constitutional Theory* (*Verfasssungslehre*, 1928). Fritz Eisler, the son of a rich Hamburg publisher, was Jewish and of Hungarian extraction. He asked to be naturalized in order to be able to take part in the war, and was killed on September 27, 1914 in northern France. Until 1933 then, Fritz's younger brother, Georg Eisler, was Schmitt's closest friend. The Eisler family continued to support Schmitt, particularly financially, as he was permanently pushed for money.

In 1915, Schmitt entered military service at the deputy general command of the military administration, where he stayed until the summer of 1919, thus avoiding being called up to the front. He thus experienced the Great War and the revolutionary situation following it from the perspective of a military jurist in Munich, a political hotspot at the time.

In 1916, Schmitt submitted "The Value of the State and the Significance of the Individual" (Der Wert des Staates und die Bedeutung des Einzelnen) for his postdoctoral *Habilitation* in Strasbourg (then still part of Germany). But the key experience and the legal theme that became his lifelong interest was the expansion of dictatorial executive powers under the conditions of a war regime and the increasing power held by the military. He began to work on the question of dictatorship.[2] The transformation of the law-governed bourgeois state into a dictatorial and executive state governed by decree would remain his central theme for the rest of his life. He combined it with a philosophical-historical analysis of the transition from the liberal and bourgeois nineteenth century to the "state [*Staat*] of the twentieth century," which he characterized as the age of the masses and of industrial technology.

In 1919 Schmitt became a full-time lecturer at the Münchner Handelshochschule, a higher education institution for business managers with an emphasis on economics. At that time, he also took part in Max Weber's seminar. For the winter term of 1921–22, he moved to Greifswald, where he took up a full professorship before moving on to Bonn University in the 1922 summer term. Over the following years, he published some of the most important writings for which he is famous today. Apart from *Political Theology* and *The Concept of the Political* (*Der Begriff des Politischen*), he completed his systematic textbook, *Constitutional Theory*. During those years, he also had important pupils over whom, as a charismatic teacher, he exerted great influence.[3] Following the theoretical work he did at Bonn, he wanted to get closer to the center of political activity, and in 1928 he moved to the Berlin Handelshochschule.

After its initial revolutionary years and the crisis of hyperinflation in 1922–23, the Weimar Republic had more or less stabilized as a law-governed bourgeois state and a "parliamentary legislative state" (*parlamentarischer Gesetzgebungsstaat*). But during the global economic crisis of 1929 the Republic was again beset by a whirlwind of crises, and as a consequence began to devolve into a system of rule by presidential decree rather than by parliament. This made the chancellor dependent on the trust of Field Marshall Paul von Hindenburg, the aged president. Schmitt had for some time observed the transition, in times of crisis, from a liberal parliamentarism to an executive regime, and from at least 1924 had argued for an extensive interpretation of dictatorial authority. As a juridical apologist for rule by presidential decree, he became an advocate of the Preußenschlag, an intervention by Chancellor Franz von Papen in the politics of Prussia to dismiss the Social Democratic government of Prussia. Schmitt represented the Reich in the ensuing trial, *Prussia v. the Reich*, probably the most important political trial of the Weimar Republic.

Schmitt as a political actor

Schmitt did not publicly declare allegiance to National Socialism before January 30, 1933, the date of Hitler's appointment as chancellor. After the "enabling law" of March 24, 1933, which gave Hitler unlimited legislative power, Schmitt immediately accepted the "legal revolution" of National Socialism as valid and legitimate, joined the Nazi Party, and quickly sought to gain influence over legal policy.

Before 1933, Schmitt had moved in varied political circles. He had had close contact with Chancellor Franz von Papen and less contact with Chancellor Kurt von Schleicher, who, as an opponent of Hitler, was murdered in 1934. Schmitt can thus be associated not only with National Socialism but also with the literary circles of the so-called Conservative Revolution, right-wing intellectual circles that pursued the project of a transformation of presidential rule into an "authoritarian state" (*autoritären Staat*). This "authoritarian" project rejected the liberal and parliamentarian republic of the 1920s, but should not therefore be equated with National Socialism.

The details of Schmitt's attitudes toward the circles around von Papen, Schleicher, and the Nazis are controversial.[4] Nonetheless, it is clear that while in Berlin from 1928 on, Schmitt became increasingly radical in his nationalism, antiliberalism, and anti-Semitism. From 1930 he formed a lifelong, if at times tense, friendship with Ernst Jünger, who, as the spokesperson of the *Frontkämpfer* (frontline soldiers) and chief representative of a "new nationalism," regarded the soldier as the prototypical figure of the twentieth century. But while Jünger distanced himself politically from National Socialism in 1933, Schmitt tried to gain influence. Through the mediation of von Papen and of his friend Johannes Popitz (then a minister), Schmitt became a member of the commission charged with drawing up the Reich Governors Law (*Reichsstatthaltergesetz*), which placed Reich representatives in the federal states and removed traditional federalism. In terms of legal policy, Schmitt's support for this was in line with his earlier arguments in favor of a *Reichsreform*, a reformation of the Reich.

Through his membership in this commission, Schmitt got to know such senior Nazi politicians as Hermann Göring and Wilhelm Frick. In his new role as the National Socialist "crown jurist," he was immediately offered professorial chairs in Heidelberg, Munich, and Berlin. In the 1933–34 winter term, he moved to Berlin University, where he taught until 1945. In 1933, Göring appointed Schmitt to the newly created Prussian Privy Council (*Preußischer Staatsrat*), which, although it soon became practically insignificant, gave Schmitt the hope of founding a "Führer Council" (*Führerrat*) that was intended to provide close access to Hitler. Schmitt saw National Socialism as a revolutionary movement and expected that this force would form new institutions beyond the existing bureaucratic state. His hope that he might be able to access the center of power as a legal advisor in the "charismatic," or personality-based, Führer-state was not altogether far-fetched but as it happened, Schmitt was disappointed. He never gained access to Hitler, and during 1933 Göring stopped contacting him. Schmitt, however, became acquainted with another National Socialist politician, Hans Frank, then Reich Commissioner for Judicial Coordination (*Reichskommissar für die Gleichschaltung der Justiz*) and later Reich Law Chief (*Reichsrechtsführer*) and governor-general of Poland (Frank's name is closely associated with the Holocaust). Over the course of three years, between 1933 and the end of 1936, Schmitt was in close contact with Frank.

We may distinguish different stages of the seizure and formation of power within the revolutionary and destructive dynamic of National Socialism. Initially, Schmitt assumed that National Socialism would stabilize or, in his own terminology, that there would be a transition from the State of Exception to a State of Normality. At that point, he believed that National Socialism could produce a constitutional state. There is controversy over the question of whether he had in mind a kind of "taming strategy" that aimed to produce a "strong" state along authoritarian and Prussian military lines. Franz von Papen, who remained vice-chancellor under Hitler until July 1934, represented a personal continuity between rule by presidential decree and National Socialism. Any hopes for a stabilization—and so an "authoritarian" rather than "totalitarian" state (a subtle distinction in any case)—became obsolete on June 30, 1934, when the Nazis murdered not only certain SA leaders but also other groups of opponents, among them the former Chancellor Kurt von Schleicher and Edgar Jung, an intellectual leader of the Conservative Revolution and an advisor of von Papen.

This was the point at which Schmitt buried any hopes for a stabilization of National Socialism and thus abandoned his former political companions in his "The Führer protects the law" ("Der Führer schützt das Recht"),[5] an article widely read as one of the most abhorrent justifications of Hitler and National Socialism. Schmitt now considered National Socialism to be a terror regime, a Leviathan in a State of Exception, but he nevertheless still offered legal apologetics for it, which, as a university teacher, he could have avoided doing without fear of punishment. He increasingly argued for aggressive anti-Semitism as providing meaning and ideological justification for National Socialism. He attempted to justify the anti-Semitic Nuremberg Laws of 1935 as "the Constitution of Freedom," and also organized a large conference on "Jews in Jurisprudence" in the autumn of 1936.[6]

Despite all this, intrigue within the Nazi Party neutralized whatever influence Schmitt, as someone close to Frank, might have had as an actor involved in legal policy formation. Such SS jurists as Reinhard Höhn and Werner Best polemicized against his earlier life and work, which, until 1933, did not at all conform to the ideological script of National Socialism. Nevertheless, from 1939 on, Schmitt regained influence in National Socialist debates over international law on the back of his work on spaces (*Großraumlehre*), which justified Nazi expansionism by presenting National Socialist Germany as a guarantor of order (*Ordnungsmacht*) for central Europe.[7]

Schmitt survived the war in Berlin. After the war, he lost his university chair and was interned between September 1945 and October 1946. In the spring of 1947, he was remanded in custody in Nuremberg for a few weeks in connection with the war crimes trials, but finally he was released. He returned to Plettenberg, his Westphalian home, and from then on into old age exerted a far-reaching influence as a private scholar through his publications and via informal channels.

Work and thought

Schmitt spoke many languages and was very widely read. He was familiar not only with the legal literature of his time, but he also had a comprehensive knowledge of art and literature, history, theology, and philosophy. A major interest was early modern and modern authors such as Hobbes and Hegel, the authors of the 1848 revolution, and the French avant-garde (Baudelaire, Bernanos). Plato and Aristotle, and also Aquinas and Kant are, by contrast, hardly mentioned. Schmitt rejected the philosophy of the Enlightenment.

One of his most faithful mentors was his doctoral supervisor at Strasbourg, Fritz van Calker. It was also in Strasbourg that Schmitt became acquainted with Paul Laband, the leading positivist scholar of state law in the Wilhelminian era. Early on, Schmitt studied the writings of Hans Kelsen and the Vienna legal school. In Munich he met Max Weber, whose work had a lasting influence on him. Schmitt was able to assimilate a wealth of intellectual influences. His numerous personal contacts and friendships, intense and often not free of tension, were also important for the ideas he forged. Many of those with whom he was in conversation were Jewish intellectuals, and Judaism remained central to Schmitt's oeuvre.

Schmitt's work developed over a long period of time, and it mostly took the form of the short treatise. Just how much unity this body of work possesses is debated. Schmitt's early work was based on fundamental legal distinctions, such as that between morality and right, law and judgment, and power and right.[8] In the early Weimar Republic, he historicized the bourgeois mentality and constitution, denied the legitimacy and integrative power of liberal parliamentary democracy, and mobilized the personalism of Christianity against the liberal legislative state.[9]

Schmitt saw the constitutional battles in the wake of 1789 as a struggle between revolution and counterrevolution, between democratic legitimacy and dictatorship. He dismissed traditional conservatism and dynastic legitimacy as the ideology of the restoration, and positioned himself alongside the counterrevolution, in part through the life and work of Juan Donoso Cortés, the nineteenth-century Spanish critic of liberalism. During the 1920s, Schmitt fought against the legitimacy of the status quo established by the Treaty of Versailles and the League of Nations.[10] He emphasized the revolutionary energy and sovereignty of the nation, addressing himself to the antiliberal and extraparliamentary movements of the Weimar Republic.[11] He systematized the distinction between liberalism and democracy to explore the notion of an antiliberal presidential democracy,[12] identified a drifting apart of legality and legitimacy, and defended a dictatorship of a president legitimized by plebiscite in order to support a transformation of the Weimar Republic into a "strong" and "authoritarian" state.[13] Throughout these writings, he aimed to elaborate a legal theory and constitutional doctrine that reconstructed valid constitutional law, legality, and legitimacy, all on the basis of political forces and "fundamental decisions" (*Grundentscheidungen*), a key concept of *Constitutional Theory*.

Schmitt's constitutional theory is also characterized by binaries: friend and enemy, power and right, State of Exception and State of Normality, liberalism and democracy, legality and legitimacy, law and measure, legislative state (liberal and parliamentarian) and executive state (legitimized by plebiscitary democracy). Schmitt sees a transition from the State of Normality to a State of Exception, and a paralysis of the law-governed bourgeois state and its transformation into the crisis regime of an "authoritarian" and dictatorial executive state.

"Theology" as postulate

As a jurist, Schmitt took on the role of analyst and hermeneutician for his contemporaries. He did not formulate strong confessional or philosophical-essentialist theses. Although he repeatedly called himself a Catholic and Christian, he did not observe the majority of the tenets of contemporary Catholicism and always argued in favor of the primacy of the state and of secular politics. And although in his programmatic treatise on *Political Theology* he rejected atheist metaphysics and the modern "philosophy of immanence"[14] and presented his "counterrevolution" as a Christian movement, he did not develop Christian doctrines but rather argued on the basis of transcendental pragmatics, in terms of necessary conditions. The state figures in anthropomorphic fashion as a person and is imagined as a sovereign. In his *Political Theology*, Schmitt states:

> The sovereign produces and guarantees the situation in its totality. He has the monopoly over this last decision. Therein resides the

essence of the state's sovereignty, which must be juristically defined correctly, not as the monopoly to coerce or to rule, but as the monopoly to decide.[15]

In this passage, Schmitt draws on Thomas Hobbes, whom he calls a "classical representative of the decisionist type," in order to argue against Max Weber. Hobbes, he says, "advanced a decisive argument that connected this type of decisionism with personalism."[16]

Political Theology develops the idea that the intellectual process of the early modern and modern periods leads from God's transcendence to conceptions of immanence that weaken the authority of the sovereign and result in the "democratic thesis of the identity of the ruler and the ruled."[17] Schmitt constructs a necessary connection between theism, personalism, and "decisionism," without, however, formulating this on the basis of theism as a theological notion; rather, he puts it forward as a hypothesis or presupposition necessitated by the authoritarian decision. For the jurist there can be no doubt: if God did not exist, then he would need to be invented for the sake of the authority of the sovereign. The morality of the intellectual, according to Schmitt, consists of the "final consequences."[18] Schmitt believed that just as atheism ultimately leads to political anarchism, the political decision in favor of authority and dictatorship implies a need for theism and religious meaning. Following Donoso Cortés, Schmitt therefore speaks in apocalyptic and counterrevolutionary terms of the State of Exception as a "decisive bloody battle."[19]

Thoughts of this kind, which can be found throughout his work, reveal Schmitt to be not a conservative and Christian thinker but a modern secularized Christian, and—primarily—a political thinker who looks at the present as a permanent battle over authority, rule, and order. This is what determines his position in post-1789 conservatism, in the Conservative Revolution of the interwar years, and as one of the key thinkers of the radical Right. Schmitt's close friendship with Ernst Jünger already suggests that he was a central figure in this group. As early as 1914, he also became acquainted with the publicist Arthur Moeller van den Bruck, another important intellectual pioneer of the Conservative Revolution, and later he also met Julius Evola. Oswald Spengler, by contrast, is rarely mentioned. Schmitt probably considered Spengler's encyclopedic deliberations on the theme of cyclical cultural decline as a betrayal by the educated bourgeoisie of the expressionist apocalyptical thought that he clearly sided with in his 1916 book on Däubler.

Schmitt's central motifs as a thinker emerge from his juridical approach. He looked at the world of politics as a battle for self-assertion (*Selbstbehauptung*), as he pointed out especially in *The Concept of the Political*.[20] But he did not affirm political power and violence, battle and war, as such; rather, as a jurist, he required the stabilization of political forms as legal relationships. In 1934 Schmitt labeled this "concrete order-thinking" (*konkretes Ordnungsdenken*).[21] This is why we find in him both an apocalyptic perspective on the State of Exception and an alarmist and dramatic perspective on the possibility of crisis characterized by recurrent worries about the erosion and disintegration of a relatively stable State of Normality into a State of Exception.

Schmitt's pessimistic crisis-centered perspective was not naturally counterbalanced by Christian belief and trust, but instead postulated God as a civil-theological political requirement. As a secularized Christian, however, Schmitt did not draw the radical conclusion of a naturalism and biologism that tended toward racism and imperialism, especially in Germany. His anti-Semitism was formulated primarily within a religious discourse. He used Christian dogmas as political myths, and affirmed the politics of myth as a kind of political propaganda. His book on *The Leviathan in the State Theory of Thomas Hobbes* (*Der Leviathan in der Staatslehre des Thomas Hobbes*) bears this out. Its subject matter is not Hobbes's philosophy but the "meaning and failure of a political symbol," as its subtitle (*Sinn und Fehlschlag eines politischen Symbols*) shows.[22]

Schmitt's theory of sovereignty also bears on gender politics. He codes the sovereign as male and anarchic situations as feminine, finding an inclination toward matriarchal myths in anarchist authors. If one wanted to link life and work at this point, one might not only attribute to the theoretician of sovereignty a strong urge to establish hermeneutic hegemony and discursive domination—an urge that is evident even at the level of style, in the epigrammatic nature of his theses and his obvious penchant for novel terminology—but also point to his licentious behavior, which, particularly in the 1920s, saw him making use of street prostitutes almost every day. Schmitt's continual use of prostitutes was a way of proving his sovereign masculinity. He also reflected on the machismo in the ritual of bullfighting, which he saw as a model of gender relations. In his diary he noted in 1923: "The fundamental affect in my life: life is a battle. Certainly. But a battle that takes place in an arena, in front of spectators, especially female spectators who have trophies ready to be presented; the feeling of a torero, a gladiator. The other idea of life as a battle: the battle of the marauding knight, the buccaneer, the pirate, the trooper [*Landsknecht*]."[23] After 1945, Schmitt referred to himself again and again as a *picaro*: a soldier of fortune trying his luck through the moments of States of Exception.

Identity politics

What is characteristic of Schmitt's work is not Catholic dogmatism but an existentialist vocabulary. He formulates his political existentialism succinctly and poignantly, especially in *The Concept of the Political*, of which there are four versions, published in 1927, 1932, 1933, and 1963. He constitutes identity by way of distancing: friendship and enmity. While *Political Theology* highlights the "decisionist" concept of the "decision," *The Concept of the Political* emphasizes the connection between decisions and the drawing of distinctions and making of identity claims. These reflections are fundamental to Schmitt's major legal work *Constitutional Theory*, which interprets positive constitutional decisions as "fundamental decisions" against constitutional alternatives.

The Concept of the Political is Schmitt's best-known and most influential work, providing both theory and practice. Schmitt sketches a "category" and a "criterion" for identification in political action (as opposed to the aesthetic realm or economic action), and seeks to identify the enemy in the political situation of 1927—this conceptually fundamental text is also a nationalist manifesto. Even the famous introductory formula, "The concept of the state presupposes the concept of the political,"[24] has this in mind: political action is "existential" and cannot be equated with the actions of a state. Political institutions are based on the political actions of citizens, on the existential forces of political self-organization. Such forces may also be directed against the state, and may, for example, identify the institutions of the Weimar Republic as their political opponent and enemy. Schmitt's later *Theory of the Partisan*,[25] which is particularly relevant today, expands on this. But *The Concept of the Political* has in mind Germany's foreign policy situation after Versailles. Schmitt says:

> The political enemy need not be morally evil or aesthetically ugly; he need not appear as an economic competitor, and it may be advantageous to engage with him in business transactions. But he is, nevertheless, the other, the stranger; and it is sufficient for his nature that he is, in a specially intense way, existentially something

different and alien, so that in the extreme case conflicts with him are possible.[26]

Schmitt also speaks of the "case of emergency" (*Ernstfall*),[27] which implies "the existential negation of another being,"[28] and he emphasizes the possibility of fighting and of real war as the "exceptional case" (*Ausnahmefall*).[29] Schmitt talks of a "war of state against state" and of "civil war,"[30] and he considers the *jus belli* of states, including the state's legal and legitimate demand for "the readiness to die and unhesitatingly to kill," as a functional condition for the political achievement of "assuring total peace within the state."[31] Schmitt affirms a "pluralism of states" and questions the humanitarian idea of a League of Nations. Following Machiavelli, Hobbes, and Hegel, he adopts a negative or "pessimistic" political anthropology, which postulates that constructive political theories should assume that humans are in need of authority and rule. Ultimately, Schmitt defends the thesis that liberal thinking ignores this precondition of a constructive politics because it is biased toward universalist ideologies. He writes:

> In a very systematic fashion, liberal thought evades or ignores state and politics, and moves instead in a typical always recurring polarity of two heterogeneous spheres, namely ethics and economics, intellect and trade, education and property.[32]

Schmitt believed that a universalist ethics typically conceals economic interests. His 1932 version of *The Concept of the Political* ends with a philosophical-historical characterization of the early modern period under the heading "The Age of Neutralizations and Depoliticizations," in which Schmitt shows how all attempts at neutralization and depoliticization end up in failure. Striving after depoliticization will only trigger new enmities and lead to the development of new ways of defining one's enemy. Liberalism, in particular, should shed the illusion that it acts unpolitically and has no political effects, and it should not consider its moral convictions and economic practices to be unpolitical.

This basis for political existentialism would alone have been enough to turn Schmitt into a classical author of the new nationalism, antiliberalism, and antiuniversalism. Schmitt always saw himself as a participant and political actor. His political theory of identity was therefore correctly received as an intervention aiming at political polarization and mobilization. However, Schmitt would have complemented this by saying that a sharp articulation of opposing views is a precondition for political acknowledgment, for the institutionalization of a conflict. This is why he later spoke of "hedged" enmity and—in *The Nomos of the Earth*—the "bracketing of war,"[33] and argued for a "nondiscriminatory" international law that would recognize war as a legal and legitimate political means. After 1945, Schmitt registered the end of "the era of statehood," and sought a new understanding of the law, one that saw it from the perspective of "land-appropriation" and the domination of space as the "unity of order and orientation."[34] As a witness of the events of the twentieth century, he described, in retrospect, the constitutional transformation of a liberal law-governed bourgeois state into an executive state whose democratic legitimacy rested on a plebiscite, and the transition from the classical nation state to a multipolar and supranational order.

Reception

Schmitt was always perceived to be an outstanding intellectual, and he enjoyed early academic success. Even during his time in Bonn, he was already seen as a controversial figure due to his juridically programmatic texts and his generous interpretation of dictatorial powers. His broad conception of legal studies as including politics and the "history of ideas," as well as his terse, proclamatory, and also associative style provoked vigorous opposition. In the debate about the orientation of state law in the Weimar Republic, Schmitt soon became the antipode to legal positivism and Hans Kelsen's "pure" theory of law. Schmitt's defense of rule by presidential decree further isolated him within his profession, and as a result his work was increasingly taken up by the antiliberal and nationalist circles of the Conservative Revolution.[35] In the debates of the early 1930s, his publications featured practically everywhere. Through his quick rise to the position of National Socialist "crown jurist," Schmitt gained influence over legal policy formation and personnel. Thus, his pupils, some of whom were brilliant themselves, soon became powerful within National Socialist jurisprudence. From 1933, beginning with Italy, France, and Spain, there was also a strong international response to his work. The worldwide influence of his constitutional theory on all kinds of authoritarian and dictatorial theories of the state cannot be separated from his National Socialist career. But Schmitt's thought was influential not only in the context of pre-1945 European Fascism, and not only in southern and eastern Europe, but also very much in South America and

Asia, including a demonstrable influence on processes of constitutional legislation.

In the context of the Federal Republic of Germany, Schmitt, as an inspiring partner in debate, influenced highly talented young intellectuals such as Reinhart Koselleck, Ernst-Wolfgang Böckenförde, and Hermann Lübbe.[36] Böckenförde read Schmitt from a liberal perspective and in the context of the State of Normality characterizing the Federal Republic, and so revived the reception of his work in legal studies. Schmitt was thus active and present not only before and after 1933 but also after 1945, into his old age. He had, so to speak, three lives: one before 1933, one after 1933, and one after 1945.

The secondary literature on him, and the systematic investigation of his life, already began before 1933 in the form of important review articles.[37] Leo Strauss, Helmut Kuhn, and Karl Löwith criticized Schmitt's *The Concept of the Political* as laying the foundations for a political existentialism, a sort of counterpart to Heidegger's *Being and Time*.[38] While Hugo Ball pursued a "theological" approach to reading Schmitt, Huber laid the foundation for the discussions of constitutional theory. For a long time after 1945, Karl Löwith's critique of "political decisionism" was particularly influential. More recently, the mimetic exegesis by Leo Strauss, who compared Schmitt with Hobbes, has increasingly been the subject of debate.

In the early Federal Republic, Schmitt was criticized as a representative of antidemocratic thinking in the Weimar Republic and as an intellectual pioneer of the "total" Führer-state. In 1964, following Löwith's criticism of Schmitt's "political decisionism," Hasso Hofmann published the first important comprehensive critique from the perspective of legal philosophy.[39] Hofmann's *Legitimacy versus Legality* (*Legitimität gegen Legalität*) saw Schmitt's thinking on legitimacy as addressing a fundamental problem in legal history. After the student revolution of 1968, the Marxist and leftwing reception of Schmitt, represented before 1933 by Otto Kirchheimer and Walter Benjamin,[40] was taken up again as part of a critique of the Federal Republic, and Marxist political economy was supplemented with the Schmittian perspective of a "political theology." In his last monograph, *Political Theology II*, Schmitt still defended himself against various "theological" appropriations of his work. In the 1970s, in old age, he again became particularly interested in conversations with Jewish intellectuals, among them Jacob Taubes and Hans Blumenberg, so that we can say that the engagement with Judaism, or with stereotypes of what Schmitt considered the "Jewish spirit," was a political-theological topic throughout his life, a lifelong riddle, or—in one of Schmitt's favorite formulations—his "own question as a form" (*eigne Frage als Gestalt*).

Following Schmitt's death in 1985, the discussions—and the available sources—changed significantly. The main texts were made available again and were widely translated. But most importantly, apart from a plethora of secondary literature, numerous crucial source texts (diaries and correspondence) were published; these changed and deepened the image of Schmitt. Among the more recent interpretations of Schmitt are both academic and nonacademic publications; there are contributions to debates in law, political science, theology, and philosophy; there are attempts to describe Schmitt's actual life and put him in historical context; there are interpretations that make marginal and selective use of his work; and there are substantial appropriations and transformations of his theories.

While today neonationalist and antiliberal authors everywhere refer to Schmitt, Schmitt himself only ever addressed his contemporaries and expressed very clearly the limits to the applicability of his work: he warned against the resurrection of old answers by later generations. An intellectual answer, he often said, "is true only once" as a concrete answer to its own time. His lack of interest in the "national question" regarding a reunification of Germany after its division in 1945 was intended as a warning: after 1945 Schmitt no longer propagated an aggressive nationalism. His complex and challenging work cannot be reduced to simple formulas and concepts; he wanted it to be understood primarily as juridical intervention. Any attempt today to appropriate Schmitt in the form of political slogans, without putting forward an analysis of the substance of today's legal situation, would not do justice to the aspirations and the status of his work.

The quality of Schmitt's work means that it ultimately requires an academic response. Since the 1990s, Schmitt has become part of the classical canon and one of the major thinkers in great debates. Jürgen Habermas has repeatedly criticized Schmitt as the main representative of German neonationalism, and reconstructed Kant's universalist conception of international law in response to Schmitt. Jacques Derrida deconstructed Schmitt's category of enmity in the service of a "politics of friendship." Giorgio Agamben adapted Schmitt's State of Exception, and Chantal Mouffe used Schmitt's antiuniversalism in her critique of globalization.[41] As a classic author of antiliberalism, statism, nationalism, and National Socialism, Schmitt's work today is pressed into service by thinkers of many different political stripes. His analysis of the transition from the liberal constitutional state to an authoritarian and dictatorial system remains relevant and informative. Today, both within Europe and beyond, there are again numerous alliances between authoritarian executive regimes and "populist" mobilizations of the masses. But Schmitt's work is also relevant to the search for new forms of politics and new strategies for obfuscation, and to the task of identifying the holders of power operating behind the scenes. Schmitt wanted to pull down the masks of power and identify the sovereign. This is the reason he became susceptible to fantasies and conspiracies. Beyond this contemporary relevance, he remains an example of German interwar radicalism, and a paradigmatic case of the entanglement of spirit and power.

Notes

1. For the vast literature on Schmitt, see www.carl-schmitt.de/neueste_veroeffentlichungen.php. See also Jens Meierheinrich and Oliver Simons, eds., *The Oxford Handbook of Carl Schmitt* (Oxford: Oxford University Press, 2016), and Reinhard Mehring, *Carl Schmitt zur Einführung*, 5th ed. (Junius-Verlag: Hamburg, 2017); *Carl Schmitt: A Biography* (Cambridge: Polity, 2014); *Carl Schmitt: Denker im Widerstreit: Werk–Wirkung–Aktualität* (Freiburg: Alber-Verlag, 2017). For jurisprudence, Michael Stolleis, *Geschichte des öffentlichen Rechts in Deutschland*, vols. 3/4 (Munich: C. H. Beck, 1999/2012), and Horst Dreier, *Staatsrecht in Demokratie und Diktatur* (Tübingen: Mohr, 2016). For historical context, Ulrich Herbert, *Geschichte Deutschlands im 20. Jahrhundert* (Munich: C. H. Beck, 2014).
2. Carl Schmitt "Diktatur und Belagerungszustand," *Zeitschrift für die gesamte Strafrechtswissenschaft* 38 (1916): 138–162; *Die Diktatur: Von den Anfängen des modernen Souveränitätsgedankens bis zum proletarischen Klassenkampf* (Munich: Duncker and Humblot, 1921); "Die Diktatur des Reichspräsidenten nach Art. 48 der Reichsverfassung," *Veröffentlichungen der Vereinigung der Deutschen Staatsrechtslehrer* 1 (1924): 63–104.
3. Especially Ernst Rudolf Huber, Ernst Forsthoff, Otto Kirchheimer, and Waldemar Gurian.
4. Ernst Rudolf Huber, "Carl Schmitt in der Reichskrise der Weimarer Endzeit," in *Complexio Oppositorum: Über Carl Schmitt*, ed. Helmut Quaritsch (Berlin: Duncker and Humblot, 1988), 33–50; Gabriel Seiberth, *Anwalt des Reiches: Carl Schmitt und der Prozess: Preußen contra Reich* (Berlin: Duncker and Humblot, 2001); Andreas Koenen, *Der Fall Carl Schmitt: Sein Aufstieg zum "Kronjuristen des Dritten Reiches"* (Darmstadt: Wissenschaftliche Buchgesellschaft, 1995); Dirk Blasius, *Carl Schmitt und der 30. Januar 1933: Studien zu Carl Schmitt* (Frankfurt: Lang, 2009);

and *Carl Schmitt: Preußischer Staatsrat in Hitlers Reich* (Göttingen: Vandenhoeck and Ruprecht, 2001).

5. Carl Schmitt, "Der Führer schützt das Recht: Zur Reichstagsrede Adolf Hitlers vom 13. Juli 1934," *Deutsche Juristen-Zeitung* 39 (1934): 945–950.
6. Carl Schmitt, "Die Verfassung der Freiheit," *Deutsche Juristen-Zeitung* 40 (1935): 1133–1135; "Die deutsche Rechtswissenschaft im Kampf gegen den jüdischen Geist," *Deutsche Juristen-Zeitung* 41 (1936): 1193–1199.
7. Carl Schmitt, *Völkerrechtliche Großraumlehre mit Interventionsverbot für raumfremde Mächte: Ein Beitrag zum Reichsbegriff des Völkerrechts* (Berlin: Deutscher Rechtsverlag, 1939).
8. Carl Schmitt, *Über Schuld und Schuldarten* (1910); *Gesetz und Urteil* (1912); *Der Wert des Staates und die Bedeutung des Einzelnen* (1914).
9. Carl Schmitt, *Politische Romantik* (1919); *Die Diktatur* (1921); *Politische Theologie* (1922); *Die geistesgeschichtliche Lage des heutigen Parlamentarismus* (1923); *Römischer Katholizismus und politische Form* (1923).
10. Carl Schmitt, *Die Rheinlande als Objekt internationaler Politik* (1925); *Die Kernfrage des Völkerbundes* (1926).
11. Carl Schmitt, *Volksbegehren und Volksentscheid* (1927); *Der Begriff des Politischen* (1927).
12. Carl Schmitt, *Verfassungslehre* (1928).
13. Carl Schmitt, *Der Hüter der Verfassung* (1931); *Legalität und Legitimität* (1932).
14. Schmitt, *Political Theology: Four Chapters on the Concept of Sovereignty*, trans. George Schwab (Cambridge, MA: MIT Press, 1985), 50.
15. Ibid., 13.
16. Ibid., 33.
17. Ibid., 49.
18. Ibid., 65.
19. Ibid., 63.
20. Schmitt, *Concept of the Political*, 33 (Chicago: University of Chicago Press, 1996).
21. Carl Schmitt, *On the Three Types of Juristic Thought* (Westport, CT: Praeger, 2004).
22. Carl Schmitt, *The Leviathan in the State Theory of Thomas Hobbes: Meaning and Failure of a Political Symbol*, trans. George Schwab and Erna Hilfstein (Westport, CT: Greenwood Press, 1996).
23. Carl Schmitt, *Der Schatten Gottes: Introspektionen, Tagebücher und Briefe 1921 bis 1924*, ed. Gerd Giesler, Ernst Hüsmert, and Wolfgang H. Spindler (Berlin: Duncker and Humblot, 2014), 482.
24. Schmitt, *Concept of the Political*, 19.
25. Carl Schmitt, *Theory of the Partisan*, trans. Gary L. Ulmen (New York: Telos, 2007), originally published as *Theorie des Partisanen* (1963).
26. Schmitt, *Concept of the Political*, 27.
27. Ibid., 35.
28. Ibid., 33.

29. Ibid., 35.
30. Ibid., 37.
31. Ibid., 46.
32. Ibid., 70.
33. Carl Schmitt, *The Nomos of the Earth in the International Law of the Jus Publicum Europaeum* (New York: Telos, 2003), 55.
34. Schmitt, *The Nomos of the Earth*, 42.
35. Stefan Breuer, *Carl Schmitt im Kontext: Intellektuellenpolitik in der Weimarer Republik* (Berlin: Akademie-Verlag, 2012).
36. See the standard work on this by Dirk van Laak, *Gespräche in der Sicherheit des Schweigens: Carl Schmitt in der politischen Geistesgeschichte der frühen Bundesrepublik* (Berlin: Akademie-Verlag, 1993). See also Mehring, *Carl Schmitt: Denker im Widerstreit*.
37. Hugo Ball, "Carl Schmitts Politische Theologie," *Hochland* 21 (1924): 263–286; Eric Voegelin, "Die Verfassungslehre von Carl Schmitt: Versuch einer konstruktiven Analyse ihrer staatlichen Prinzipien," *Zeitschrift für öffentliches Recht* 11 (1931): 89–109; Ernst Rudolf Huber, "Verfassung und Verfassungswirklichkeit bei Carl Schmitt," *Blätter für Deutsche Philosophie* 5 (1931/1932): 302–315; Otto Kirchheimer and Nathan Leites, "Bemerkungen zu Carl Schmitts 'Legalität und Legitimität,'" *Archiv für Sozialwissenschaft und Sozialpolitik* 69 (1932): 457–487.
38. Leo Strauss, "Anmerkungen zu Carl Schmitts 'Der Begriff des Politischen,'" *Archiv für Sozialwissenschaft und Sozialpolitik* 67 (1932): 732–749; Helmut Kuhn, "Carl Schmitt 'Der Begriff des Politischen,'" *Kantstudien* 38 (1933): 190–196; Karl Löwith (Pseudonym: Hugo Fiala), "Politischer Dezisionismus," *Internationale Zeitschrift für Theorie des Rechts* 9 (1935): 101–123.
39. Hasso Hofmann, *Legitimität gegen Legalität: Der Weg der politischen Philosophie Carl Schmitts* (Neuwied: Luchterhandt Verlag, 1964).
40. Reinhard Mehring, "Otto Kirchheimers Promotionsakte," in *Kriegstechniker des Begriffs: Biographische Studien zu Carl Schmitt*, ed. Reinhard Mehring (Tübingen: Mohr, 2014), 31–46, 137–152.
41. Jürgen Habermas, "Kant's Idea of Perpetual Peace: At Two Hundred Years' Remove," in *The Inclusion of the Other* (Cambridge: Polity, 1999), 165–201; "Does the Constitutionalization of International Law Still Have a Chance?" in Jürgen Habermas, *The Divided West* (Cambridge: Polity, 2006), 113–93; Jacques Derrida, *The Politics of Friendship* (London: Verso, 2005); Giorgio Agamben, *The State of Exception* (Chicago: Chicago University Press, 2005); Chantal Mouffe, ed., *The Challenge of Carl Schmitt* (London: Verso, 1999).

4

Julius Evola and Tradition

H. Thomas Hakl (Translated by Joscelyn Godwin)

JULIUS EVOLA HARDLY ever spoke about his outer life and wrote little about it. His autobiography, *The Path of Cinnabar* (*Il cammino del cinabro*), describes almost exclusively his inner development.[1] The uncertainties begin with his origins. He was born in Rome on May 19, 1898. Despite what standard short biographies say, he most probably did not stem from the Sicilian nobility. Both parental lines originated in Cinisi (in the province of Palermo), and were certainly not ennobled.[2] The title of baron, frequently used even on some official documents, could date from a provocative Dadaistic pose of his youth, when he was known for his dandyish behavior. However, we can state that Evola never referred to himself as a baron.

Evola was born at a very disturbed time. The Risorgimento (revival), with its unification of Italy and the rise of the middle classes, had also prepared the country for the rise of Fascism. An alternative religiosity in Italy led to the emergence of Theosophy, Anthroposophy, and awareness of Eastern religions. In philosophy, Benedetto Croce and Giovanni Gentile's idealism served as a counterweight to Marxism.

Early work and thought

Evola's intellectual activity can be divided into several phases, and this chapter will discuss its key concepts and resultant writings. Despite his multiple fields of interest, Evola's worldview has a clear and discernable structure. Many fundamental ideas, primarily that of transcendence, remained valid and visible as they continually developed and seized on each new field of interest.

Intellectual foundations

Although Evola was raised in Catholicism, he turned against it and felt attracted to writers such as Oscar Wilde, Gabriele D'Annunzio, and Arthur Rimbaud. At the same time he pursued technical and mathematical interests. His early readings of Friedrich Nietzsche and Otto Weininger were especially influential, together with the philosophy of Carlo Michelstaedter, whose cousin Emilio was friends with the young Evola.

The influence of these three thinkers cannot be overestimated, for they were not only decisive in Evola's youth but also in later life. Nietzsche gave him his uncompromising, aggressive attitude, his revulsion toward the "humility" and "bourgeois moralism" of Christianity, as well as his opposition to "egalitarianism, democratic ideals and conformism."[3] However, Evola did not embrace Nietzsche's *Übermensch* (superman) ideal, at least not until later on, finding it dominated by the naturalistic, biological element, and utterly lacking the transcendent.[4]

Otto Weininger's influence carried equal weight. His work obviously affected Evola's attitude to the female sex and to Judaism (of which Weininger, though of Jewish origin, was extremely critical), also embracing ethical principles ("Truth, purity, fidelity, sincerity towards oneself: that is the only acceptable ethic")[5] and even political views, rejecting popularism in the broadest sense. Above all it is the attitude of "virility" in the sense of courage, daring, and steadfastness, so characteristic of Evola, that goes back to Weininger, who in his book *Sex and Character* (*Geschlecht und Charakter*) proposed that everyone carries both masculine and feminine elements, and that no purely masculine or feminine type exists. He identified the feminine element with sexuality and motherhood, and regarded Judaism as marked by it.

Carlo Michelstaedter, who came from a Jewish family in northeastern Italy, committed suicide at the age of twenty-three after finishing his book *Inner Conviction and Rhetoric* (*La persuasione e la rettorica*), apparently believing that his philosophical discoveries could go no farther. By "inner conviction" Michelstaedter understood an absolute self-sufficiency of the "I." As long as this did not rest exclusively on oneself but depended on some "other," it was subjected to the "necessity" of external circumstances and therefore had no freedom. True freedom lay only in autarchy.

Evola called these three thinkers the "holy damned," because none of them, for all their genius, was equal to the power and force of their own conceptions. Two of them committed suicide while still young; the third became insane. Evola was convinced that it was their own inner tension that destroyed them because they lacked the spiritual element—the deep, inner connection with the transcendent—that is unshakable and above and beyond anything earthly. And as Evola says, this decisive drive to transcendence had "manifested itself from my early youth."[6] Upon his return from the First World War, Evola too was thrown into an existential crisis and contemplated suicide. He lost his longing for extinction when he suddenly grasped a passage from the Buddhist Pali Canon.[7] It said that he who believes that his own extinction is final extinction has in no way understood true extinction.[8]

Evola came to a transcendent experience of the "I" through spiritual experimentation, reinforced by inhaling ether. It changed his life and forever after gave him the firm grounding that allowed no inner deviation. He describes this consciousness expansion as an "idea of peremptory, absolute, and resounding certainty," adding "When I compare it to my previous and habitual consciousness, only one image comes to mind: the most lucid, conscious state of wakefulness in comparison to the deepest, most hypnotic and torpid state of sleep."[9] This was the basis for the unshakable quality of his views, despite all the hazards of his life. His many ambitious mountaineering excursions in the Alpine glacier region helped to deepen this attitude. Climbing mountain peaks was for him a symbol of the ascent to the divine.[10]

Futurism and Dadaism

Evola's philosophical and literary interests brought him into the artistic circle around the Italian Futurists Giovanni Papini and Filippo Tommaso Marinetti, and Evola himself soon began to paint. Papini introduced him to Eastern spirituality and above all to Meister Eckhart. In one of his earliest writings, *Essays on Magical Idealism* (*Saggi sull'idealismo magico*) Evola cites Eckhart's statement that one should not do one's work for the sake of heaven, God, or salvation, that is, not for anything outside, but always without asking why.[11] This saying stands as a leading principle of Evola's entire life: action done irrespective of success or of the plaudits or opposition of others. Eckhart also wrote: "God and Being are the same.

But if I know God directly thus, then *I* must become *him* and *he* must become *me* . . . so completely one that this *he* and this *I* are one thing." This may be the origin of Evola's recurrent urge in his esoteric writings toward "identity with God" (deification), often criticized as hubris and "supermanhood."[12]

Evola soon broke with Futurism, whose polemical attacks against the bourgeois had so attracted him. "What disturbed me in Futurism was its sensualist overtones: its lack of inwardness, its noisy and exhibitionist character . . . with its chauvinistic nationalism."[13] He then turned to the incipient Dada movement. A friendship developed with Tristan Tzara, Dada's prime mover, documented by thirty surviving letters from Evola to the Franco-Romanian artist.[14] Dadaism was far more radical than Futurism, and like Far Eastern philosophy spoke of an identity of the I with the Non-I. In his essay *Abstract Art* (*Arte astratta*) Evola speaks of art as coming out of a *higher* consciousness.[15] Dadaism could, however, not satisfy his metaphysical thirst, and in 1922, at the age of twenty-four, he ended not only his Dadaistic period but also, abruptly and finally, his artistic career. Even so, he is reckoned today as one of the foremost representatives of Italian Dadaism and is valued by collectors, with paintings in Roman and Brescian museums.[16]

The philosophical phase and the Far East

Evola dates this phase to about 1923–27, although his two main philosophical works—*Theory of the Absolute Individual* (*Teoria del l'individuo assoluto*) and *Phenomenology of the Absolute Individual* (*Fenomenologia dell'individuo assoluto*)—were published later.[17] His philosophy goes back to German idealism (especially Fichte and Schelling) and beyond that to Plato. Evola called it "magical idealism," a term from the Romantic poet Novalis, in which one again detects his transcendent impulse.

Evola's question is one of the oldest in philosophy. He seeks the absolute point of certainty on which to build his structure of thinking. In view of his earlier transcendent experience of the I, there could only be one certainty for him: the I itself—naturally not the everyday ego but the transcendent foundation of one's own personality. Called the "absolute individual" and likened to the Indian *ātman*, this is for Evola not only the "center of universal responsibility"[18] but also expresses a perfect fullness of power, which necessarily grows from absolute knowledge and is at the same time boundless freedom.

During this phase, Evola was also deeply involved with the religious and esoteric writings of the Far East. It was already evident in his *Essays on Magical Idealism* (*Saggi sull'idealismo magico*) how important he found the *Tao Te Ching*.[19] His philosophy thus broke the usual academic boundaries and reached far into spiritual traditions. Equally important was his study of the Hindu scripture *Bhagavad Gita*, whose statements could only reinforce Evola's natural leaning toward the *Kshatriya* warrior class. He concluded that the outward battle simultaneously symbolizes the inward battle against one's own weaknesses and negative qualities.[20]

Evola's next book, *Man as Power* (*L'Uomo come Potenza*),[21] which appeared in 1925, formed the link between his philosophical period and the following "magical" one, in which he strove, after his theorizing, for an active and practical breakthrough to transcendence. Evola's all-important concept of power, which also applied to politics and which he interprets in the sense of Tantrism and Taoism, must be firmly distinguished from "force" or "violence." Power and force stand for him as contraries, for power loses its own being when it has to resort to material means, that is, to force, rather than working completely from itself, out of its inner superiority and hence "magically." In his first political work, *Pagan Imperialism* (*Imperialismo pagano*) he stated that "superiority is not based upon power, but power upon superiority. To need 'power' is impotence."[22]

A very important relationship of Evola's was with the Italian Arturo Reghini, a Pythagorean and a Freemason, who introduced him to alchemy, magic, and the pagan tradition of Rome. In 1927 Evola and Reghini founded the magical and initiatically oriented "Group of Ur."[23] Beside individual practices there was also "group work" by the leading members, aimed at creating a "subtle" entity for magically influencing Mussolini, who had spoken of the "Return of the Empire after fifteen centuries to the destined hills of Rome,"[24] which was also Evola's and Reghini's ambition, in the sense of their *Pagan Imperialism*. But the Catholic Church, which Mussolini needed for his regime, naturally did not want a pagan Rome. This led to the Lateran Accords of 1929 between the Vatican and Mussolini, exploding this dream of the Group of Ur.

The Group of Ur was fundamentally concerned not just with self-transformation and integration into the transcendental realm but also with the resultant higher dignity and freedom. An actual ontological change of state (initiation) was necessary for obtaining the intended identity with God (deification). Connected with this was the achievement of an unbroken continuum of consciousness, which ideally would even extend beyond (bodily) death.

The integral tradition

It was also through Reghini that in the mid-1920s Evola came into contact with the idea of the "integral tradition" in the sense of the French esotericist René Guénon, where "integral" distinguishes it from simple tradition as the preservation of old customs and mores. Evola was quickly seized by the idea, but he differed from Guénon in his active and combative character. He saw himself as belonging to the warrior or *Kshatriya* caste, and not, like Guénon, as a contemplative Brahmin. This activist attitude also explains Evola's controversial effort as an esotericist to influence practical politics. The fruit of Evola's intensive study of the integral tradition is what is probably his best-known book, *Revolt Against the Modern World* (*Rivolta contro il mondo moderno*).[25] The book is in two parts: part 1 sets out the theoretical principles and explains what constitutes the integral tradition; part 2 offers an "occult" history of the world.

Evola presents the integral tradition as a universal and timeless (perennial) *Weltanschauung*, whose origin lies in the transcendent, beyond humans, peoples, and history. It is primordial, unitive, and all-encompassing. All metaphysical worldviews and important religions derive from it. Since the integral tradition claims a "divine" origin, it is also the final authority for its adherents; it cannot be questioned, never alters, and sets the absolute norm that everything should follow. It is clearly determined from "above." The modern world, in the form of Western civilization and technology, which rests on merely material, physiochemical bases and is thus determined from "below," is seen as the exact contrary of this tradition.

The integral tradition, never perfectly realizable on Earth and thus only an ideal to be striven for, rests on strictly hierarchical thinking, whereby the highest rank approaches the transcendent. The stages descend through progressive materialization. From this hierarchy of the absolute primacy of everything spiritual, there inevitably derive a series of incompatible contrasts with modernity, dominated as it is by the idea of equality. For example, the leadership in a traditional society can belong only to someone who can act as link to transcendence, for only "there" can the meaning and purpose of such a society be found. A priest-king corresponds most closely to this idea of a leader:

> Every traditional society is characterized by the presence of beings who, by virtue of the innate or acquired superiority over the human condition, embody within the temporal order the living and efficacious presence of a power that comes from above. One of these types of beings is the *pontifex* . . . Pontifex means "builder of bridges" . . . connecting the natural and supernatural dimensions. . . . In the world of Tradition the most important foundation of authority and of the right of kings and chiefs, and the reason why they were obeyed, feared and venerated, was essentially their transcendent and nonhuman quality.[26]

A further consequence of this spiritually organized hierarchy is the division of humans according to their inner capability of approaching traditional spirituality and transmitting it, clearly manifested in the Hindu caste system. Further characteristics of the traditional world are the predominance of ritual, initiation, and consecration, together with completely different concepts of time and space, considered not quantitatively but qualitatively, according to their affinity with transcendence.

The second part of *Revolt Against the Modern World* describes the "decline" from an originally spiritual and traditional culture down to the modern world. Thus, following Greco-Roman and Vedic reports, Evola speaks of a hyperborean center that was localized in prehistoric times in the Arctic, and where Nordic "god-men" ruled until "Cosmic" catastrophes forced them to leave their homeland, thereby spreading their upward-directed ("heavenward"), solar, and heroically masculine view of life throughout most of the world. On the other side there had arisen the downward-directed ("earthward"), lunar, and matriarchal cultures of the southern peoples, leading to warfare but also to miscegenation with northerners. The influence of Jakob Bachofen is evident here, though Evola turned his worldview completely upside down.[27]

Over descending cycles, the solar element in the West is said to have lost more and more of its power. A final flickering of tradition is still detectable in medieval Catholicism, because this leaned less towards Christian humility than towards a sacred imperialism.[28] For Evola, the Renaissance and especially the French Revolution mark further stages of decline. Modernity would finally plunge into collectivism, anarchy, and materialism, as already prophesied in Indian scriptures (*Vishnu-purāṇa*). World history thus appears not as evolution but as devolution, to the point of the Iron or Dark Age (*kālī-yuga*) of today. A true restoration of tradition would be possible only after the utter collapse of the modern world. There can be no gradual transition between traditional and modern culture because they are utterly separate and have developed entirely different concepts of time, value, and the sacred.

The much-honored German expressionist poet Gottfried Benn, reviewing *Revolt Against the Modern World*, called it "an epochal book. Whoever has read it will be changed."[29]

Politics

Evola's political philosophy is understandable only through his premise of the primacy of the transcendent, as mentioned earlier. It rests on hierarchical thinking and finds its expression in the "organic state," as presented in Evola's chief political work, *Men Among the Ruins (UGli uomini e lerovine*, 1952).[30] Its presupposition is a center resting on transcendent principles, which—in contrast to totalitarianism—permeates all elements of the state from above to below due to its higher spiritual power alone. As in Plato, the first duty of the state is to lead citizens to higher goals.

At the same time, Evola took issue with the concept of the nation, since this was determined merely by biological and cultural parameters; instead, he advocates a spiritual-monarchical empire. The core ideas of this work were already summarized for Evola's closest adherents in his short book *Orientations (Orientamenti)*.[31]

Evola's first political essay appeared in 1925 in the anti-Fascist newspaper *Lo Stato Democratico (The Democratic State)*, and already had all the ingredients that would mark his later political works: first, opposition to democracy, since this depended on quantity, not on quality, and lacked the spiritual element. But it also opposed the ruling Fascist regime as being too "populist" and likewise devoid of any spirituality. He called the Fascist revolution a "caricature of a revolution" (*ironia di rivoluzione*). Evola wrote all this in the hope of reforming a Fascism striving for strict control, and of being able to correct it in the direction of his pagan, spiritual, and imperial idea. It was a project that could never succeed.

Italian Fascism had arisen from the often violent "Fasci italiani di combattimento" (Italian battle groups), founded in 1919, which transformed into a political party in 1921. In 1922 there came the triumphal "March on Rome," whereupon it formed a coalition government with conservatives and nationalists. Mussolini, who had originally belonged to the Socialist Party, became prime minister, and in 1925 a single-party dictatorship was established.

In 1928 Evola's *Pagan Imperialism* was published, as a polemical focusing of his political views. The book caused lively controversy, especially in the Vatican, whose influence Evola had sharply criticized. After the end of the Group of Ur, Evola founded the journal *La Torre* (*The Tower*), which was closed down after only six months. The cause was his attacks on Mussolini's campaign for increasing the birthrate and his uncompromising attitude to the "plebeian" regime.

Evola abroad

Seeing no further possibility for himself and his political ideas in Fascist Italy, Evola undertook extensive journeys throughout Europe to meet representatives of political directions that matched his own sacral, holistic, antiliberal and anti-Bolshevist positions. Among them were representatives of Germany's "Conservative Revolution" and the founder of Romania's Iron Guard, Corneliu Codreanu.[32] While visiting Romania, Evola came into contact with Mircea Eliade, the historian of religion and philosopher, who had early on embraced some of Evola's ideas and with whom he remained in contact later.

Evola also met the political theorist Carl Schmitt and the poet Gottfried Benn, and gave lectures in Germany. He met Schmitt several times, and letters to him even exist from the postwar era. Evola followed Schmitt's ideas closely,[33] but their outlooks were too different to allow for a reciprocal influence, not least because of Schmitt's Catholicism. Evola appreciated Schmitt, both because they belonged to the same tradition of conservative thinkers and also because they were linked by their esteem for the antiliberal political philosopher Juan Donoso Cortés.

Evola and Ernst Jünger seem never to have met. Evola wanted to translate Jünger's *The Worker* (*Der Arbeiter*), because he saw the "worker" as an elemental force against bourgeois society. However, he did not agree with some aspects of the work and settled for an adaptation of it, supplied with his own commentaries.[34] Evola certainly did not agree with the later works in which Jünger turned more to humanistic and democratic ideas.[35] Although Evola translated Spengler's *The Decline of the West* into Italian in 1957, he wrote that Spengler's writing influenced him in no way and criticized Spengler for his lack of a metaphysical standpoint.[36]

It was mainly the apparent leanings of National Socialism toward the Germanic past and to ancient symbols, as well as its emphasis on loyalty, discipline, and readiness for sacrifice, that led Evola to a closer approach to Germany and especially to the SS, which he admired—at least to begin with—as a spiritual warrior order. A claim from Italian police reports that Evola was acquainted with Heinrich Himmler, who was fascinated by old German esoteric teachings and wanted to lead the SS as a chivalric order, is unconfirmed. There is however evidence that he was in contact with the *Ahnenerbe* (Research Community for Ancestral Heritage), the research institute founded by Himmler and the *völkish* ideologist Herman Wirth. The point of contention was above all the Führer Principle, which, in Evola's view, lacked any legitimacy from a transcendent authority, referred only to the people, and consequently had to act in a demagogic fashion. Evola also opposed the purely biological racial principle, as well as the whipping-up of nationalist feelings.[37]

Evola's attempt to gain a corrective influence over German politics via the SS was a complete failure. Already in 1938 an SS document described Evola, because of his divergent views, as a "reactionary Roman and a fantasist," together with the directive to observe his subsequent activity. With that, his efforts for a sacralized politics failed in Germany, as they had in Italy.

Evola's racial doctrines

In the mid-1930s another chance occurred for Evola to gain political influence. Mussolini expressed himself in positive terms about Evola's thesis of a "spiritual" racism and invited him for discussions. Evola had applied his holistic concept of man as consisting of body, soul, and spirit to racial doctrine, and spoke of a bodily race, a soul race, and a spiritual race. These would not necessarily coincide in the same individual. As Evola wrote in July 1931, "The preservation or restoration of racial unity (in its narrow sense) may be everything in an animal. But it is not so in man."[38] Mussolini wanted to use Evola's racial doctrine as a counterweight to the "materialistic and biological" racism of National Socialism, but the project failed because resistance in both countries was too strong.

Evola's anti-Semitism requires discussion. He saw the Jews as a symbol of the materialistic and economic domination of humanity, as conceived by the German sociologist Werner Sombart.[39] The early influence of Otto Weininger, with his dictum "Judaism is the spirit of modern life," now came to fruition.[40] After his suicide in 1903, Weininger had acquired a worldwide circle of admirers, including Jews. Evola's anti-Semitism was neither religious nor primarily biological. In emotional moments he often repudiated his own guidelines, though. He expressed himself positively on orthodox Judaism and especially Kabbalah, and ensured that his esoteric book-series *Horizons of the Spirit* (*Orizzonti dello spirito*) would publish the great Jewish scholar of Kabbalah, Gershom Scholem.

The postwar period

After the downfall and arrest of Mussolini in 1943 and his subsequent rescue by German troops, Evola was present as interpreter at discussions between Mussolini and Hitler at Hitler's headquarters in Rastenburg, East Prussia (now Kętrzyn, Poland). The resulting Salò Republic, however, fulfilled Evola's expectations even less than the original Fascist state that had now collapsed.[41] As American troops were marching on Rome in 1944, Evola fled to Vienna. His relations with individual Fascist leaders were well known, and toward the end of the Fascist regime he had also been in contact with the Nazi Security Service (*Sicherheitsdienst*).[42] The nature of these contacts remains unexplained. In Vienna he planned to write a *Secret History of Secret Societies*, probably having access to the documents that the German authorities had seized from Masonic lodges. This plan, however, was not realized.

During one of the final bombing raids on Vienna in 1945, Evola suffered a serious spinal injury, which caused him to be confined in a wheelchair to the end of his life. After three years in Austrian and Italian hospitals and sanatoria he returned to Rome, where he resumed his activity as a writer. Beside his own writing, Evola was obliged by financial need to extensive activity as a translator. This included, among others, works by Gustav Meyrink, Mircea Eliade, Arthur Avalon, D. T. Suzuki, Oswald Spengler, Gabriel Marcel, Otto Weininger, and Ernst Jünger.

Soon after his return to Rome, Evola became the spiritual focus of a group of mostly young followers, who tried to emulate his sharply formulated spiritual and political views. In April 1951 he was accused of being the "intellectual instigator" of secret neo-fascist terrorist groups, and of "glorifying Fascism." After six months in custody he was acquitted.

Evola died in 1974, appreciated only by a few, in a small Roman apartment provided by a benefactress. Following his last will and testament he was cremated, and his ashes deposited in a glacier cleft on Monte Rosa.

Postwar writings

In 1958 a further major work appeared: *The Metaphysics of Sex* (*Metafisica del sesso*).[43] Evola saw sex as almost the only possibility for today's man to get some sense of a transcendent "higher world." For thereby man most readily lets his everyday "I" fall away and can open himself to transcendent spheres.

Evola's political attitude finally altered—partly because a practical application of his ideas seemed impossible given the lack of qualified followers—to an *apoliteia*, an attitude exempt from mundane political efforts. This concept, originating with the Stoics, is found in Evola's most controversial book, *Ride the Tiger* (*Cavalcare la tigre*),[44] which sold well. It is the most pessimistic and misunderstood of Evola's books. There are two possible meanings to *apoliteia*. One sees it as a call to complete retreat from all politics; the other holds that political activity is still possible, but that one should not allow oneself to be inwardly affected by it. Many took this as meaning that one must act absolutely uncompromisingly. In the years of unrest among Roman youth, when leftist students also began to read Evola, opinions—already exacerbated by the Cold War—became ever more radical and street fighting more violent, with many killed.

A few young people saw the book as even justifying terrorist activities, although Evola had expressly stated that this was a book intended "for a particular human type," and that it "does *not* concern the ordinary man of today."[45] It was meant only for those who feel that they belong to the "world of Tradition." An excellent discussion of this issue is Gianfranco de Turris's *Praise and Defence of Julius Evola: The Baron and the Terrorists*.[46] Evola also wrote in the journal of the New Order Study Center (*Centro Studi Ordine Nuovo*).[47] A series of terrorist attacks was long blamed on certain members of this order, but many now attribute most of these attacks to the "strategy of tension," a controversial episode of the Cold War.[48] Evola, then, was hardly the spiritual leader of the terrorists as some have portrayed him, though individual actors did read him.

Later reception

Although Evola was never a member of the Fascist Party, his involvement with Fascism, National Socialism, and anti-Semitism had the result that after the Second World War he was at first little read, except by his dedicated enemies or followers. Only after his death, and since the late 1980s, has he again been widely discussed. Translations into French were published first. Italians who had fled from Italy to France and England also contributed to the dissemination. An ever-increasing number of translations have now made Evola widely known outside Italy, including all of Eastern Europe and some Near-Eastern and South American regions.

The success of these publications is in part connected to Evola's almost "magical" writing style, which is on the one hand precise and logical, and on the other hand able to evoke "eternal" myths. Evola's use of myth connects him to J. R. R. Tolkien's trilogy *The Lord of the Rings*, which revived interest in archetypal forces, with their polarization between good and evil. It thereby also opened a door to Evola's world of Tradition. Authors such as the mythologist Joseph Campbell, and the *Star Wars* films, reaching millions of viewers, also contributed to the process. In Italy there was a successful movement called "Campo Hobbit," in which students who wanted to get beyond the old rightist ideas came under the influence of former Evola admirers, such as Marco Tarchi.[49]

Evola was first published by esoteric publishers. In Italy it was Edizioni Mediterranee, the country's largest esoteric publisher, who obtained Evola's copyrights. In the German-speaking world, Ansata Verlag published the first German translations. In the Anglophone world, Inner Traditions, the largest esoteric publisher in the US, marketed Evola in English. Then, in 2010, Evola's political works began to appear from Arktos in London. Only in France was Evola's promotion divided between publishers of esotericism and religious history on the one hand, and on the other, the predominantly political house of Pardès in Puiseaux. The root of Evola's wide-ranging reception seems to lie primarily in the power of myth and esotericism, then, and not in his political persuasiveness.

Today, however, works outlining Evola's worldview and political ideas, with their successful blend of myth with social questions, sell in greater numbers than the esoteric writings. His linguistic radicalism and uncompromising statements have often touched the nerves of a youth culture which, after the uprisings of 1968, wanted to combat capitalist finance and the excesses of consumer culture. Youth of both rightist and leftist tendencies shared this furious opposition. Hence a parallel has even been suggested between the statements of Evola and Marcuse.[50] Evola has also entered into the alternative music scene with groups like Blood Axis, Von Thronstahl, Allerseelen, or Ain Soph, though it is unclear whether they really share Evola's worldview, or just use his name.

Ironically, a further cause for Evola's wider reception is the often fierce reaction of his philosophical opponents to the increasing publication of Evola's works. Most notably, Umberto Eco's enraged commentaries reached far and wide, thanks to his fame, and led to more curiosity and higher sales for Evola.

Conclusion

Can one truly say that Evola is the most significant thinker of the Italian Right? It is correct inasmuch as Evola was perhaps the only intellectual to have offered a comprehensive rightist challenge to the dominant anti-Fascist worldview. But it is also wrong, because only a few representatives of the Right accept Evola's equation of the Right with tradition. Many, like the New Right in Italy, even speak of this as a "politically disabling myth." Evola's worldwide reception by the radical Right came at a cost, since, as the legal philosopher Anna Jellamo says, "it necessarily led to a partial or even reductive view."[51] Taking single elements of Evola's works as equivalent to the whole has often resulted in a flawed criticism, due to such limited or reductive views. Any political reading of Evola needs above all to notice the primacy of the transcendent.

Notes

1. Although there are already around eighty books on Evola, most of which are political, there is still no comprehensive biography covering Evola's multifarious interests.
2. Further details in H. T. Hakl, "Julius Evola: War er nun Baron—oder doch nicht?" *Gnostika* 60 (May 2017): 75–83.
3. Julius Evola, *The Path of Cinnabar* (London: Integral Tradition, 2009), 10.
4. Julius Evola, "Sorpassamento del Superuomo," in *Il nihilismo attivo di Federico Nietzsche* (Rome: Europa Libreria, 2000), 26–40. First published 1934.
5. Otto Weininger, *Sex and Character* (New York: A. L. Burt Co., 1906), 159.
6. Evola, *Path of Cinnabar*, 6.
7. *Majjhima-nikāya* I, 1.
8. Evola, *Path of Cinnabar*, 15–16.
9. Julius Evola (Iagla), "Experiences: The Law of Beings," in *Introduction to Magic* (Rochester, VT: Inner Traditions, 2001), 167–172.
10. Julius Evola, *Meditations on the Peaks* (Rochester, VT: Inner Traditions, 1998).
11. Julius Evola, *Saggi sull'idealismo magico* (Todi–Rome: Atanòr, 1925).
12. Hans Thomas Hakl, "Deification as a Core Theme in Julius Evola's Esoteric Works," *Correspondences* (forthcoming).
13. Evola, *Path of Cinnabar*, 13.

14. Ibid., 19–20.
15. Assessorato alla Cultura, Regione Lombardia, *Julius Evola e l'Arte delle Avanguardie*. Mostra Palazzo Bagatti-Valsecchi, October 15–November 29, 1998.
16. Ibid.
17. Julius Evola, *Teoria dell'individuo assoluto* (Turin: Bocca, 1927); *Fenomenologia dell'individuo assoluto* (Turin: Bocca, 1930).
18. Ibid., 12.
19. Julius Evola, *Saggi sull'idealismo magico* (Todi–Rome: Atanòr, 1925), 100.
20. Julius Evola, *Revolt Against the Modern World* (Rochester, VT: Inner Traditions, 1995), 116–117.
21. No English translation. Only Evola's second work on Tantra has been translated as *The Yoga of Power* (Rochester, VT: Inner Traditions, 1992).
22. English translation: https://de.scribd.com/document/359983564/Julius-Evola-Pagan-Imperialism 36.
23. Renato Del Ponte, "Julius Evola and the Ur Group," *Introduction to Magic* (Rochester, VT: Inner Traditions, 2001). This is the first of the three volumes of Ur-Krur monographs. The second is forthcoming. For details, see Hans Thomas Hakl, "Julius Evola and the Ur Group," *Aries* 12, no. 1 (2012): 53–90.
24. https://youtu.be/r6NdDMg8DTQ
25. Julius Evola, *Rivolta contro il mondo moderno* (Milano: Hoepli, 1934); *Revolt Against the Modern World* (Rochester, VT: Inner Traditions, 1995).
26. Evola, *Revolt Against the Modern World*, 7.
27. Evola translated and commented on extracts from Bachofen's work in 1949 as *Le madri e la virilità olimpica* (Milan: Bocca, 1949).
28. Evola's aversion to Christianity is not complete but directed above all against its modern currents. Significant former followers of his have found their way, thanks to his teachings, to a traditionally aware Christianity.
29. Gottfried Benn, review of *Erhebung wider die moderne Welt* by Julius Evola, *Die Literatur* 37 (1934/35): 283–287.
30. Julius Evola, *Men Among the Ruins* (Rochester, VT: Inner Traditions, 2002). The sole English academic work on Evola's political writings, which also competently treats his philosophical but unfortunately not his esoteric writings, is Paul Furlong, *Social and Political Thought of Julius Evola* (London: Routledge, 2011). See also H. T. Hansen [Hakl], "Julius Evola's Political Endeavors," in Evola's *Men Among the Ruins* (Rochester, VT: Inner Traditions, 2002), 1–106. A well-informed but very critical position regarding Evola's political views is Francesco Cassata, *A destra del fascismo* (Turin: Bollati Boringhieri, 2003).
31. Julius Evola, *Orientamenti*. English translation on https://www.counter-currents.com/2015/01/orientations.
32. Summary in H. T. Hansen [Hakl], *Julius Evola et la révolution conservatrice allemande* (Montreuil-sous-Bois: Les Deux Étendards, 2002).
33. *Lettere di Julius Evola a Carl Schmitt 1951–1963* (Rome: Fondazione Julius Evola, 2000). Includes three essays on Schmitt by Evola.

34. Julius Evola, L' "Operaio" nel pensiero di Ernst Jünger (Rome: Armando, 1960).
35. Evola, Path of Cinnabar, 221.
36. Ibid., 206.
37. Julius Evola, Fascism Viewed from the Right (London: Arktos, 2013).
38. Julius Evola, "Stirpe e spiritualità," in Vita Nova (1925–1933) (Rome: Settimo Sigillo, 1999).
39. Werner Sombart, Die Juden und das Wirtschaftsleben (Leipzig: Duncker and Humblot, 1911).
40. Weininger, Sex and Character.
41. Evola's fundamental report is in "Con Mussolini al Quartier Generale di Hitler" in Mito e realtà del fascismo, ed. Gianfranco de Turris (Rome: Fondazione Julius Evola, 2014), 133–151.
42. See Dana Lloyd Thomas, Julius Evola e la tentazione razzista (Mesagne: Giordano, 2006); Gianfranco de Turris, Julius Evola, un filosofo in guerra 1943–1945 (Rome: Mursia, 2016).
43. Julius Evola, The Metaphysics of Sex (New York: Inner Traditions, 1983).
44. Julius Evola, Ride the Tiger (Rochester, VT: Inner Traditions, 2003).
45. Ibid., 2. Even Paul Furlong, a political scientist at the University of Cardiff, who is certainly no friend of Evola but reads him in the original language, writes that Evola "emphasizes that this is a specifically spiritual discussion." Mark Sedgwick also shows great discrimination in his very detailed chapter, "Terror in Italy," in Against the Modern World: Traditionalism and the Secret Intellectual History of the Twentieth Century (New York: Oxford University Press, 2004), 179–189.
46. Gianfranco de Turris, Elogio e difesa di Julius Evola: Il Barone e i terroristi (Rome: Edizioni Mediterranee, 1997). The book is admittedly written by the president of the Evola Foundation in Rome but has a foreword by Giorgio Galli, a leftist political scientist at Milan University. Galli writes (9) that he undertook this foreword after long doubts, "because he was convinced that the documentation contained in it was complete and makes the point regarding a question of indubitable historical value."
47. Julius Evola, I Testi di Ordine Nuovo (Padua: Edizioni di Ar, 2001).
48. Daniele Ganser, NATO'S Secret Armies: Operation GLADIO and Terrorism in Western Europe (Abingdon: Routledge, 2005).
49. Apiù Mani, Hobbit / Hobbit (Rome: LEDE, 1982); Alessandro Portelli, "Tradizione e meta-tradizione," in Fascismo oggi (Cuneo: Istituto Storico della Resistenza, 1982), 287–310.
50. Giano Accame, "Evola e Marcuse," in Il fascismo immenso e rosso (Rome: Settimo Sigillo, 1990), 137–142.
51. Anna Jellamo, "J. Evola, il pensatore della tradizione," in La destra radicale (Milan: Feltrinelli, 1984), 215–247.

PART II

Modern Thinkers

5

Alain de Benoist and the New Right

Jean-Yves Camus

ALAIN DE BENOIST was born in 1943 in Saint-Symphorien, near Tours, France. He is considered the main thinker of the so-called French New Right (*nouvelle droite*), an intellectual movement established in France in 1968 in order to rethink European identity and challenge both then-dominant Marxism and the mainstream liberal Right. Since the early 1990s, the French New Right has been influential beyond France, especially in Italy, Germany, and Belgium, and has inspired Alexander Dugin in Russia. Part of the American radical Right and "Alt Right" also claims to have been inspired by de Benoist's writings. Although this is questionable, de Benoist and Dominique Venner are also seen as the forefathers of the "identitarian" movement in Europe. De Benoist has published one hundred and six books and more than two thousand articles, which have been translated into fourteen languages.[1] He is the editor of the annual publication *Nouvelle école* (*New School*) and the editorial writer for the monthly magazine *Eléments*, the two flagship publications of the French New Right. He is also the director of a quarterly publication, *Krisis*.

The goal of de Benoist and the French New Right is similar to that of the 1930s Non-Conformists (a French group that called for a nontotalitarian "new order")[2] and is even closer to that of the German Conservative Revolution, on which they draw heavily. De Benoist was introduced to the Conservative Revolution by Ernst Jünger's former secretary, Armin Mohler, while the latter was a journalist in Paris.[3] True to his Conservative Revolutionary beliefs, de Benoist still sets himself the goal of having a critical approach toward the mainstream conservatism that is, in the French context, heir to the Gaullist party and to the authoritarian Right of the nineteenth century.[4] He agrees with mainstream conservatives on such matters as keeping traditional Western values and having a holistic vision of society,[5] but strongly rejects free-market economics, the primacy of human rights, and the Christian heritage.

Career

De Benoist generally keeps quiet about his private life.[6] He is married to a German-born wife and has two children. His avowed passion is collecting books (and reading them), his private library containing 250,000 volumes. De Benoist, who is keen on genealogy, says his father belonged to the nobility, with roots from the Middle Ages in what is now Belgium. His mother came from the lower middle class, her ancestors being fishermen and peasants from Normandy and Brittany. Jean-Yves Le Gallou, another intellectual figure in the French New Right, writes that the reason for de Benoist's avowed contempt for the bourgeoisie lies in this family background,[7] and de Benoist himself admits that his socially mixed family made him aware at an early age that he could not bear the upper class's contempt for the common man.

From the age of fifteen, de Benoist was attracted to the nationalist Right, at first in the context of the war in Algeria and the return to power of General de Gaulle. He started work as a journalist by contributing to Henry Coston's magazine *Lectures françaises* (*French Readings*) in 1960,[8] but always stayed away from Coston's belief in conspiracy theories (especially involving Freemasonry and the Jews) and his strident anti-Semitism. Often using the pseudonym "Fabrice Laroche" (and later "Robert de Herte," as well as a few others) he found a political home in activist movements such as the Federation of Nationalist Students (Federation des étudiants nationalistes, FEN) and Europe-Action, which fought to keep Algeria French.

After Algeria became independent in 1962, de Benoist was among those who decided to break with the useless street activism of the fringe extreme Right and to focus on "metapolitics," borrowing Antonio Gramsci's idea that ideological hegemony is a precondition for political victory. De Benoist explains that "all the big revolutions in history did no more than transpose into facts an evolution that had already taken place in minds, in an underlying manner."[9] Both parliamentary politics and street activism can only have short-term consequences and, if one really wants one's ideas to shape society, one has to work on ideas first. This, and de Benoist's belief that petty French nationalism had to be replaced by European nationalism, led him to become the main founding member of GRECE (Groupement de recherche et d'études pour la civilisation européenne/Research and Study Group for European Civilization), the intellectual think tank of the French New Right.[10] GRECE had a political influence on conservative and liberal parties between 1975 and 1980, and later gave birth to sister movements in, among others Italy (Nuova Destra with Marco Tarchi), Germany (Neue Rechte, with Henning Eichberg and today, the weekly *Junge Freiheit*, to which de Benoist contributes), Flanders (with Luc Pauwels and the magazine *TeKos–Tekste, Kommentaren en Studies*) and the French-speaking part of Belgium (GRECE-Belgique with Georges Hupin and then Robert Steuckers).[11] It also has an influence in the US, where he was introduced and published by the late Paul Piccone of the New Left magazine, *Telos*, starting in 1992–93.

In 1979 and 1993, two press campaigns in the French liberal media damaged de Benoist's influence in France by alleging that he and GRECE were "closet Fascists" or even "Nazis" who hid their beliefs in a racist, antiegalitarian *Weltanschauung* aimed at reformulating *völkisch* ideas in a seemingly acceptable way by replacing the hierarchy of races with "ethnodifferentialism." Since that time, although still a frequent commentator on French politics and as such someone who keeps an interest in the role of the Front national (National Front), de Benoist has focused on his intellectual activity, trying to be the key thinker of a nonconventional Right and a critic of globalization, postmodern society, and—above all—the "ideology of sameness." He rejects politically correct anti-racism on the grounds that it ultimately leads to the eradication of the very same "right to be different" that it seeks to implement. His criticism of globalization and free-market economics has led him to translate and publish such nonconformist Marxists or Progressives as Costanzo Preve[12] and Danilo Zolo. Since 1988, through the quarterly magazine *Krisis*, he has also tried to build a bridge between the New Right and some of the academics who write in *La Revue du MAUSS*,[13] and has positively received the thought of Christopher Lasch, with whom he agreed on participatory democracy and the criticism of the globalized elites.[14] Another consequence of his radical stand against capitalism is that he supports "degrowth"— the ecology-oriented policy of downsizing production and consumption. This goes hand in hand with his post-2000 evolution toward advocating localism and deliberative democracy.

Key ideas

The key idea throughout de Benoist's intellectual journey has been, through the use of metapolitics, to think the ways and means that are necessary in order for European civilization, based on the cultural values shared on the continent until the advent of globalization, to thrive and be perpetuated. De Benoist's work and thought are not always identical to that of GRECE and the French New Right, even though he embodies both movements and sets the tone of their development. GRECE and the French New Right, because they are schools of thought, encompass a variety of beliefs and attitudes. For example, de Benoist admires the mid-twentieth-century novelist and political writer Raymond Abellio and his concept of gnosis but, unlike other French New Right figures, he is not a perennialist and (other than with regard to aesthetics) has been little influenced by Julius Evola or René Guénon. He is undoubtedly a pagan, as can be seen in his 1981 book *On Being a Pagan* (*Comment peut-on être païen?*)[15] but his opposition to monotheism is voiced in a softer tone than that of Pierre Vial, or the late Maurice Rollet and Jean Mabire, members of GRECE who are committed to *völkisch* values, including a focus on Nordicism. Understanding de Benoist's intellectual journey means accepting that he is a thinker, not a mere compiler, and that his views are his own, as is shown by his distancing himself from Guillaume Faye, who had been a member, then a top official of GRECE from 1970 until 1986. When Faye published *The Colonization of Europe: Speaking Truth about Immigration and Islam* (*La Colonisation de l'Europe: discours vrai sur l'immigration et l'Islam*) in 2000, de Benoist disavowed Faye's "strongly racist" ideas with regard to Muslims.[16]

This being said, de Benoist's core values are those of the French New Right, which he embodies. His work and thought can be summed up in three key ideas. The first is the criticism of the primacy of individual rights, which he sees as a consequence of eighteenth-century humanism, later embodied in the principles of the French Revolution and of the American Founding Fathers (he is very critical of the "American dream"). However, he is no less opposed to nationalism, as he thinks both ideologies derive from the "metaphysics of subjectivity."[17] His second core idea is that the main danger the world is now facing is the hegemony of capital, combined with the pursuit of self-interest which is typical of the postmodern era. As a result, de Benoist has told his (mostly rightist) readers that although he is not a Marxist, he sees some truth in what Karl Marx wrote in *Das Kapital*, both with regard to the nature of capitalism and to the reality of conflicting class interests.[18] Contrary to what his opponents from the radical Right believe, there is no such thing as a "leftist" move in his thought: he stays true to the anti-capitalist tradition of the National Revolutionaries and that of the Communitarian Socialists and, furthermore, his opposition to the unlimited expansion of the free market stems from his belief that consumerism and finance contribute to the erasure of peoples' identities. The first and foremost distinction he makes is not between the "working class," although he acknowledges that it does exist, and the "bourgeoisie," but between the "haves" and the "have nots," the "new dominant class" and the "people."[19]

Another consequence of his cherishing ethnic and cultural identities is that de Benoist stands for the political autonomy of each and every such group. When applied to Europe, this third central idea means that he is opposed to the nation state (in the case of France, the centralized "Jacobin" state) and favors a federal Europe built on the principle of subsidiarity—that is, the recognition of the existence of communities, whether based on ethnicity, language, religion, or gender. De Benoist frequently refers to the ideas of Johannes Althusius in *Politics Methodically Set Forth* (*Politica methodice digesta*, 1603), and also shows sympathy toward the idea of "national personal autonomy" (*nationale Selbstbestimung*) developed by Otto Bauer, Karl Renner, and the interwar Austro-Marxists, who envisioned replacing the nation state with the "ethnopluralist" concept of gathering individuals belonging to a distinct ethnic or ethnoreligious group into a nonterritorially based association of persons.

He has been criticized by those who see him as a (neo-)Fascist for wanting to replace the nation state with a juxtaposition of homogenous ethnic entities, thereby denying rights to those who hold dual or multiple identities. This forgets that de Benoist, in *We and the Others* (*Nous et les autres*, 2006), defines identity as dialogical, in the sense of Martin Buber's *Ich-Du* concept of interaction between individuals.[20] He explains that one's identity is made of two components: an "objective part" that comes from one's background (ethnicity, religion, family, nationality) and a "subjective part" that one can chose according to one's personal wishes, experiences and interactions with others. Ultimately, according to de Benoist (and contrary to what ideologues of race contend), identity is not fixed once and for all, but is a process in evolution.[21]

Finally, although de Benoist believes that knowledge of one's genealogy and local (ethnic, religious) traditions is a duty, and that such traditions need to be passed on to following generations, he also criticizes what he calls "the pathology of identity"—the political use of identity which often leads the populist Right to focus exclusively on "us versus them" policies. However, he is also very critical of the moral imperative of cosmopolitanism imposed by the Left and the liberal Right. The French scholar Pierre-André Taguieff sees the New Right as prone to "mixophobia," to fear of miscegenation.[22] One can challenge this, and de Benoist seems to be sincere when he writes that he stands against all forms of phobia, if that word means refusing to take into account the complexity of reality, leading to "systematically and irrationally hating" a specific group or ideology.[23]

One of the most interesting aspects of his work is that while he often refers positively to Carl Schmitt's distinction between friend and enemy as the core issue of politics,[24] and while he also emphasizes the importance of keeping alive the knowledge of pre-Christian Europe,[25] he does not scapegoat immigrants, whom he ultimately thinks are victims of globalization and the hegemony of capital over the diversity of cultural values. He is critical of non-European mass immigration because he thinks that it leads to "pathological consequences" in European societies, but he does not embrace Islamophobia, and explains that immigration is first of all a consequence of big companies being greedy for profits and preferring to import cheap labor.[26]

Finally, while some former leading figures of GRECE (such as Pierre Vial) still cling to the anti-Jewish clichés of the *völkisch* movement, there is no reason to believe he is an anti-Semite. Suspicion that he is one derives from the false idea that he remains committed to each and every word he previously wrote, while in fact reading his works shows that his thought is in constant evolution. When it comes to the question of biologically diverse races, for example, de Benoist said, in 1974, that "there is no superior race. All races are superior and each of them has its own genius."[27] This implies that de Benoist believes that race is a biological reality. Nevertheless, as early as 1991, *Eléments* explained that among its editorial staff "the rejection of Modern Individualism . . . has come to the forefront, instead of too systematic a critic of egalitarianism, and too systematic anti-egalitarianism can lead to social Darwinism, which might justify free-market economy."[28]

Inspirations

De Benoist's exit from the nationalist extreme Right was influenced by Dominique Venner and his seminal work *For a Positive Critique* (*Pour une critique positive*, 1964), which explained why activism was a dead-end street and called for a break with petty French nationalism, putting the defense of European civilization first. When he was a contributor to *Europe-Action* between 1963 and 1967, de Benoist discovered the work of the philosopher Louis Rougier, especially his rebuke of Christianity as an egalitarian and thus subversive doctrine, which he claimed was responsible for uprooting the hierarchical but tolerant social model derived from the old pagan wisdom of Europe. At that time, de Benoist acknowledged his debt to Rougier's rationalism, as opposed to Jean-Paul Sartre's Existentialist philosophy, adding that he also drew on the French biologist Jean Rostand, with whom he shared a belief in eugenics, which he opposed to the utopia of innate equality between individuals.

There is no doubt that, at this early stage of his life, de Benoist was very much in tune with the white-supremacist ideology of Europe-Action, as shown by his 1966 book *Rhodesia, Land of the Faithful Lions* (*Rhodésie, pays des lions fidèles*), penned under his pseudonym "Fabrice Laroche" and coauthored with François d'Orcival, then a militant in the Federation of Nationalist Students and now a leading and highly respected mainstream conservative journalist. After the loss of the French empire, worldwide decolonization, and the lost civil war in Algeria, de Benoist's generation—that of young men and women born during or after the Second World War—was not attracted to white supremacy by a coherent neo-Fascist ideology: they rather felt compelled to defend a "Western civilization" that they saw as being challenged by the rise of the Third World and by communism. It is in this context that de Benoist, starting at the time of Europe-Action, developed his idea of promoting European identity based on ethnicity as a "third way" between the materialism of the US and that of the communist USSR. However, unlike Jean Thiriart (who advocated a European nation with only one pan-national, centralized state), he chose to stand for building a Europe of smaller ethnic nations, alongside the ideas disseminated within the radical Right by Jean Mabire,[29] later a member of GRECE, who in turn had borrowed the idea from the novelist and former collaborator Marc Augier.[30]

By the mid-1970s, de Benoist had set himself the goal of leaving fringe politics and making his voice heard among Right-leaning intellectuals, who were in the minority in academia, and felt the urge to reshape the political landscape during the presidential term of Valéry Giscard d'Estaing (1974–1981) in favor of a more organic, holistic and elitist democracy. De Benoist's magnum opus is often thought to be his 1978 prize-winning book *Seen from the Right* (*Vu de droite*),[31] which aimed at being an anthology of contemporary rightist thinking, with a slant toward the behavioral sciences, in line with the then scientistic and positivist orientation of GRECE. In this mammoth book, one can already see the major influences on de Benoist's thought. He started by distancing himself from the mainstream Right, writing that "at the time of publishing, the ideas supported in this book stand on the Right. They do not necessarily belong to the Right. I can even imagine a situation when they would stand on the Left."[32] He then undertook to map the intellectual landscape of the postmodern era as seen from the Right, but in strong opposition to the free-marketers and proponents of laissez-faire who, like Margaret Thatcher and Ronald Reagan, were to become beacons of mainstream conservative thought. The key sentence in this book, which gives an in-depth insight into de Benoist's worldview, is: "I hereby define *the Right*, by pure convention, as a positive thing; and the progressive homogenization of the world, extolled and effected by two thousand years of egalitarian ideology, as a negative thing."[33]

First and foremost, de Benoist is inspired by Friedrich Nietzsche, whom he discovered around 1959 while still in high school.[34] He says his encounter with Nietzsche was a "revelation" that lasted until the late 1970s, when he became familiar with the philosophy of Martin Heidegger and undertook to re-read Nietzsche in this light. De Benoist sees those two authors as complementary. Initially, he was attracted to Nietzsche's idea of the "death of God," as well as to his call for the advent of "the men with the longest memory." After having also been influenced by Nietzsche's idea of the Will to Power (*der Wille zur Macht*), he came to think (with Heidegger) that the Will to Power can degenerate into "the will to will," a form of impotency. Also, he first adhered to the idea explained in *Thus Spoke Zarathustra* (*Also sprach Zarathustra*) that one value system is no more worthy than another, but later decided that Heidegger was right in saying that Nietzsche clung too much to the realm of values, and that the only way to escape from nihilism is not to change values, but to go beyond them. De Benoist also reflected on the notion of truth in Nietzsche and Heidegger's philosophy, eventually finding more depth in Heidegger's distinction, in *Being and Time* (*Sein und Zeit*), between truth and *aletheia* ("disclosure").

Other major influences on de Benoist's thought are the writings of the French philosopher Georges Sorel on violence and action, as well as his anti-bourgeois stand and his call to the general strike as a myth that would awaken the instinct of fighting in a decaying society. This leads us to mention three other authors, Oswald Spengler, Arthur Moeller van den Bruck, and Ernst Jünger, who are associated with the Conservative Revolution.[35] From Spengler's *The Decline of the West*, de Benoist borrows elitism, skepticism about the role of reason in history, cultural pessimism and the fear that technical progress may annihilate man. Tomislav Sunić emphasizes that the New Right heavily relies on Spengler's assumption that mankind does not exist as such, that "each culture passes through various cycles" and that there is no universal history, just "the plurality of histories and their unequal distribution in time and space."[36] In Moeller van den Bruck, de Benoist loves the young conservative rebel and the man who believes he lives in times of transition (or in an *interregnum*) when new cleavages will take place and bring along something which stands above socialism and conservatism, which will enable "new peoples" (as opposed to "old peoples") to shape the world.

Finally, Jünger, whom de Benoist knew personally, is certainly the influence who was closest to him. De Benoist describes Jünger as a man with four lives who was in succession "the soldier on the front, the worker, the rebel, and the Anarch."[37] He sees him as a model man who embodies heroism in wartime action and also the sense of honor. He thinks Jünger was right in his criticism of technology, which draws the warrior away from fighting in a chivalrous way, and he shares his belief that the experience of war can give birth to a new kind of man who will overthrow the old order of society. Undoubtedly, de Benoist agrees with Jünger's claim that the First World War had produced a sense of community between soldiers at the front belonging to all classes of society. He also supports his aesthetic and voluntarist conception of productivity and, last but not least, he might even identify himself with the one who resorts to "the forest passage" (the title of one of Jünger's major works, *Der Waldgang*); de Benoist writes that Jünger's rebel is a man who "cannot be identified with one system or another, even the one for which he fights." He adds that "he is not at ease in any of them,"[38] and that seems very much to be a reliable self-description, up to the point where de Benoist seems to see himself as Jünger's archetypal Anarch—that is, the man who has reached the point of not even needing to walk the forest passage, because he "is content to have broken all ties [with power]." His praise of the Anarch reflects his fear that we are heading toward an Orwellian society in which individuals will be under the control of the Big Brother state.

Early reception in France

Until the beginning of the 1970s, de Benoist's intellectual activity was known only in France and only to those with an interest in GRECE, a rather small group of senior civil servants, professionals and mostly non-academic intellectuals. It was launched in January 1968, before the student riots of May 1968. The first mention of GRECE appeared in the French left-wing satirical weekly *Le Canard enchaîné* in December 1972, asking quite seriously whether the group was neo-Nazi. In 1974, another attack on GRECE and de Benoist came from the monarchist New Royalist Action (Nouvelle action royaliste) and a group of Catholic traditionalists who wrote a far-fetched investigative work denouncing the New Right and its thinkers as dangerous promoters of anti-Christian principles, namely eugenics, paganism and white supremacism (as opposed to the universalism of Christianity).[39] Ultimately, the authors linked de Benoist and the New Right to the ideology of the Third Reich.

The New Right and its major thinker were subject to a much bigger and hotter controversy in France during the summer of 1979, after de Benoist and other key members of GRECE succeeded in gaining access to the editorial board of *Le Figaro Magazine* and *Valeurs actuelles* (*Current values*), two standard-bearer magazines of the mainstream conservative Right, reaching a combined readership of over one million. The strategy of the New Right was then to influence the mainstream conservative parties—that is, the neo-Gaullist Rassemblement pour la République and the moderate, right-of-center Union pour la Démocratie française—by providing their leadership with a set of concepts that, if adopted, would ultimately have make the mainstream conservative Right drop its commitment to key values such as equality, human rights, the welfare state and Judeo-Christian culture.

Liberal intellectuals tried to counter the rise of de Benoist and the New Right in the political debate with an impressive campaign launched in June 1979 by the daily *Le Monde*, and followed by more than five hundred articles claiming that GRECE and its leader had connections with racist movements such as the (British) Northern League, quoting some crude quotes on race from early issues of *Eléments* and trying to show that de Benoist's interest in the history of the Indo-European peoples was in the intellectual tradition of Nazi archeologists such as Hans F. K. Günther.[40] Since the press campaign of 1979, de Benoist continues to be suspected in France of being a "closet racialist" and many on the Left still cling to the belief that, despite his repeated criticism of racism and his many writings and explanation of how and why he has changed his mind on this and other topics, he has remained a devoted white supremacist. This misses the point. By the time of the 1979 campaign, de Benoist had already left behind his Nietzschean philosophy of man and the kind of racism which implies a hierarchy of ethnic groups in favor of what Pierre-André Taguieff calls the "differentialist" approach,[41] that is, the idea that each and every ethnic group has its own culture which is worth preserving, so much that the best way to preserve it is by avoiding different cultures on the same soil.

This ideological move explains how de Benoist and GRECE were received positively by a segment of the French conservative Right in 1978–81. After General de Gaulle left power in 1969 and died one year later, the Gaullist ideology, born out of the wartime Resistance, was also about to die. With less general acceptance that the state had to play a role in the economy (for example by redistributing wealth as a reward for constant growth), and with mass non-European immigration becoming a political issue, the emergence of the New Right under de Benoist's aegis was seen by several prominent conservative politicians as an unique opportunity to promote a nativist, pro-market, identitarian agenda which would appeal to the most Right-leaning voters, who were not yet attracted National Front, which was founded in 1972, and was until 1983–84 a tiny group of extremists tainted by their connection with the collaboration with the Nazi occupiers of France.

When thinking this way, the likes of Michel Poniatowski, Alain Griotteray, Philippe Malaud and other stalwart leaders of President Giscard's center-right party made a double mistake. First, they wrongly presumed that de Benoist and GRECE were in tune with the libertarian agenda of *Club de l'Horloge*, a think tank founded in 1974 by senior civil servants originating from GRECE such as Yvan Blot, Henry de Lesquen and Jean-Yves Le Gallou. This proved to be wrong, as de Benoist was then at the stage when he put an emphasis on the criticism of the free-market economy. The second mistake that the staunch supporters of the Europe-United States axis working with Giscard made is that they failed to foresee that de Benoist, being preoccupied with the decadence of Europe and the dream of his continent becoming an empire-superpower, was very unlikely to become the "organic intellectual" of those very same parties that were pushing for more European integration and closer ties with NATO.

Later reception

At the end of 1982, de Benoist and other contributors to *Figaro Magazine* who were close to GRECE were forced to leave it and, although de Benoist kept on contributing to the now-defunct monthly magazine *Spectacle du monde* (*World spectacle*), his link with the mainstream political Right was broken, and he chose to live as an independent writer. If there is an "earlier" and a "later" reception of his thought in France, the breakpoint was first the 1979 press campaign, then the hegemony of free-market economics and social conservative thought within the post-Gaullist Right, and only marginally because of the coming to power of the Left in 1981. In fact, de Benoist and GRECE were never really acceptable in mainstream French conservative politics, except when some conservatives used them as ghost-writers in order to give an intellectual backbone to their anti-egalitarian agenda.

From the start, the social democratic Left and the Communists opposed de Benoist and GRECE because they saw them as continuing in the tradition of Fascism. However, the real problem is that several of the core ideas which are still at the heart of de Benoist's *Weltanschauung* are totally alien to the issues which are the key to electoral success. A gap between de Benoist and the mainstream Right that cannot be bridged results from the belief that today's European peoples are all offshoots of the same stock (that is, the Indo-European people), and from the contention that the monotheistic religions are totally alien to European culture, and the opposition to Christianity.

Since the mid-1980s, the ideology of GRECE has been interpreted in France in opposite ways. Most liberals from the Left and Right have refused to engage in intellectual debate with de Benoist: following the celebrated leftist philosopher Bernard-Henri Lévy, they contend that his anti-egalitarian ideology disqualifies him as a thinker, and accusations of anti-Semitism in a "hidden form" are still commonplace. The first mainstream intellectual academic who agreed to debate with de Benoist was Pierre-André Taguieff, the foremost scholar of the New Right, and this caused such an uproar that in 1993 a manifesto was published in the daily *Le Monde* warning his fellow (Left-leaning) academics against the pernicious influence of GRECE and the danger of "normalizing" de Benoist.[42]

De Benoist was more successful in persuading contributors from the other side of the spectrum to contribute articles to *Krisis*, among them Jean Baudrillard, Raymond Boudon, Sebastian Budgen, Massimo Cacciari, the Left-wing economist André Grjebine, the columnist Jean-François Kahn, and Jean-Pierre Laurent, a scholar of perennialism. In addition, de Benoist publicly met in 1992 with prominent cadres of the Communist Party's think tank, the Institut de Recherches Marxistes (Institute for Marxist Research), who were consequently disavowed by the Party's official organ, *L'Humanité-Dimanche*.[43]

The launch of a newly-designed edition of *Éléments* in 2015 seems to have diminished the isolation of the French New Right. Together with de Benoist's flagship editorial, respected academics from the Catholic conservative Right such as Pierre Manent, social democrats such as Jacques Julliard, and philosophers such as Marcel Gauchet (he coeditor of the influential quarterly *Le débat*) agreed to be interviewed, and although they have been criticized for having done so, the harshness of attacks against the magazine and its inspirer is not as great as it once was.

De Benoist has been extensively translated into Italian and German since the early 1980s. After he was discovered by young militants belonging to the oppositional faction of Giorgio Almirante's then neo-Fascist party, the Movimento Sociale Italiano (Italian Social Movement, MSI), they used his thought, among other things by launching *Elementi* in 1978 to rejuvenate the party's doctrine by escaping narrow-minded reference to the Fascist past, albeit without repudiating it in its entirety. Later on, the Italian New Right (Nuova destra) was able, because of the very specific local culture of dialog between radicals from both Left and Right, to infuse some of its ideas into the Alternative Left and the post-Fascist Aleanza Nazionale (National Alliance), a partner in the coalition government led by Prime Minister Silvio Berlusconi from 1993 onwards. In Germany, his ideas were disseminated by the magazine *Elemente* from 1987, and then, on a much wider basis, by *Junge Freiheit*, a bridge between the national-conservatives and the nationalist, anti-multiculturalism party, Alternativ für Deutschland (Alternative for Germany, AfD). The reception of de Benoist has been marginal in the United Kingdom, where historian Roger Griffin has argued that the New Right was aimed at preserving Fascist culture under the claim of metapolitics.[44]

One controversial topic is de Benoist's reception in Russia, especially by the Eurasianist writer Alexander Dugin. De Benoist met Dugin, then a member of the nationalist Patriotic Front Pamyat, in 1989, and traveled to postcommunist Russia in 1992, meeting with Dugin again, and with the nationalist Right and the communist opposition to President Yeltsin.[45] De Benoist has since published a book with Dugin,[46] who was a speaker at the convention of GRECE for the first time in 1991, and for the last time in 2016.[47] De Benoist and Dugin share a common opposition to American influence in Europe and a belief in the role of Russia's "heartland" in geopolitics, but Dugin is more attracted to Guénon and Evola than is de Benoist.

It is striking that in France, the New Right has failed in its goal of promoting an economic and social organicist doctrine opposed to individualism and globalization, despite the short period when, with Bruno Mégret in an influential position during the late 1980s, the National Front drew on its ideas. Under Marine Le Pen, this influence remains so far as the criticism of the global ruling class, the condemnation of financial capitalism and the support for a multipolar world are concerned, but the National Front has taken a very different direction from de Benoist in promoting the republican model of assimilating minorities to the *Leitkultur* (hegemonic common culture) as a solution to the multicultural society. De Benoist's writings are aimed at an intellectual readership and cannot easily be translated into the populist language of Le Pen.

Conclusion

Drawing from Antonio Gramsci's works has proved to be a mixed success for de Benoist and GRECE, although on a theoretical level they were able to refresh both the radical and the mainstream Right with their antiegalitarian thought. De Benoist was instrumental in lessening the influence on the French Right of Action française (French Action) and its interwar leader Charles Maurras, whose reactionary and often Catholic fundamentalist followers he saw as blocking the adaptation of the Right to the contemporary world.[48] Alain de Benoist has planted seeds as a philosopher which will eventually take roots later on, most probably contributing to critical thinking on both sides of the political spectrum than in the mainstream, and even the populist Right.

Notes

1. *Alain de Benoist: Bibliographie 1960–2010* (Paris: éditions Les amis d'Alain de Benoist, 2009). Most of his later works are available on the internet: see http://www.alaindebenoist.com/textes/.

2. Inspired by Alexandre Marc, Robert Aron, Arnaud Dandieu, and Emmanuel Mounier, the Non-Conformists rejected totalitarian ideologies as an answer to the crisis of the 1930s and called instead for a "new order" going beyond individualism and liberalism.
3. Mohler's 1949 dissertation on this topic was published in France as *La révolution conservatrice en Allemagne: 1918–1932* (Puiseaux: Editions Pardès, 1993). Mohler spoke at GRECE conventions as early as 1975.
4. In the December 2017 edition of *Eléments*, he speaks in favor of a "Revolutionary-Conservative solution" to the contradiction between mainstream conservative values and the political impotence of conservatives because of their alliance with the liberal Right.
5. In the sense of Louis Dumont's *Essais sur l'individualisme* (Paris: Editions du Seuil, 1983). Dumont makes a distinction between egalitarian individualism, whose roots can be found in Christianity, and "individualism of the singular," which is specific to traditional societies.
6. De Benoist has published an account of his life (*Mémoire vive*, Paris: Editions de Fallois, 2012) and a sort of diary titled *Dernière Année: Notes pour conclure le siècle* (Lausanne: L'age d'homme, 2001).
7. Jean-Yves Le Gallou, "'Mémoire vive' de Alain de Benoist," August 17, 2013, https://www.polemia.com/memoire-vive-de-alain-de-benoist/.
8. Coston was one of the most strident prewar anti-Semites, then a collaborationist. He was obsessed with the Jewish-Freemasonic conspiracy theory, to which he devoted his postwar writings as well.
9. De Benoist, *Les idées à l'endroit* (Paris: Hallier, 1979), 62.
10. Together with, among others, the Italian journalist, Giorgio Locchi, his fellow countryman Antonio Lombardo, French students becoming academics Jean-Claude Rivière, Pierre Bérard, Pierre Vial, and the journalist Jean-Claude Valla. *Nouvelle école*, August-September 1968, 86.
11. Steuckers was once de Benoist's assistant before breaking away and launching his own movement, Synergies européennes (European Synergies).
12. Costanzo Preve, *Eloge du communautarisme: Aristote–Hegel–Marx* (Paris: Editions Krisis, 2012).
13. The review of the Anti-Utilitarian Social Science Movement (Mouvement anti-utilitariste en sciences sociales, MAUSS) of the academic economists Serge Latouche and Alain Caillé.
14. Christopher Lasch: *The Revolt of the Elites: And the Betrayal of Democracy*. (New York: W. W. Norton, 1995).
15. First published in Paris by éditions Albin Michel in 1981, it was translated into English as *On Being a Pagan* (Atlanta, GA: Ultra, 2004) with a foreword by Stephen Flowers, also known as Edred Thorsson, an Odinist writer.
16. In an interview with the Italian monthly *Area*, politically close to Aleanza Nazionale, March 2000.

17. De Benoist, interview with Nietzsche Académie, October 14, 2013, http://nietzscheacademie.over-blog.com/article-alain-de-benoist-120592080.html.
18. See his most exhaustive critic of capitalism in Alain de Benoist, *Critiques, Théoriques* (Paris: L'Age d'Homme, 2002).
19. De Benoist, *Le moment populiste* (Paris: PGDR, 2017). This book was written "in memory of Paul Piccone and Costanzo Preve."
20. See Martin Buber, *I and Thou*. (New York: Charles Scribner's Sons, 1937).
21. In a conference held in Barcelona, and available on the *Krisis* website (http://www.revue-krisis.com/2017/08/identites-alain-de-benoist.html), de Benoist contends that "We are first and foremost what we have become, and it is on this basis that we can project ourselves into the future. There is no identity without transformation and the important thing is to look at those two concepts in a non-contradictory way."
22. Pierre-André Taguieff, *La force du préjugé* (Paris: La Découverte, 1988), 337.
23. De Benoist, "Phobies en tous genres et point Godwin: l'Etat se defend comme il peut," March 3, 2014, http://www.bvoltaire.fr/phobies-en-genre-points-godwin-letat-se-defend-il-peut/.
24. See Carl Schmitt, *Der Begriff des Politischen* (Berlin: Duncker and Humblot, 1932). De Benoist was introduced to Schmitt's thought by Julien Freund, a French sociologist who had sympathy for the New Right.
25. See his book *Les traditions d'Europe* (Arpajon: éditions du Labyrinthe, 1996), a compendium of articles published in the bulletin of GRECE.
26. On immigration leading to "social pathologies" and on his condemnation of Islamophobia, see his interview with Dugin's website *Katehon* (26 August 2016), at http://katehon.com/fr/article/alain-de-benoist-burkini-il-faut-aborder-frontalement-la-question-de-limmigration. On the link between immigration and capitalism, see Alain de Benoist, *Survivre à la pensée unique* (Paris: Krisis, Paris, 2015),140–143.
27. See his interview in *Eléments* 8–9 (1974).
28. *Eléments* 72 (Winter 1991), 23.
29. Benoit Marpeau, "Le rêve nordique de Jean Mabire," *Annales de Normandie* 43, no. 3 (1993): 215–241. De Benoist later published a bibliography of Mabire, who is considered an iconic figure of the identitarian and radical Right neopagan movements, Alain de Benoist, *Bibliographie de Jean Mabire* (Pont-Authou [Normandie]: Editions Héligoland, 2008).
30. Mabire notes his debt to Augier (who wrote as "Saint-Loup") in Jean Mabire, "Ils ont rêvé l'Europe des patries charnelles," *Réfléchir et Agir* 17 (2006), http://www.terreetpeuple.com/les-eveilleurs-de-peuples-memoire-15/156-jean-mabire/422-ils-ont-reve-leurope-des-patries-charnelles-par-jean-mabire.html.
31. In the fifth edition, published in 2001, the author claims sales of 25,000, a huge figure for a 590-page volume conveying ideas that were against the tide of post-1968 liberal ideology.

32. De Benoist, *Vu de droite* (Arpajon: Editions du Labyrinthe, 2001), xii.
33. De Benoist, *Vu de droite*, xii. English translation by Robert A. Linndgren, taken from *View from the Right* (NP: Arktos, 2017).
34. De Benoist, interview with Nietzsche Académie.
35. De Benoist, *Quatre figures de la Révolution Conservatrice allemande–Werner Sombart–Arthur Moeller van den Bruck–Ernst Niekisch–Oswald Spengler* (Paris: Editions Les amis d'Alain de Benoist, 2014).
36. Tomislav Sunić, *Against Democracy and Equality: The European New Right* (NP: Arktos Media, 2011), 95. The title of this work implies that the New Right rebukes democracy, and the fact that de Benoist wrote the foreword seems to acknowledge that he shares Sunic's own antidemocratic worldview. Instead, one can say he opposes modern, representative democracy and stands for direct democracy, on the ground that participation is more fundamental than representation.
37. De Benoist, "Types et figures dans l'oeuvre d'Ernst Junger: Le Soldat du front, le Travailleur, le Rebelle et l'Anarque," lecture in Rome, May 1997, https://www.centrostudilaruna.it/types-et-figures-dans-loeuvre-dernst-junger-le-soldat-du-front-le-travailleur-le-rebelle-et-lanarque.html.
38. De Benoist, "An Introduction to Ernst Jünger," *Occidental Quarterly* 8, no. 3 (Fall 2008): 53.
39. Georges Naughton; *Le choc du passé: Avortement, Néo-Nazisme, Nouvelle morale* (La Celle Saint-Cloud: GARAH, 1974).
40. Before the start of GRECE, de Benoist had authored a small book, *Les Indo-Européens* (Paris: G.E.D., 1965), devoted to the Indo-European roots of Western civilization, and Günther, an academic who had been involved in Nazi "race research," was briefly on the academic board of *Nouvelle école*, the first issue of which was published in 1968, the same year he died.
41. See Taguieff's seminal book, *La Force du préjugé: Essai sur le racisme et ses doubles* (Paris: La Découverte, 1988).
42. "Appel à une Europe de la vigilance contre l'extrême droite," *Le Monde*, July 13, 1993.
43. Martine Bulard, "Le refus de l'amalgame," *L'Humanité-Dimanche*, July 15, 1993.
44. Roger Griffin, "Between Metapolitics and Apoliteia: The Nouvelle Droite's Strategy for Conserving the Fascist Vision in the 'Interregnum'" *Modern and Contemporary France*, no. 8 (2000): 35–53.
45. Anton Shekhovtsov, "Alexander Dugin and the European New Right, 1989–1994," in *Eurasianism and the European Far Right: Reshaping the Europe–Russia Relationship*, ed. Marlene Laruelle (Lanham, MD: Lexington Books, 2015), 35–53.
46. Alexandre Douguine, *L'appel de l'Eurasie: Conversation avec Alain de Benoist* (NP: Avatar éditions, 2013).

47. Being under sanctions from the United States but not from the European Union, because of his involvement in the Ukrainian conflict, Dugin was obliged to speak via a satellite link from Moscow.
48. In "Maurras écrivain, artiste, poète," *Bulletin Charles Maurras,* April 2001, de Benoist writes that Maurras was a man of the nineteenth century.

6

Guillaume Faye and Archeofuturism

Stéphane François

GUILLAUME FAYE, BORN in 1949, is responsible for the doctrinal renewal of French nativism and, more widely, for the development of the European-American radical Right, including its concept of "archeofuturism," which was forged in the middle of the 1990s, combining postmodern philosophy, some elements of Western counterculture, and racism. Faye defined archeofuturism as the acceptance of technological-scientific advances in a society that has remained traditional. He believed that postmodern philosophy sanctions this alliance as the union of the Promethean, referring to the "Faustian soul" and the "most ancient memory,"[1] and the "reconciliation between Evola and Marinetti."[2] This union also doubles up for the dismissal of modernity, born from the Enlightenment, and of conservatism, since modernity shows signs of fracture and conservatism leads to nothing. To support his case, he points to the surge of Islam as the expression of an archaic form of belief and civilization.

Faye's thought extends beyond the French context, and his work has been read and discussed by both European and American activists. In this sense, Faye is a key thinker of the European-American radical Right. His activism spanned across two periods. During the first of these he was a member of GRECE (Groupement d'Études et de Recherches de la Civilisation Européenne) between 1970 and 1986, and is considered its second theorist after Alain de Benoist. At the time, he defended a somewhat pro-Arab Conservative Revolutionary thought. But after withdrawing from political activism between 1987 and 1996 to work in the French media, he made a comeback in the second period as an important theorist of nativism, using a discourse focused on Islam and Arab Muslim migration. Faye is a complex and sometimes baffling figure. Because of this, our comments are structured in three parts. First, we retrace his biography and professional development. We then analyze the two main periods of his activism. Finally, we examine his influence on the French, European, and American radical Right.

Between political activism and the media

Faye occupies a special place in the small world of the radical Right. He was born on November 7, 1949, in Angoulême, a medium-sized city in southwest France. He was raised in a well-off bourgeois family close to the authoritarian and nationalistic "Bonapartist" Right. Unlike many of the founding members of GRECE, he did not come from a family that had collaborated with the Nazis during the Second World War. He also did not campaign as part of the groups that defended the French presence in Algeria or in nationalist circles. He studied instead at the Paris Institute of Political Studies ("Sciences Po," one of France's elite schools). Between 1971 and 1973 he ran the Circle Pareto and the Association GRECE.[3] He campaigned for the latter in 1970. A gifted speaker and bright theorist, in the 1980s he became a permanent member of GRECE, where he acted as Secretary for Studies and Research and one of its principal authors, writing for most journals of the New Right—*Eléments, Nouvelle école* (*New School*), *Orientations*, and *Études et recherches* (*Studies and Research*). During the 1970s and 1980s, he also worked as a journalist and published in several major French national and counterculture newspapers and magazines.

Faye's intellectual reference points included French figures such as Henri Lefebvre, Jules Monnerot, Robert Jaulin, Julien Freund, Michel Maffesoli, Gilles Deleuze, and Guy Debord; German figures, including Friedrich Nietzsche, Hegel, Martin Heidegger, Arnold Gehlen, Jürgen Habermas, Georg Simmel, Ferdinand Tönnies, and Carl Schmitt; British figures such as Herbert Spencer and Robert Ardrey; and the American Christopher Lasch. He recognized just one single influence from the radical Right, that of the Italian journalist and philosopher Giorgio Locchi, who played a key role in the development of the first doctrines of GRECE.

Faye participated in the dissemination of nativist and Conservative Revolutionary themes, including the defense of cultural and biological identity, European nationalism, anti-Americanism, antiliberalism, and the dismissal of immigration in the name of respecting ethnic-cultural particularism and differences. He also helped spread ideas that had been defended before him by various nationalist-revolutionary or neo-Nazi groups. Spiritually he was close to a form of paganism, which he defined as an almost ideal religion that allows a rigid, holistic and organic society, respect for natural and cosmic cycles, and for "beliefs and sensitivities."[4] More particularly, he believed that paganism is a rooted and differentialist religion ("the logic that 'everyone is to remain where they belong'") and a solution to a "mixophile" and leveling universalism.[5] This aspect is key in Faye's thought. He was close to the pagan trend within GRECE and participated in the Oath of Delphi, first delivered in 1979 upon the initiative of Pierre Vial, then General Secretary of GRECE. The oath was taken in Delphi, in front of the Stoa in the presence of several European pagan and radical activist members of GRECE: it declared the promise made by these activists to fight for European identity.

From the end of the 1970s, Faye became a promoter of the strategy of "metapolitics." His first text on this dates from 1978, ten years after the foundation of GRECE,[6] and eight years after he became a member of GRECE. After the failure of the attempt of entryism within the *Figaro Magazine*, he continued to promote this strategy, also after his return to activism in the late 1990s. He was not, however, the founding theoretician of this strategy, which is consubstantial from the birth of GRECE in 1968. The founders of GRECE—of whom Guillaume Faye is not one[7]—wanted from the beginning to insist on this point; metapolitics *is* the essence of GRECE.[8]

As a result of intellectual and financial disagreements with Alain de Benoist, Faye was marginalized within GRECE. As a result, he left the organization in the spring of 1987. He distanced himself from the activism of the New Right to focus on his work in the media. In parallel to his activities in the press (using his own name or pseudonyms), he hosted a show on a large French radio station on which he entertained his listeners with hoaxes and a provocative spirit. Between 1991 and 1993 he also took part in a general-interest program broadcast by a French state channel. And he also claims to have acted in pornographic films. He published three books intended for the general public. Finally, he wrote stories for comic strips, something that he had already started doing in 1985. Since at the time he was not hostile to homosexuality and transsexualism, he wrote for a magazine on homosexuality, where, in the name of paganism, he often praised teenage homosexuality.[9]

He went back into politics in 1998 after writing *Archeofuturism* (*L'Archéofuturisme*), a key book published by L'Æncre, a major publisher of the French radical Right; it was followed by the publication of *The Colonization of Europe* (*La Colonisation de l'Europe*) in 2000. He became more involved with the activities of various radical Right networks. He organized conferences with sympathizers of GRECE, with supporters for the restoration of the monarchy in France, with young Catholic traditionalists and with neopagans. In 2000 came the attacks by Alain de Benoist and his sympathizers, who accused Faye of racism. This was an unfortunate time for Faye and his publisher L'Æncre: following the publication of *The Colonization of Europe*, they were both sued for incitement to racial hatred. At the request of de Benoist, Faye was finally ousted from GRECE in May 2000 by an assembly of executive members. Subsequently, Faye became involved in nativist circles, participating in the group Terre et Peuple (Land and People), founded by former GRECE members Pierre Vial, Jean Mabire, and Jean Haudry, until he was expelled in 2007 following the publication of his book *The New Jewish Question* (*La nouvelle question juive*).

Guillaume Faye's thought

Intellectually, Faye was a member of GRECE and who is hard to categorize. He did not feel the nostalgia for the *völkisch*. He did not share the interests of the theorists of the "Integral Tradition" such as Julius Evola or René Guénon, in pagan esotericism or in any attempts to reinvent pagan cults. He was neither reactionary nor modern since "traditions are made to be redacted, absorbed, selected; since so many of them are carriers of the viruses that are going wild today. As for modernity, it probably has no future."[10] On the contrary, he insisted on the need to restore the term "archaic" to its original meaning as the foundation, the beginning. According to Faye, archaism is different from an attachment to the past because it is not a historical counterrevolutionary regression.[11] In fact, Faye believes that his thinking is not "antimodern" but "nonmodern." He views those who are antimodern and counterrevolutionaries as constructs that reflect modernity and share the same biases, including a linear conception of time, even though he defended, following Nietzsche, a spherical conception of time.[12] Faye is, thus, halfway from the "culturalist" and "biological" currents of GRECE. He was strongly influenced by French postmodern philosophers and sociologists, in particular Michel Maffesoli. As mentioned earlier, he participated in the dissemination of an identity that was both cultural and biological. Unlike most activists of the radical Right, he is not hostile to hypermodernity and the liberation from morality, to which he devoted two books: *Sex and Ideology* (*Sexe et idéologie*) in 1983, and *Sex and Deviance* (*Sexe et dévoiement*) in 2011. In 1983, he wrote that in a pagan society the coexistence of different sexualities (including sexual asceticism, orgiasm, debauchery, deviance, homosexuality) is permitted because they correspond to highly structured social functions.[13] His conception of sexuality was "liberated," "pagan." It went against the sanctimonious discourse that dominated the Right and acted as the carrier of a cultural revolution, undermining the foundations of the Christian ethic. More particularly, this liberated but highly structured form of sexuality was a catharsis from the rules of an extremely rigid society, which controls "the reproduction of the species and the transmission of progeny."[14] This, as we will see, was a vital issue for him. Thus, sexual freedom facilitates the acceptance of an authoritarian regime.

His first books, published in the beginning of the 1980s, were both a critique of consumerist society and a rejection of the standardization and Westernization of the world.[15] This is one of his major intellectual constants. In the early 1980s he defended a radical differentialism to the point of calling for the return of non-European immigrants to their civilizational area since the right to difference, according to him, was the dismissal of the multiracial society as one that is "multiracist." He also condemned multiculturalism and what he called "ethnomasochism." In the 1990s, he made his discourse even more radical, writing that the cultural struggle of the Right activist remains the defense of European ethnocentrism.[16]

Like some leftist theorists, in particular those of the Frankfurt School, Faye believes that Europe has been colonized by American values. His subsequent dismissal of the US firmly situated him in the revolutionary-nationalist current, even though he also dismissed nationalism in favor of European nationalism. This influence can be found in his geopolitical views, his early condemnation of the "American-Zionist Axis," and proposed alliance with Arab regimes, in particular Ba'thists. In 1985, he believed that there were Zionist "opinion circles" in France that prompted French governments to break ties with the Arab regimes, which he viewed as France's natural allies. Moreover, he defended the idea of taking action against "Zionist lobbies" in the US that wished to influence the global geopolitics that supported the state of Israel.[17]

After his comeback to the political arena, however, Faye reversed his position: he now supported Israel and the US against the Arab and Muslim world. In fact, he became an important ideologue of nativism with a vehemently anti-immigration and anti-Islamic discourse in the name of defending the ethnic interests of Europeans. Since the late 1990s, he has championed a racialism that is reminiscent of the 1900s to the 1930s. He has made references to "loyalty to values and to bloodlines."[18] As a follower of the "right of blood," he hopes for a natalist and eugenic campaign favoring high birthrates for ethnic Europeans. He has defined ethnocentrism as the mobilizing conviction that is specific to long-living peoples and the idea that where one belongs is central and superior, and that one must preserve one's ethnic identity to endure the course of history.[19] He has also adopted the Darwinist theme of the "struggle for survival" and the law of the fittest, considering other civilizations as enemies to be eliminated.[20] For Faye, this racial Darwinism must promote European ethnocentrism as the source of world civilization.[21] By his own admission, the books that he published upon his return to political activism were an appeal to the "ethnic awareness" of Europeans who must defend their biological and cultural identity in order to preserve their civilization in the course of history.[22] Faye has developed the idea that non-European migration (African, Arab Muslim, and Asian) is colonizing Europe through high birthrates among these ethnic groups: for him, what is at work is an ethnic substitution. Islam has undertaken the conquest of Europe to impose its values, which are contrary to those of European paganism, while the supposed greater delinquency of young migrants is only the beginning of an ethnic civil war (here we find the ethological idea of war over territory).[23] If his current discourse is a complete reversal from his positions in the early 1980s, when he called for an European-Arab alliance to fight against US hegemony, he still condemns the Americanization of morals through culture and food practices as eroding the identities and sovereignty of Europeans, substituting an American mythology and imaginary for those of Europeans.[24] Yet he has recognized that the US is not the "main enemy." For Faye, the adversary is made up of "alien non-native masses colonizing Europe, their collaborators (foreign states or a fifth column) and Islam."[25] The transformation of his thinking is evident.

Finally, Faye also wishes to quell liberal democracy in order to confront the "convergence of catastrophes," to use the title of one of his books, which he wrote using the pseudonym Guillaume Corvus.[26] He believes that the Western countries are threatened by various perils: a cancer spreading across the European social fabric, demographic decline, the threat of a chaotic South, the global financial crisis, the rise of religious fundamentalism and in particular Muslim extremism, the ethnoreligious clash between North and South, and the worsening of uncontrolled pollution. To avoid civilizational and ecological collapse, he proposes putting in place an authoritarian regime under the auspices of a "born chief," a dictator defined as a providential man who knows how to take the right decisions in emergency situations, knows how to set his peoples in motion, and protects his peoples' identity and ancestry.[27] Yet, if there is a risk of ecological disaster, he does not believe, unlike radical environmentalists, whom he has qualified as "naïve," in an endangered nature. Rather, he argues that only humanity is endangered, since the Earth will be able to recover from the climate upheaval.[28]

An increasingly discussed body of work

Faye has maintained long-standing links with various groups and figures. As early as the 1980s, his work was translated into Italian, German, and Spanish, thus in countries where there is a long-standing tradition of New- Rightist and revolutionary-nationalist groups. Several of his books were translated between 1980 and 1985: *The System to Kill the Peoples, The New Consumer Society, New Ideological Issues*, and *Little Lexicon of the European Partisan*, coauthored with the Belgian activists Pierre Freson and Robert Steuckers.[29] His articles were also translated in the German and Italian versions of *Elements* and *New School*. During this first period, Faye participated in university symposia in Greece[30] and in Belgium.[31] He even taught the sociology of sexuality at the University of Besançon, France. But above all, he has spoken at conferences organized by European New Right groups. During his media period, he abandoned these activities. Nonetheless, his first books and articles in this new period continued to be translated and discussed not only by European activists but also by American activists of the movement that was later called the "Alt Right."[32]

His reputation grew abroad after his return to politics. In the beginning, between 1998 and 2006, he renewed his links with the nativist milieux of GRECE and nationalist-revolutionary networks. He participated in meetings and symposia organized by the activists of "Eurosiberia," a sort of federal empire bringing together the peoples of the "white race" in Europe and in North America, organized in 2005 in Spain, and in 2006 in Russia. In Spain, he found himself alongside some very radical activists on the margins of Nazism, including Italians such as Gabriel Adinolfi, and Germans such as Pierre Krebs (whose work he translated and published in German in the 1980s), Andras Molau, and Ernesto Mila. In Russia, he once again stood alongside Pierre Krebs, the Spaniard Enrique Ravello, the Frenchmen Pierre Vial and Yann-Ber Tillenon, former executive members of GRECE; the Greek Eleftherios Ballas; the Ukrainian Galina Lozko; and, finally, the Russians Vladimir Ardeyev, Anatoly Ivanov, and Pavel Tulaev. The goal of these meetings was to put in place a structure to defend the "future of the white world:" the Council of the peoples of European origin, bringing together German, Austrian, Spanish, Flemish, French, Italian, Portuguese, Russian, Serbian, Walloon, and Quebecois splinter groups. Subsequently, during an international conference on "The Future of the White World," which took place in Moscow in June 2006, Faye proposed an alliance between Eurosiberia and all the white peoples of European origin. He referred to the "notion of Septentrion" to create "ethnospheres," namely "groups of territories ruled by peoples who are ethnically related."[33] This concept is based on the idea that the "ethnic foundations of a civilization rest on its biological roots and those of its peoples."[34] He has, therefore, become an important figure of "national-westernism." This idea was taken up and discussed by the Alt Right website Counter-Currents.[35] In the light of this white supremacism, it is not surprising that Faye is frequently cited in the American neo-Nazi website of the Racial Nationalist Library, alongside the French revisionists Robert Faurisson and Maurice Bardèche;[36] since 2006 he has taken part in the meetings of the *American Renaissance* association.

During this period, there were more translations of Faye's work, which became closely linked to its vehemently anti-Muslim and anti-Islam content. His most important works in this second period were in English, published by Arktos Media, a radical London-based publisher with links to the Alt Right; they included *Archeofuturism, The Colonization of Europe, Why We Fight, The Convergence of Catastrophes, Sex and Deviance,* and *Archeofuturism 2.0*,[37] all of which were also translated into other languages.[38] These works have been reviewed on the website and publications of Counter-Currents. However, the publication in 2007 of *The New Jewish Question* caused a split with his older friends who were usually anti-Semites: the revolutionary-nationalist Europeans and nativists from GRECE considered him to be overly "Zionist." His nonhostile positions toward Israel and Judaism prompted both Holocaust deniers and Catholic traditionalists to dismiss him.

Finally, Fayes's views were also discussed in *Télos*, a journal that came out of the American "New Left." The journal's stance became increasingly close to the French New Right during the 1990s. Its founder, Paul Piccone, asserted during his presentation of the special issue dedicated to the French New Right that it was not a threat and that it was necessary to engage with it in a dialog. [39] Following the publication of this issue, the exchange took place, not with Faye but with Alain de Benoist. If Faye shared some of the reference points of the American New Left (e.g., Jürgen Habermas, Carl Schmitt, and Martin Heidegger), he had different views not only on the question of power, whose instrumental reason, he believed, can act as a tool, but also on the question of racism. Paul Piccone supported the idea of the New Right as a sort of "new New Left," yet GRECE had nothing leftist, since it only used the revolutionary-national strategy of the Far Left of the Far Right.[40] An author who was favorable to GRECE, Michael Torigian,[41] published an article on the New Right in *Télos* in 1999.

Since his return to political activism, Faye has remained a key theorist of nativism. His dismissal of Islam and Arab Muslim migration met a favorable public in the US, where the radical Right has been sensitive to this issue since 9/11. Like Alain de Benoist, Faye and the French New Right have been reading American thinkers since the creation of GRECE in 1968, despite their anti-Americanism.[42] These readings have given birth to a reciprocal exchange of intellectual reference points and discussions.

Notes

1. Guillaume Faye, *L'Archéofuturisme* (Paris: L'Æncre, 1998), 42–43.
2. Ibid.
3. Pierre-André Taguieff, *Sur la Nouvelle Droite: Jalons d'une analyse critique* (Paris: Descartes & Cie, 1994), 205.
4. Guillaume Faye, "Les Titans et les Dieux: Entretien avec G. Faye," *Antaïos* 16 (2001): 116.
5. Ibid., 116.
6. Guillaume Faye, "Le G.R. E. C. E. et la conquête du pouvoir des idées," *Pour un Gramscisme de droite: Actes du XVIe colloque national du GRECE* (Paris: GRECE, 1978).
7. *Nouvelle École*, August-September 1968, 86, published the list of the founders of GRECE.
8. Anne-Marie Duranton-Crabol, *Visages de la Nouvelle droite: le GRECE et son histoire* (Paris: Presses de Sciences Po, 1988); Pierre-André Taguieff, *Sur la*

Nouvelle droite: Jalons d'une analyse critique (Paris: Descartes & Cie, 1994); Stéphane François, *Les Néo-paganismes et la Nouvelle Droite (1980–2006): Pour une autre approche* (Milan: Archè, 2008).

9. Stéphane François, *Les Paganismes et la Nouvelle Droite*; Pierre Verdrager, *L'Enfant interdit: Comment la pédophilie est devenue scandaleuse* (Paris: Armand Colin, 2013).
10. Faye, *L'Archéofuturisme*, 10–11.
11. Ibid., 66.
12. Ibid., 168.
13. Guillaume Faye, *Sexe et idéologie* (Paris: Le Labyrinthe, 1983), 25.
14. Faye, *L'Archéofuturisme*, 103.
15. Guillaume Faye, "Pour en finir avec la civilisation occidentale," *Éléments pour la civilisation européenne* 34 (1980): 5–11; *Le Système à tuer les peuples* (Paris: Copernic, 1981); *La NSC, la nouvelle société de consommation* (Paris: Le Labyrinthe, 1984); *L'Occident comme déclin* (Paris: Le Labyrinthe, 1984); *Nouveau discours à la nation européenne* (Paris: Albatros, 1985).
16. Guillaume Faye, *Pourquoi nous combattons: manifeste de la résistance européenne* (Paris: L'Æncre, 2001), 73.
17. Faye, *Nouveau discours à la nation européenne*, 106.
18. Faye, *Pourquoi nous combattons*, 113.
19. Ibid., 117.
20. Ibid., 76.
21. Ibid., 118.
22. Ibid., 78.
23. Ibid., 20–21.
24. Ibid., 55–56.
25. Ibid., 57.
26. Guillaume Corvus (pseudonym), *La convergence des catastrophes* (Paris: Diffusion International Éditions, 2004).
27. Faye, *Pourquoi nous combattons*, 69.
28. Corvus, *La Convergence des catastrophes*, 201.
29. Guillaume Faye, *Le Système à tuer les peuples*, translated into Italian as *Il sistema per uccidere i popoli* (Milan: Edizioni dell'uomo libero, 1983) and *Il sistema per uccidere i popoli* (Milan: Società editrice Barbarossa, 1997); Faye, *La NSC*, translated into Italian as *La Nuova Societa dei consumi* (Milan: Edizioni dell'uomo libero, 1985); Faye, *Nouveau discours à la nation européenne*, translated into German as *Rede an die europäische Nation* (Tübingen: Hohenrain, 1990); Faye, *Les Nouveaux enjeux idéologiques* (Paris: Le Labyrinthe, 1985), translated into German as *Die neuen ideologischen Herausforderung, en Mut zur Identität: Alternativen zum Prinzip der Gleichheit* (Struckum: Verlag für ganzheitliche Forschung und Kultur, 1988); Guillaume Faye, Pierre Freson, and Robert Steuckers, *Petit lexique du partisan*

européen (Esneux: Eurograf, 1985), translated into Spanish as *Pequeño léxico del militante europeo* (Valencia: Iskander, 1996), and *Pequeño léxico del partisano europeo* (Barcelona: Nueva Republica, 2012).

30. The "symposia of Athens" organized by Jason Hadjinas between 1982 and 1985.
31. On European-Arab links organized by the University of Mons in 1985.
32. Stéphane François, *Au-delà des vents du Nord: L'extrême droite française, le pôle nord et les Indo-Européens* (Lyon: Presses Universitaires de Lyon, 2014), 233–245.
33. Faye, *Pourquoi nous combattons*, 119.
34. Ibid., 128.
35. Greg Johnson (2010), "Project Septentrion: The Last Line of Defense," Counter-Currents 2010, accessed July 11, 2017, http://www.counter-currents.com/2010/08/project-septentrion.
36. "En français," *Racial Nationalist Library*, accessed August 8, 2017, http://library.flawlesslogic.com/french.htm.
37. Guillaume Faye, *Archeofuturism* (London: Arktos Media, 2010); *Why We Fight: Manifesto of European Resistance* (London: Arktos Media, 2011); *Convergences of Catastrophes* (London: Arktos Media, 2012); *Sex and Deviance* (London: Arktos Media, 2014); *The Colonisation of Europe* (London: Arktos Media, 2016); *Archeofuturism 2.0* (London: Arktos Media, 2016); *Understanding Islam* (London: Arktos Media, 2017).
38. *Archéofuturisme* was translated into Spanish as *El Arqueofuturismo* (Barcelona: Titania, 2008) and into Italian as *L'Archeofuturismo* (Milan: Società editrice Barbarossa, 2000); *Pourquoi nous combattons* was translated into German as *Wofür wir kämpfen: Manifest des europäischen Widerstandes: das metapolitische Hand-und Wörterbuch der kulturellen Revolution zur Neugeburt Europas* (Kassel: Ahnenrad der Moderne, 2006) and into Czech as *Pročbojujeme: manifest evropského odporu: metapolitický slovník* (Prague: Delsky potapěč, 2016).
39. Paul Piccone, "The French New Right: New Right–New Left–New Paradigm?" *Telos* 98–99 (Winter 1993).
40. Stéphane François, 2014, *Au-delà des vents du Nord: L'extrême droite française, le Pôle nord et les Indo-Européens* (Lyon: Presses Universitaires de Lyon, 2014).
41. Torigian was close to the European-American radical Right and wrote in the white-supremacist press under the pseudonym of Michael O'Meara.
42. For example, Paul Gottfried, Raymond Cattell, Arthur Jensen, Donald Swan, Wesley George, Roger Pearson, Kevin MacDonald, Roger Griffin, Samuel Francis, and Jared Taylor.

7

Paul Gottfried and Paleoconservatism

Seth Bartee

PAUL GOTTFRIED IS the founder of the "paleoconservative" wing of the American conservative movement, and the author of twelve books dealing with subjects as broad as conservatism in the US, European intellectual history, fascism, the German jurist Carl Schmidt, and the German-Jewish émigré political philosopher Leo Strauss. Gottfried is a late second-generation postwar conservative intellectual who began publishing monographs in the 1980s. He did not belong to the early formative years that saw the publication of books such as Russell Kirk's *The Conservative Mind*, Richard Weaver's *Ideas Have Consequences*, and Leo Strauss's *Natural Right and History*.[1] By the late 1970s and 1980s, neoconservative intellectuals and Protestant activists challenged the traditionalist ideas that animated the works of Russell Kirk and the Southern Agrarian wing of the Right.[2] The traditionalism of Kirk and the Agrarian wing often gathered around ideas such as regionalism, the enduring value of Western civilization, and the role of Christianity as it was animated in the structure of the Roman Catholic Church. Neoconservatives and Protestant evangelicals were committed to broadening the appeal of the Republican Party and the ideology of conservatism beyond its traditionalist roots, which Gottfried disliked. The traditionalists were often associated with Watergate, and opposition to the New Deal and the Civil Rights Act of 1964. Although the conservative movement in America could date its beginnings only to the immediate post–Second World War years, the neoconservatives, according to Gottfried, were destroying vital intellectual elements of the traditionalist wing of the Right. These necessary elements included the Right's capacity to argue from history, or within a tradition, without having to rely on the progressivism of the American Left. This might include an American southerner's right to defend the primacy of antebellum southern culture without being labeled a bigot or racist. Gottfried is troubled by the fact that conservatives have adopted and modified identity politics for their purposes, which also means that they now are no different from the leftist politics of the Democratic Party.[3]

Postwar conservatism

American conservatism prior to Ronald Reagan included many different strands. Additionally, early conservative intellectuals in the late 1940s and 1950s were often disconnected from American politics. Russell Kirk was not seriously involved in American politics until the campaign of Barry Goldwater in 1964. The émigré wing of conservatism included the likes of the historian Eric Voegelin and the Catholic thinker Thomas Molnar, and also the Southernist Richard Weaver, who were never terribly public about their politics in the US. This changed in the 1960s after the defeat of Goldwater in 1964 and following the conclusion of the Vietnam War. The neoconservatives, who were often ex-Marxist and Jewish, popularized their brand of conservatism in publications such as the *Wall Street Journal* and *Commentary*, using their influence to move conservatism from an isolationist stance on foreign policy to one that was determined to bring an end to communism abroad. For decades, it was thought by most historians and observers that conservatism was a monolithic entity. But during the presidency of George W. Bush, conservatives began to reveal the fracture that had existed for decades because of disagreement about both the Second War in Iraq and Bush's embrace of "compassionate conservatism" as espoused by neoconservatives and Protestant evangelicals.[4]

Gottfried's life

There is a small irony in Paul Gottfried not becoming a neoconservative intellectual, although he claims there is nothing ironic about his choice. The stereotypical neoconservative is a well-educated Jewish former Marxist who rejected the Marxism associated with Stalin in favor of an anticommunism which did not include the regionalisms of the old

Right. More broadly, "neoconservative" came to mean those conservative intellectuals affiliated with the rise of Ronald Reagan and both Bush presidencies. During the 1960s, neoconservatives broke ranks with the Democratic Party once it began to identify with the New Left, the counterculture, and a foreign policy considered to be anti-Israeli.[5] In a 1980 article in *Commentary*, Midge Decter argued that many of the liberation movements, especially gay liberation, had found a way to upend bourgeois morality for heterosexual men by freely flaunting their liberated lifestyles in front of families.[6] While the neoconservatives were opposed to these new radical movements, they belonged to an urban culture that many of the first American New Right thinkers such as Russell Kirk and Mel Bradford had abandoned long before. Kirk was most open in his opposition to urban living in his books where he celebrated himself as a "northern agrarian" living in the "stump country" near the Canadian Lakes region of Michigan.[7]

Gottfried does not easily fit into either category of neoconservative or traditionalist. He was not raised in the countryside or in a thriving metropolis but in the manufacturing city of Bridgeport, Connecticut.[8] This fact alone might not seem like an important detail except that the founding neoconservative intellectuals, such as Irving Kristol, often considered the father of neoconservatism, Gertrude Himmelfarb, and Norman Podhoretz all grew up in Brooklyn and remained within the New York intellectual scene. It is also worth mentioning that the neoconservatives were also intimate with the New York literati as a result of their work in the *Partisan Review* and through teaching affiliations in New York City.[9] Gottfried's upbringing in a working-class, white ethnic neighborhood produced more difference than likeness with neoconservatives.[10] Yet, Gottfried's family was not without means; he reports that his father was a respected businessman and a fire commissioner in Bridgeport. Gottfried's father was from Budapest, part of his family having come from Austria. This meant that the young Gottfried grew up familiar with the German language, and he has published widely in German and English.[11]

Gottfried earned a bachelor's degree from Yeshiva University in New York City. At Yeshiva, he studied rabbinic law, as well as New York Jewish culture.[12] Following graduation from Yeshiva, he found himself a graduate student at Yale, where he reported never feeling quite at home. In his autobiography, *Encounters*, he writes, "I . . . have remained a Hebrew rather than Rabbinic Jew or a passionate Zionist. . . . The Jews, mostly from New York, raged with anger against the 'fascist' war of president Lyndon Johnson, but when the Six-Day War between Israel and its neighbors erupted, they became a vocal war party."[13] For Gottfried, the neoconservatives represented the many ironies of both conservatism and being an American Jew on the Right. On the one hand, a Jewish conservative had everything an individual of a traditionalist persuasion needed, with a history that went all the way back to ancient Mesopotamia and its pastoral patriarchs, but a progressive impulse seemed to keep them from embracing the traditionalism of the New Right. The celebration of customary practices that often defined the work of traditionalists was absent from the ex-Marxist wing of conservatism. Mostly, Gottfried's graduate school days at Yale were "uneventful," and the only life-changing associations at the institution were his connection with the Yale Party of the Right and time studying with Herbert Marcuse of Frankfurt School fame.[14]

Early career and the Bradford affair

Gottfried's path from a self-described Republican Party activist to a paleoconservative is a twofold journey. Gottfried struggled to find academic work because of his traditionalism, as described in *Encounters*.[15] Later, his opinions on social issues and foreign policy made him suspect to neoconservative academics because of his criticisms of the politics of the Republican Party, and his eventual affiliation with *Telos* in the 1980s and 1990s. The *Telos* group formed in 1968 as a New Left publication and group, only to turn toward conservatism by the 1980s and 1990s. *Telos*, led by Paul Piccone, for many years hosted a flurry of well-known intellectuals including both Christopher Lasch and Gottfried, who were not members of the original group. Gottfried believes his appeal to *Telos* was based on his isolation in the conservative movement.[16] Nostalgia and the idea of lost opportunities also played a key role in Gottfried's thinking about the history of conservatism in the US. If the conservative movement was the safe place for rightists all of persuasions before the 1980s, Gottfried opined, it became less friendly to debates concerning political correctness because of the neoconservative influence during the Reagan years. Therefore, Gottfried felt no compunction about joining a faction of which shared his same concerns.

Gottfried's reminiscence was not unwarranted, given the influx of neoconservatives into conservatism and the Republican Party during Ronald Reagan's first term as president. The historian George

Nash has shown that the neoconservative wing grew increasingly in universities and the publishing world throughout the 1960s and 1970s. The neoconservatives later challenged the Goldwaterites who supported escalated use of military force in Vietnam, and a reduced role of government in the US.[17] This influx of Jewish ex-radicals into the conservative movement also resulted in the purging of the traditionalist wing of conservatism from influencing the Republican Party and its major publication, *National Review*.[18] Once the neoconservatives' influence trickled down from the Republican Party to publications and think tanks, their dominance became apparent.[19] What seemed like a minor debate in the 1960s between two conservative intellectuals—Harry Jaffa and M. E. (Mel) Bradford—created sparks on the pages of conservative journals during what is now remembered as "The Lincoln Wars."[20] The first historian to contextualize American conservatism, George Nash, referenced the sparring between Jaffa, a student of the political philosopher Leo Strauss, and traditionalist conservatives such as Frank Meyer, Russell Kirk, Wilmoore Kendall, and Bradford. The controversies amounted to an important but mostly ignored debate concerning the nature of America's founding. Supporters of Jaffa argued that the founding was primarily democratic while traditionalists saw the creation of the US as a special moment in history limited to a particular people and culture. Jaffa's followers believed the original founding was flawed while most traditionalists had no issue with the founding or with antebellum Southern criticisms of the expansion of democracy and industrialism.[21]

These competing forces fleshed out in an unforeseen set of events following the election of Ronald Reagan as president in 1980. Just as conservatives celebrated the landslide victory of the former California governor over the incumbent Jimmy Carter—something that had not happened since Herbert Hoover lost to Franklin Roosevelt in 1932— conservative intellectuals split over the position for the chair of the National Endowment for the Humanities (NEH).

The division between neoconservatives and traditionalists started in the Lincoln Wars. Mel Bradford, a humanities professor and admirer of the antebellum South, was nominated to become chairman of the NEH. Bradford was a supporter of Reagan and a recognized humanist. However, a campaign instigated by the neoconservative intellectuals helped oust Bradford from consideration in favor of William Bennett, based on a footnote in a book where Bradford had compared Abraham Lincoln to Adolf Hitler.[22] Bennett was reported to have voted in the Democratic primary in

1980, and Bradford was thereby labeled a racist for his dislike of Lincoln.[23] Neoconservatives, especially the Jaffaites, look at Lincoln as the key figure that renewed a flawed process for creating a constitution.[24] This seemingly small event split conservative intellectuals and launched Gottfried's career as a paleoconservative.

Gottfried's work

Gottfried's early work reflected his dissertation interests pertaining to aspects of German culture and history. His chosen field of study even revealed a bravado and willingness to go against the expectations of conservative historians of this period as well. While there are seeds of his key beliefs in his first book, *Conservative Millenarians: The Romantic Experience in Bavaria*, he now dismisses that 1979 work as unrefined and unrelated to his mature body of literature.[25] The observer, however, can find an evident shift in his scholarship following Bradford's bruising at the hands of the neoconservatives. In 1983 Gottfried published an article "On Neoconservatism" for the conservative journal *Modern Age*. In this article, Gottfried argued that neoconservative intellectuals had accepted Lyndon Johnson's Great Society programs and liberal arguments for hiring quotas, and therefore wanted only to make sure that the federal glut went to the Right instead of the Left.[26] Yet, Gottfried still held out hope in 1983 that the neoconservatives might become friendly to traditionalists despite the falling out about the chair of the NEH just years earlier.

Gottfried's historicism

Throughout his career, Gottfried became more critical of conservatism as both an ideology and in political practice. His intellectual journey in the conservative movement can be divided into three periods. In the first part of his career (1980 and 1990) Gottfried served as a highbrow critic of conservatism but from within the mainstream of the movement. The second phase of Gottfried's career began in the early 1990s culminating the publication of his Marxism trilogy in the middle of the 2000s. This most fruitful intellectual period was defined by his friendship with Christopher Lasch and close association with the *Telos* group. Lasch was a former New Leftist turned "right-wing populist" by the 1980s. A midwestern-born historian, Lasch spent most of his career directing graduate students at the University of Rochester in upstate New York.[27] The third phase of

Gottfried's career started in 2008, as founder of the H. L. Mencken Club, and as an activist moving farther away from the conservative mainstream.

Gottfried's first major work and his grand opus is *The Search for Historical Meaning: Hegel and the Postwar Right*. This is one of the most important, and underappreciated, conservative books ever written for its recognition of the theoretical weaknesses in the founding generation of the postwar American New Right. These supposed weaknesses included a brief but fruitful fusion of conservative intellectuals that included traditionalists, libertarians, and Straussians striving to either preserve things lost from premodernity or to roll back some aspect of the New Deal order.[28] *The Search for Historical Meaning* was written at a moment of conservative victory—Ronald Reagan was serving his second term as president following his 1984 reelection landslide. Despite Gottfried's unwelcomed criticisms, the conservative sociologist Robert Nisbet complimented *The Search for Historical Meaning* as not just a theoretical work but also a reminder that the conservative movement was rooted in the ideas of historicism.[29] In other words, the conservative movement was supposed to curb liberalism's desire to universalize the American political project. Nisbet, like Gottfried, believed that the neoconservatives were making a similar mistake by universalizing the language of conservatism.[30]

The Search for Historical Meaning stood out because Gottfried questioned the legacy of Leo Strauss as a genuine conservative intellectual. Debates between Straussian intellectuals and members of the New Right had taken place as early as the 1960s, but often Strauss himself was absent from these conflicts. The philosopher died in 1973 and never witnessed the growth of "Straussianism" that flourished in the 1980s and beyond.[31] Nisbet wrote that thinking historically was key to the original project of the New Right because of its recognition that the American founding was exceptional . . . but limited to the US alone. Gottfried's ultimate claim is that the neoconservatives universalized the American experience in the language of human rights.[32]

Yet, in *The Search for Historical Meaning* Gottfried revealed a tension within conservatism that only astute observers noticed. When George Nash published *The Conservative Intellectual Movement in America Since 1945*, he presented a picture of conservatism that showed polite disagreement instead of the fierce sectarianism that had often prevailed in conservative circles.[33] As Jennifer Burns revealed in her 2004 review of Nash's *The Conservative Intellectual Movement*, the book has become a classic as a primer on conservatism even though few scholars have actually engaged Nash's arguments directly.[34] Gottfried further boiled down these differences to reveal, as he did later in his career, that conservatism was far less conservative and less theoretically sound than Nash had shown it to be. He agrees with the mid-twentieth-century thinker Louis Hartz when he claimed that America did not have a genuine conservative tradition because it lacked a background in the kind of feudalism Europe experienced during the Middle Ages.[35]

First, Gottfried thought, conservative intellectuals wrongly rejected historicism because of its association with Nazism. However, denunciation of all forms of historicism was costly for conservatives because it left them without a weapon against the progressive impulse of liberalism. For years, paleoconservatives have been highlighting conservative Republican presidents' failures to defund the Department of Education, overturn Roe v. Wade, and significantly scale down the size of government. One of his greatest insights was that German-influenced historicism had merely been replaced by the terminology of "Burkeanism" and "Western Civilization." In other words, Kirk and others modified Burkeanism to mean localism, regionalism, and a general escape from the progressive impulse of liberalism while Burkeanism in its original context was associated closely with Romanticism and not populism.[36] Contemporary Burkeanism was committed to the same kind of thinking without connecting itself to German thought. The main thrust and conclusions of *The Search for Historical Meaning* was that the traditionalist wing of conservatism had permanently injured its cause by accepting Leo Strauss's rejection of historicism as an implicit anti-Semitic idea linked to the Holocaust and National Socialism.

Just two years following the publication of *The Search for Historical Meaning*, Gottfried coauthored *The Conservative Movement* (1988) with the libertarian thinker Thomas Fleming. *The Conservative Movement* was one of the first histories of the movement since George Nash published *The Conservative Intellectual Movement in America Since 1945* in 1976.[37] Nash's story of the conservative movement as a fusionist convergence of various strands of conservatism seemed to stand up to criticism in 1976, but twelve years later this no longer seemed to be the reality. In fact, Gottfried and Fleming challenged the fusionist thesis that all conservative intellectuals worked under the same umbrella by demonstrating the ideological divergences between various kinds of conservatives.

The turning point in Gottfried's career, and one that was unforeseen, was his interaction with the *Telos* group. As the *Telos* group made a conservative turn away from the liberalism of the 1960s counterculture, they did not openly support the Republican Party or lock arms with *National Review* magazine founder and conservative icon William F. Buckley Jr. What they did do was to form close associations with Paul Gottfried and Christopher Lasch as they shifted toward paleoconservatism, which really represented the rejection.

Gottfried explains that under the direction of Paul Piccone, he was welcomed into the group as they embraced populism. Piccone's group already included the self-proclaimed right-wing populist Christopher Lasch, who openly criticized the new class of global elites who worked to create international governance of the world without consideration of the traditional mores that bonded society together.[38] It was during this era that Gottfried also began formulating his most prescient criticisms of both contemporary versions of liberalism and conservatism.

In 1999, six years after the death of his friend Christopher Lasch, Gottfried published the first book of what became known as his Marxism trilogy. The three monographs that make up this triumvirate are *After Liberalism: Mass Democracy in the Managerial State*; *Multiculturalism and the Politics of Guilt: Toward a Secular Theocracy*; and *The Strange Death of Marxism: The European Left in the New Millennium*. These texts amount to a formidable examination of the trajectory and ostensible collapse of nineteenth-century liberalism, as it reverted to what Gottfried calls the democratic-multicultural "managerial state" in the postbourgeois era. *After Liberalism* is a genealogy of liberalism where Gottfried shows that liberalism has become progressively more disconnected from its bourgeois foundations in nineteenth-century Europe. For Gottfried, liberalism is perpetually adrift because intellectuals on the Left have labeled themselves internationalists, localists, revolutionaries, and so on without disrupting the chain of leftist ideology in America.[39]

The main thesis in Gottfried's work is that all modern political ideas have become unmoored from their historical settings. He borrowed this idea from Christopher Lasch who believed that American political parties adopted a progressive axiomatic approach to politics.[40] Lasch believed that all modern political ideologies are utilized by a new class of elites looking to subsume all identity into a perverse jousting match for administrative supremacy.[41] One can think of the contemporary political upheavals in both the US and in Europe as revealing elite class rivalries concerning administrative supremacy. Gottfried's main difference with Lasch is that the former University of Rochester professor saw hope in a kind of intellectual populism, while Gottfried believes that democracy depends on centralization leaving little hope for genuine dissent. It is possible that as a conservative intellectual who faced career difficulties, Gottfried witnessed what he considered the impossibility of a compromise between progressive politics and the Right's desire to soak in traditions considered antiquated by the Left.

Multiculturalism and the Politics of Guilt was published in 2002.[42] It concerns the supposed therapeutic dogmatism that props up the managerial state. By "managerial state," Gottfried means the class of global elites that oversee the affairs of government. This new class of elites, unlike their earlier forefathers the early twentieth-century progressives, have less at stake because they are often far removed from the American middle class. Gottfried points to the Frankfurt School theorists Theodore Adorno and Gunnar Myrdal as examples of therapeutic thinkers advocating for societal reeducation for anyone dissenting from the ideology of liberal democracy. Adorno's 1950 *Authoritarian Personality* and Myrdal's 1944 *An American Dilemma: The Negro Problem and Modern Democracy* both reveal a new casting of liberalism, which belongs to a genre of literature that applied Freudian psychoanalysis to the treatment of societal ills.[43] In other words, these works served not as narrative histories that told a story but as history used to solve problems. Again, building upon the work of Lasch, Gottfried posits that contemporary philanthropic and paragovernment organizations borrowed these ideas and thus maintain a therapeutic ideology to ward off dissent. In the final work of the Marxism trilogy, *The Strange Death of Marxism*, Gottfried finalizes his arguments against managerial liberalism.[44]

Initially, and contrary to popular representations, Gottfried claimed that the US, and not Europe, is the most influential liberal influencer in the world. This has been so since the Frankfurt School theorists left Europe, according to Gottfried, and returned with their ideas radicalized by American democratic practices.[45] The most provocative of Gottfried's claims were that the historical Marxists in Europe failed to grasp why the working class did not embrace revolution. Instead of allowing the conservatism and traditionalisms of the working classes to prevail, neo-Marxists abandoned their rigid orthodoxy and began supporting Third World liberation movements when the hope of a genuine revolution in Western Europe failed.[46] At the root of Gottfried's criticisms of late modernity and liberalism is the belief that democracy needs the centralizing impulse of the state to maintain its aims, which increases with each year and electoral cycle. Ultimately, Gottfried's wider but unspoken belief is that liberalism is an authoritarian ideology not content to remain within the borders of politics as it seeks to become a permanent and undisputed civil religion.

By the time that Gottfried had published the final volume of the Marxism trilogy in 2005, conservatism was in the process of splintering. The second Bush presidency made many conservative intellectuals shudder.[47] Many rightists opposed the Second Iraq War and President Bush's insistence on using the federal government to spread democratic principles domestically and abroad. Gottfried and other paleoconservative intellectuals, in dismay at the state of the movement, began forming new paleo-Right organizations with the goal of renewing something lost from the first generation of American conservatives. Gottfried and a Catholic University philosophy professor, Claes Ryn, formed the Academy of Philosophy and Letters, but split soon afterwards because of differences concerning axiomatic approaches to conservatism. The division resulted in Gottfried's belief than anyone of a conservative persuasion, religious or not, should be able to join the Academy of Philosophy and Letters. Ryn, a bourgeois Swedish Anglophone philosopher, disagreed with Gottfried's populism, as Gottfried would allow almost any dissenter from liberalism into his organization if it meant grinding the wheels of the state to a halt.[48] However, when it became apparent that several who wanted to join the Academy of Philosophy and Letters had affiliations with neo-Confederate groups, Gottfried and Ryn parted ways.[49]

It is during this period that Gottfried revisited conservatism for a third time. In *Conservatism in America: Making Sense of the American Right* (2007), Gottfried finalized his criticisms of the conservatism movement.[50] Here Gottfried chided conservative intellectuals for failure to see that historicism was the missing ingredient to provide a real alternative to liberalism. Several new and additional elements highlight this work, with one being that American conservatives often rejected European conservatism, and relied heavily on imagination and not enough on the historical record.

In 2008, Gottfried's H. L. Mencken Club met for the first time in Baltimore, Maryland, in a convention hotel near the Baltimore-Washington International Airport at the same location where the Academy of Philosophy and Letters met until 2017. The Academy of Philosophy and Letters would meet in the summer, and the H. L. Mencken Club met in the fall. Its meetings were attended by those who had often been associated with the conservative movement at one time, but had either become intellectually removed from it or found one of its leaders (such as William Buckley) to be less than virtuous characters. Peter Brimelow, a former editor of Buckley's *National Review*, described Buckley as a self-interested and egotistical person interested only in preserving his power in the conservative movement and not being intellectually committed to true conservative principles.[51] The first several years of the H. L. Mencken Club drew renowned conservative intellectuals from all over the spectrum including the Catholic political philosopher Patrick Deneen, a former Republican presidential candidate Patrick Buchanan, and Richard Spencer, later the leader of the Alt Right. However, Gottfried never embraced white nationalism nor attended any of Spencer's protests.[52]

It was known that the H. L. Mencken Club allowed conservatives to present who took both race and biology as key factors in their conception of conservatism, even if Paul Gottfried did not.[53] Yet, Gottfried defended his kind of conservatism by calling it "right-wing pluralism." By right-wing pluralism, Gottfried meant that he wanted to offer both an organization and venue where conservatives of all stripes could converse openly. Gottfried said these conservatives were without power institutionally and politically. For example, these kinds of conservatives could be neo-Confederates, who were, he believed, harmless since they held onto a worldview that had been demolished long ago. Gottfried says that rooting out these types of "reactionaries" is a ridiculous plan because they are "harmless" figures without any real social power.[54]

Gottfried's association with the Alt Right was more of a stepping-stone for Spencer than it was an end point for Gottfried. Spencer found himself at odds with several mainstream conservative organizations before meeting Gottfried and attending H. L. Mencken Club meetings. Spencer originally created a blog he called *The Alternative Right*, which was not just a blog for interviews but also for thoughts on anything Spencer considered worthy of his efforts.[55] Jacob Siegel's November 2016 *Tablet* article linked Gottfried directly to Spencer as his mentor, but this seems to be a nefarious claim as Spencer was never a student of Gottfried.[56] In fact, Gottfried reports that Spencer stopped attending H. L. Mencken Club meetings in favor of creating his own organizations such as The National Policy Institute and Washington Summit Publishers. Spencer stopped attending the meetings of his H. L. Mencken Club years before his reputation garnered national attention, according to Gottfried.[57]

The formation of the H. L. Mencken Club is also a canonical creation and a reaction against Burkean conservatives who looked to Europe for inspiration. Russell Kirk and others have been important in reintroducing Edmund Burke into the canon of conservatism. However,

Kirk's claim that the US had a kind of Burkean founding was not without criticism and controversy even among conservative intellectuals.[58] Gottfried only recently connected conservatism to the mind and actions of the Baltimore journalist, editor, and writer H. L. Mencken. Mencken questioned the popular idols of American life during the first half of the twentieth century, as well as the creation of the twentieth-century welfare state.

Mencken was not a conservative and never identified as one, as that terminology was not in popular usage during his lifetime. However, the sage of Baltimore offers hope for contemporary American conservatives. He was a critic of the New Deal and decried the fundamentalism represented by evangelical progressive William Jennings Bryan. For Gottfried, Mencken represents a high critic of ideology without succumbing to the need to be admired. Accordingly, Gottfried affirms Mencken's skepticism of democracy and egalitarianism.

In this way, Gottfried has successfully returned conservatism to the Right. In other words, the conservative movement that the post–Second World War organized is now fracturing again. Gottfried is returning conservatism to its classical liberal and laissez-faire atomism and is doing so with texts at the center of his worldview. Yet, Gottfried is not an atheist like Mencken and finds the genuine conservative tradition in the US to be one that is Protestant. Following the publication of Gottfried's autobiography with a traditionalist conservative publisher in 2009, he began publishing works that were explicitly reactionary,[59] in the sense that they were outside of the conservative mainstream with the intent of upsetting status quo conservatism.

Beginning in 2012, Gottfried began writing for publishers who were linked to right-wing elements not associated with the mainstream of the Republican Party. Arktos published a compilation of his essays in 2012 and, in 2015, Gottfried edited a book titled *The Great Purge: The Deformation of the Conservative Movement* with Richard Spencer. *The Great Purge* included a host of authors associated with the H. L. Mencken Club such as Lee Congdon, Keith Preston, James Kalb, and William Regnery. The idea of purge works in cooperation with a Menckenian persona of reaction against the mainstreams of both conservatism and liberalism. The genesis of this story often begins with the neoconservative surge during the 1960s and 1970s when these ex-Marxists began criticizing the counterculturalism of the Left and the civil rights movement.[60] The influence of neoconservative intellectuals increased throughout the 1970s and into 1980s when we find them impacting key conservative think tanks such as the Heritage Foundation, the American Enterprise Institute, the Philadelphia Society, along with *National Review*, and more. These same ex-Marxists also founded their own journals that included *Public Interest* and took over *Commentary* magazine with Norman Podhoretz editing the publication for decades.[61]

The idea of political correctness is one that pervades these works. For Gottfried and his Menckenians, the therapeutic idealization of culture destroys everything it touches. Mostly, it has distorted the true historical narrative of conservatism. In 2012, he published *Leo Strauss and the Conservative Movement in America*. This monograph serves as a revision of Strauss, and his role in conservatism, which he is generally disassociated from in most accounts. A main reason for writing this account was to reveal Strauss to be a kind of sinister element within conservatism instead of a gentle philosopher whose ideas were expropriated by his students.

According to Gottfried, Leo Strauss was a philosopher who sowed the seeds of progressivism in the conservative movement by finding a philosophical plot that would disturb historicism of the conservative movement. Gottfried's main theoretical criticism of Strauss and Straussianism is that their conservatism "does not require historical imagination or any serious acceptance of the possibility that others, separated by time and circumstance, were not like themselves, namely religious skeptics who would have celebrated their good fortune in being able to live in a materialistic democracy."[62] It is with these criticisms that Gottfried demonstrates his importance to the conservative movement. Gottfried is returning conservatism back to the Right when it served as both a laissez-faire and philosophy of skepticism toward progressivism and democracy.

Gottfried's return to the Right

Gottfried holds a rare place in American conservatism. He met and knew many of the key first generation of American conservatives such as Russell Kirk. And he came of age in a time when the conservative movement first splintered during the NEH controversy between the paleoconservatives and the neoconservatives. Yet, Gottfried was an academic, not an independent scholar, and therefore occupied a space that the likes of Kirk, Whittaker Chambers, and William F. Buckley never inhabited. For this reason, Gottfried encountered the *Telos* group, and most importantly Christopher Lasch as he was moving away from liberalism.

There are many compilations and genealogies of the conservative movement. Gregory Schneider published *The Conservative Century: From Reaction to Revolution* in 2009. Schneider's book is important in that he shows that conservatism often defies definition.[63] In his final chapter, Schneider addressed the issue that conservatism was often stuck between the desire for political prowess and principle. For Gottfried and the paleoconservative supporters, it was not so much that principles had been destroyed, but that the theoretical foundation was never in place to begin with. Gottfried repeats the irony of political conservatism and its intellectual equivalencies:

> Although some Fox-news viewers and some subscribers to magazines like *National Review* have deeply ingrained loyalty to the Republican Party and to Republican talking points, one must ask whether these senior citizens agree with the leftward drift shown by widely featured conservative celebrities on salient social issues. How many Southern white senior citizens are pleased to hear Charles Krauthammer, Bill Kristol, Rich Lowry, and Max Boot come out passionately in favor of dismantling Confederate memorial statues?[64]

Gottfried's paleoconservatism has not necessarily spurred the rise of the Alt Right. If anything, Spencer gravitated toward Gottfried primarily because the Yale graduate offered a platform for networking among ostracized paleoconservatives in the H. L. Mencken Club. Gottfried's record reveals a historian who has struggled to spread his warnings to fellow conservatives long before terminology and labels such as Alt Right were thought about. In an effort to be heard, Gottfried linked himself to certain figures that a student of Herbert Marcuse would never associate with. Neither is the father of paleoconservative a pundit that can be dismissed for lack of education and refinement. Gottfried has the rare ability to write a well-respected monograph, and then change tone and publish polemics on the level of H. L. Mencken. It is the combination of both abilities that Gottfried has returned conservatism from its Cold War manifestations back to the Right where skepticism and disillusionment with late modernity are the only two principles worth maintaining.

Notes

1. Most historians agree that Russell Kirk's *The Conservative Mind: from Burke to Eliot* (Washington, DC: Regnery, 1995); Richard Weaver's *Ideas Have Consequences* (Chicago: University of Chicago Press, 1948); Leo Strauss's *Natural Right and History* (Chicago: University of Chicago Press, 1953); and Whittaker Chambers's *Witness* (New York: Random House, 1953) make up the essential canon of texts for the New Right.
2. See Daniel Oppenheimer, *Exit Right: The People Who Left the Left and Reshaped the American Century* (New York: Simon and Schuster, 2016).
3. See Paul Gottfried, *The Search for Historical Meaning: Hegel and the Postwar American Right* (DeKalb: Northern Illinois University Press, 1986).
4. See Marvin Olasky, *Compassionate Conservatism: What It Is, What It Does, and How It Can Transform America* (New York: Free Press, 2000).
5. See Michael Kimmage, *The Conservative Turn: Lionel Trilling, Whittaker Chambers, and the Lessons of Anti-communism* (Cambridge, MA: Harvard University Press, 2009); and Matthew Berke, "Neoconservatism," in *A Companion to American Thought*, ed. Richard Wightman Fox et al. (Malden: Blackwell Publishers, 1998), 484–486.
6. See Midge Decter, "The Boys on the Beach," *Commentary*, September 1, 1980, https://www.commentarymagazine.com/articles/the-boys-on-the-beach/.
7. Russell Kirk, *The Sword of Imagination: Memoirs of a Half-century of Literary Conflict* (Grand Rapids, MI: William B. Eerdmans Pub., 1995).
8. See Paul Gottfried's autobiography, *Encounters: My Life with Nixon, Marcuse, and Other Friends and Teachers* (Wilmington, ISI Books, 2009).
9. See Alexander Bloom, *Prodigal Sons: The New York Intellectuals and Their World* (New York: Oxford University Press, 1986); and Alan Wald, *The New York Intellectuals: The Rise and Decline of the Anti-Stalinist Left From the 1930s to the 1980s* (Chapel Hill: University of North Carolina Press, 1987).
10. Gottfried, *Encounters*, 13–15.
11. Paul Gottfried, e-mail message to author, November 6, 2017.
12. Gottfried, *Encounters*, 22–23.
13. Ibid., 23–24.
14. For a short biography of Gottfried, read Seth Bartee's, "What You Need to Know about Paul Gottfried," *Front Porch Republic*, September 13, 2013, accessed October 1, 2016, http://www.frontporchrepublic.com/2013/09/what-you-need-to-know-about-paul-gottfried/.
15. Gottfried, *Encounters*, 30–31.
16. Gottfried, message to author, December 24, 2017.
17. George Nash, *The Conservative Intellectual Movement in America Since 1945* (New York: Basic Books, 1976).
18. Kimmage, *Conservative Turn*.

19. See Paul Gottfried, *Leo Strauss and The Conservative Movement in America: A Critical Appraisal* (New York: Cambridge University Press, 2012). The expansionist narrative of neoconservative dominance is a key theme in paleoconservative historiography.
20. See Daniel McCarthy, "The Right's Civil War," *American Conservative*, July 23, 2013, accessed June 29, 2017, http://www.theamericanconservative.com/articles/the-rights-civil-war/.
21. See Nash, *Conservative Intellectual Movement*, 344–347.
22. McCarthy, "The Right's Civil War."
23. For another account of these happenings see Paul Murphy, *The Rebuke of History: The Southern Agrarians and American Conservative Thought* (Chapel Hill: University of North Carolina Press, 2001), chaps. 7 and 8.
24. See Harry Jaffa, *Crisis of the House Divided: An Interpretation of the Issues in the Lincoln-Douglas Debates* (Seattle: University of Washington Press, 1959).
25. Alex Smith in discussion with the author, March 2012.
26. Paul Gottfried, "On Neoconservatism," *Modern Age* 27 (1983): 36–41.
27. See Eric Miller, *Hope in a Scattering Time: A Life of Christopher Lasch* (Grand Rapids, MI: Wm. B. Eerdmans, 2010).
28. There are two American New Rights. The original New Right was the group in the 1950s, with the other being the Evangelical Right during the 1980s. See Raymond Wolters, "New Right," *First Principles*, June 5, 2011, http://www.firstprinciplesjournal.com/articles.aspx?article=725.
29. Gottfried, *Search for Historical Meaning*.
30. See Robert Nisbet, *History of the Idea of Progress* (New York: Basic Books, 1980).
31. There are several schools of thinking about the legacy of Leo Strauss. One school represented in Laurence Lampert, *The Enduring Importance of Leo Strauss* (Chicago: University of Chicago Press, 2013), sees Strauss as disconnected from postwar conservatism. In Harry Jaffa's, *Crisis of the Strauss Divided: Essays on Leo Strauss and Straussianism, East and West* (Lanham, MD: Rowman and Littlefield Publishers, 2012), he shows Straussianism as a sectarian conflict between competing schools of philosophically inclined conservatives. Paul Gottfried's *Leo Strauss* (Cambridge: Cambridge University Press, 2013) connects Strauss directly to conservatism and neoconservative politics.
32. Gottfried, message to author, December 27, 2017.
33. George Nash reflected on the publication of this book in 2016. See Nash, "The Conservative Intellectual Movement in America: Then and Now," *National Review*, April 26, 2016, http://www.nationalreview.com/article/434548/conservative-intellectuals-george-nash.
34. See Jennifer Burns, "In Retrospect: George Nash's The Conservative Intellectual Movement Since 1945," *Reviews in American History* 32, no. 3 (2004): 447–462.
35. See Louis Hartz, *The Liberal Tradition in America: An Interpretation of American Political Thought since the Revolution* (New York: Harcourt, Brace, 1955).

36. Gottfried, *Search for Historical Meaning*, chap. 7.
37. Paul Gottfried and Thomas Fleming, *The Conservative Movement* (Boston: Twayne Publishers, 1988).
38. For a general history of the *Telos* group see Timothy W. Luke and Ben Agger, eds., *A Journal of No Illusions: Telos, Paul Piccone, and the Americanization of Critical Theory* (New York: Telos Press Pub., 2011). Also see Gottfried, *Encounters*, chap. 5.
39. Paul Gottfried, *After Liberalism: Mass Democracy in the Managerial State* (Princeton, NJ: Princeton University Press, 1999).
40. Christopher Lasch, *The Revolt of the Elites and the Betrayal of Democracy* (New York: W. W. Norton, 1996).
41. Ibid.
42. Paul Gottfried, *Multiculturalism and the Politics of Guilt: Toward a Secular Theocracy* (Columbia: University of Missouri Press, 2002).
43. See Theodore Adorno, *The Authoritarian Personality* (New York: Harper, 1950), and Gunnar Myrdal, *An American Dilemma: The Negro Problem and Modern Democracy* (New York: Harper and Brothers, 1944).
44. Paul Gottfried, *The Strange Death of Marxism: The European Left in the New Millennium* (Columbia: University of Missouri Press, 2005).
45. Ibid., chaps. 1 and 2.
46. Ibid., chap. 3.
47. For contemporary debates among conservative intellectuals, see Joel Aberbach, *Understanding Contemporary American Conservatism* (New York: Routledge, 2017).
48. See the H. L. Mencken Club founding statement, "About he H. L. Mencken Club," accessed October 14, 2017, http://hlmenckenclub.org/about/.
49. See, "Mission State of Academy of Philosophy and Letters," accessed October 14, 2017, https://philosophyandletters.org/about/.
50. Paul Gottfried, *Conservatism in America: Making Sense of the American Right* (New York: Palgrave, 2007).
51. See Peter Brimelow, "The WFB Myth," presentation, Annual meeting of the H. L. Mencken Club, Baltimore, MD, November 5, 2011.
52. Paul Gottfried in discussion with the author, December 2017.
53. Ibid., March 2012.
54. Ibid., March 2012.
55. See Alternative Right (blog), https://alternative-right.blogspot.com/. This is not the original blog that Spencer hosted.
56. See Jacob Siegel, "The Alt-Right's Jewish Godfather," *Tablet*, November 29, 2016, http://www.tabletmag.com/jewish-news-and-politics/218712/spencer-gottfried-alt-right.
57. The H. L. Mencken Club website, which keeps a record of past conference speakers, shows that Spencer last attended a meeting as a speaker in November 2013.

58. For a summary and intellectual history of these controversies see Seth Bartee, "Imagination Movers: The Construction of Conservative Counter-Narratives in Reaction to Consensus Liberalism" (PhD diss., Virginia Polytechnic Institution and State University, 2014).
59. See Paul Gottfried and Richard Spencer ed., *The Great Purge: The Deformation of the Conservative Movement* (Whitefish, MT: Washington Summit Publishers, 2015) and *Revisions and Dissents: Essays* (DeKalb: Northern Illinois University Press, 2017).
60. See Norman Podhoretz, *Making It* (New York: Random House, 1967).
61. See Alan Wald, *The New York Intellectuals: The Rise and Decline of the Anti-Stalinist Left From the 1930s to the 1980s* (Chapel Hill: University of North Carolina Press, 1987).
62. See Bartee, "Imagination Movers," 301.
63. See Gregory Schneider, *The Conservative Century: From Reaction to Revolution* (Lanham, MD: Rowman and Littlefield, 2009).
64. See Paul Gottfried, "The End of the Conservative Movement," *Lew Rockwell*, September 1, 2017, https://www.lewrockwell.com/2017/09/paul-gottfried/end-conservative-movement/.

8

Patrick J. Buchanan and the Death of the West

Edward Ashbee

PATRICK J. BUCHANAN WAS born in Washington, DC, in 1938. Although he later embraced the abrasively populist, paleoconservative politics of the outsider during his quixotic bids for the presidency, he first spent almost two decades serving in Republican administrations.

Buchanan's childhood and adolescence were shaped by the ordered hierarchies of a mid-twentieth-century white urban neighborhood and the Roman Catholic Church. His father, an accountant, was among those "white ethnics" (Buchanan and his siblings claimed a German, British, and Irish lineage) who had become disaffected with the Democrats by the time Franklin Roosevelt began his third term of office in 1941.[1] Within Buchanan's boyhood community there was a sense of profound, instinctual loyalty to the US, but at the same time there were strong feelings of exclusion from, as well as subordination to, its governing institutions. In his autobiography, *Right from the Beginning*, Buchanan recalls his days at Blessed Sacrament School in Washington, DC: "even though we lived in the nation's capital, I cannot recall a single 'field trip' in eight years to visit the monuments or institutions of government. While we were all proud to be Americans, running the country was somebody else's job."[2]

This is a telling claim conveying a deep sense of resentment against the "somebody else" that administered and staffed the American state. That resentment haunted Buchanan's later politics and, if anything, became stronger over time. As he grew up, the WASP "establishment" elites appeared in the eyes of the Right to overreach themselves through relentless bureaucratic expansionism, large-scale social engineering, and, more dramatically, the betrayal of American interests during the Cold War. For Buchanan, McCarthyism was not only a bid to unmask "red" espionage or subversion but also a legitimate populist revolt against a corrupt, self-serving, and disloyal political class. The McCarthy movement, and Buchanan saw it as a movement, began a process of challenging that class, the progressive-liberal state and the governing New Deal ideology, that was built over the decades that followed:

> McCarthy was cheered because for four years he was daily kicking the living hell out of people most Americans concluded should have the living hell kicked out of them. . . . Never again, after Tail Gunner Joe, would liberalism be entrusted with the governance of the United States.[3]

Political career

After working as a journalist and editorial commentator, and backing Senator Barry Goldwater's 1964 presidential campaign, Buchanan served his political apprenticeship with Richard Nixon. Following his participation in the Nixon campaign team, he became a special assistant in the White House and would retain a very substantial degree of personal loyalty to Nixon over the decades that followed. While the Nixon administration was later disavowed by many conservatives because of its enlargement of government, the introduction of direct economic controls, and the rapprochement with China, Nixon was in Buchanan's eyes an outsider who, like McCarthy before him, was brought down by the political "establishment."[4]

For Buchanan, Nixon was not just a victim. Although toppled, he had started to chart a new electoral course for his party. Together with Nixon's first vice president, former Maryland governor Spiro Agnew, Nixon had begun the process of turning Republicanism, which in the wake of desegregation was already drawing white southerners into its voting bloc (the "Southern strategy"), toward the white working class in other regions of the country. George Wallace's 1968 campaign as presidential candidate for the American Independent Party, when he won 13.5 percent of the popular vote, had powerfully demonstrated that nationalism, a populist suspicion of governing elites, and the raising of issues such as immigration, law and order, and affirmative action, many of which had racial connotations, could potentially make substantial inroads across white working-class communities in much of the country.[5] Nixon's strategy drew on the Wallace campaign, and as it took shape, references to the "silent majority" and "Middle American Radicals" (MARs), on which Buchanan would later build, began to enter the political lexicon.

After a brief period in the Ford White House following Nixon's resignation, Buchanan built his credentials as an independent columnist and commentator contributing to CNN's *Crossfire* and *The McLaughlin Group*. At the beginning of Reagan's second term he joined the White House as Director of Communications, although the lack of a developed macropolicy agenda, the mediating role of the Chief of Staff, and Reagan's hands-off style impeded Buchanan's ability to shape events. Reportedly, the more abrasive asides and additions that Buchanan sought to add to Reagan's speeches were routinely edited out.[6]

Buchanan established himself as a television and syndicated print-media commentator during the period after he left the Reagan White House in February 1987. At the same time, without using the term, he openly embraced many of the ideas that defined paleoconservatism. The move owed much to his long-held sense of being an outsider, a feeling that Republican administrations had been undermined, and an increasingly visible impatience with the de jure and de facto constraints that characterize the US political process.[7] Indeed, during his period in the Reagan White House, Buchanan had reveled in some of the covert and illegal activities that collectively constituted the Iran-Contra scandal. At the same time, changing demographics, processes of deindustrialization, long-run cultural shifts, and the rise of new social movements all appeared to pose threats to the integrity of the nation. The demise of the Soviet bloc removed the rationale for the US's global military commitments and opened up political opportunities for those who sought a foreign policy based upon a much more narrowly realist understanding of national interest.

There was some speculation within certain fairly narrow circles of conservatives active in movement organizations that Buchanan might seek the Republican nomination in 1988. In the event, Vice President George H. W. Bush had a relatively straightforward path to both the party nomination and the presidency. Thoughts of Buchanan making a run in 1988 came to little, and those opposed to party elites were instead represented in the fight for the Republican nomination by the Christian Broadcasting Network tele-evangelist Reverend Pat Robertson, who went on to found the Christian Coalition.

Buchanan did, however, contest the 1992 Republican primaries. A trigger factor may have been the decision by David Duke, founder of the Knights of the Ku Klux Klan and an avowed white supremacist who had served in the Louisiana state legislature, to contest the primaries, thereby opening up the process. Buchanan's entry into the race and his campaign of support for "American culture" brought him to national attention and allowed him to establish a forceful presence among the Republicans' voters.[8] He secured 37.5 percent in New Hampshire and 35.7 percent in Georgia, thereby denting President George H. W. Bush's electoral credibility and beginning a process that would culminate in Bush's defeat in November 1992 at the hands of Bill Clinton. His speech to the Republican national convention in Houston gave formal support to Bush but invoked an image of a country under siege from, above all else, its domestic enemies. Buchanan again sought the Republican presidential nomination four years later, winning four states and gaining just over a fifth of the total Republican primary vote in a crowded field.

Buchanan's third and final bid in 2000 descended into farce. In the wake of Ross Perot's third-party presidential bids (the Texan billionaire had won 19 percent of the popular vote in 1992), the Republican and Democratic duopoly seemed to have been fractured. Furthermore, the Republican primaries appeared locked into a battle between Governor George W. Bush and Senator John McCain. The Reform Party that Perot founded had, because of its 1996 performance, secured funding from the Federal Election Commission (FEC). Given all of this, and despite his long-established partisan loyalties, Buchanan abandoned the Republicans and sought the Reform Party nomination. However, the party then fractured between supporters of Buchanan, Donald Trump (who was toying with the possibility of running), and John Hagelin, a physicist with a background in transcendental meditation. Legal battles ensued, and although Buchanan eventually secured the FEC funds, the party's nomination for the election remained in doubt. In the end, individual states determined whether Buchanan or Hagelin should represent the Reform Party on the ballot. Buchanan was therefore listed as an Independent in a significant number of states and secured just 0.4 percent of the popular vote.

After 2000, Buchanan continued to support The American Cause, which he had together with his sister established a base organization in 1993, and maintained his role as an author and columnist. His commentaries appeared regularly in journals such as the core paleoconservative magazine *Chronicles*, published by the Rockford Institute, which after a fractious split with neoconservatives became a principal point of reference for paleoconservatives, and *The American Conservative*, a journal that he cofounded in 2002. However, although still cited by the mainstream media, Buchanan lost his position as a commentator with MSNBC in 2012 as the racial and ethnic basis of his thinking became yet more pronounced.[9]

Buchanan's thinking

How should Buchanan's politics be understood? He was above all else a popularizer of paleoconservatism. In contrast with figures such as Paul Gottfried and Thomas Fleming, former editor of *Chronicles*, and other paleoconservative intellectuals, Buchanan had the ability to reach beyond the narrow confines of activists and translate relatively dense intellectual arguments into a form that could serve as a basis for political mobilization.

Because he sought to popularize a broad tradition rather than the works of specific thinkers, Buchanan did not put forward a tightly structured worldview. Indeed, he did not generally take sides when there were tensions between those within the paleo camp who leaned toward libertarianism but still saw hierarchies and nations as a necessary basis for social order, and those who sought more of a role for the state in structuring the polity. Instead, he simply depicted paleoconservatism as a return to "first principles," and his commentaries often straddled the stresses and ambiguities in paleoconservative thought.[10]

Buchanan's paleoconservatism claimed to have inherited the mantle of those conservatives that had been largely banished or at least confined to the margins of the conservative movement after the defeat of Senator Robert Taft in the 1952 Republican presidential nomination battle. They had taken a stand against both the New Deal and the US's growing global commitments but were beaten back by fears of Soviet expansionism and through the determination of William F. Buckley's journal, *National Review*, to define and limit the conservative movement's boundaries.

National Review came to serve as a gatekeeper, distinguishing the legitimate conservative movement, structured around the free market, traditional moral conservatism, and the US's role in the front line of the battle against global communism, from both older conservative strands, such as those that had backed the America First Committee and had opposed military intervention in Korea, and the Right that took shape in the 1950s and 1960s.[11] This comprised organizations such as the John Birch Society, the Liberty Lobby, and the Citizens' Councils that were formed in the southern states. These campaigned against desegregation, took a stand against the United Nations, fanned fears of both communism and supranationalism, and at times edged toward conspiracism and anti-Semitism. Because of his role in defining the boundaries of legitimate conservatism and "excommunicating" dissident voices, Buckley was sometimes described as conservatism's "pope."

The associations between the paleoconservatism that Buchanan embraced and the pre-1950s Right tell only a small part of the story, however. In practice, Buchanan's paleoconservatism also rested upon the belief that there is an American nation structured around a white, European heritage. From this perspective, the US is defined by, and drawn from, national folkways and mores rather than abstract affirmations of principle such as the Declaration of Independence. At the same time, however, paleoconservatism distances itself from England and Englishness and instead celebrates the "white ethnic" communities drawn from Ireland, Scotland, and the countries of central Europe. In doing so, it not only expresses and conveys antipathy to racial and ethnic minorities but also to the WASP elites that seemed to represent Anglo-Saxon hegemony over those with a central and Southern European lineage.[12]

Alongside this, there is also a stress upon localism, sectionalism, and regionalism. Indeed, Buchanan's paleoconservatism adjoins and at times merges with neo-Confederate claims that not only assert the distinctiveness of the South but also invoke the role that, at least mythically, the antebellum South gave to order, tradition, place, as well as what they regard as its rejection of materialism, and its anticapitalist ethos.

Buchanan's paleoconservatism also drew upon a critique of the "managerial class." Although the concept is usually associated with James Burnham and neoconservatism, its significance in paleo thinking rests upon the ways in which it suggests that property-owning capitalism rooted in local communities and the regions has been displaced by a "placeless" class of managers, which is tied together with the political class and has globalist aspirations.

Furthermore, although there are ambiguities in paleoconservative perspectives, identity and place trump economics and the market. Indeed, in paleoconservative eyes, the economic nationalism that they championed rested upon the subordination of the market to the nation. For paleoconservatives (and at this point there was a divide with the paleolibertarians such as Murray Rothbard who, although seeking a structured and ordered form of liberty, placed more stress on the market), there was thus a case for protectionism and the management of trade. In his 1998 book, *The Great Betrayal*, Buchanan sought to rehabilitate the control of imports as a core Republican tradition and tie it to the preservation of nationhood.

Buchanan's paleoconservatism was also a conscious reaction against a relatively new breed within the conservative movement. Neoconservatives who had broken with the Democrats during Lyndon Johnson's presidency stressed the principles upon which the US was founded and their universal relevance. They also argued that the US should use the "unipolar moment" brought about by the collapse of the USSR to reshape the globe to bring down dictatorships and spread liberal democracy and the market order. In contrast, Buchanan rejected the concept of a universal nation constructed around a "proposition." He also called for a "new nationalism" which he directly counterposed to neoconservative globalism. While he staunchly defended American military might, he sought to rein in its ambitions. Indeed, he went so far as to call for the withdrawal of US troops from their overseas bases: "If Kim Il Sung attacks, why should Americans be the first to die?"[13] The responses to the Iraqi invasion of Kuwait in August 1990 highlighted some of the rifts within conservatism. While the war had many cheerleaders, Buchanan spoke out against it and took aim at the neoconservatives. The war, he asserted, was being fought at the behest of Israel and served no vital American interest. Democracy should not be forcibly exported or universalized. Indeed, democracy could take root only in certain conditions. As he posted in the wake of the "Arab Spring": "When George W. Bush declared that the peoples of the Middle East should decide their future in democratic elections, Lebanon chose Hezbollah, the Palestinians chose Hamas, the Egyptians the Muslim Brotherhood."[14]

Nonetheless, although Buchanan's paleoconservatism is structured around a broad critique of the contemporary US and its place in the world, the notion of an American nation based upon a distinctly white lineage and heritage remains pivotal as a starting point. A deeply felt sense of white dispossession is never far from the surface. Indeed, white identity and identitarianism tie the American future together with the fate of the West. Buchanan's thoughts about the prospects for the native population across the continents were conveyed in their most developed form in his 2001 book, *The Death of the West*.

The Death of the West

Paradoxically, while eschewing the US's global role as a standard-bearer for liberal-democratic values and speaking in terms that are often dubbed isolationist, *The Death of the West* not only invoked an American nation but, as the title suggests, also sought to address the history and future of the West much more broadly. Indeed, it portrayed the countries of Europe as well as the US as being in the front line of the assault.

Europeans, by which Buchanan means whites, faced an unprecedented threat. Fertility rates had, he noted, fallen dramatically. Enlarged state social provision and the hedonistic individualism of the counterculture embraced by the baby-boom generation had undermined the family and removed the need for children. Thus, by 2050, people of European ancestry will constitute just a tenth of the world's population.[15] It was a demographic process, Buchanan argued, comparable with effects of the Black Death.

There were specific reasons why white European women kept "out of the maternity ward."[16] The new or postindustrial economy drew women toward careers and a college education. As real median wages declined, the "family wage," whereby men earned sufficient to maintain a wife and children, had been eroded. The collapse of the established moral order and the spread of feminism reshaped popular culture: "millions are influenced by feminist ideology and its equation of marriage with prostitution and slavery, and that ideology has persuaded many to put off marriage and not to have children."[17]

Buchanan's critique edges toward conspiracism at this point. Feminism and other forms of cultural assault on traditional Western institutions can, it was said, be traced back to deliberate and coordinated forms of action by those with Marxist goals. He cites Antonio Gramsci's representations of counterhegemonic strategies and the writings of the Frankfurt School. In explaining the death of the West, the Frankfurt School was, Buchanan considered, "a prime suspect and principal accomplice."[18]

The fall of the birthrate went together with an unwillingness to assert the distinctiveness of Western values and a loss of national purpose: "But if Europeans are so uninterested in self-preservation that they refuse to have enough children to keep their nations alive, why should Americans defend Europe—and perhaps die for Europe?"[19] In contrast, Islam had vigor and purpose. The decline of Christian church congregations in Europe has been matched by growing numbers attending mosques.

Similarly, the US faced the consequences of mass Hispanic migration. Contemporary migrants came for simple economic reward rather than allegiance to the American nation. And they share, Buchanan maintains, "a new ethnic chauvinism": "Why should Mexican immigrants not have greater loyalty to their homeland than to a country they broke into simply to find work? Why should nationalistic and patriotic Mexicans not dream of *reconquista?*"[20]

As in Europe, the demographic restructuring of the US has electoral consequences. Immigration had given the Democratic Party a renewed lease on life, insofar as immigrants lean heavily Democratic, and has also raised the possibility of separatism. California is "on its way to becoming a predominantly Third World state."[21]

Alongside all of this, mass immigration poses a direct challenge to established understandings of nationhood. Whereas the nation was traditionally brought together and defined by a people with the same ancestors, speaking a common language, united by a religious faith, attached to the same principles of government, as well as sharing customs and mores, it is being reconfigured so that it simply rests upon principles of government.[22] The rest has been discarded. This, however, provides a very weak and fragile basis for nationhood, particularly given low levels of engagement with the political process.

Buchanan and the paleoconservative critique

Buchanan established himself as by far the US's most prominent popularizer of paleoconservative claims. Alongside *The Death of the West*, he is the author of at least twelve other books and coauthor of many others. He has written innumerable commentaries.

Many of these reproduced familiar paleoconservative themes. Buchanan echoes the ideas developed by fellow columnists and commentators. These included in particular Joe Sobran (who despite his paleoconservative leanings wrote for *National Review* until fired in 1993 amid accusations of anti-Semitism) and Samuel T. Francis. Francis put forward paleo thinking in its most rounded and conceptual form but also represented a bridge to openly white-identity groupings and interests such as those within the orbit of *American Renaissance*.[23]

While distancing himself from conspiracy theories, the paramilitarism that characterized the farther reaches of the American Right, and southern secessionism, Francis spoke of a white social revolution.[24] He looked toward those whom the sociologist Donald Warren had termed "Middle American Radicals" (MARs).[25] The concept merged class and race together insofar as MARs were drawn from whites on the lower, but not the lowest, rungs of the economic ladder. MARs, Francis asserted, were under threat from large-scale corporate capitalism, globalizing processes, and minority groups. Nonetheless, they had a role akin to that assigned to the proletariat in classical Marxist thinking. They were the only social force that could develop an authentically American counterculture and thus over time redeem the nation.[26]

Buchanan did not, however, simply reproduce claims such as these, although they inform many of his commentaries. Perhaps because of the role that Roman Catholicism played in his life, or perhaps because he recognized that Protestant evangelicals were a core Republican constituency playing a pivotal role in some primary states, Buchanan gave much more weight to cultural issues than many others within the paleo camp. This brought him closer than many others within paleo circles to the organizations and networks that collectively constituted the Christian Right.[27] He repeatedly returned to issues such as abortion, gay and lesbian rights, and other themes associated with what he considered moral decline. His 1992 Republican primary campaign included a television advertisement directed against the National Endowment for the Arts funding for work that "glorified homosexuality," and in the mid-1980s he described AIDS as retribution for "defying the natural order." His 1992 address to the Republican national convention hailed "the Judeo-Christian values and beliefs upon which this nation was built." He lambasted abortion, same-sex marriage, efforts to restrict school prayer, and "radical feminism." The address tied Bill and Hillary Clinton together:

> The agenda Clinton & Clinton would impose on America—abortion on demand, a litmus test for the Supreme Court, homosexual rights, discrimination against religious schools, women in combat—that's change, all right. But it is not the kind of change America wants. It is not the kind of change America needs. And it is not the kind of change we can tolerate in a nation that we still call God's country.[28]

In contrast, others within paleoconservative ranks, including Samuel Francis, distanced themselves from what saw as the limited political scope of cultural conservatism and the Christian Right: "If they ever ended abortion, restored school prayer, outlawed sodomy and banned pornography, I suspect, most of its followers would simply declare victory and retire."[29]

Impact and effects

While, along with his other books, *The Death of the West* won plaudits within paleoconservative and white nationalist circles, there was a much less plauditory tone among mainstream conservatives. Writing in *National Review*, Jonah Goldberg pointed to the coded language that offered "let-outs" but masked what was in sum a call for white supremacy, Buchanan's eclectic use of statistics, the loose and undefined references to the "Third World," and his confusion of correlation and causation.[30] For many conservatives, Buchanan had, since his embrace of paleoconservatism, not offered a "dark" vision of conservatism but instead undermined the efforts of the Right to win adherents in those minority communities, which had (at least at that point) seemed essential to the Republican Party's electoral future.[31]

Buchanan's overall influence cannot, however, be measured by the character of book reviews. Instead, his significance is twofold. First, his polemics and campaigns blurred the dividing lines and distinctions that had largely defined the American Right since the 1950s. As mentioned earlier, Wiliam F. Buckley and his *National Review* served a gatekeeping function by "excommunicating" white nationalism, conspiracy theories, and opposition to American "empire building" from the ranks of the conservative movement. Samuel Francis was to allege that the "permissible boundaries of discourse" were tightened as neoconservatism gained ground and dissidents were still being "purged" in the 1990s.[32] Nonetheless, there was an important shift. Buchanan's primary campaigns gave him credibility and meant that he could not be dismissed in the same way as the "kooks" had been sidelined in the 1950s. His paleoconservatism contributed, along with Richard Herrnstein and Charles Murray's 1994 book, *The Bell Curve*, which drew attention to recorded differences in IQ between racial groupings, and anti-immigration polemics such as Peter Brimelow's *Alien Nation* (1995), to the structural weakening of the boundaries between different sections of the Right. Indeed, paleoconservatism at times merged with white nationalism as biological representations of race, such as those put forward by Samuel Francis and in *American Renaissance*, were not necessarily legitimized but gained a place at the table: "The civilization that we as whites created in Europe and America could not have developed apart from the genetic endowments of the creating people, nor is there any reason to believe that the civilization can be successfully transmitted to a different people."[33]

Similarly, Buchanan's references to Israel seemed to open the way for shifts in the character of the Right's discourses and its treatment of anti-Semitism. He often seemed to single out Jews and assert that they unduly influenced US policy. His critique of the Gulf War included not only the assertion that it was being promoted by Israel and its backers in the US but also those who would likely die would be "kids with names like McAllister, Murphy, Gonzales and Leroy Brown."[34] Alongside this, Buchanan also seemed ready to adopt an unduly realist approach to twentieth-century history in asserting that an accommodation should have been reached with Nazi Germany, as he did in *Churchill, Hitler, and the Unnecessary War: How Britain Lost its Empire and the West Lost the World*.[35] While never subscribing to Holocaust denial, he questioned the numbers killed at Treblinka and appeared unduly zealous in his defense of alleged Nazi war criminals.[36]

By bringing in these strands back in from the cold, Buchanan's campaigns and commentaries undermined the gatekeeping role of *National Review*. It was further weakened during the years that followed by shifts and changes in the character of the media that allowed white nationalism, paleoconservatism, paleolibertarianism, and forms of conspiracism that were at times informed by anti-Semitism to merge with new strands such as the "manosphere" (together forming the Alt Right) and engage with the mainstream right on far more equal terms.

Second, Buchanan's electoral showing in the 1992 (when former Ku Klux Klan leader David Duke also stood) and the 1996 primary campaigns suggested that there was a significant constituency among grassroots Republicans or at least those who could be drawn into the Republican primary electorate for a message structured around a reassertion of the nation state and hostility to both globalist elites and immigration. His speeches and commentaries highlighted the extent to which the party was winning across a substantial share of the white working class from the Democrats, although these realignment processes were taking place at a faster rate in the South than the North.[37] Nonetheless, after 1996, and while the white working class was in numerical terms an increasingly important part of the Republican electoral bloc, nationalism and right-wing populism were politically marginal. For the most part, at both presidential and congressional level, candidates were associated with either economic conservatism, thereby stressing the capacity of an untrammeled market to generate growth and prosperity, or social conservatism that rested on issues such as abortion and same-sex marriage.

A few candidates such as former Pennsylvania senator Rick Santorum and Arkansas governor Mike Huckabee sought to fuse the social conservatism of the Christian Right with populist themes. They attacked political elites and sought to invoke blue-collar interests. For example, in late 2007 Huckabee spoke in explicitly paleoconservative terms: "The Wall Street-to-Washington axis, this corridor of power, is absolutely, frantically against me. . . . The president ought to be a servant of the people and ought not to be elected to the ruling class."[38] In 2008, the Republicans' vice presidential candidate, Governor Sarah Palin, sometimes also wandered well beyond the bounds of cultural conservatism and hinted at an economically populist message although it remained a long way removed from the defining axioms of paleoconservatism. However, while Palin's quasi-independent campaign served as a temporary rallying point, there was no electoral breakout.

For his part, Buchanan maintained a more than steady literary output, although his electoral credibility was damaged beyond repair by his third-party bid in 2000. While he continued, despite advancing age, to appear as a news channel commentator until 2012, he never regained the prominence of his *Crossfire* days.

Nonetheless, once the 2016 presidential campaign was underway, comparisons were became quickly drawn between Buchanan and Donald Trump as well as the Alt Right. There were, of course, differences, and Trump's campaign also owed a debt to Ross Perot's presidential bids.[39] Although there was, as noted earlier, a profound pessimism underpinning Buchanan's claims, which was echoed in the vision of "American carnage" around which Trump's 2017 inaugural address was structured, Trump would emphasize the ways in which, with sufficient leadership skill and acumen, the challenges facing the country could be swiftly overcome. There is also a wide political gulf between Buchanan's conservative Catholicism and Trump's and the Alt Right's treatment of cultural questions. For the most part, Trump steered away from cultural issues and in particular the use of bathrooms by the transgendered, which had been a defining issue for many Christian Right organizations in 2016 although, having said that, Trump was able to capture the backing of grassroots white evangelicals at an early stage in the primaries. He also accommodated them once he took office. Furthermore, while some detected an anti-Semitic edge to the Trump campaign's advertisement indicting Wall Street and the financial sector, a much stronger odor of anti-Semitism attached itself to Buchanan during the 1990s, and he forcefully opposed many of the policies pursued by Israel. In contrast, Trump has stood resolutely by Israel, and his election was warmly welcomed in Jerusalem.

Nonetheless, although he questioned Trump's focus and self-discipline and also wondered aloud if American decline had become irreversible, Buchanan still threw his support behind Trump. In a portrait of Buchanan that assessed the parallels, *Politico Magazine* recalled the power of Buchanan's oratory, reminded its readers about his place in the history of the American Right, and at the same time acknowledged the debt that Donald Trump owed him:

> This rhetoric . . . not only provided a template for Trump's campaign, but laid the foundation for its eventual success. Dismissed as a fringe character for rejecting Republican orthodoxy on trade and immigration and interventionism, Buchanan effectively weakened the party's defenses, allowing a more forceful messenger with better timing to finish the insurrection he started back in 1991. All the ideas that seemed original to Trump's campaign could, in fact, be attributed to Buchanan.[40]

Notes

1. Patrick J. Buchanan, *Right from the Beginning* (Washington, DC: Regnery Gateway, 1990), 30.
2. Ibid., 63–64.
3. Ibid., 93–95.
4. Ibid., 95.
5. Martin Durham, *The Christian Right, the Far Right, and the Boundaries of American Conservatism* (Manchester: Manchester University Press, 2000), 152.
6. Timothy Stanley, *The Crusader: The Life and Tumultuous Times of Pat Buchanan* (New York: Thomas Dunne Books, 2012), 106–110.
7. Durham, *Christian Right*, 155.
8. Samuel T Francis, *Revolution from the Middle* (Raleigh, NC: Middle American Press, 1997), 60.
9. George Hawley, *Right-Wing Critics of American Conservatism* (Lawrence: University Press of Kansas, 2016), 190.

10. Justin Raimondo, *Reclaiming the American Right: The Lost Legacy of the Conservative Movement* (Wilmington, DE: ISI Books, 2008), 263.
11. Martin Durham, "On American Conservatism and Kim Phillips-Fein's Survey of the Field," *Journal of American History* (December (2011): 758.
12. Edward Ashbee, "Politics of Paleoconservatism," *Society* 37, no. 3 (March 2000): 75–84.
13. Raimondo, *Reclaiming the American Right*, 266.
14. Patrick J. Buchanan, "Is Democracy in a Death Spiral?" *Patrick J Buchanan–Official Website*, April 21, 2017, accessed November 6, 2017, http://buchanan.org/blog/democracy-death-spiral-126837.
15. Patrick J. Buchanan, *The Death of the West: How Dying Populations and Immigrant Invasions Imperil Our Country and Civilization* (New York: Thomas Dunne Books, 2001), 11.
16. Ibid., 32.
17. Ibid., 40.
18. Ibid., 87.
19. Ibid., 109.
20. Ibid., 129.
21. Ibid., 140.
22. Ibid., 144.
23. Francis spoke at *American Renaissance*'s founding conference in 1994 (AR Staff, "Sam Francis in His Own Words," *American Renaissance*, April 2005, accessed November 5, 2017, https://www.amren.com/news/2011/02/sam_francis_in/.) Nonetheless, *American Renaissance*, of which Jared Taylor is founder and editor, regarded Buchanan as part of "non-racial Right" and it provided little coverage of his campaigns until 1999. Jared Taylor "What the Non-Racial Right Thinks," *American Renaissance*, April 2004, accessed November 5, 2017, https://www.amren.com/archives/back-issues/april-2004/.
24. Leonard Zeskind, *Blood and Politics: The History of the White Nationalist Movement from the Margins to the Mainstream* (New York: Farrar, Straus and Giroux, 2009), 290.
25. Francis, *Revolution from the Middle*, 61.
26. Ibid., 146.
27. Having said that, although Buchanan may have won significant swathes of grassroots white evangelicals during his electoral bids, he was less successful in winning the backing of leading figures within the Christian Right or its organizations. By the 1990s, such organizations eschewed insurgency and were increasingly pursuing a strategy based upon strategic lobbying and political bartering with Republican elites.
28. Patrick J. Buchanan–Official Website, *1992 Republican National Convention Speech* (Patrick J. Buchanan–Official Website, 2017) http://buchanan.org/blog/1992-republican-national-convention-speech-148.

29. Ashbee, "Politics of Paleoconservatism," 80.
30. Jonah Goldberg, "Killing Whitey," *National Review*, February 25, 2002, accessed August 29, 2017, http://www.nationalreview.com/article/205150/killing-whitey-jonah-goldberg.
31. Durham, *Christian Right*, 154.
32. Hawley, *Right-Wing Critics*, 39–40.
33. Ashbee, "Politics of Paleoconservatism," 76. Those who seek to defend Buchanan from charges of close associations with white supremacists point to his selection of Ezola Foster, an African American conservative, as his running mate in the 2000 presidential election campaign.
34. Nathan Glazer, "The Enmity Within," *New York Times*, September 27, 1992, accessed August 21, 2017, http://www.nytimes.com/books/00/07/16/specials/buckley-anti.html.
35. Patrick J. Buchanan, *Churchill, Hitler, and the Unnecessary War: How Britain Lost its Empire and the West Lost the World* (New York: Random House, 2008).
36. Newsweek, "Is Pat Buchanan Anti-Semitic?" *Newsweek*, December 22, 1991, accessed August 25, 2017, http://www.newsweek.com/pat-buchanan-anti-semitic-201176.
37. Thomas B. Edsall, "White Working Chaos," *New York Times*, June 25, 2012, accessed August 19, 2017, https://campaignstops.blogs.nytimes.com/2012/06/25/white-working-chaos/?_r=0.
38. Rick Macgillis, "Rick Santorum, Closet Populist?" *New Republic*, December 29, 2011, accessed August 30, 2017, https://newrepublic.com/article/99017/the-other-huckabee-santorum-connection.
39. Joshua Green, *Devil's Bargain: Steve Bannon, Donald Trump and the Storming of the Presidency* (New York: Penguin Press, 2017), 37.
40. Tim Alberta, "The Ideas Made It, but I Didn't," *Politico Magazine*, May–June, 2017, accessed August 22, 2017, http://www.politico.com/magazine/story/2017/04/22/pat-buchanan-trump-president-history-profile-215042.

9

Jared Taylor and White Identity

Russell Nieli

SAMUEL JARED TAYLOR—WHO prefers to go by his middle name, Jared—was born in 1951 in Kobe, Japan, to Christian missionary parents from Virginia, and who instilled in their son the Christian ideal that all human beings are equally children of God. He attended all-Japanese schools throughout most of his childhood and early adolescence, where he learned to speak Japanese like a native. He would subsequently earn much of his living as a Japan expert, translator, and consultant to international corporations wanting to do business in the land of his birth.

After attending Yale University, where he obtained a BA in 1973 with a major in philosophy, Taylor spent three years in France, getting an MA degree in international economics from the Paris Institute of Political Studies. During what he calls a brief "vagabond" period that interrupted both his undergraduate and later graduate college years, he traveled extensively in West Africa learning about its people and improving his French in Francophone regions of the continent. He is said to speak excellent French. In the 1980s Taylor was the West Coast editor for *PC Magazine* and worked as a business and finance consultant.[1] Between 1978 and 1981 he worked as an international banker for Manufacturers Hanover Trust Company in New York City. One could hardly imagine a background more likely to turn a young man into a liberal, internationalist, cosmopolitan, and defender of a globalist perspective.

Sometime in his early thirties, however, Taylor began to reassess the cosmopolitan and liberal internationalist viewpoint that so many of the people around him professed and that he had absorbed without serious reflection. We may all be children of God, and learning about cultures and peoples different from one's own can be life enriching, but Taylor came to believe that a stubborn fact of human nature is that human beings are tribal in their feelings and associations, and that they differ—often quite substantially—in their talents, folkways, temperaments, and capacities for different kinds of civilization. "The more one travels and really becomes acquainted with people of different nations," he would later write, explaining his personal odyssey, "the more one begins to understand just how different they actually are."[2] Much of these differences are the result of differing cultural histories and differing patterns of social conditioning, but in his later years Taylor came to believe that the differences also have a large genetic component that is not easily changed. Reproductively isolated continental populations ("races") differ not just in their outward physical features but also in many psychological and temperamental features as well. Such differences, Taylor believes, can have profound effects on the kinds of societies the different racial groups create.[3]

These new beliefs set Taylor apart not only from his earlier self but from the dominant opinion among the European and American elites with whom culturally, intellectually, and educationally he has so much in common. His views are dismissed as wicked and dangerous with the claim often made that they are the kinds of beliefs that led to slavery, the Jim Crow system of segregation, and the racial views of the Nazis. Taylor rejects these claims and believes much is to be gained from greater candor and honesty in the public discussion of controversial racial issues. There is often a contradiction, he claims, between what white elites and other white people say in public and what they really believe; this state of affairs, he contends, has prevented white-majority societies like the US from successfully addressing their most pressing racial problems.[4]

White identitarianism and white racial advocacy

In November 1990 Taylor launched *American Renaissance* magazine, which, together with its parent company, the New Century Foundation, became the major vehicle for circulating his "identitarian" and "white racial advocacy" ideas. For more than twenty years *American Renaissance* existed as a subscription-based monthly newsletter, ceasing publication in its print format in 2012 to become a daily webzine that featured articles of interest to white identitarians, most taken from other outlets, including newspapers, periodicals, and other websites.

From its inception, *American Renaissance* offered literate, highbrow, and intelligently argued defenses of white racial advocacy and the view that white people in America have legitimate racial interests in the same way that black and Hispanic people do. The early newsletter typically contained two or three extended feature articles, short descriptions of current events which were generally ignored by the mainstream media but likely to be of interest to white identitarians and white nationalists (provocatively titled "*O Tempora, O Mores!*"), and a "letters to the editor" column. Many of the early articles were written by Taylor himself, under his own name or under several different pen names, and were intended to put white racial advocacy on a higher intellectual plain than that of the white skinheads and Klansmen who often dominated media images of those speaking out on behalf of the racial interests of white people.

"Today in America, there are hundreds of organizations that speak for blacks, Hispanics, Asians, and American Indians, but virtually no one speaks for us," Taylor proclaimed in the lead editorial of *American Renaissance*'s first issue. White people, Taylor argued, have been engaging in a kind of unilateral disarmament allowing other racial groups to organize in order to further their own racial interests while whites became helpless victims of self-interested racial lobbies and racial pressure groups, and the cowardly white liberals who give in to them. "While other racial and ethnic groups work tirelessly to advance their group interests—often at our expense—we alone," he protested, "are not to think of ourselves as a people with our own ideals and aspirations."[5] *American Renaissance* was created to put an end to this, and since its inception Taylor has worked tirelessly to further this goal.

Racial identity, Taylor says, is something that comes naturally to almost all people, and there is nothing wrong or evil about this. "Members of a race do not need objective reasons to prefer their own group," he writes in his book *White Identity*, published in 2011. "They prefer it because it is theirs."[6] Taylor goes on to explain that preferences for one's own race need not imply hostility toward other races any more than a parent's affection for his own child implies hostility to the children of others. One's own children, however, must come first in the hierarchy of affection and concern.

Black and Hispanic people understand all this, Taylor says, as seen in blacks calling each other "brothers" and Latinos *la raza* (the race). White people too understand this, Taylor claims, at least if they are judged by how they act rather than by what they say. Whites, he notes, often leave long-established neighborhoods when the proportion of whites drops below a certain comfort level—and when they move, it is usually to neighborhoods or regions of the country where whites dominate.[7] Whites and nonwhites, Taylor says, differ only in that it is socially permissible for the nonwhites to express preferences to live and interact primarily among their own racial kind, but not for whites. When whites, he explains, do express feelings of racial solidarity akin to that of blacks and Hispanics, they are often denounced in the harshest of terms. Taylor's white racial advocacy and white identitarianism is intended to open up space in America's public discourse where white people can express their true feelings about themselves and their race without being demonized or penalized for doing so.[8]

A related theme in Taylor's writings is the importance of racial, linguistic, and cultural homogeneity for a nation's stability. "For a nation to be a nation—and not just a crowd—it must," he observed just before the breakup of the Soviet Union, "consist of people that share the same culture, language, history, and aspirations. It is in this sense that Norway, France, and Japan are nations, and that the Soviet Union or Yugoslavia are not."[9] From its inception and throughout the 1950s, America was a nation, Taylor says, as it was fairly homogeneous in language and culture and had an overwhelming white majority. The two historical exceptions to this homogeneity, he adds, were the Native Americans and the former African slave population, members of whom were rarely accepted by the whites as citizens or people like themselves.[10]

The ongoing challenge these groups have posed to the creation of an integrated America, Taylor believes, confirms his fundamental claim that for a nation's internal harmony and stability, racial and ethnic diversity is a curse, not a blessing. "We're all now more or less obliged to say," he writes, "'Oh! Diversity is a wonderful thing for the country,' whereas practically every example of tension, bloodshed, and civil unrest around the world is due [precisely to diversity]."[11] He reasons from this that America's top priority today should be limiting—or ending— all nonwhite immigration to American shores, which has increased exponentially since the changes in the country's immigration laws in 1965. Multiracial, multiethnic, multilinguistic societies are inherently unstable and more conflict-ridden than more demographically homogeneous ones, Taylor believes, and a major goal of Taylor's white identitarian efforts is to get this idea widely circulated. It is an invidious double standard, Taylor charges, when liberal intellectuals think it legitimate for nonwhite-majority countries like Japan to oppose massive immigration that would fundamentally alter the demographics of their nations, while denying the same choice to countries like the US where whites have always been in the majority. Not surprisingly, in virtue of Donald Trump's strong immigration restrictionist stance during his 2016 presidential campaign, Taylor enthusiastically supported Trump, even though he usually disliked the presidential candidates of both major political parties.[12]

Group Differences: Japanese, Africans, Europeans, and Jews

In the 1980s, Jared Taylor became known as a "Japan expert" at a time when much of the world was focused on the extraordinary rise of Japan to economic dominance in Asia. Taylor published at this time *Shadows of the Rising Sun*, a widely acclaimed book on Japanese culture, business practices, and folkways. While highly critical of certain aspects of Japanese culture—especially its excessive conformism and rigid hierarchical attitudes—Taylor left no doubt about his admiration for the Japanese and the modern society they created after the Second World War. Indeed, he saw Japanese society, which he had come to know so intimately, as superior in many ways to other modern societies, and more successful in solving most of the social problems that afflict America and the West. "Japan has come the closest of any nation in the world to solving the problems of crime, unemployment, inflation, and poverty,"[13] he wrote in 1983, and his views have changed little in the decades since then. Japan's extraordinarily low crime rates, its stable political organizations, its high standards of living, its success in international business, its high rates of literacy, its outstanding transportation infrastructure, its high levels of public health and long life expectancy, and its low levels of communal strife and corruption—all these, Taylor says, are at least partially a consequence of Japan's racial and cultural homogeneity.[14]

"Linguistically, culturally, and racially, Japan is homogeneous," Taylor writes, and as a result it is spared a host of problems that trouble America. Since there is only one race there is no racism, he says, and no need for quota-hiring schemes, antidiscrimination laws, multicultural curriculums, bilingual education, court-ordered busing, racial preferences in universities, or the tyrannies of political correctness. And the Japanese know, he writes, "that an American-style immigration policy would change everything. They want Japan to remain Japanese."[15]

After completing *Shadows of the Rising Sun* Taylor came to believe that while racial and cultural homogeneity, along with a generally accepted moral code encouraging dedication to the common good, were important factors in Japan's postwar success story, there was much more to Japan's success story than these factors, critically important though they were. Foremost among the missing pieces to the puzzle, he came to believe, were genes. Starting in the mid-1980s, Taylor began to take a keen interest in the developing fields of evolutionary biology and evolutionary psychology, especially in the work of three controversial academic psychologists: Richard Lynn (University of Exeter and University of Ulster, United Kingdom), J. Philippe Rushton (University of Western Ontario, Canada), and Helmuth Nyborg (University of Aarhus, Denmark). Each of these would later be invited to speak at one of his *American Renaissance* conferences. All three believe that as modern *Homo sapiens* ventured forth out of Africa perhaps sixty or seventy thousand years ago, they encountered challenges to survival and reproduction much more cognitively demanding than life on the warm African savannah. The colder climates of more northerly latitudes, where year-round plant foods were no longer available, placed a premium on the ability to delay gratification, to plan for a more distant future structured by extreme seasonal weather changes, to develop thermally efficient clothing and shelters, and to develop cooperative techniques for taking down large land animals for food. These ecological challenges, they contend, had the effect of winnowing out those of lesser cognitive capacities, future planning abilities, and the ability to delay gratification. Those who survived these more challenging environments passed on to their progeny the superior genes that enabled them to succeed in the struggle for life.[16]

Taylor came to believe that this "cold-and-variable-climate" hypothesis explains why Northern Asians, including the Japanese, have higher IQs than Southern Asians and most European populations. It also explains, he believes, why African populations and their New World descendants—most of whose ancestors were never subjected to the more cognitively challenging environments of northern climes—lag so far behind both Northern Asians and Europeans on such measures as IQ scores, economic and scientific achievement, general economic development, and the capacity for long-range planning. There may be other factors involved in the difficulties African populations have in creating technologically advanced civilizations, Taylor acknowledges, but evolutionary genetics, he insists, is a big part of the story. The same is true, he believes, for the relative technological backwardness of Middle Eastern and South American populations, though their general intelligence is usually placed by the IQ sources Taylor relies upon considerably higher than that of Sub-Saharan Africans.[17]

None of Taylor's claims have proven more incendiary—especially to liberal audiences—than these. But Taylor defends himself against charges of white racial chauvinism or white supremacism. While he believes Europeans may have a larger proportion of creative geniuses than Asians (for reasons not entirely understood), he insists that they are clearly not the smartest people on the planet in terms of what the psychometricians call "g" or general intelligence. The rapid advance of Asian American students at the most selective US universities, Taylor believes, partially reflects this superiority. "I think Asians are objectively superior to whites by just about any measure that you can come up with in terms of what are the ingredients for a successful society," he once said in an interview.[18] Taylor also seems to believe—although he hasn't spoken about this nearly as much as he has spoken about Asians—that the Ashkenazic Jews stand at the top of the intelligence pecking order, above both whites and Northern Asians. All of the academic psychologists who have influenced his thinking report the IQs of the Ashkenazim above that of any other ethnic group and believe superior intelligence explains the outstanding Jewish achievement in such cognitively demanding fields as mathematics, physics, economics, chess, and a host of natural sciences.[19]

The relationship of Taylor's *American Renaissance* group to Jews is in some ways atypical of other white advocacy groups in America, including other primarily intellectual organizations like Greg Johnson's Counter-Currents and Kevin MacDonald's *Occidental Quarterly*. Taylor welcomes Jews to his organization, has had several Jewish speakers at *American Renaissance* conventions, and seems genuinely to like Jews on a personal level. Taylor would surely like to see more Jews, at least European Jews, join the ranks of supporters of *American Renaissance*. While he regrets the fact that so many American Jews are hostile to the white identitarian views he espouses, he believes Jews can be won over and could become powerful allies.[20]

His embrace of Jews has led to tensions within his white-identity movement since it includes at least some people openly hostile to Jews and to the pernicious effect they claim Jews have had on white interests in America. For what seems like tactical reasons, Taylor has sought neither to officially welcome, censure, nor expel from his movement those openly espousing anti-Semitic viewpoints. Such a neutral stance, however, has not always produced the group harmony Taylor clearly desires. At one *American Renaissance* convention, an open clash erupted between David Duke, an avowed enemy of Jews and their influence in America, and Michael Hart, a Jewish astrophysicist who shares many of Taylor's views on race and American society.[21]

Family-Values Conservatism and Classical Liberalism

Between *Shadows of the Rising Sun* (1982) and *White Identity* (2011), Taylor published another major book, *Paved with Good Intentions* (1992), which set forth the socially conservative and "traditional values" side of his thinking.[22] Although it focuses on the downward spiral of the black underclass in America, and on the unwise government policies that he believes have contributed to it, this second book eschews the genetic-based understandings of these developments that would play so prominent a role in *White Identity* and many of his *American Renaissance* articles. There is no genetically grounded "race realism" in this work, and in many ways it resembles the kind of critiques of welfare and other public policies to be found in books by the leading conservative and libertarian writers of the time.[23]

When asked in an interview why he did not talk about genetic differences in this second book, he replied that if he had talked about IQ differences "it probably would have been impossible to get the book published." The question of race-based differences in mental and behavioral traits, he said, "is still very much a radioactive subject."[24] There were many important things to be said about race relations and public policies in the US aside from genes, Taylor reasoned, and *Paved with Good Intentions* was his outlet for presenting them. The book sold fairly well to a mainstream conservative and libertarian audience, something not true of the overtly "race realist" *White Identity*. Taylor's misgivings about getting his genetic-based views on race published proved prescient; despite great efforts, no mainstream publisher could be found to publish *White Identity*, which had to be brought out by his own New Century Foundation.

Paved with Good Intentions starts out on the same major theme that preoccupied Democratic senator Daniel Patrick Moynihan in his 1965 report, *The Negro Family: The Case for National Action*.[25] "There is scarcely a social problem in this country that would not be well on its way toward solution," Taylor wrote in his own book's introduction, "if Americans adopted a rule their ancestors lived by and took for granted: They did not have children until they had a spouse and an income."[26] Marriage has completely disappeared from many black communities, Taylor noted, but such social decay was rapidly spreading among whites as well, where illegitimacy and marriage breakups were approaching the levels of those among blacks twenty-five years earlier that had so alarmed Moynihan.

Taylor attributed these developments to a variety of changes that took place in the 1960s, including more generous and more permissive welfare payments for single mothers, the destigmatization of out-of-wedlock births, the decline in the "shotgun wedding" tradition, and, in the case of blacks, the development of an all-pervasive blame-casting and excuse-making mentality that many white liberals reinforced. On this last point, Taylor claimed that telling blacks their problems are mostly the result of unremitting white racism denies to them the confidence they need to feel in control of their lives, robs them of a sense of personal responsibility and personal efficacy, teaches them to hate whites, and leads them to believe that improvement in their condition must await changes in white attitudes and behavior. Such a message, Taylor says, not only has a poisonous effect on black-white race relations but is devastating in terms of recognizing the kinds of changes that are needed for blacks to effect their own improvement.[27]

Paved with Good Intention contains lengthy discussions of government-mandated racial preference policies, which Taylor sees as manifestly unfair to the better qualified white and Asian applicants for jobs and university positions. In addition, such policies, Taylor claims, reinforce among the members of the supposed beneficiary groups the idea that advancement in America comes not from hard work and genuine achievement, but from investment in one's status as victim and sufferer from past oppression. "Our crusade to undo the mischief of the past," Taylor writes, "has done mischief of its own, and by formally discriminating against whites, it has stood both justice and the law on their heads."[28]

Taylor believes that all laws requiring racial preferences should be abolished, but like libertarians and classical liberals, he goes farther and opposes most antidiscrimination laws, believing that government should not be telling private institutions how they should be conducting their business. He objects to laws interfering with the rights of private citizens and private associations—including private colleges—to conduct their affairs any way they choose, without having to please anyone else. Freedom of association should be accorded to private persons, private employers, private colleges, and the like, without government interference. These associational rights were the traditional rights of Englishmen, Taylor says and, until the last century, were traditional rights of most Americans. "I think everything from the Civil Rights Act of 1964 onward," he says, "is an unconscionable invasion of federal government power into what should be private decision making."[29]

Taylor is consistent in his thinking on this in that, unlike defenders of the Old South, he believes government-mandated segregation laws were unjust: with freedom, people will tend to harmoniously self-segregate on their own, he believes. He sees laws prohibiting interracial marriage, which almost all southern states retained until they were declared unconstitutional by the Supreme Court in 1967, as patently unjust. Taylor thus combines with his white racial advocacy strong elements of traditional "values conservatism" and classical liberal understandings of individual associational rights.

American leaders of the past as race realists

A recurring theme in Taylor's writings and public talks is his claim that the ideas on race and racial identity that became dominant in America in the latter decades of the twentieth century are historical anomalies and out of tune with both common sense and human nature. They are also, he tries to demonstrate, inconsistent with the views of many of the leading statesmen of America's past, including Thomas Jefferson and Abraham Lincoln. Lincoln and Jefferson both believed, he points out, that a freed black population could never live together in harmony with the dominant white population in the US, and to this extent, he insists, they were "race realists" just like he is. Jefferson's and Lincoln's pronouncements on these matters are frequently quoted in *American Renaissance* articles and elsewhere. Jefferson is cited:

> Nothing is more certainly written in the book of fate than that these people [blacks] shall be free; nor is it less certain that the two races, equally free, cannot live in the same government. Nature, habit, opinion has drawn indelible lines of distinction between them.[30]

Likewise, Lincoln is quoted:

> We have between us [whites and blacks] a broader difference than exists between almost any other two races. Whether it is right or wrong I need not discuss, but this physical difference is a great disadvantage to us both, as I think your race suffers very greatly, many of them by living among us, while ours suffers from your presence. In a word we suffer on each side. If this is admitted, it affords a reason at least why we should be separated.[31]

Lincoln and many other opponents of slavery in his time, Taylor points out, supported the American Colonization Society, which sought to convince free blacks to return to Africa or some other suitable location and establish their own society free from white interference or white oppression. Lincoln asked Congress several times to appropriate money for this purpose. Taylor insists that while Lincoln's views on race are considered retrograde by contemporary standards, they were realistic and true to human nature in a way that most current thinking on race is not.[32]

Most American leaders of the past also believed, Taylor explains, that racially homogeneous societies have a much easier time establishing harmonious relations among their people than racially mixed ones. This, says Taylor, is why the first naturalization act passed by Congress in 1790 allowed only "free white persons" to become citizens. He quotes in this context from a letter Harry Truman once wrote to his future wife about the undesirability of race mixing ("I am strongly of the opinion Negroes ought to be in Africa, yellow men in Asia, and white men in Europe and America"),[33] as well as from *Federalist Paper* 2 in which its author, John Jay, saw heaven's blessing in the relative racial, religious, and cultural homogeneity of the American people: "Providence has been pleased to give this one connected country to one united people—a people descended from the same ancestors, speaking the same language, professing the same religion, attached to the same principles of government, very similar in their manners and customs."[34] Most of America's leading men throughout the eighteenth, nineteenth, and early twentieth centuries, Taylor claims, held views on race similar to his own. And those views were more in tune with the truth on these matters, he insists, than the views that have become dominant since the victories of the civil rights movement in the 1960s. The latter, he holds, combine fantasy, wishful thinking, and in some cases the cold, self-interested logic of nonwhite groups seeking to replace whites as America's dominant population.

The tensions and instabilities inherent in multiracial societies

The belief that race consciousness is an important factor in human affairs is not confined to Taylor or his readers. Where Taylor differs from others is in the extreme salience he accords to race consciousness and the intractability of the tensions and disharmonies he believes it inevitably creates in multiracial societies. When people of different races and ethnicities live together in the same space and under the same government, there is no end, Taylor claims, to the problems created. Even under the most favorable of circumstances, he believes, multiracial societies are always plagued with intergroup tensions and disharmonies that are impossible to avoid.

Taylor expressed these beliefs most clearly in a discussion with the psychologist Arthur Jensen (University of California, Berkeley):

> It is my view that a sense of racial difference, even independent of actual measurable differences, is sufficiently great so that any society that attempts to build a multiracial nation is setting up what may be an insuperable obstacle for its own development. I think that to an unfortunate degree the mere fact of racial differences is something that human beings are almost always conscious of. For that reason, a society such as the United States, that is deliberately and explicitly trying to build a society on the notion that race can be made not to matter—which is in fact the unspoken assumption in America today—is doomed to failure.[35]

This has remained Taylor's settled belief from the very beginning of *American Renaissance*, and although he has high regard for the Japanese and other Northern Asians, as did the young Harry Truman, he wants them to remain in Asia, not to overwhelm white people in America. He is even more concerned that Mexicans, Africans, Afro-Caribbeans, and members of various Hispanic and Middle Eastern groups remain in the lands they currently occupy and not flood the US as immigrants.

Southern regional conservatism

Jared Taylor's basic ideas show a clear affinity for, and to some extent have developed out of, a distinct "Southern regional conservatism" in America, which has roots going back to the American Civil War, the

Reconstruction period, and the era of legalized segregation in the states of the Old Confederacy. It was a form of conservatism forged by the very peculiar situation of the American South, and the South's anomalous position within a broader American society that affirmed principles of universal human rights and rejection of legal distinctions based on ethnicity and race. "Compared to every other country in Western civilization," the Swedish economist Gunnar Myrdal wrote in a 1942 study of race relations in the American South, the US "has the most explicitly expressed system of general ideals in reference to human interrelations. This body of ideals is more widely understood and appreciated than similar ideals are anywhere else."[36] Myrdal famously described these ideals as constituting an American Creed, one drawing upon the biblical notion that all human beings are children of God, and the proclamation in the Declaration of Independence that "all men are created equal" and have inalienable human rights. It was largely in reaction to these ideals, Myrdal explains, that a distinctly white Southern form of social and political conservatism developed that began in the nineteenth century in the struggle over slavery. This Southern conservatism continued into the next century in defense of segregation and in opposition to the US government's attempt to integrate schools and other aspects of southern life.[37]

In the period before the popularity of Darwinian evolutionary theory, prominent Southern writers, including John C. Calhoun, George Fitzhugh, and William Harper, developed arguments based on traditionalist and pragmatic grounds for white supremacy, racial segregation, and the subordination of blacks in the slaveholding South.[38] In a substantially modified form, the legacy of these thinkers would be carried over and gain even greater saliency in the twentieth century as biological understandings of racial differences came to dominate racial thinking among interwar American eugenicists and racialists, including Lothrop Stoddard, author of *The Rising Tide of Color against White World-Supremacy*, and Madison Grant, author of *The Passing of the Great Race*.[39] Both of these writers were influential in gaining support for the 1924 US Immigration Act that tried to maintain the demographic dominance in America of whites from northern Europe.

Stoddard and Grant were each the object of celebratory articles in *American Renaissance*,[40] and seem to have influenced Jared Taylor, at least insofar as they reinforced his own maturing racialist views. While Taylor strongly rejects white supremacy in the sense of whites ruling over unwilling blacks, these and a number of other twentieth-century racialists confirmed Taylor's belief that members of different racial groups are better off developing themselves in separate homelands rather than in mixed-race polities or territorial states. Peaceful political and territorial separation, he believes, may be the best solution to racial problems both in America and elsewhere.[41] More contemporary southern conservatives who have influenced Taylor's racial views include the late Samuel Francis, a journalist who spoke at every *American Renaissance* conference until his death in 2005, and the southern attorney Sam Dickson, who has also been a regular speaker at Taylor's conferences. The combination of southern regional conservatism and Taylor's experience of living in racially homogeneous—and extraordinarily peaceful—Japan has undoubtedly had a formative effect on his thinking about race.[42]

Going Global: Joining Forces with the European New Right

In recent years Taylor has sought alliances with members of several populist and New Right groups in Europe that share his concern for white identity, ethnic nationalism, and preserving white-majority populations in areas of the globe where they now exist and are demographically threatened by large influxes of nonwhite immigrants. He has hosted on his website and his annual conferences European supporters of France's National Front, Britain's UKIP, Austria's Freedom Party, Germany's Alternativ für Deutschland (Alternative for Germany, AfD), and the Flemish national party Vlaams Belang (Flemish Interest, VB). Taylor himself has traveled extensively in Europe and given speeches and interviews in both French and English in support of ethnonationalism and white-identity politics.

Taylor seems to have a special affinity for the French New Right author Guillaume Faye, three of whose books he reviewed favorably in the pages of *American Renaissance*. Taylor clearly hopes his own ethnonationalism and white identitarianism will go global and eagerly seeks allies among like-minded Europeans. "Racially conscious Americans," he wrote in a review of Faye's *Why We Fight*, "invariably see European identitarians as allies in a worldwide struggle."[43] In the future this struggle is likely to become only more intense, Taylor predicts, as immigrants from nonwhite, Third World countries continue to migrate in huge numbers to the more prosperous white nations. Like Faye, he believes the white people of the planet need to overcome what he sees as their open-borders insanity and suicidal "ethnomasochism" (Faye's term), and join in the fight for their racial, cultural, and demographic survival.

Over the last three decades, Taylor has assiduously dedicated his energies to this struggle. He has been one of the dominant intellectual forces on America's radical Right. He may well have been as central to structuring the fledgling movement in the 1990s as the late William F. Buckley Jr. was in the 1950s and 1960s in structuring post–World War II American conservatism. The growing Alt Right movement in America today owes a great deal to Taylor's past efforts.

Notes

1. See the entries under "Jared Taylor" in Wikipedia, en.wikipedia.org, and at the website of the Southern Poverty Law Center, www.splcenter.org.
2. "Allerlei Interviews Jared Taylor," n.d., https://www.amren.com.
3. Samuel Taylor, "Race and Intelligence," *American Renaissance*, November 1992; Samuel Taylor, "Genetics, Personality, and Race," *American Renaissance*, August 1993; Thomas Jackson, "Why Some Nations are Rich and Others are Poor," *American Renaissance*, August 1993. In his numerous *American Renaissance* articles between 1992 and 2012, Samuel Jared Taylor wrote using both his middle name and first name. He also used pen names, the most common being "Thomas Jackson." All of the back issues in the print format are available electronically (though without the original pagination) on the *American Renaissance* website, www.amren.com, under "Archives–Print Back Issues."
4. Jared Taylor, "Is a Multiracial Nation Possible," *American Renaissance*, February 1992; Samuel Taylor, "Who Still Believes in Integration," *American Renaissance*, September-October, 1993; Jared Taylor, "The Myth of Diversity," *American Renaissance*, July-August, 1997.
5. Jared Taylor, "Who Speaks for Us?" *American Renaissance*, November 1990; Samuel Taylor, "The Right of Self Defense: Why White Racial Consciousness is Necessary and Moral," *American Renaissance*, January 1994.
6. Jared Taylor, *White Identity: Racial Consciousness in the 21st Century* (NP: New Century Books, 2011), 288–290.
7. Taylor, "Who Still Believes in Integration."
8. Interview with Jared Taylor, in Carol Swain and Russ Nieli, *Contemporary Voices of White Nationalism in America* (New York: Cambridge University Press, 2003), 88–89; Samuel Taylor, "The Right of Self Defense: Why White Racial Consciousness is Necessary and Moral," *American Renaissance*, January 1994.
9. Jared Taylor, "Who Speaks for Us?" *American Renaissance*, November 1990.
10. Jared Taylor, "Is a Multiracial Nation Possible?" *American Renaissance*, February 1992.

11. Interview with Jared Taylor, in Swain and Nieli, *Contemporary Voices of White Nationalism*, 101.
12. Zack Beauchamp, "A Leading White Nationalist Says It Plainly: Trump's Victory Was about White Identity," www.vox.com, November 21, 2016.
13. Jared Taylor, *Shadows of the Rising Sun* (New York: William Morrow, 1983), 288.
14. Writing under the pen name Steven Howell, Taylor elaborates on this theme in "The Case of Japan (Part II)," *American Renaissance*, October 1991. The article begins "Japanese society is a perfect example of the advantages of ethnic homogeneity."
15. Taylor, *White Identity*, 288–290. See also Taylor's article on the Japanese in *American Renaissance*, "In Praise of Homogeneity," August 2007.
16. See Richard Lynn, *Race Differences in Intelligence: An Evolutionary Analysis* (Augusta, GA: Washington Summit Publishers, 2006); J. Philippe Rushton, *Race, Evolution, and Behavior* (Port Huron, MI: Charles Darwin Research Institute, 2000); Helmuth Nyborg, "What Made Europe Great and What Could Destroy It," *YouTube*, August 9, 2017; Helmuth Nyborg and Arthur Jensen, "Black-White Differences on Various Psychometric Tests: Spearman's Hypothesis Tested on American Armed Services Veterans," *Personality and Individual Differences* 28 (2000):593–599.
17. Jared Taylor, "Race and Intelligence: The Evidence," *American Renaissance*, November 1992; Jared Taylor, "Race Realism and the Alt Right," Counter-Currents, October 25, 2016, www.counter-currents.com; Jared Taylor, "Egalitarian Orthodoxy: Noble Fiction or Noxious Poison," *VDare.com*, June 24, 2008.
18. Interview with Jared Taylor, in Swain and Nieli, *Contemporary Voices of White Nationalism in America*, 102.
19. See especially Richard Lynn, *The Chosen People: A Study of Jewish Intelligence and Achievement* (Whitefish, MT: Washington Summit Publishers, 2011).
20. Jonathan Tilove, "White Nationalist Conference Ponders Whether Jews and Nazis Can Get Along," *Forward*, March 3, 2006; Anti-Defamation League, "Jared Taylor/American Renaissance," www.adl.org.
21. Southern Poverty Law Center, "Mainstream Scholars Attend Racist Conference Hosted by Jewish Astrophysicist," *Hatewatch*, March 18, 2009.
22. Jared Taylor, *Paved with Good Intentions* (New York: Carol and Graf, 1992).
23. See Charles Murray, *Losing Ground: American Social Policy 1950–1980* (New York: Basic Books, 1984); Thomas Sowell, *Compassion Versus Guilt* (New York: William Morrow, 1987); and Myron Magnet, *The Dream and the Nightmare: The Sixties' Legacy to the Underclass* (New York: Encounter Books, 2000).
24. Interview with Jared Taylor, in Swain and Nieli, *Contemporary Voices of White Nationalism in America*, 94–95.
25. Daniel Patrick Moynihan, *The Negro Family: The Case for National Action* (Washington, DC: US Government Printing Office, 1965).

26. Taylor, *Paved with Good Intentions*, 18.
27. Ibid., 14–17, 83–85, 106–108, 120–121, 210–215, 248–279, 281–290, 352–358.
28. Ibid., 17–18.
29. Interview with Jared Taylor, interview in Swain and Nieli, *Contemporary Voices of White Nationalism in America*, 101.
30. Thomas Jefferson, Autobiography Draft Fragment, February 8, 1821, from the Thomas Jefferson and William Short Correspondence, edited by Gerald W. Gawalt, Manuscript Division, Library of Congress, online at www.jrbooksonline.com.
31. Abraham Lincoln, "Address on Colonization to a Deputation of Negroes," August 14, 1862, in *Collected Works of Abraham Lincoln* (Ann Arbor: University of Michigan Digital Library Production Services, 2001), 5:371, online at www.quod.lib.umich.edu.
32. Jared Taylor, "The Racial Revolution," *American Renaissance*, May 1999.
33. Letter from Harry S. Truman to Bess Wallace, June 22, 1911, Truman Papers, Family, Business, and Personal Affairs Papers, 1911, online at www.trumanlibrary.org.
34. John Jay, "Concerning Dangers from Foreign Force and Influence," *The Federalist* 2, from *The Complete Federalist Papers*, www.let.rug.nl.
35. Jared Taylor, "A Conversation with Arthur Jensen," *American Renaissance*, September 1992.
36. Gunnar Myrdal, *An American Dilemma* (New York: Harper and Row, 1962), 3.
37. Taylor's views on Myrdal's *An American Dilemma* are presented in "Sowing the Seeds of Destruction: Gunnar Myrdal's Assault on America," *American Renaissance*, April 1996; and "Integration Has Failed (Part 1)," *American Renaissance*, February 2008.
38. See for instance, Russell Kirk, *The Conservative Mind* (Chicago: Henry Regnery, 1960), 172–210; and A. J. Beitzinger, *A History of American Political Thought* (New York: Dodd Mead and Company, 1972), 370–375.
39. Lothrop Stoddard, *The Rising Tide of Color against White World-Supremacy* (New York: Charles Scribner's Sons, 1920); Madison Grandt, *The Passing of the Great Race* (New York: Charles Scribner's Sons, 1916).
40. On Lothrop Stoddard, see James P. Lubinskas, "A Warning from the Past," *American Renaissance*, January 2000; and "Lothrop Stoddard and the Color Line," *American Renaissance*, January 16, 2015. On Madison Grant, see George McDaniel, "Madison Grant and the Racialist Movement," *American Renaissance*, December 1997; and Thomas Jackson, "Nordic Man Comes to the New World: Madison Grant on the American People," *American Renaissance*, December 2001.
41. Jared Taylor, "How Can We Solve the Race Problem," *American Renaissance*, September 26, 2017.

42. Taylor discusses the great advantages of ethnic and racial homogeneity in "Diversity Destroys Trust," *American Renaissance*, September 2007; and with specific reference to Japan in "In Praise of Homogeneity: The Japanese Know How to Run a Country," *American Renaissance*, August 2007.
43. Jared Taylor, "Why We Fight," *American Renaissance*, February 16, 2012 (review of Guillaume Faye's book by that title). See also Jared Taylor, "The Colonization of Europe," *American Renaissance*, June 10, 2016 (review of Guillaume Faye's book by that title); and Thomas Jackson (pen name for Jared Taylor), "Life after the Collapse: How Whites Will Emerge from the Rubble," *American Renaissance*, February 2011 (review of Guillaume Faye's *Archeofuturism*).

10

Alexander Dugin and Eurasianism

Marlene Laruelle

SINCE THE MID-1990S, Alexander Dugin has been the best-marketed of all Russian ideologists, both in Russia and in the West. His prolific character and his ability to publish in very diverse media outlets and speak to different audiences, combined with the Western obsession with him, have kept him in the media spotlight both in Russia and abroad. Well-read in mainstream philosophy and the humanities, Dugin is an impressive aggregator of radical Right ideologies. He brings together doctrines from diverse origins—*völkisch* occultism, Traditionalism, Conservative Revolution, French New Right, and Eurasianism—and openly calls for a renewal of the Russian nationalist doctrinal stock by drawing on European traditions. He has also mastered several levels of discourse: academically respectable texts with references to Max Weber and Michel Foucault, geopolitical analysis for news outlets, and hate pamphlets for radical websites. Like Antonio Gramsci and Alain de Benoist, Dugin believes that the only way to influence politics is to first conquer the intellectual field and set the agenda. He does not conceal his ultimate goal: "a meta-ideology, common to all the enemies of the open society."[1]

Life and Background

In 1980, at just nineteen years old, Dugin encountered what remained of the Yuzhinsky Circle, a dissident group that emerged in the 1950s around the novelist Yurii Mamleev, and was later joined by the poet Yevgenii Golovin, the philosopher Geidar Dzhemal, and the poet Vladimir

Stepanov. At first, the Circle believed that the answer to the Soviet regime would be found not in a rival political ideology but in metaphysics and the search for another level of reality. This initial path allowed for the discovery and assimilation of the main thinkers of Traditionalism, René Guénon and Julius Evola; German Conservative Revolution theories; *völkisch* occultism; and postwar rightist doctrines from Italy and Latin America. Golovin, the Circle's main inspiration, appreciated the carnival-like character of references to Nazism: he presented the Circle as an "SS Black Order," established a hierarchy among the members, and instituted a Masonic-style initiation ritual—with the addition of alcohol. All these elements were part of an ironic denunciation of the political correctness of the late Soviet regime and its ideological rigidity. Over three decades, the Yuzhinsky Circle evolved, experiencing everything from Mamleev's encounter with radical Right metaphysics and Golovin's discovery of the political side of Traditionalism to Dugin's revisiting of the *völkisch* occultism of Herman Wirth and his attempts to transform it into an engine for political activism.[2]

In 1991, during the last months of the Soviet Union, Dugin became close to the conservative Soviet writer Alexander Prokhanov, who had been known in the 1980s as the "songbird" of the Soviet General Staff. At the time, Prokhanov was desperately attempting to formulate a new patriotic ideology, which would forestall the country's collapse and unify the diverse antiperestroika groups. Dugin joined the editorial board of Prokhanov's weekly newspaper *Den'* (*Today*). Using this prominent platform, he was able to test many of his ideological combinations and observe which ones resonated with public opinion. *Den'* was banned during the October 1993 political standoff between Boris Yeltsin and the Supreme Soviet, and renamed *Zavtra* (*Tomorrow*). Along with the writer Eduard Limonov, Dugin also played a major role in launching the countercultural National Bolshevik Party (NBP), but progressively left the countercultural movement to reach out to the political establishment.[3]

In the second half of the 1990s, Dugin secured support from several high-level senior officials on the General Staff of the Russian armed forces, who funded his major work, *The Foundations of Geopolitics: Russia's Geopolitical Future* (*Osnovy geopolitiki: Geopoliticheskoe budushchee Rossii*).[4] Commissioned by General Igor Rodionov, minister of defense in 1996–97, and first published in 1997, the book had been reissued four times by 2000 and enjoyed a large readership in Russian academic and political circles. *Foundations of Geopolitics* became Dugin's calling-card for reaching out to military circles and the establishment more broadly. Thanks to its success, he was invited to teach at the Military Academy of the General Staff of the Armed Forces of the Russian Federation and became advisor for geopolitical affairs to Gennadii Seleznev, then chair of the Duma and a member of the Communist Party.[5] Through his book, Dugin also influenced the two main anti-Yeltsinian political figures of that time, Communist Party of the Russian Federation leader Gennadii Zyuganov and Vladimir Zhirinovskii, whose cultivated imperialist eccentricities made him one of the most famous farcical and caricatured media products to come out of post-Soviet Russia.[6] Since then, the popularity of Dugin's book has declined somewhat, but it is still considered a major—if contested—reference for the contemporary Russian school of geopolitics.

In the 2000s, Dugin underwent a first "crossing of the desert" with the disappointing performance of his small Eurasian Party in 2001, followed by the very moderate success of the International Eurasianist Movement (IEM), launched in 2003. The IEM was quite effective in bringing together pro-Eurasianist figures abroad, especially in Turkey;[7] it achieved a lesser degree of success in the post-Soviet republics and among some of Russia's Muslim leaders.[8] However, the IEM failed to unite the Russian political establishment; it appealed only to lower-level figures, mostly retired ambassadors and mid-level civil servants. The IEM's low membership testified to Dugin's inability to secure public support within state structures and mainstream political institutions.

It was only in 2008 that Dugin succeeded in penetrating an established institution—Moscow State University (MSU)—with the support of the scandal-plagued dean of the Sociology Department, Vladimir Dobrenkov, a Soviet-style philosopher and proponent of a nationalist agenda.[9] Dugin created the Center for Conservative Research within the Sociology Department, though he never received tenure and taught there only as an adjunct. The Center's declared objective was to counter the growing success of liberal universities, namely the Higher School of Economics, and reinforce the reputation of MSU as a bastion of conservatism by "developing and establishing a conservative ideology in Russia" and educating the next generation of "scholarly cadres."[10]

Dugin reached a new peak of success between 2012 and early 2014, when the Kremlin opened the door for all conservative ideologues to appear more visibly on state-controlled media. The government's first objective was to drown out the liberal opposition that emerged during the anti-Putin protests of 2011–12, and then to legitimize its position on the

Ukrainian crisis, the annexation of Crimea, and the Donbas insurgency. Dugin rapidly became one of the main proponents of Novorossiya—the notion that eastern Ukraine's destiny is to (re)join Russia.[11] This time, his success was even more brief: too radical in celebrating a nationalist "Russian Spring" that vehemently criticized the Putin regime for refusing to organize a "national revolution," Dugin lost both his access to mainstream media and his status at MSU. Officially, it was his violent—even if maybe metaphorical—call to "kill, kill, kill" Ukrainian nationalists[12] that led him to lose his position at the university.

As this brief history illustrates, Dugin has been unable to secure himself a position within the Kremlin's institutions: he has never been a member even of the Civic Chamber, coopted by the authorities, and it was only in 2014 that one of his protégés, Valerii Korovin, was able to get himself elected to it. Since 2015, Dugin has been undertaking a second "crossing of the desert," with support coming almost exclusively from the Orthodox business mogul Konstantin Malofeev. Thus far, Dugin has been thwarted in his aspiration to become the "gray cardinal" of the regime. Contrary to the claims of many Western commentators, Dugin is not a member of the Kremlin's inner ideological circles. He is an external figure who can be used or rejected as needed but remains more "out" than "in."

Work and Thought

Dugin is a complex theorist. He is a chameleon thinker, and can adapt his discourse to different publics, speaking as a convinced proponent of Russian statehood and great power before an audience of Russian civil servants or senior military leaders while calling for unlimited violence against the current political order when he communicates with countercultural groups. He is very much a *bricoleur*, creatively using what is currently fashionable to elaborate a (pseudo-)philosophical metanarrative that is quite unique in its syncretism, even eclecticism. He is a prolific author, with about thirty monographs and textbooks, as well as the founder of numerous websites: *evrazia.org* as a news portal on Eurasia, *evrazia.info* for the IEM, *evrazia.tv* for podcasts of events, *arcto.ru* for the philosophical and religious aspects of his doctrine, *Rossia3.ru* for the Eurasian Union of Youth, *eurasianaffairs.net* for publications in English, and so on.

Inspirations

Dugin's thinking is articulated around five ideological traditions. His first inspiration comes from the *völkisch* occultism of Wirth and the Ahnenerbe (Research Community for Ancestral Heritage, an SS-sponsored research institute, which Wirth cofounded but was then excluded from),[13] with references to Aryanism, Hyperborea, Thule, and conspiracy theories. One of his attempts to anchor this in the Russian context was to dissociate "Fascism" as the historical enemy of Russia—which makes almost full consensus in today's Russian society, still deeply shaped by the memory of the Second World War—from some ideological elements from Nazi Germany and other Far Right regimes. For instance, he rehabilitates the Russophile tradition of National Socialism by identifying several pro-Russian forces in Nazi Germany, which he labels a "Eurasian order" in order to show that they share similar geopolitical perceptions with Russian Eurasianism.

The second tradition Dugin refers to is Traditionalism, inspired by René Guénon and—to an even greater degree—by Julius Evola, with whom he shares the vision of a new world to emerge from the ruins of the previous one.[14] Dugin's third doctrinal reference is rooted in the German Conservative Revolution of the 1920s and '30s: he admires the National Bolshevik Ernst Niekisch as well as all authors linked to the German *Geopolitik* at the turn of the twentieth century, such as Karl Haushofer. He also refers regularly, but to a lesser extent, to Ernst Jünger, and Carl Schmitt. Over the past decade, he has become a fervent proponent of Martin Heidegger, in whom he had been interested since his youth, and contributed to his rehabilitation in Russia. Like the German philosopher, Dugin references Dostoyevsky; he also echoes Heidegger's view of the United States as the ultimate expression of Western culture and of Russia as the new dawn that will soon emerge.[15]

Dugin also borrows from the French European New Right, a reframing of radical Right theories under the influence of some leftist doctrines that incorporates anticapitalist rhetoric as well as regionalist and ecological stances.[16] He has developed complex but long-lasting relations with Alain de Benoist in France, Claudio Mutti in Italy, and—to a lesser extent—with several other identitarian or National Bolshevik groups in France, Belgium, Germany, and Central European countries, as well as in the United States.[17]

Last but not least, a fifth component of Dugin's *Weltanschauung* can be found in classical Russian Eurasianism from the interwar period, constructed around the notion of Russia as the pivot of a specific civilization, Eurasia. Eurasianism states that Russia has an imperial nature by essence, based on its continental identity and the need to interact with, and control the steppic world, and that a form of religious autocracy constitutes its primordial political system.[18] Also present, though to a lesser degree, are some nineteenth-century conservative Russian thinkers, such as Konstantin Leontiev and Nikolai Danilevskii, and even more marginal allusions to Soviet cultural figures or representatives of leftist doctrines. Russia-centric references are clearly peripheral for Dugin, with the sole exception of Eurasianism and Orthodoxy—in particular, the Old Believer Church (born from schism with a reformed Orthodox Church in the seventeenth century); of which he is a member.[19]

Key concepts

A tremendously prolific and eclectic thinker, Dugin has been playing with multiple concepts and doctrinal traditions. Two sets of concepts appear in his work.

The first one includes geopolitics and the notion of Eurasia. Dugin affirms that the regeneration of the Russian nation will be realized by the total—and totalitarian—transformation of the Russian state on the international scene. The birth of a new mankind is therefore intimately linked not to a biological and cultural entity, that is, the nation (as in classic Nazi and Fascist doctrines), but to a state, Russia, and a civilization, Eurasia. This explains why radically revisionist transformational geopolitics remains at the core of Dugin's worldview, an integral part of its philosophical arsenal: Eurasian geopolitics is seen as the concrete implementation of a revolutionary solution for post-Soviet Russia.[20] Dugin is convinced that Europe's "tellurocracies" (continental powers), particularly Germany, should cooperate with Russia to defeat the "thalassocratic" (maritime) world exemplified by the British Empire and now the United States.[21] He sees *Geopolitik* as simultaneously a holistic and totalitarian science and as a *Weltanschauung*: "Geopolitics is a vision of the world. It is therefore better to compare it not to sciences, but to systems of sciences. It is situated on the same level as Marxism, liberalism, etc., i.e. systems of interpretation of society and history."[22]

The second set of concepts belongs to the Conservative Revolution. Contrary to classic conservatism, which calls for slow, gradual changes, or immobilism, the Conservative Revolution wants to counter liberalism by a new kind of revolution that would push forward conservative values. It thus combines conservative worldviews with revolutionary means, and in many aspects prefigures and parallels the Nazi and Fascist regimes. Dugin advanced his own version of Conservative Revolution in his 2009 book, *The Fourth Political Theory* (*Chetvertaia politicheskaia teoriia*), which he presented as a new, critical stage for his political thought. In it, he stated that he had definitively renounced what he calls the second and third political theories (communism and nationalism/fascism; the first theory is liberalism). He considers that liberalism is, in many aspects, a totalitarian ideology because of its absolute normative character, and he proposes on the contrary to celebrate—in a very Herderian way—the diversity of civilizations and their primordial incommensurability.

The fourth political theory, he wrote, proposes a complete break with the first three because it no longer seeks to accommodate modernity but denies it in its entirety. In spite of these declarations of novelty, Dugin limits himself to reproducing the definition of Arthur Moeller van den Bruck: "Conservatives who have preceded us have sought to stop the revolution; we must take the lead."[23] Dugin recognizes for instance that the drama of the fourth political theory is that "it was hidden behind the third (Nazism and Fascism). Its tragedy is to have been overshadowed historically by the third, and being allied with it, given the impossibility of conducting an ideological war on three fronts [against liberalism, communism and nationalism/Fascism]."[24]

Around this dual core of geopolitics/Eurasia and Conservative Revolution, Dugin has deployed several other concepts. Inspired by Jünger and Evola, he cultivates the cult of war as a unique regenerative tool to destroy the old world and create a new one. His apocalyptic vision has been particularly acute since the start of the Ukrainian crisis, which he sees as the final war between the West and Russia and the only way for a new Russia to be reborn from its liberal ashes. He nurtures several ancient myths from the *völkisch* and Evolian repertoire, including that of Hyperborea/Thule, with its Aryan undertones, as well as the notion of an ancient caste of warriors that will reemerge and take the lead of the new world.[25] He also celebrates more specifically Russian figures such as Baron von Ungern-Sternberg, a White lieutenant-general who converted to Buddhism. Ungern-Sternberg committed bloody mass atrocities during the Russian Civil War, and hoped to re-create a Genghis-khanid empire in Siberia. He embodies Dugin's call for empire and the realization of Russia's Eurasian destiny in Asia, as well as his metaphysics of war.

Dugin calls for a regenerated Europe, detached from any US influence, proud of its ancient identity, and of which Russia would be an integral part. He remains ambiguous on his relationship to race. He denies classic racism and white supremacists theories, but, inspired by Evola, he advocates "spiritual racism," and considers that races are the soul of peoples, endowing them with innate qualities that reveal certain philosophical principles. He further visualizes a Europe unified in the defense of so-called "traditional values." For instance, in 2012, defending the new antigay law in Russia, Dugin declared that Russia "is not a liberal country, nor does it pretend to be such," and thus it refuses "to apply liberal ideology in the form of obligatory laws, against normalization and juridical legitimization of what is considered a moral and psychological perversion."[26] Unsurprisingly, given his illiberal positioning, Dugin was one of the most vocal supporters of Donald Trump during the 2016 election campaign in the US, going so far as to call on him to launch a "Nuremberg of liberalism."[27]

However, unlike many figures of the US and European New Right, Dugin is not an Islamophobe: he believes that Shi'a Islam is a natural ally of Russia/Eurasia—it belongs to the Indo-European tradition—and that some revolutionary aspects of Sunni Islam can be compatible with the principles of the fourth political theory. Yet he shares many of the New Right's ambiguities toward the Jewish world. He sees in Israel a successful example of a Conservative Revolution that he admires, but condemns virulently the "subversive forces" of Judaism and Freemasonry. The 2014 Ukrainian crisis rejuvenated his anti-Semitic language: on Western radical Right websites, Dugin condemned "cosmopolitan financial elites" and Ukrainian "Jewish oligarchs." He extends support to a certain intellectualized white nationalism but refuses concrete violence: "When white nationalists reaffirm Tradition and the ancient culture of European peoples, they are right. But when they attack immigrants, Muslims, or the nationalists of other countries . . . or when they defend the United States, Atlanticism, liberalism or modernity, or when they consider the white race as being the highest and other races as inferior, I disagree with them completely."[28]

Reception

Dugin's greatest success in reaching a genuinely broad audience in Russia dates back to the mid-1990s, with his *Foundations of Geopolitics*. He played a critical role in promoting geopolitics and conferring on it academic respectability in the Russian university system, as well as in offering the broader public a geopolitical vision of Russia's natural and legitimate great power status. Yet his other doctrines remain largely untouched by this success and have influenced only a small group of supporters, mostly in countercultural circles. This outreach is primarily done by websites, as well as by the so-called New University—launched in 1998 on Dugin's initiative—which diffuses Traditionalist ideas through classes with former Yuzhinsky Circle disciples and their intellectual descendants.

If Dugin was a trendy author in Russia in the second half of the 1990s, he has progressively lost his appeal. With only thirty-six thousand followers in 2017, his Twitter account is dramatically underfollowed for a figure who claims to be an ideological agenda-setter. Through his multiple websites and the publication of textbooks prominently displayed in bookstores, he still retains some influence among Russian students and intellectual groups interested in geopolitics, conspiracy theories, and alternative history—domains that flourish in Russia, especially in provincial cities. But in terms of shaping the newspeak of the Putin regime, he has been bypassed by many other ideological producers, who offer less esoteric doctrines more in tune with the needs of the presidential administration. Dugin plays a relatively modest role even in Prokhanov's latest attempt to shape the Kremlin's language: the Izborsky Club, launched in 2012.[29]

Between 2008 and 2014, Dugin focused on producing textbooks—a commercially profitable market—and devoted much of his energy to structuring a so-called "conservative curriculum" which could be integrated into university programs. It offered students traditional courses (geopolitics and social sciences, international relations, introduction to structuralism, sociology of Russian society, introduction to religious studies, and introduction to philosophy), as well as less conventional disciplines (sociology of the imagination, sociology of geopolitical processes, deep sociology, ethnosociology, and postphilosophy).[30]

Contrary to the belief of those Western commentators who view him as "Putin's guru," Dugin has little direct access to the highest echelons of the presidential administration; he is not part of the Kremlin's main institutions, nor of their socializing mechanisms. Available public sources do not document direct contacts between Dugin and the presidential administration. Putin and Dugin reportedly met a few months after the former's accession to power,[31] and Dugin was also a part of the entourage that accompanied Putin on his visit to Mount Athos, the Orthodox Christian holy site in Greece, in May 2016, but we have no detailed information on Dugin's supposed personal connections with the Kremlin's "gray cardinals," nor with the president or deputy president of the presidential administration—figures such as Alexander Voloshin, Vladislav Surkov, and Viacheslav Volodin. Surkov, in particular, is known to harbor personal hatred for Dugin's esoteric imperialism.

Dugin can, however, rely on some go-betweens, and there are several identifiable niches connecting him to certain segments of the Kremlin's kaleidoscope. As a member of the branch of the Old Believer faith that has been reintegrated into the Moscow Patriarchate, Dugin has been able to cultivate close relations with some political circles within the Russian Orthodox Church. His personal connection with the Orthodox businessman Konstantin Malofeev secure him both status and revenues. Through the Yuzhinsky Circle, which has hosted numerous countercultural figures, Dugin has also been in contact with many media personalities: musicians, artists, and journalists. To this day, he retains the support of two major figures on Russia's media landscape: Mikhail Leontiev, long regarded as one of Putin's preferred television presenters, and now press officer of the oil giant Rosneft, and Ivan Demidov, the founder of the Orthodox television channel *Spas*, which has given Dugin a regular televisual platform.

Over the past thirty years, Dugin can point to just two periods of success. The first one came in the second half of the 1990s, when his influence among military circles reached its peak, thanks to his decision to move away from the countercultural National Bolshevik Party and reconnect with Alexander Prokhanov and his networks in the military and the security services. Dugin was thus able to teach at the Academy of the General Staff, as well as work as a consultant for some Duma committees. His greatest achievement was probably becoming Seleznyev's advisor in 1998, since it was the only time that he was part of policymaking. But his success was short-lived: in the early 2000s, Dugin found himself in deep opposition to Putin, then perceived as a liberal and pro-Western statesman, and felt himself sidelined by the groundswell of support for Putin and the latter's ability to recapture patriotic feelings and the nationalist narrative. He gained new visibility from 2008 to 2014, after having penetrated the Moscow State University, and reached the peak of his media influence in 2012–14, during Putin's third mandate "conservative turn." Soon afterward, he once again lost any solid institutional status and outreach ability due to his excessively radical positioning during the Ukrainian crisis.

Dugin's reception outside Russia

Paradoxically, Dugin has had more success abroad than in Russia. His ability to speak several European languages, to translate and be translated, contributes to this visibility.[32] One of the first Russian figures to build bridges with the European radical Right, Dugin has, since the early 1990s, been able to rely on a large network of supporters in France and Italy for Western Europe, in Greece and Hungary for Central Europe and the Balkans, as well as in the United States among the so-called Alt Right.

In France and Belgium, Alain de Benoist familiarized Dugin with New Right doctrine. The Belgian Robert Steuckers, another GRECE alumnus, proved to be an even greater influence on Dugin, introducing him to works by the major authors of German geopolitics, such as Karl Haushofer, as well as to contemporary conspiracy theories about US world domination. Steuckers was also the one to rally Dugin behind National Bolshevism and to connect it to the European Liberation Front, originally founded by Francis Parker Yockey and Otto Strasser and reanimated in the early 1990s by movements such as Nouvelle Resistance, with figures like Christian Bouchet in France and José Antonio Llopart in Spain. Dugin also drew inspiration from meeting Jean Thiriart, a fervent supporter of a unified Euro-Soviet space, who at that time led a small National-European Community Party (*Parti communautaire national-européen*). In Italy, his friend Claudio Mutti has inspired several pro-Russian and pro-Islam movements, and launched several Eurasianist initiatives loosely connected to Lega Nord.

In the 2000s, Dugin consolidated new support in Hungary, especially among the radical Right party Jobbik (Right Choice), and in Greece, with links both with the radical Left party SYRIZA (Coalition of the Radical Left) and with the radical Right party Golden Dawn (Chrysí Avgí), sharing the same combination of Orthodoxy and *völkisch* occultism as his own. Dugin has also reached out beyond Europe. In the United States, he developed contacts with members of the Alt Right movement. Several white-supremacist activists such as Preston Wigington, Matthew Heimbach, and the conspiracy theorist Alex Jones, all interviewed him or invited him for Skype conferences: being on the US sanctions list following the Donbas insurgence, Dugin cannot travel to the United States. In 2011, he established contacts with Brazil, including an online debate with the journalist and Traditionalist thinker Olavo de Carvalho, a disciple of René Guénon and Frithjof Schuon, who is close to some Islamist movement, and currently in exile in the United States. Dugin traveled to Brazil in early 2013, visiting several universities, where he met with Heidegger-focused circles and was introduced to the thought of Vicente Ferreira da Silva.

Conclusion

Dugin remains the main introducer, translator, mediator, and aggregator of radical Right theories in post-Soviet Russia. In the three decades since perestroika, he has been able—both literally (he reads the main European languages, and speaks excellent French and English and good German) and intellectually translate a broad literature in order to nativize it and adapt it to the Russian context. Dugin should be read not only as an ideological *bricoleur* but an intellectual chameleon. He adapts his doctrinal stock to the current fashions of the time, giving, at first glance, the impression that he regularly changes his mind. But this *bricolage* is motivated, above all, by his unceasing drive to court a new readership, as well as by the need to secure niches in the publishing market.

Dugin's unfailing loyalty to European doctrines makes him unique in contemporary Russia. He has approached this rich intellectual domain with different lenses: first the esoteric one (Guénon and Evola), which he mastered during his dissident years with the Yuzhinsky Circle, followed by the geopolitical lens (European New Right and Haushofer-style German *Geopolitik*), and, most recently, the philosophical one, which has Heidegger as its iconic figure. Guénon's Traditionalism and Orthodox-themed religious prose are used as metaphysical arguments to justify the choice of a religious, revolutionary autocracy as Russia's national ideology. The framing of Eurasianism allows Dugin to instrumentalize a term that has familiarity and prestige among the Russian public and thus associate a Russophile and "clean hands" radical Right doctrine with Russia's future.

Dugin epitomizes the space created in contemporary Russia for ideological entrepreneurship. He is the only figure to have selected European radical Right doctrinal traditions as his product for ideological marketing, and his success in Russia has been limited. His efforts to influence Russia's broader geopolitical narrative have prospered, but his work to introduce doctrinal content inspired by the European radical Right has not. The ideological contexts in which he has flourished have been the ones where he has acted as a chameleon, claiming to be in tune with the rest of society—Russia's great power status and leading role in its Eurasian "near abroad," Soviet-style patriotism, and reference to Europe and conservative values as Russia's own identity. Meanwhile, he has failed to anchor new ideological toolkits—be they *völkisch* occultism, Guénon's and Evola's Traditionalism, or the German Conservative Revolution—in Russian public opinion or in the minds of Kremlin decision makers. Only some aspects of the French and European New Right have been integrated into Moscow's narrative—namely, the need for a unified and continental Europe that integrates Russia but excludes the United States—but these ideas are drawn not from the New Right itself but from more mainstream populist parties (which explains the Kremlin's willingness to co-opt them). Abroad, in contrast, Dugin is interacting closely with New and Alt Right groups and their leaders, reaching out to a large number of European and American movements.

Notes

1. Aleksandr Dugin, *Tampliery proletariata: Natsional-bol'shevizm i initsiatsiia* (Moscow: Arktogeia, 1997), http://www.e-reading.club/chapter.php/85175/5/Dugin_-_Tamplery_Proletariata.html.
2. Marlene Laruelle, "The Iuzhinsky Circle: Far-Right Metaphysics in the Soviet Underground and Its Legacy Today," *Russian Review* 75, no. 4 (2015): 563–580.
3. Fabrizio Fenghi, "Making Post-Soviet Counterpublics: The Aesthetics of Limonka and the National-Bolshevik Party," *Nationalities Papers* 45, no. 2 (2017): 182–205.
4. On Dugin's book, see John B. Dunlop, "Aleksandr Dugin's 'Neo-Eurasian' Textbook and Dmitrii Trenin's Ambivalent Response," *Harvard Ukrainian Studies* 25, no. 1–2 (2001): 91–127.
5. For further details on Dugin's connections with military circles, see Dunlop, "Dugin's 'Neo-Eurasian' Textbook," 94 and 102.
6. Andreas Umland, "Aleksandr Dugin's Transformation from a Lunatic Fringe Figure into a Mainstream Political Publicist, 1980–1998: A Case Study in the Rise of Late and Post-Soviet Russian Fascism," *Journal of Eurasian Studies* 1 (2010): 144–152.
7. See Vügar İmanbeyli, "Failed Exodus: Dugin's Networks in Turkey," in *Eurasianism and European Far Right: Reshaping the Europe-Russia Relationship*, ed. Marlene Laruelle (Lanham, MD: Lexington, 2015), 145–174.
8. Aslambek Aslakhanov, then-advisor to the Russian president; Eduard Kokoity, president of the self-proclaimed Republic of South Ossetia; and Talgat Tadzhuddin, chairman of the Central Spiritual Board of Muslims.
9. Vadim Rossman, "Moscow State University's Department of Sociology and the Climate of Opinion in Post-Soviet Russia," in *Eurasianism and European Far Right: Reshaping the Europe-Russia Relationship*, ed. Marlene Laruelle (Lanham, MD: Lexington, 2015), 55–76.

10. "Razvitie i stanovlenie konservativnoi ideologii v Rossii s oporoi na nauchnye kadry," Center for Conservative Research, http://konservatizm.org/about.xhtml.
11. Marlene Laruelle, "The Three Colors of Novorossiya, or the Russian Nationalist Mythmaking of the Ukrainian Crisis," *Post-Soviet Affairs* 32, no. 1 (2015): 55–74.
12. The video in which Dugin made this call is available at www.youtube.com/watch?v=R_63IswcVnA.
13. Michael H. Kater, *Das "Ahnenerbe" der SS 1935–1945: Ein Beitrag zur Kulturpolitik des Dritten Reiches* (Munich: R. Oldenbourg Verlag, 2006).
14. Andreas Umland and Anton Shekhovtsov, "Is Dugin a Traditionalist? 'Neo-Eurasianism' and Perennial Philosophy," *Russian Review* 68 (October 2009): 662–678. See also Mark Sedgwick, *Against the Modern World: Traditionalism and the Secret Intellectual History of the Twentieth Century* (New York: Oxford University Press, 2004), as well as Andreas Umland, "Classification, Julius Evola and the Nature of Dugin's Ideology," *Erwägen, Wissen, Ethik* 16, no. 4 (2005): 566–569.
15. See Aleksandr Dugin, *Martin Khaidegger: filosofiia drugogo nachala* (Moscow: Akademicheskii proekt, 2010); Aleksandr Dugin, *Martin Khaidegger: vozmozhnost' russkoi filosofii* (Moscow: Akademicheskii proekt, 2011). On Dugin's Heideggerianism, see Jeff Love and Michael Meng, "Heidegger and Post-Colonial Fascism," *Nationalities Papers* 45, no. 2 (2017): 307–320.
16. See Peter H. Merkel and Leonard Weinberg, eds., *The Revival of Right Wing Extremism in the Nineties* (London: Frank Cass, 1997).
17. More details in Anton Shekhovtsov, *Russia and the Western Far Right: Tango Noir*. Routledge Studies in Fascism and the Far Right (London: Routledge, 2017).
18. Anton Shekhovtsov, "Aleksandr Dugin's New Eurasianism: The New Right à la russe," *Religion Compass* 3–4: (2009): 697–716; Marlene Laruelle, *Russian Eurasianism: An Ideology of Empire* (Washington, DC: Woodrow Wilson Press/Johns Hopkins University Press, 2008).
19. Dugin joined the Old Believer Church in 1999. He presents the Russian schism of the seventeenth century as the archetype of Traditionalist thought, born of rejection of the secularization of Orthodoxy, which he dates to around the same time as that given by Guénon for the end of Tradition in the West (after the end of the Thirty Years' War in 1648).
20. Anton Shekhovstov, "The Palingenetic Thrust of Russian Neo-Eurasianism: Ideas of Rebirth in Aleksandr Dugin's Worldview," *Totalitarian Movements and Political Religions* 9, no. 4 (2008): 491–506.
21. On Haushofer, see David T. Murphy, *The Heroic Earth: Geopolitical Thought in Weimar Germany, 1918–1933* (Kent, OH: Kent State University Press, 1997).
22. Aleksandr Dugin, *Osnovy geopolitiki: Geopoliticheskoe budushchee Rossii* (Moscow: Arktogeia, 1997), 12.
23. Aleksandr Dugin, *Chetvertaia politicheskaia teoriia* (Moscow: Amfora, 2009), cover blurb.
24. Ibid., 209.

25. See, for instance, Aleksandr Dugin, *Misterii Evrazii* (Moscow: Arktogeia, 1996), as well as *Znaki velikogo norda* (Moscow: Veche, 2008).
26. Aleksandr Dugin, "The Long Path: An Interview with Alexander Dugin," *Open Revolt*, May 17, 2014, http://openrevolt.info/2014/05/17/alexander-dugin-interview/.
27. Aleksandr Dugin, "Donald Trump: The Swamp and Fire," *Katehon*, November 14, 2016, http://katehon.com/article/donald-trump-swamp-and-fire.
28. Aleksandr Dugin, "On 'White Nationalism' and Other Potential Allies in the Global Revolution," The Fourth Political Theory, http://www.4pt.su/en/content/white-nationalism-and-other-potential-allies-global-revolution.
29. Marlene Laruelle, "The Izborky Club, or the New Conservative Avant-Garde in Russia," *Russian Review* 75, no. 4: 626–644.
30. A list of the lectures and their bibliographies is at available at "Kursy," Center for Conservative Research, http://books.4pt.su/issues/kursy.
31. Charles Clover, *Black Wind, White Snow: The Rise of Russia's New Nationalism* (New Haven, CT: Yale University Press, 2016).
32. Shekhovtsov, *Russia and the Western Far Right*.

11

Bat Ye'or and Eurabia

Sindre Bangstad

IN SO-CALLED "COUNTER-JIHADIST" circles in Europe and the US, the Egyptian-born Swiss-Israeli popular author Bat Ye'or (Gisèle Littman, née Oreibi) is widely seen as the doyenne of "Eurabia" literature. She has rightly been described as a "key ideologue" in the international counter-jihadist movement.[1] The Eurabia literature comes in different varieties and formulations, but Bat Ye'or's version describes an ongoing secret conspiracy, which involves both the European Union and Muslim-majority countries in North Africa and the Middle East working under the auspices of the Euro-Arab Dialogue (EAD) established in the 1970s, and aimed at establishing Muslim control over a future Europe or "Eurabia."

Bat Ye'or's work was little known beyond the radical Right fringes before al-Qaida's attacks on the US on September 11, 2001. Her writings are now often mistakenly referred to as the work of a historian and academic among her sympathizers, who include Ayaan Hirsi Ali, Bruce Bawer, Niall Ferguson, Irshad Manji, Melanie Phillips, Robert Spencer, and Mark Steyn. Of these, it is noteworthy that only Ferguson, a professor at Stanford University, is a serious academic. Although Bat Ye'or actually appropriated the term "Eurabia" already created in the 1970s, she can undoubtedly be credited with having popularized it as a conspiracy theory through quasi-academic titles such as *Eurabia: The Euro-Arab Axis*[2] and *Europe, Globalization, and the Coming Universal Caliphate*.[3]

Through its dissemination on various "counter-jihadist" websites and in the work of the "counter-jihadist" Norwegian blogger "Fjordman" (pen name of Peder Are Nøstvold Jensen),[4] Bat Ye'or's work inspired the Norwegian right-wing terrorist Anders Behring Breivik, who executed the worst terrorist attacks in modern Norwegian history in 2011.[5] In Norway, Bat Ye'or's work and the Eurabia conspiracy theories that underpin it have long been promoted by the government-funded NGO Human Rights' Service (HRS).[6] The director of HRS, Hege Storhaug, and the HRS have long-standing links with Norway's Progress Party (Fremskrittspartiet), a coalition partner in the post-2013 government, which has campaigned on a platform of exclusivist nationalism and opposition to Muslim immigration to Norway since 1987. State subvention of the HRS in a situation in which anti-Muslim sentiment has become both widespread and mainstream in the Norwegian population at large offers the Progress Party supportive media platforms as well as a means by which to satisfy the most radical part of its electoral constituency. A recent national representative survey from Norway finds that 30 percent of those surveyed consent to the view that "Muslims want to take over Europe," 39 percent consenting to the view that "Muslims are a threat against Norwegian culture," and 28 percent declaring that they have an "aversion to Muslims." The survey finds that these attitudes are far more widespread among Norwegians with electoral preferences for the Progress Party than among the voters of any other party.[7] Bat Ye'or is also widely read among, and has long-standing relations with, Serbian ultranationalists, the Israeli Far Right, and many radical Right activists in Western Europe and the US. It is difficult to assess Bat Ye'or's international impact and influence beyond counter-jihadist and radical Right circles. She is now quite old and has, by virtue of her limited public presence among the more social-media-savvy new intellectuals of the radical Right, faded from view in recent years. But it is hard not to see traces of the influence of some of the ideas and tropes she and her likeminded fellow travelers have put into circulation over the past thirty years, especially in their mainstreaming in the Trump administration's various "Muslim bans."

Life and context

Bat Ye'or (Hebrew for "Daughter of the Nile") is a pen name for Gisèle Littman. Littman has at times claimed that she cannot disclose her real name out of "security concerns,"[8] but her real name and identity have long been a matter of public record. Littman was born the daughter of an Italian-French couple under the name of Gisèle Oreibi in the upper-class area of Zamalek in Cairo, Egypt, in 1933. Oreibi's father was an Italian Jew who had fled his native Italy under Mussolini. Like many Jews in

Egypt, the Oreibis left Egypt in the aftermath of the 1956 Suez War as conditions for Egyptian and foreign Jews worsened in the wake of the newly formed Israeli state's support for the failed British and French-led invasion of the Suez canal zone,[9] and during the rise of Arab nationalism under Nasserite decolonization.[10] In the light of Bat Ye'or's later attitudes to Islam and Muslims, it does not seem unreasonable to suggest that the trauma of the Oreibis' and other Egyptian Jews' exodus from Egypt was formative for her.

Bat Ye'or is reported to have attended undergraduate courses at University College London in the UK in 1958 and at the University of Geneva in Switzerland in 1960. In fact, she never obtained any academic degrees from either of these institutions. She is, in the words of Adi Schwartz of the Israeli newspaper *Haaretz*, who in a 2006 profile of Bat Ye'or's work referred to her 2005 *Eurabia* monograph as "The Protocols of the Elders of Brussels," "not an academic and has never taught at any university."[11]

At the age of twenty-six, in 1959, Bat Ye'or married the British Jewish historian David G. Littman (1933–2012) and became a British citizen. A year later, in 1960, she moved to Lausanne in Switzerland with her husband. The couple had three children.[12] Bat Ye'or's husband, David, and his close associate René Wadlow represented the Association for World Education and the World Union for Progressive Judaism at the United Nations Commission on Human Rights (UNHCR) in Geneva, Switzerland, for many years.

Littman and Bat Ye'or were also involved in Operation Mural, a secret operation led by the Israeli foreign intelligence services Mossad, which in 1961 managed to evacuate some 530 Moroccan Jewish children to Israel from Morocco via Switzerland under cover of an NGO, Swiss Aid to North African Children (Ouevre Suisse de Secours aux Enfants de l'Afrique du Nord). Morocco, like most other Arab countries, did not recognize the State of Israel after Moroccan independence from France in 1956. Hence, Moroccan Jews who wanted to emigrate or undertake *aliyah* to Israel (and who were encouraged to do so by the Jewish Agency) were prevented from doing so because the Moroccan government would not issue exit visas for Israel. Moroccan Jews faced increasing hostilities and persecution linked to the rise of Arab nationalism after the Suez crisis.[13] Operation Mural involved the Littmans posing as Christians in Morocco, and led to David G. Littman later being awarded the "Hero of Silence" decoration by the Israeli president Shimon Peres in 2009. It is clear from the late Littman's own publications and his coauthorship of one of his wife's books[14] that he shared his wife's convictions regarding both Eurabia and "dhimmitude." Bat Ye'or has throughout her publishing career mainly published in French, and a number of her works had been translated, edited, and coauthored by her late husband.

Although a 1980 French publication of Bat Ye'or's on the "dhimmis of Islam" was referenced by the historian and later neoconservative Bernard Lewis in a footnote to his widely cited 1984 monograph *The Jews of Islam*,[15] Bat Ye'or's publications by and large existed in a state of obscurity prior to al-Qaeda's 9/11 terrorist attacks on the US. Mark Sedgwick rightly notes that "her work is not highly regarded by professional historians."[16] The aftermath of the 9/11 attacks led to her invitation to address the Congressional Human Rights Caucus in 2002, as well as to present lectures at the universities of Georgetown, Brown, Yale, and Brandeis that same year. Her website makes much of these appearances to bolster her supposed academic credentials. To the consternation of a number of the distinguished international scholars invited, Bat Ye'or also made an appearance at an academic conference on anti-Semitism at the Vidal Sassoon Memorial Center for the Study of Antisemitism at the Hebrew University of Jerusalem in 2006.[17]

Bat Ye'or's personal links and ideological affiliations with anti-Muslim extremists, and her provision of anti-Muslim ideas and sentiments, are long-standing. In an interview with a US-based counter-jihadist publication from 2011, Bat Ye'or claimed to have coined the neologism "dhimmitude," a term first recorded as having been used by the Lebanese Maronite civil war president Bashir Gemayel in 1982.[18] In an interview with a sympathetic online media outlet in 2011, Bat Ye'or alleged that her term "dhimmitude" had become known to Gemayel through "mutual friends" earlier that year.[19]

The civil war in Lebanon from 1976 to 1991 provides an important rhetorical and ideological template for Bat Ye'or. Here, she casts Israel's Lebanese allies among Maronite Christians as defending an allegedly "Western" "Judeo-Christian" civilization against the "barbarian hordes" of Muslims, and advances the civil war in Lebanon as a harbinger of a future that awaits Europe unless Eurabia is stopped in its tracks. This claim of a historical civilizational "unity" between Christians and Jews is problematic in the light of centuries of European Christian and Christianist persecution, discrimination, and exclusion of European Jews until after World War II, and the very fact that the very notion of a shared "Judean-Christian tradition" was coined by American Lutheran and Catholic theologians opposed to fascism in Europe as late as the 1930s.[20] By the 1950s, however, the notion of a shared tradition uniting Jews and Christians had migrated to the mainstream American conservative Right and was used as an ideological instrument against communism, in a similar manner as it is used today by radical Right activists and politicians as an ideological instrument against Islam and Muslims.[21] The notion allows Bat Ye'or to portray terrorism—almost whenever and wherever perpetrated by Muslims—as a shared threat uniting Christians and Jews in Europe and elsewhere—and as intimately linked to alleged wider Muslim ambitions of conquest and rule, thus casting the contemporary state of Israel as a foremost defender and avant-garde of Western European Enlightenment, and having shared interests with the people, if not the leaders, of Europe.

Bat Ye'or is also able to rhetorically cast historically secular and nationalist Palestinian movements such as the PLO and Fatah as "Islamic" and "Muslim" pure and simple, so that the civil war in Lebanon, as well as the Palestinian struggle for independence since 1948, are rewritten as simply a struggle for Muslim "global domination." In Bat Ye'or's view, echoing the view of the former Israeli prime minister Golda Meir, "Palestinians" simply do not exist, the term being an alleged historical fabrication by Arabs bent on denying Israeli Jews' historical rights to a state. Bat Ye'or's theories are—as observers have noted—unthinkable without reference to the idea of Israel as a frame around which all global politics ultimately revolve.[22] In this, Ye'or's work ultimately and paradoxically mirrors the work of the many pro-Palestinian activists—whether secular nationalist or Islamist—who often reduce Middle East politics to the question of Palestine.

In the context of the attempted genocide of Muslims in Bosnia in the 1990s, Bat Ye'or also moved in the circles of Serbian ultranationalists and their Western European and American supporters. In the midst of the Balkan Wars in the 1990s, she spoke to the Lord Byron Foundation for Balkan Studies in Chicago. This foundation was established by Alfred Sherman, a one-time advisor to the British conservative prime minister Margaret Thatcher and a respected member of Britain's Jewish community, and Srdja Trifkovic, a close associate of and political advisor to Serbian ultranationalists Radovan Karadžić and Biljana Plavšić. Bat Ye'or had by this time begun to be widely read by Serbian ultranationalist intellectuals. In 1994 she declared to *Midstream*, a Jewish monthly journal in the US, that Bosnia was a "spearhead" for the impending "Islamization" of Europe.[23]

Her speech to the Lord Byron Foundation in Chicago in 1995 was titled "Myths and Politics. The Tolerant Pluralistic Islamic Society: Origin of a Myth." Bat Ye'or's contrived and tendentious representation of Bosnian Islam, with its long-standing secular and pluralistic traditions, stands in stark contrast with the ethnographic work of anthropologists on Bosnian Muslims before and during the Bosnian War.[24] Her speech would later be reproduced in its entirety in Breivik's 2011 cut-and-paste tract *2083: A European Declaration of Independence*.[25] The radical Right and counter-jihadist authors who inspired Breivik were all authors who promote Eurabia theories. The term "Eurabia" is mentioned in Breivik's *2083* no less than 171 times.[26] In blogposts dating back to 2009, Breivik names Bat Ye'or, Robert Spencer, and Fjordman as his main sources of inspiration.[27]

It was Fjordman, by far the most influential on Breivik's ideas of these three,[28] who introduced the work of Littman in Norwegian mainstream media in the form of an op-ed in the Norwegian tabloid *Verdens Gang* as early as in 2003.[29] Fjordman was introduced to Bat Ye'or and Robert Spencer at a counter-jihadist conference in commemoration of the slain Dutch right-wing populist Pim Fortuyn in The Hague in 2006.[30] Fjordman subsequently maintained a regular correspondence with his main source of inspiration, Bat Ye'or.[31]

Another central media and organizational platform for the wider international dissemination of Bat Ye'or's work—especially in the Nordic countries—has been the Copenhagen-based Danish International Free Press Society (IFPS) and its associated media outlets and publications. Bat Ye'or is a board member of the IFPS, run from Copenhagen by the former Danish newspaper editor and historian Lars Hedegaard. The IFPS was established in 2009 as an extension of its Danish precursor, the Danish Free Press Society, itself established in 2004 in the aftermath of the so-called "cartoon crisis" of 2005–6. The board of directors and the board of advisors of the IFPS is a virtual who's who of international actors and intellectuals in the counter-jihadist movement, including the editor of the *Brussels Journal* Paul Beliën; the editor of the blog *Gates of Vienna* Edward S. May; Andrew Bostom, Helle Merete Brix, Brigitte Gabriel, Frank Gaffney, Ibn Warraq, Daniel Pipes, Roger Scruton; the editor of *Jihad Watch* Robert Spencer; Mark Steyn; and Geert Wilders. Hedegaard, who was first convicted but later acquitted for hate speech under the Danish General Penal Code for statements to the effect that "Muslims are rapists" in 2009/10, survived an assassination attempt at his home in Copenhagen in 2013.

Part of Bat Ye'or's appeal in these circles no doubt derives from the fact that her work has been published by some academic publishers in the US, and that her works, although anchored in generalizations and conspiracy theories,[32] often mimic the prose style and the scholarly apparatus of serious academic texts. There is also a discernable tendency in counter-jihadist circles to play up nonexistent academic credentials in an intertextual process of mutual citation, and to ascribe legitimacy to authors who demonstrate a certain level of command of transliterated Arabic, readily discernable in the case of Bat Ye'or.

Major works and concepts

Bat Ye'or is the author of eight books, six of which are available in English. Her first book was *The Jews of Egypt: An Overview of 3,000 Years of History* (*Les Juifs en Egypte: Aperçu sur 3000 ans d'histoire*), a short seventy-five page booklet published in Geneva in 1971 under the pen name "Yahudiya Masriya" (Arabic for "Egyptian Jewess"). Her major works include *The Dhimmi: Jews and Christians under Islam* in 1985; *The Decline of Eastern Christianity: From Jihad to Dhimmitude: Seventh-Twentieth Century* in 1996; *Islam and Dhimmitude: Where Civilizations Collide* (coauthored with David G. Littman) in 2001; *Eurabia: The Euro-Arab Axis* in 2005; and *Europe, Globalization, and the Coming of the Universal Caliphate* in 2011. Bat Ye'or has also published a number of essays in more obscure French and Italian journals, as well as contributed to volumes edited by anti-Muslim activists such as Robert Spencer.[33]

Though anti-Muslim sentiment has long been a staple of Bat Ye'or's work, it has arguably undergone a process of increasing "radicalization" and is in her later works increasingly untethered from any serious academic scholarship on Islam and the Muslim world. As has become commonplace in radical literature and discourse on Islam and Muslims in Europe and the US in recent years, Ye'or treats "Islam" and "Muslims" as self-evident transhistorical, transnational, and determinative entities.[34] Although references to the work of Bernard Lewis still appear, the "radicalization" in Bat Ye'or's recent work means that her texts increasingly depend on authors and intellectuals who share her worldviews and political orientations. One may regard the counter-jihadist genre in which Bat Ye'or moves as a form of hypertext in which authors such as Oriana Fallaci and Robert Spencer appear over and over again, along with Bat Ye'or herself, as if they constituted authoritative sources on Islam, Muslims, and the Muslim world.

Eurabia

The concept of "Eurabia" is a key concept in Bat Ye'or's last three books. The term was popularized by the Italian journalist Oriana Fallaci in her widely translated 2004 book *The Force of Reason* (*La forza della ragione*) and picked up by the Stanford historian Niall Ferguson in a 2004 *New York Times* op-ed essay with the same title,[35] but the term itself was not coined by any of these authors. It originated with an obscure and by all accounts unsuccessful French literary and cultural journal, *Eurabia*, published by the European Committee for the Coordination of Friendship Associations with the Muslim World (Comité européen des associations d'amitié avec le monde arabe) in 1975. According to Sedgwick,[36] Bat Ye'or first adopted the term and the meaning she gives it in 2002, following an article by the Israeli-Canadian reporter Sam Orbaum in the Israeli newspaper *Jerusalem Post*.[37]

The original journal *Eurabia* published only four issues in 1975 before it ceased publication, but for Bat Ye'or the term is nothing less than the cornerstone of an Arab Muslim and EU-led conspiracy to establish Muslim control over Europe and an Islamic caliphate. By virtue of this conspiracy, hidden from public view yet discernable and decipherable for select "seers" like Bat Ye'or herself, Europe has evolved from "a Judeo-Christian civilization" to a "post–Judeo-Christian civilization that is subservient to the ideology of jihad and the Islamic powers that propagate it."[38] This whole conspiracy, and the monumental shifts engendered by it, results from "the oil crisis of 1973 when the European Economic Community (EEC), at the initiative of France and the Arab League, established the Euro-Arab Dialogue (EAD)."[39] The main villain of Bat Ye'or's account is France. In light of what is known about the relations between French political elites and the average Muslim and Arab in postwar France, and especially during and after the Algerian War of Independence,[40] it might seem surprising that these very same elites should have conspired with Arab Muslim leaders in spearheading a covert "Islamization of Europe." But for Bat Ye'or, since 1973, "the EAD has been in the vanguard of engineering a convergence between Europe and the Islamic states of North Africa and the Middle East."[41] Eurabia is ultimately directed against Israel and its closest Western ally, the US, and reflects "increasing Islamic penetration of Europe and its growing influence on European policy." "Euro-Arab culture is permeating, even overwhelming, all levels of Western European society."[42]

There are any number of EU-employed and associated "Eurabians" secretly working to further the Eurabia conspiracy, for the "faceless networks of a huge administration uniting the EU and the OIC (Organization of The Islamic Conference)" have managed to create "a Kafkaesque world functioning as a totalitarian anonymous system" that maintains "political correctness and censorship."[43] Exactly how this feat of political and societal influence is achieved by structurally and often financially weak postcolonial states, which are linked in highly ambiguous ways to Muslim populations in Europe, is not addressed in any detail by Bat Ye'or. She seems either unaware of or unconcerned by the mirroring in her anti-Muslim Eurabia theories of the anti-Semitic *Protocols of the Learned Elders of Zion*.[44]

Dhimmitude

Another key concept for Bat Ye'or is the concept of "dhimmitude." The term is derived from the Arabic term for historically protected "peoples of the book" under Islamic rule—the *dhimmi*—but is in fact a neologism. For Bat Ye'or, the term refers to an "obligatory submission [of non-Muslim peoples] by war or surrender to Islamic domination."[45] "The study of dhimmitude, then, is the study of the progressive Islamization of Christian civilizations," according to Bat Ye'or.[46]

Bat Ye'or first introduced the term in her 1991 monograph *The Decline of Eastern Christianity under Islam*. In Bat Ye'or's conception, dhimmitude includes "the whole web of disabling political, historical, sociological, and cultural circumstances that enmesh a Christian or Jewish population that has been brought under Islamic hegemony."[47] It even refers to a state of mind in contemporary Western societies, which does not "develop all at once" but is rather a "long process that involves many elements and a specific mental conditioning."[48] One can be living in dhimmitude without knowing it, given that "the psychological impact of intellectual terrorism" is such that the West had, according by Bat Ye'or, already "entered into a phase of dhimmitude without realizing it" by 1996.[49] The apocalyptic strains of this line of argument are apparent.

Jihad

The term "jihad," understood not as Muslims themselves understand it (as polyvalent and contextual)[50] but as "war" against "infidels" pure and simple is, furthermore, a key term for Bat Ye'or. Jihad, in Bat Ye'or's rendering, is what defines and determines Islam's and Muslims' essence. It is a transhistorical and transcultural essence that is hereby defined. Bat Ye'or argues that "wherever the ideology of jihad and its precepts have not been rejected, Muslims relate to non-Muslims within its conceptual framework."[51] The elaboration of the concept and doctrine of jihad "developed by Muslim theologians and jurists beginning in the eighth century established the relationship between Muslims in terms of belligerency, armistices, and submission." It is, according to Bat Ye'or, "a fundamental part of Islamic jurisprudence and literature, since it is through jihad that the Islamic community is developed and expanded"—a "collective duty" to be pursued "by military means or peaceful efforts—propaganda, speech, or subversive activities—within a non-Muslim nation."[52] For Bat Ye'or, dhimmitude is nothing but "the direct outcome of jihad."[53]

This essentialist rendering of the concept of jihad in the lives of Islam and Muslims past and present of course raises the question of why Muslims and Christians have in historical contact zones on the whole managed to live remarkably peacefully together, and why Muslims could historically be both allies and foes of Christians and Western empires, colonialism, and world wars.[54] But such empirical details are of little interest in the grand scheme that Bat Ye'or constructs, in which it is an article of faith that whenever people of Muslim background engage in warfare, it is down to an essential motive derived from Islamic tradition, rather than matters relating to politics, interests, or resources.

Conclusion

Bat Ye'or's representations of Islam and Muslims are, for all her claims to be writing history, profoundly ahistorical. There is, however, a constant throughout Bat Ye'or's work, which opposes the myth of an interfaith utopia past or present to the idea of a non-Muslim choice between either willing "submission to Islam" (as in dhimmitude) or opposition and resistance to it. It is in this sense that it is hardly surprising that Bat Ye'or's theories have come to inspire violent acts by individuals who self-identify with the counter-jihadist movement of which she is a central part.

Notes

1. Arun Kundnani, "Blind Spot? Security Narratives and Far-Right Violence in Europe," ICCT Research Paper, 2012; Hope Not Hate, *The Counter-Jihad Movement: Anti-Muslim Hatred from the Margins to the Mainstream* (London: Hope Not Hate, 2012), https://web.archive.org/web/20121011225433/http://www.hopenothate.org.uk/counter-jihad/.
2. Bat Ye'or, *Eurabia: The Euro-Arab Axis* (Madison, NJ: Farleigh Dickinson Press, 2005).
3. Bat Ye'or, *Europe, Globalization and the Coming of the Universal Caliphate* (Madison, NJ: Farleigh Dickinson University Press, 2011).
4. Sindre Bangstad, "Eurabia Comes to Norway," *Islam and Christian-Muslim Relations* 24, no. 3 (2013): 369–391.
5. Sindre Bangstad, *Anders Breivik and the Rise of Islamophobia* (London: Zed Books, 2014).
6. Sindre Bangstad and Frode Helland, *Serving the Norwegian State with Islamophobia: The Case of Hege Storhaug and Human Rights Service (HRS)* (forthcoming).
7. Christhard Hoffman and Vibeke Moe, eds., "Holdninger til jøder og muslimer i Norge 2017," HL-Centre report, 2017.
8. Adi Schwartz, "The Protocols of the Elders of Brussels," *Haaretz*, June 20, 2006, https://www.haaretz.com/1.4919785.
9. Joel Beinin, *The Dispersion of Egyptian Jewry: Culture, Politics, and the Formation of a Modern Diaspora* (Berkeley: University of California Press, 1998).
10. Craig S. Smith, "Europe's Jews Seek Solace on the Right," *New York Times*, February 20, 2005, http://www.nytimes.com/2005/02/20/weekinreview/europes-jews-seek-solace-on-the-right.html, stated that the then twenty-four-year-old Gisèle Oreibi was formally expelled from Egypt along with her parents. This was never the case, but she did arrive in London as a stateless person in 1957.
11. Schwartz, "The Protocols of the Elders of Brussels."
12. John W. Whitehead, "Eurabia: The Euro-Arab Axis–An Interview with Bat Ye'or," *Oldspeak*, June 9, 2005, https://www.rutherford.org/publications_resources/oldspeak/eurabia_the_euro_arab_axis_an_interview_with_bat_yeor.
13. Michael M. Laskier, "The Emigration of the Jews from the Arab World," in *A History of Jewish-Muslim Relations: From the Origins to the Present Day*, trans. Jane Marie Todd, ed. Michael B. Smith, Abdelwahab Meddeb, and Benjamin Stora (Princeton, NJ: Princeton University Press, 2013), 415–433.
14. Bat Ye'or and David Littman, *Islam and Dhimmitude: Where Civilizations Collide*, trans. Miriam Kochan (Madison, NJ: Farleigh Dickinson Press, 2001).
15. Bernard Lewis, *The Jews of Islam* (Princeton, NJ: Princeton University Press, 1984), 194.

16. Mark Sedgwick, "The Origins and Growth of the Eurabia Narrative," undated and incomplete draft manuscript provided to the author.
17. According to the coverage of this conference in the Israeli newspaper *Haaretz*, it was a French Muslim academic who reacted to Littman's appearance and lecture at this conference. See Schwartz, "The Protocols of the Elders of Brussels." The author of this essay has however been in contact with non-Israeli academics of Jewish background who were present at this conference, and who deemed her presence and appearance there "bizarre." *Haaretz*'s rendering of what transpired at this conference appears to be attributable to Wistrich's comments. Wistrich, a leading scholar of antisemitism, had by the time of inviting Littman to this conference also involved himself in the production of Islamophobic ideas and sentiments: he is listed as the academic advisor on the controversial 2005 documentary *Obsession: Radical Islam's War Against the West*, funded and produced in the US by the so-called Clarion Fund. According to the sociologist Cristopher A. Bail, the Clarion Fund was a "non-profit organization funded in 2006 to 'educate the American public on the most urgent threat of radical Islam.'" Its advisory board "featured prominent members of anti-Muslim organizations such as Frank Gaffney . . ., Daniel Pipes . . . and Walid Phares." The film "made frequent comparisons between radical Islamic groups and the Nazis, claiming to provide an "insider's view of the hatred . . . radicals are teaching . . . and their goal of world domination." Christopher A. Bail, *Terrified: How Anti-Muslim Fringe Organizations Became Mainstream* (Princeton, NJ: Princeton University Press, 2015), 83.
18. Sydney H. Griffith, review of *The Decline of Eastern Christianity: From Jihad to Dhimmitude: Seventh–Twentieth Century*, by Bat Ye'or, *International Journal of Middle East Studies* 30, no. 4 (1998): 619–621.
19. Jerry Gordon, "An Egyptian Jew in Exile: An Interview with Bat Ye'or," *New English Review*, October 2011, http://www.newenglishreview.org/custpage.cfm/frm/98500/sec_id/98500.
20. Mark Silk, "Notes on the Judeo-Christian Tradition in America," *American Quarterly* 36, no. 1 (1984): 65–85.
21. M. J. C. Warren, "Why 'Judeo-Christian Values' are a Dog-Whistle Myth Peddled by the Far Right,' *Conversation*, November 7, 2017, http://theconversation.com/why-judeo-christian-values-are-a-dog-whistle-myth-peddled-by-the-far-right-85922.
22. Pål Norheim, "Hvem stakk av med arvesølvet?" *Vagant* 4, 2012, http://www.vagant.no/hvem-stakk-av-med-arvesolvet/.
23. Michael A. Sells, "Christ Killer, Kremlin, Contagion," in *The New Crusades: Constructing the Muslim Enemy*, ed. Emran Qureshi and Michael A. Sells (New York: Columbia University Press, 2003), 363, 382.
24. Tone Bringa, *Being Muslim the Bosnian Way: Identity and Community in a Central Bosnian Village* (Princeton, NJ: Princeton University Press, 1995).

25. Bangstad, *Anders Breivik and the Rise of Islamophobia*, 150.
26. J. Van Vuuren, "Spur to violence? Anders Behring Breivik and the Eurabia conspiracy," *Nordic Journal of Migration Research* 3, no. 4 (2013): 205–215, DOI: https://doi.org/10.2478/njmr-2013-0013.
27. Andrew F. Brown, "Anders Breivik's Spider Web of Hate," *Guardian*, September 7, 2011, https://www.theguardian.com/commentisfree/2011/sep/07/anders-breivik-hate-manifesto.
28. Vidar Enebakk, "Fjordmans radikalisering," in *Høyreekstreme ideer og bevegelser i Europa*, ed. Øystein Sørensen, Bernt Hagtvet, Bjørn Arne Steine (Oslo: Dreyer), 45–101; Peter Jackson, "The Licence to Hate: Peder Jensen's Fascist Rhetoric in Anders Breivik's Manifesto 2083: A European Declaration of Independence," *Democracy and Security* 9, no. 3 (2013): 247–269.
29. Peder Are Nøstvold Jensen, "Islam og det åpne samfunn," blog post, *Verdens Gang Debatt*, August 21, 2003, http://vgd.no/index.php/samfunn/innvandring-rasisme-og-flerkultur/tema/465438/innlegg/.
30. Bruce Bawer, *The New Quislings: How the International Left Used the Oslo Massacre to Silence Debate About Islam* (London: Harper Collins, 2012).
31. Simen Sætre, *Fjordman: Portrett av en anti-islamist* (Oslo: Cappelen Damm, 2013).
32. Cass Sunstein, *Conspiracy Theories and Other Dangerous Ideas* (New York: Simon and Schuster, 2013).
33. Robert Spencer, *The Myth of Islamic Tolerance: How Islamic Law Treats Non-Muslims* (Amherst, MA: Prometheus Books, 2005).
34. For a genealogy and critique of the notion of the so-called Muslim world, see Cemil Aydin, *The Idea of the Muslim World* (Cambridge, MA: Harvard University Press, 2017).
35. Niall Ferguson, "The Way We Live Now: 4-4-04; Eurabia?" *New York Times Magazine*, April 4, 2004, http://www.nytimes.com/2004/04/04/magazine/the-way-we-live-now-4-4-04-eurabia.html.
36. Sedgwick, "Origins and Growth."
37. Samuel Orbaum, "Resentment and Revenge," *Jerusalem Post*, April 26, 2002. Cited by Sedgwick, "Origins and Growth."
38. Bat Ye'or, *Eurabia*, 9.
39. Ibid., 10.
40. Todd Shepard, *The Invention of Decolonization: The Algerian War and the Remaking of France* (Ithaca, NY: Cornell University Press, 2006).
41. Bat Ye'or, *Eurabia*, 10.
42. Ibid., 11.
43. Ibid., 20.
44. See Reza Zia-Ebrahimi, "When the Elders of Zion Relocated in Eurabia: Conspiratorial Racialization in Antisemitism and Islamophobia," *Patterns of Prejudice* 52, no. 4 (2018): 314–337.
45. Bat Ye'or, *Eurabia*, 148.

46. Ibid., 149.
47. Griffith, "Review of Bat Ye'or," 621.
48. Spencer, *The Myth of Islamic Tolerance*, 31, citing Bat Ye'or, *Decline of Eastern Christianity*.
49. Bat Ye'or, *Decline of Eastern Christianity*, 219.
50. See John Kelsay, *Arguing the Just War in Islam* (Cambridge, MA: Harvard University Press, 2009) for a good study of the concept of jihad in Islamic history.
51. Bat Ye'or, *Eurabia*, 31.
52. Ibid., 32.
53. Ibid., 31.
54. See Aydin, *The Idea of the Muslim World*; Caroline Frankel, *Osman's Dream: The Story of the Ottoman Empire 1300–1929* (London: John Murray, 2006); Eugene Rogan, *The Arabs: A History* (London: Penguin Press, 2012); and David Motadel, *Islam and Nazi Germany's War* (Cambridge, MA: Harvard University Press, 2015).

PART III

Emergent Thinkers

12

Mencius Moldbug and Neoreaction

Joshua Tait

IN 2007, CURTIS YARVIN began his weblog *Unqualified Reservations* in order to "build a new ideology."[1] Through dozens of posts as "Mencius Moldbug," the San Francisco–based software engineer developed a heady critique of democracy and the nature of knowledge. Seeking to break free from a "thought control" system dominated by soft-headed progressive elites, Moldbug rejects the "virus" of democracy. As an alternative philosophy, Moldbug fuses radical libertarian thought with authoritarianism as "neoreaction." Only a reassertion of authority and hierarchy against democracy and egalitarianism will halt society's catastrophic decline.

Moldbug is an early example of important new trends in radical Right thought and activism. His blog broached long-taboo themes within the mainstream American Right that have since gained currency among the Alt Right and even the Trump White House. He pioneered anonymous, online, antiprogressive activism through his blend of bleak political analysis and irreverent humor, prefiguring the Alt Right. Beyond the small movement of explicit neoreactionaries, Moldbug has links with the prominent radical Right website Breitbart, the former White House chief strategist Steve Bannon, and the influential billionaire investor Peter Thiel. Moldbug has helped popularize a burgeoning American right-wing turn against democracy and traditional conservative norms, and helped normalize racialist views previously absent from American conservatism. Moldbug is a new type of radical Right activist at odds with the conservative mainstream: young, coastal, anonymous, secular, male, and adept at manipulating digital technologies to advance an antiprogressive agenda.

The *Unqualified Reservations* blog garnered Moldbug's outsized influence for an anonymous blogger. He became the founding theorist of the "neoreactionary" movement, an online collection of writers determined to theorize a superior alternative to democracy. At least one neoreactionary colleague considers Moldbug "one of only a few political writers today who will be read one hundred years from now."[2] *Social Matter*, the "flagship Neoreactionary web magazine," and neoreaction.net, which collects Moldbug's work together with his influences and acolytes, are two of several interlinked online communities that regard Moldbug's work as an important rediscovery of the reactionary tradition.[3]

Sometimes called the "Reactionary Enlightenment," neoreaction is an alchemy of authoritarian and libertarian thought. As a neoreactionary, Moldbug resents the trajectory of modern history but doesn't share the "shipwrecked mind" typical of some reactionaries who project idealized visions onto the past, hoping to restore it by radical means.[4] Neoreactionaries consider the past instructive, perhaps even superior to the present, but are essentially futurists. Moldbug has a complex relationship to the Enlightenment values that dominate in mainstream American political thought. Unlike irrationalist thinkers like Julius Evola and Alain de Benoist, Moldbug believes in secular, observable reality clearly understandable by reason; his major complaint with progressivism is its alleged falsification of reality. Nor is he a "throne and altar" thinker. His ideal society is cosmopolitan and socially free. However, Moldbug also rejects key political ideals of the Enlightenment. He opposes human equality and the promises of democracy.

Neoreaction's vision is antihumanist and nihilistic. Moldbug thinks overwhelmingly in terms of systems and the grand, almost mechanistic, operation of laws, principles, and trends. His thought generally has little room for human agency. People, he argues, act within rigid structures, driven by basic motivations. The complexities of human behavior and society barely exist in his pursuit of the perfectly engineered political system. Nor does his focus on systems and rational behavior leave much room for the intricacies and durability of historically specific social norms, like business practices or kin relationships, lending Moldbug's thought a certain artificiality.

Moldbug strikingly shows how new web-based media promulgates radical Right ideas to new audiences. The web has fostered anonymous subcultures of socially disaffected people, fostering predominantly male antiprogressive subcultures.[5] Moldbug is both an influence on this class and an early instance of it. His antiprogressive critiques justify these groups' rejection of society. And because Moldbug largely uses online sources to develop his arguments, he also reflects new trends in right-wing thought and activism made possible by the internet's drastic lowering of barriers to entry into mass communication. Since 2010 online antiprogressive activism has grown dramatically. Digital activism takes many forms: verbal fights in the comments sections of major websites; Twitter "armies" of users sharing content en masse or targeting individuals for abuse. During the 2016 presidential election, radical Right activists generated thousands of darkly comic and politically loaded images or "memes" to attack Hillary Clinton. Sometimes online targeting becomes criminal with threats of violence and leaks of personal details.

There are important tensions in Moldbug's thought. He advocates hierarchy, yet deeply resents cultural elites. His political vision is futuristic and libertarian, yet expressed in the language of monarchy and reaction. He is irreligious and socially liberal on many issues but angrily antiprogressive. He presents himself as a thinker in search of truth but admits to lying to his readers, saturating his arguments with jokes and irony. These tensions indicate broader fissures among the online Right.

Technolibertarian Foundations

Part of Moldbug's mystique is that he comes from the "Brahmin" social class that, he claims, dominates the US. He was born in 1973 into a highly-educated secular Jewish family connected with the Ivy League and State Department. Moldbug spent parts of his childhood abroad, mainly in Cyprus, before returning to the US around 1985.[6] Shortly after, he was selected to participate in Johns Hopkins's longitudinal Study of Mathematically Precocious Youth. He entered college in 1988, graduating from Brown in 1992 before dropping out of the Computer Science Division of the University of California at Berkley.[7]

Moldbug was shaped by 1980s and 1990s Silicon Valley programmer and internet subculture. Before neoreaction, he explored libertarianism, a worldview that "in many-blossomed efflorescence" is the "pervasive *Weltanschauung*" of the overwhelmingly male American high-tech culture.[8] As Paulina Borsook argues, libertarianism fits with tech culture for several reasons. First, engineers like Yarvin are typically sorted through competitive academic programs, which they consider analogous to the competition imagined in a libertarian society. Secondly, their world is rational, rule-bound, and solvable. Within the subculture, computer software and hardware are the dominant metaphors for society. Such thinking dovetails with the ironclad assumptions about human and market behavior of the Austrian School of Economics led by Ludwig von Mises. Tech culture's systems focus also accords with libertarianism's concentration on efficiency and "solving" government. Finally, tech culture venerates science, treating human biology as determinative and confirming their mechanistic assumptions about humanity.

Silicon Valley libertarians are not nostalgic for a mythical past. Working with cutting-edge technology gives programmer culture a futurist bent that combines widespread enthusiasm for science fiction with the promises of the early internet. Science fiction has long been used for political experimentation: seminal writers like Ursula Le Guin and Robert Heinlein consciously used the genre to explore libertarian concepts and imagine possible alternative regimes. For early adopters, the internet was a digital libertarian society. It offered privacy, free-thinking, and ordered but essentially free interaction.[9] These themes became technolibertarian priorities and saturate Moldbug's mature writing.

Embracing Reaction: From Misesian to Carlylean

Moldbug's intellectual trajectory was a rightward march. He shifted from the liberalism of his family, through the cultural libertarianism of Silicon Valley, in and out of mainstream American conservatism and radical libertarianism, and ultimately arrived at neoreaction. Much of Moldbug's political evolution happened online, where he had access to right-wing texts and avenues to pursue a study in right-wing thought. Moldbug read numerous key thinkers of mainstream American conservatism.

The libertarian University of Tennessee law professor and blogger Glenn Reynolds introduced Moldbug to the radical libertarian tradition, informed by the early twentieth-century Austrian-American economist Ludwig von Mises.[10] One of Mises's most important American popularizers, Murray Rothbard, excoriated government intervention, advocating an anarcho-capitalist alternative.[11] Mises and the Austrian School reject empiricism in favor of deductive reasoning from assumptions about human behavior and economic principles. This "applied logic" economics coheres with Moldbug's engineering mind-set. For Moldbug, Mises "is a titan" and

"Rothbard is a giant."[12] However, although he continues to embrace important aspects of libertarianism, Moldbug's reading of the nineteenth-century Scottish philosopher Thomas Carlyle convinced him that without authoritarianism, libertarianism was ineffectual at best and destructive at worst.

Moldbug's first break with democracy came through Rothbard's intellectual successor, Hans-Hermann Hoppe. In his 2001 book, *Democracy: The God that Failed*, Hoppe argued that in order to appease voters, democratic leaders have every incentive to exhaust resources and mismanage the economy for short-term gains. Democracy, he argues, causes long-term civilizational decline. By contrast, because monarchies are the private domain of monarchs, they are incentivized to maximize profits over the long-term. Moreover, conflicts between monarchies are shorter and less destructive than democratic conflicts, partly because prolonged warfare risks damaging the monarch's property.[13] Moldbug laments that Hoppe is "a sound formalist at every layer up to the top," but rejects "sovereign property as a royalist plot."[14] For Moldbug, Hoppe's failure of nerve illustrates the extent of the progressive hegemony that prohibits people from entertaining nonconsensual politics.

Another of Moldbug's principal influences was the conservative theorist James Burnham, whose thought informs Moldbug's "realism" and attention to power structures. Burnham argued that politics cannot be understood by studying rhetoric, where aims are metaphysical and unachievable. "Real" politics occurs through actions and power manipulation. In *The Machiavellians*, a chapter of which Moldbug reproduced in full on his blog, Burnham argued that good political thought reasons inductively from the past and present to reach conclusions about the struggle for power.[15] Burnham placed himself in the tradition of the Italian post-Marxist "Elitists" Gaetano Mosca, Robert Michels, and Vilfredo Pareto. This loose group's central theme was the "iron law of oligarchy:" beneath democratic or socialist rhetoric, societies are dominated by elites. Accordingly, Burnham came to believe that managing elites to maximize liberty and "civilization" for nonelites was the essential task of political actors.

Drawing Hoppe and Burnham's antidemocratic insights together with radical libertarianism, Moldbug made a final leap into reaction with his discovery of Thomas Carlyle. "Carlyle is the greatest of all," he rhapsodized, "because his vision is the broadest." While "Mises is almost never wrong," Carlyle is wrong "frequently." The Scotsman's "strokes are big. He excavates with a pick, not a dental drill. But there is really nothing in Mises' philosophy that is not in Carlyle; and the converse is not the case." Moldbug endorses Carlyle's stress on order above all else, embracing Carlyle's belief that the conflict between left and right is ultimately "the struggle between order and chaos." "Evil is chaos; good is order. Evil is left; good is right."[16] Moldbug jokes that *Unqualified Reservations* is a "late, decadent, second-rate imitation of Carlyle."[17]

In many ways, Moldbug remains committed to radical libertarianism, but he believes libertarianism has failed because it presupposes order. Without order, agitating for liberty creates chaos and violence, which inhibits freedom far more than the state does. By prioritizing order above all, Moldbug left behind Mises and Rothbard—even Hoppe and Burnham—and embraced reaction.

Unqualified Reservations and the Desert of the Real

Yarvin's only work as Moldbug is the blog *Unqualified Reservations*, which he began in 2007. Moldbug's critique of the mainstream American Right emerged in response to seven years of American conservatism comfortable with the role of the federal government. The failure of American nation-building in Iraq and Afghanistan reinforced his antidemocratic inclinations, just as the federal response to the 2008 financial crisis offended his libertarian sensibilities. The jubilation around Obama's candidacy, and then the Obama presidency, fueled Moldbug's resentment and confirmed his belief in history's inevitable leftward trajectory.

The now-defunct blog used the online medium effectively. It featured frequent updates, sometimes strung together as a series. The basic structure of Moldbug's major posts was a critique of progressive hegemony loaded with "jolts" to wrench readers free from its grasp, followed by a justification of antidemocratic politics, a sketch of an alternative system, and a program for neoreactionaries. Moldbug adopted a conversational and referential tone, alluding to science, history, sci-fi, and political and mathematical theory. Through ubiquitous hyperlinks (largely Wikipedia and Google Books, but also right-wing websites and blogs), Moldbug shared these references with his reader, developing a web of common allusion and meaning. Because each post was published separately, Moldbug built his arguments publicly, sometimes in conversation with readers. One result of this process was frequent terminological reinvention. Although his conclusions remained fairly consistent, Moldbug created numerous neologisms for social classes, problems, and solutions in an attempt to generate language free of "progressive" taint. The overall effect of the language and style of his blog is of joining a conspiracy and entering a world of illicit knowledge.

Moldbug offers a totalizing explanation of elite liberal domination that justifies right-wing rejection of mainstream news sources and academia. Beneath the rhetoric of democracy, the progressive political and social order is an "intellectual political machine" that dictates acceptable and unacceptable thought. Moldbug initially called this regime "Orwellian" (elsewhere he more accurately calls it Gramscian and Moscan, alluding to Marxist and post-Marxist thinkers who argued that elites produce cultures to justify their dominance). Unlike Orwell's Oceania, progressive hegemony is decentered, self-regulating, even elegant, but acutely pernicious. It "has no center, no master planners," but reproduces an intellectual elite class whose control over "mass opinion creates power. Power diverts funds to the manufacturers of opinion, who manufacture more," perpetuating progressive control.[18]

Moldbug calls this "feedback loop" "the Cathedral." He argues that progressive elites have established "universalism," a secularized liberal Protestantism, as the implicit state religion. Universalism's pervasiveness and assumed infallibility infuriate him: he objects "most of all to the insidious way in which the Cathedral has managed to mutate its way around the 'separation of church and state' in which it so hypocritically indoctrinates its acolytes."[19] Molbug's fixation on free thought reflects the concerns of his technolibertarian milieu taken to conspiratorial conclusions.

Moldbug's epistemological critique is typically associated with the Left.[20] But unlike left-wing antifoundationalists comfortable with relativistic concepts of knowledge, Moldbug does not reject the concept of objective reality. Reflecting the polarized approach to knowledge in American politics, Moldbug, like the mainstream American Right, is committed to universal truth.[21] He argues that the Left constructs false knowledge that obscures actual reality and attacks the alleged progressive control of the media and institutions of power. In doing so, he extends the long-standing conservative claim that biased, left-wing media and scholarship is damaging the US.[22] But Moldbug goes much further. He argues that democracy and political equality, values common to the American Left and Right, are fraudulent productions of the Cathedral.

To shock readers free from progressive control, Moldbug uses thought experiments and presents contemporary problems in alien ways. To illustrate the power dynamics inherent in constructing knowledge, for example, he imagines a Nazi Wikipedia reliant on Nazi-approved sources. Many of Moldbug's arguments, especially those critical of the Left, are mainstream conservative positions repackaged in calculatedly provocative terms. To critique affirmative action he describes a society with a protected class of "nobles," gradually revealed to be African Americans. Like many American conservatives, he dismisses climate change science as an unfalsifiable government-funded boondoggle.[23]

Moldbug's treatment of race, however, skirts and exceeds mainstream conservative acceptability.[24] Moldbug views "human neurological uniformity" and antiracism as central pillars of universalism. During the 2008 presidential election, he decried the "fundamentally predatory nature of the black power movement" created by civil rights programs. Minority crime, in particular, preoccupies Moldbug. He returned to the subject repeatedly on his blog, highlighting the alleged burying of the problem of black violent crime by the universalist media.

His blog uses some racial epithets to defy politically correct language conventions.[25] He also put some relatively mainstream conservative positions in inflammatory terms. He argued that if civil rights programs were applied to America's "WASP-Ashkenazi" population, a group of "genuine genetic elites with average IQs of 120" it would "take no more than two generations to produce a culture of worthless, unredeemable scoundrels." Since these programs were "applied to populations with recent hunter-gatherer ancestry and no great reputation for sturdy moral fiber," the result was "absolute human garbage."[26] Moldbug's point—that welfare and affirmation action programs have deleterious effects on those they are intended to help—is uncontroversial on the right, but Moldbug phrases his claim to incite.[27]

Moldbug's racial comments suggest a broader trend: the anonymity of the internet allows him and others who have followed in his wake to revel in taboo language, ideas, and activities. Violating social norms is a kind of liberation for Moldbug: entertaining these ideas is to break from the Cathedral. Moldbug provides a theoretical justification for the extremely transgressive anonymous message boards and political "shitposting" that has manifested online in the past decade.[28]

The complete ideological transformation required to cast off the Cathedral is alienating, Moldbug admits, but intoxicating. Moldbug calls this process "taking the 'Red Pill,'" a reference to the film *The Matrix* (1999) in which the protagonist chooses between swallowing a red pill and escaping a dull digital prison or accepting a blue pill to remain in ignorant normalcy. The Red Pill trope is common among web-based right-wing and antifeminist movements, from the racialist Alt Right to politicized "gamers," "pick-up artists," and the "involuntarily celibate," (incels). Angela Nagle suggests it is an especially potent symbol for the growing number of alienated men. The Red Pill idea rationalizes their isolation and justifies their antiegalitarianism.[29]

The Real Enemy is Democracy

Moldbug believes that under the Cathedral's spurious commitment to equality and justice is a system of power manipulation. Neoreaction's basic assumption is that humans desire power. Interpreting democracy through this framework, Moldbug claims that democracy's appeal is that it disperses power widely, indulging the mass desire for useless fragments of power. Since power-seeking is pervasive, society trends toward greater division of power and a concomitant erosion of order. Democracy is a "dangerous, malignant form of government which tends to degenerate, sometimes slowly and sometimes with shocking, gut-wrenching speed, into tyranny and chaos." Within the Cathedral, it is rational to obey the rules of the system. Ambitious individuals are incentivized to embrace progressive dogma, hence a class of Brahmin progressive elites.

Moldbug rejects the classic republican premise that divided sovereignty constrains governments. Instead, he argues that each branch of government metastasizes, expanding the size and the scope of the state. Strong governments with clear hierarchies, however, remain small and narrowly focused. With this insight, Moldbug justifies authoritarianism on libertarian grounds. The minimal state is achieved by making government strong, not by weakening it.

Neoreactionaries look to non-Western states as alternatives. Moldbug admires Deng Xiaoping for the Chinese leader's pragmatic, market-oriented authoritarianism, and praises Singapore as a successful authoritarian regime.[30] By contrast, he sees the US as soft on crime, economically delusional, and dominated by Brahmins. The subjects of democracy cannot recognize its flaws. They have "been taught to worship democracy." Elections give the illusion of responding to social demands but are false safety valves that mask progressive control. Since power-seeking is basic to human nature, democratic drift is chronic. "Cthulu may swim slowly," Moldbug wrote, alluding to the hideous Lovecraftian deity, "but he always swims left."[31]

Neoreaction's decline story bemoans the defeat of reactionary regimes and expansion of progressive dominance in the US and around the world. Although he does not endorse them, Moldbug argues that Wilhelmine and Nazi Germany fought defensive wars against progressive global conquest. He depicts the American Revolution as rabble-rousers violently opposed to responsible Tories and, drawing on libertarian Confederate-apologia, construes the American Civil War as the violent imposition of progressivism on the South.[32] On the flip side, the progressive marriage between "Harvard" and government that forms the Cathedral came in two stages. In the 1870s and 1880s, the Liberal Republican civil-service reforms politicized the American academic class. Franklin Roosevelt, a classic libertarian villain, completed the merger of academia and politics through the New Deal and its "brains trust."[33]

Moldbug's treatment of historic reactionary regimes also features antidemocratic caveats that distinguish neoreaction from other movements. Fascism and Nazism were right-wing phenomena, to be sure, but Moldbug maintains that they were historically specific, democratic distortions of the Right's core truth. Order and authority are commonsensical but unpopular. Advancing order and authority through democracy typically means joining it with another motivating force like anti-Semitism or nationalism. Nationalism of any kind, including white nationalism, is dangerous precisely because it is democratic. Moldbug's revisionist histories place the blame for the horrors of the twentieth century squarely at the feet of democracy.

What Is to be Done?

The fact that egalitarian rhetoric conceals the rule of progressive elites is Moldbug's starting point. The solution is for political discourse to match real power dynamics. Although he moved away from the term, Moldbug proposed "Formalism"—the formal recognition of realities of power—as an alternative ideology. Denuded of rhetoric, Americans are "serfs" and the "US is just a corporation . . . not a mystic trust consigned to us by the generations."[34] After laying the realities of political power bare, Moldbug began "solving" the "engineering problem" of political organization.

There are two aspects of Moldbug's ideal regime: the political structure and the civil society it engenders. In effect, Moldbug imagines a radical libertarian utopia with maximum freedom in all things *except politics*. The ideal economic order is a thoroughgoing acceptance of

Misesian microeconomics. Moldbug proposes nationalizing every asset and node of power in exchange for cash and then either privatizing them at auction or destroying them, creating a cash-rich, entirely privatized society.[35] Moldbug envisages an "open society" of free thought and behavior constrained by rigorously enforced laws protecting contracts and preventing violence.[36] Many of Moldbug's views on social issues are conventionally libertarian—he has written in favor of same-sex marriage, the toleration of private religion, private drug use, and against race- or gender-based discriminatory laws (although he self-consciously proposed private welfare and prison reforms that resembled slavery). Within a correctly engineered authoritarian order, Moldbug assumes that maximum economic freedom produces the best society. There are libertarian precedents for this assumption, especially the libertarian Right's engagement with Augusto Pinochet's Chile in the 1970s and 1980s.

The libertarian aspect of Moldbug's thought is overshadowed by his antiprogressivism and stark Carlylean authority. Because the most ordered system is a unitary command structure with a clear hierarchy, Moldbug's model for a new political order is the corporation. He proposes that the state is privatized to incentivize profit-maximizing governance by "shareholders" (large owners) who vote for a CEO-monarch. More Steve Jobs than Henry VIII, the monarch has absolute authority but serves at the shareholders' pleasure. Moldbug calls this corporate-monarchy regime "neocameralism." By limiting politics to this narrow domain, Moldbug reasons it creates space for a libertarian paradise.[37] Moldbug calls himself a "Jacobite" and favors the restoration of the House of Stuart, but the details of his futurist monarchy are less important than the thrust toward the total privatization and authoritarianism.[38]

Drawing on an implicit machine metaphor, he argues that society needs a "hard reset" not gradual political reform. But Moldbug's strategy for the destroying the Cathedral further distinguishes him from other right-wing movements. He forbids neoreactionaries from engaging in any form of activism, "violent or harmless, legal or illegal, fashionable or despicable." Even voting is borderline. Instead, Moldbug advocates "the Steel Rule of Passivism." He counsels readers that "since you believe others should be willing to accept the rule of the New Structure, over which they wield no power, you must be the first to make the great refusal."[39] Moldbug's rationale is that progressivism feeds on right-wing opposition. By remaining passive, neoreaction "starves" progressivism of a necessary enemy. Without a "loyal opposition," "progressivism collapses into sclerosis." Eschewing politics also safeguards neoreaction from cooption by those attracted to power, "vaccinat[ing] itself against Hitler."[40]

Moldbug concedes that destroying progressivism is implausible. But he thinks that with the internet it is possible. He suggests the collapse of the Soviet Union as a model to follow. The sclerosis of the American government and the disjuncture between power structures and political rhetoric will naturally undermine confidence in the state. But indoctrinated Americans also needed a visible alternative. The neoreactionary's task is to create a clear and obvious alternative or "Schelling Point." The first steps are challenging the Cathedral intellectually and theorizing an alternative. Moldbug distills his plan into the mantra "Become worthy; Accept power; Rule." Having begun the creation of the Schelling Point, in 2013 Moldbug drastically reduced his blogging and, after two years of silence, announced in April 2016 that *Unqualified Reservations* had "completed its mission."[41]

Harbinger and Archetype

It can be difficult to gage the seriousness of Moldbug's project. On the one hand, his droll tone and outlandish statements make it tempting to dismiss him as a prank. There is some evidence to this effect. The Kindle versions of his posts are published by the winkingly named TRO LLC. In one particular post, Moldbug discusses at length Daniel Defoe's *The Shortest Way with the Dissenters*, a 1702 pamphlet that parodied Tory propaganda to discredit the Right.[42] It is possible that Moldbug highlighted the pamphlet to indicate the reality of his blog.

However, Moldbug should be taken seriously. Despite some outlandishness, his core critiques and basic proposals are consistent, and his use of exaggeration is purposeful. Neoreaction treats taboo thought as liberation, and Moldbug's use of comedy and transgression make sense within this framework. His real identity was revealed online around 2012, and his tech work has occasionally suffered as a result. Two tech-expos disinvited him in 2015 and 2016 causing minor controversy, and Moldbug-Yarvin has since defended *Unqualified Reservations* under his own name.[43]

Even if Yarvin had not done this, there would be reason to reckon with Moldbug. Regardless of his intent, *Unqualified Reservations* developed a dedicated following who read Moldbug seriously. Moldbug's approach reflects the online turn toward absurdist memes and "trolling," the act of inciting outrage by adopting provocative beliefs or actions. Simultaneously ironic and sincere, trolling makes it impossible to disentangle the serious from the intentionally provocative. If Moldbug is a prototroll, his blog is intended to challenge society and cause teeth-gnashing in mainstream publications like the *Atlantic* and the *Nation*. Most importantly, antiprogressive arguments resembling Moldbug's have entered the public square. Moldbug was a harbinger of an antiprogressive trend most apparent in the 2016 presidential election.

Donald Trump and his surrogates sounded neoreactionary notes in their condemnation of progressivism and the media. According to *Politico*, the Breitbart executive chairman and Trump advisor Steve Bannon read and admired Moldbug's work, which confirmed Bannon's conviction that liberal technocrats were destroying "Western Civilization." Though criticism of progressivism and liberal media bias have long histories in mainstream conservatism, Trump and Moldbug are distinct for their tone, use of alternative media types, and disrespect for prevailing norms.

But neoreaction is also at odds with some of conservatism's core tenets. Moldbug's philosophy is hyperindividualistic, thoroughly deracinated from the regional, national, and religious identities conservatives traditionally emphasize. He rejects patriotism, constitutionalism, and populism. Most of the conservative Right venerates a narrow vision of America's political tradition utterly distinct from Moldbug's vision of corporate feudalism.

Moldbug's relationship with white nationalism is also thorny. He is "not exactly allergic to" white nationalist writers and accepts racialist claims about "human biodiversity" but disavows it for political reasons. While racialist thought may be "a sensible description of a general problem," it suggests erroneous solutions. White nationalism is misguided because it emphasizes race rather than intelligence. More importantly, identitarian politics are flawed because they are democratic and counterproductive because they energize the Left.[44] Neoreactionaries have distanced themselves from the Alt Right and white-identity politics. Nick Land, another neoreactionary thinker, says he does not "think the Alt-Right (in America) is very serious."[45] Privately, however, Moldbug has suggested that this distancing is a tactical consideration. In a message to Milo Yiannopoulos, then a Breitbart reporter, on how to relate to neo-Nazis, Moldbug counseled Yiannopoulos to "deal with them the way some perfectly tailored high-communist NYT reporter handles a herd of greasy anarchist hippies. Patronizing contempt." Although disdainful of the neo-Nazi Right, Moldbug sees them as a part of a broad right-wing assault on the Left. Neoreaction's dismissal of neo-Nazism is cultural and tactical, but not entirely ideological. "The liberal doesn't purge the communist because he hates communism," Moldbug told Yiannopoulos. He purges them "because the communist is a public embarrassment to him." Neo-Nazis are losers "and losers rub off."[46]

Where Moldbug has been most influential is among radical libertarians and in burgeoning online subcultures. His overt anti-democracy is a departure for American libertarianism but has a small but growing influence, especially following the 2008 financial crisis. Prominent libertarian investors Balaji Srinivasan and Peter Thiel have echoed Neoreactionary themes about seceding from the US for tech-CEO dictatorships.

Moldbug's relationship with the investor-entrepreneur Thiel is his most important connection. Thiel has considerable influence within mainstream and libertarian circles. He was seriously considered for a cabinet position in the Trump White House, sits on the boards of several major companies, including Facebook, and is a majority shareholder in Palantir, a major intelligence contractor. Thiel invested in Yarvin's tech company and wrote while recommending *Unqualified Reservations*, that he "no longer believe[s] that freedom and democracy are compatible."[47] In 2016 Moldbug privately boasted that he had been "coaching Thiel" who is "fully enlightened" but "plays it very carefully."[48] Moldbug exemplifies an important trend in radical libertarianism: a grim view of contemporary society but supreme confidence in technology and the private sector to supersede traditional politics.

Moldbug is perhaps best understood as an online archetype. Especially with the growth of social media and the availability of video technology, many right-wing activists have adeptly harnessed the web to create and propagate their philosophies. The unprecedented platform of the internet provides a space and audience for their world-historical theories. What Moldbug captured in his verbose posts was a growing sense of social frustration among mostly white, middle-class males resentful of diminished economic and social fortunes in a diverse, economically slowing, post–Third Wave feminist society. This frustration manifests itself as misanthropic superiority. *Unqualified Reservations* was the "highbrow" predecessor and later companion to the transgressive anti-"politically correct" metapolitics of nebulous online communities like 4chan and /pol/. Moldbug represents a new type of thinker inseparable from the internet. Moldbug was among the first of this new type of digital ideologue, but he is far from the last.

Notes

1. Mencius Moldbug, "A Formalist Manifesto," *Unqualified Reservations* (blog) (hereafter *UR*), April 23, 2007, http://unqualified-reservations.blogspot.com/2007/04/formalist-manifesto-originally-posted.html. Moldbug's identity is now public knowledge, but his blog posts are cited as he posted them under his *nom de web*.
2. Justine Alexandra Roberts Tunney, introduction to *A Gentle Introduction to Unqualified Reservations*, by Mencius Moldbug (New York: TRO LLC, 2009), vii.
3. www.socialmatter.net.
4. Mark Lilla, *The Shipwrecked Mind: On Political Reaction* (New York: New York Review of Books, 2016), ix–xxi.
5. Angela Nagle, *Kill All Normies: The Online Culture Wars from Tumblr and 4chan to the Alt-Right and Trump* (Washington, DC: Zero Books, 2017).
6. Mencius Moldbug, "How I Stopped Believing in Democracy," *UR*, Jan 31, 2008, http://unqualified-reservations.blogspot.com/2008/01/how-i-stopped-believing-in-democracy.html.
7. SMPY at JHU Precollege Newsletter, no. 10, Sept 1, 1988, 2. Found at https://digital.library.unt.edu/ark:/67531/metadc268929/m1/2/; Curtis Yarvin, Richard Bukowski, and Thomas Anderson, "Anonymous RPC: Low-Latency Protection in a 64-Bit Address Space," in *Proc. Of the 1993 Summer Usenix Conference*, 175–186, June 1993.
8. Paulina Borsook, *Cyberselfish: A Critical Romp Through the Terribly Libertarian Culture of High Tech* (New York: PublicAffairs, 2000), 3.
9. Ibid.
10. Mencius Moldbug, "OL8: A Reset is Not a Revolution," *UR*, June 5, 2009, http://unqualified-reservations.blogspot.com/2008/06/ol8-reset-is-not-revolution.html.
11. George Hawley, *Rightwing Critics of American Conservatism* (Lawrence: University of Kansas Press, 2016), 145–178; George H. Nash, *The Conservative Intellectual Movement in America since 1945* (Wilmington, DE: ISI Books, 2006), 497–499.
12. Mencius Moldbug, "From Mises to Carlyle: My Sick Journey to the Dark Side of the Force," *UR*, February 4, 2010, https://unqualified-reservations.blogspot.com/2010/02/from-mises-to-carlyle-my-sick-journey.html.
13. Hans-Hermann Hoppe, *Democracy—The God That Failed: The Economics and Politics of Monarchy, Democracy, and Natural Order* (New Brunswick, NJ: Transaction, 2002).
14. Mencius Moldbug, "OLXII: What Is to be Done?," *UR*, July 2, 2008, http://unqualified-reservations.blogspot.com/2008/07/olxii-what-is-to-be-done.html.
15. James Burnham, *The Machiavellians: Defenders of Freedom* (New York: John Day, 1943).
16. Moldbug, "From Mises to Carlyle."

17. Mencius Moldbug, "A Gentle Introduction (part 4)," *UR*, January 29, 2009. http://unqualified-reservations.blogspot.com/2009/01/gentle-introduction-to-unqualified_29.html.
18. Mencius Moldbug, "OLXIV: Rules for Reactionaries," *UR*, July 17, 2008, http://unqualified-reservations.blogspot.com/2008/07/.
19. Mencius Moldbug, "OL9: How to Uninstall a Cathedral," *UR*, June 12, 2008, https://unqualified-reservations.blogspot.com/2008/06/ol9-how-to-uninstall-cathedral.html.
20. For example, Michel Foucault, Jacques Derrida, or Judith Butler.
21. Andrew Hartman, *A War for the Soul of America: A History of the Culture Wars* (Chicago: University of Chicago Press, 2015), 113.
22. Nicole Hemmer, *Messengers of the Right: Conservative Media and the Transformation of American Politics* (Philadelphia: University of Pennsylvania Press, 2016).
23. Mencius Moldbug, "OL5: The Shortest Way to World Peace," *UR*, May 15, 2008, http://unqualified-reservations.blogspot.com/2008/05/ol5-shortest-way-to-world-peace.html; "A Gentle Introduction (part 3)," *UR*, January 22, 2009, http://unqualified-reservations.blogspot.com/2009/01/gentle-introduction-to-unqualified_22.html.
24. Hawley, *Rightwing Critics*, 67–70.
25. Mencius Moldbug, "Why I Am Not a White Nationalist," *UR*, November 22, 2007, http://unqualified-reservations.blogspot.com/2007/11/why-i-am-not-white-nationalist.html.
26. Mencius Moldbug, "A Gentle Introduction (part 4)," *UR*, January 29, 2009, http://unqualified-reservations.blogspot.com/2009/01/.
27. Hartman, *War for the Soul of America*, 113–114.
28. Nagle, *Kill All Normies*, 28–39.
29. Ibid., 86–100.
30. Mencius Moldbug, "OL7: The Ugly Truth about Government," *UR*, May 29, 2008, http://unqualified-reservations.blogspot.com/2008/05.
31. Moldbug, "A Gentle Introduction (part 1)."
32. Moldbug, "A Gentle Introduction (part 7)," *UR*, March 5, 2009, http://unqualified-reservations.blogspot.com/2009/03/gentle-introduction-to-unqualified.html.
33. Moldbug, "A Gentle Introduction (part 6)," *UR*, February 19, 2009, http://unqualified-reservations.blogspot.com/2009/02/gentle-introduction-to-unqualified_19.html.; "OL8."
34. Moldbug, "A Formalist Manifesto."
35. Moldbug, "A Gentle Introduction (part 4)."
36. Moldbug, "OL4: Dr Johnson's Hypothesis," *UR*, May 8, 2008, http://unqualified-reservations.blogspot.com/2008/05/ol4-dr-johnsons-hypothesis.html.
37. Moldbug, "How Dawkins Got Pwned [sic] (part 6)," *UR*, November 1, 2007, http://unqualified-reservations.blogspot.com/2007/11/how-dawkins-got-pwned-part-6.html.

38. Moldbug, "OL8." (see n8)
39. Moldbug, "A Gentle Introduction (part 9a)," *UR*, September 3, 2009, https://unqualified-reservations.blogspot.com/2009/09/gentle-introduction-to-unqualified.html.
40. Ibid.
41. Moldbug, "Coda," *UR*, April 18, 2016, http://unqualified-reservations.blogspot.com/2016/04/.
42. Moldbug, "OL5: The Shortest Way to World Peace," *UR*, May 15, 2008, http://unqualified-reservations.blogspot.com/2008/05/ol5-shortest-way-to-world-peace.html."
43. Curtis Yarvin, "Why You Should Come to LambdaConf Anyway," *Medium*, March 27, 2016, https://medium.com/@curtis.yarvin/why-you-should-come-to-lambdaconf-anyway-35ff8cd4fb9d.
44. Ibid.
45. George Hawley, *Making Sense of the Alt-Right* (New York: Columbia University Press, 2017), 45–50.
46. Joseph Bernstein, "Alt-White: How the Breitbart Machine Laundered Racist Hate," *BuzzFeedNews*, October 5, 2017, https://www.buzzfeed.com/josephbernstein/heres-how-breitbart-and-milo-smuggled-white-nationalism?utm_term=.ptROyy5xq#.kcGyRRPNv.
47. Peter Thiel, "The Education of a Libertarian," *Cato Unbound*, April 13, 2009, https://www.cato-unbound.org/2009/04/13/peter-thiel/education-libertarian; Corey Pein, "Mouthbreathing Machiavelli's Dream of a Silicon Reich," *Baffler*, May 19, 2014, https://thebaffler.com/latest/mouthbreathing-machiavellis.
48. Bernstein, "Alt-White."

13

Greg Johnson and Counter-Currents

Graham Macklin

GREG JOHNSON IS editor-in-chief of Counter-Currents, an esoteric and metapolitical website created in 2010 "as a space for a dialogue in which a new intellectual movement, a North American New Right, might emerge."[1] Counter-Currents also provides "a critique of liberal modernity in North America in the light of Traditionalism and the ideas of the European New Right."[2] Both his website and publishing imprint, which bears the same name, attest to Johnson's enduring concern: "metapolitics"—a precursor to politics, which aims to provide the "correct" ideological foundations upon which to erect a cultural and intellectual movement in North America capable of affecting "real" political change that will, ultimately, underpin the establishment of a white "ethnostate."

Biographical details are scant, though one can trace an outline of Johnson's early intellectual trajectory through various published interviews. His father was a staunch Democrat and union member. Born in 1971, Johnson gravitated toward libertarianism in high school, imbibing the work of Ayn Rand as a college freshman: "I was a bit of a boy Objectivist . . . for a couple of years because of that," he recalled. Interested in philosophy, his reading propelled him beyond Rand toward paleoconservatism and, ultimately, white nationalism. Johnson was "somewhat pro-Zionist" in his early twenties, and despite admiring the ideas of Leo Strauss in graduate school, increasingly perceived a "definite Jewish bias" in neoconservatism, becoming, he recalled, "more keyed into the Jewish slant on things." Johnson's increasingly anti-Jewish

Weltanschauung crystallized after encountering the controversy surrounding Heidegger's National Socialism. For Johnson, this "really called forth a lot of rhetorical thuggery . . . on the part of Jewish commentators, and it just didn't sit well with me." Having argued with Jewish graduate students about this, Johnson subsequently evoked a parallel between his own anti-Semitic acculturation and that undergone by Hitler. Relating the passage from *Mein Kampf* in which the future Führer claims to have spent hours debating and, he believed, demolishing the arguments of Viennese Jewish socialists only to see them carry on regardless, impervious to his logic, Johnson stated: "That's when I knew this guy [Hitler] was telling the truth. That was so powerful. I'd seen that with my own eyes."[3]

The subsequent publication of Heidegger's *Black Notebooks (Schwartze Hefte)*, in which he recorded his private philosophical musings, later confirmed to Johnson that Heidegger believed he might shape an intellectually coherent foundation for National Socialism and thereby help it understand its own "inner truth and greatness" with regards its role in "the confrontation of historical man with global technological civilization." For this reason, Heidegger had an enduring influence upon the New Right and on Johnson personally.[4] Indeed, Johnson claims that "the outline of a post-totalitarian, postmodernist New Right first emerges in these diaries of a dissident National Socialist."[5] Heidegger also served as an intellectual bridge in Johnson's own development. A favorite Heidegger scholar was Thomas Sheehan of Stanford, whose work introduced Johnson to Alain de Benoist and Julius Evola.[6]

After studying for a philosophy PhD,[7] Johnson moved to Atlanta, Georgia. In late 1999 or early 2000 a chance meeting with Joshua Buckley, a former skinhead who subsequently edited *Tyr*[8] (a radical Traditionalist, neopagan journal devoted to "Myth–Culture–Tradition") proved pivotal: "Not just eye-opening, world-opening." So fortified, Johnson took the plunge, transitioning from private intellectualizing to political engagement. His first step was attending a lecture given by the British Holocaust denier David Irving in September 2000.[9]

Thereafter Johnson immersed himself in radical Right political and cultural publishing, an activity from which he now makes his living.[10] In late 2000, Johnson began to think about creating a metapolitical journal to advance white nationalist politics, but he considered this need fulfilled with the establishment in 2001 by the Charles Martel Society of *The Occidental Quarterly* (*TOQ*), a white nationalist periodical offering "Western Perspectives on Man, Culture, and Politics."[11] He became *TOQ*'s editor in 2007, establishing the journal's online presence, *TOQ Online*, together with Michael J. Polignano, who, as a student, had achieved some notoriety for defending racial genetic difference in *Emory Wheel*, Emory University's student newspaper.[12]

Having departed acrimoniously from the editorship of *TOQ* in April 2010,[13] Johnson and Polignano cofounded Counter-Currents.[14] Despite the personal rancor accompanying his departure from *TOQ*, Johnson acknowledges that his current venture represents a continuation of this intellectual initiative.[15] Johnson originally intended Counter-Currents to become a major voice for European New Right thought in North America, publishing English translations of work by the French New Right ideologues Alain de Benoist and Guillaume Faye. However, *Arktos*, a similar European metapolitical venture founded in November 2009, beat Counter-Currents to the punch. Their coup forced Johnson to "reconfigure" and "reconceive" his original plans, though he hoped the two complementary ventures would work together in future to avoid duplication of effort.[16]

Work and thought

Johnson holds that the New Right's opponents constantly deconstruct its ideals, traditions, and worldviews, and that "we are suffering mightily from it." Through metapolitical activism, he hopes to reverse this "continual intellectual dissection" and to practice "some deconstructing of [our] own."[17] The Counter-Currents website, the fulcrum of Johnson's activities, provides a platform for a sustained intellectual assault on liberal social democracy and those values embodied by Christianity and liberalism, which are to be replaced by "a new moral hierarchy" (or the return to a "traditional" one) that "prizes the striving of life for differentiation, struggle and excellence."[18]

To promote this new moral hierarchy, Counter-Currents features an array of original metapolitical articles, poetry, cultural criticism, reviews, translations, and interviews with prominent ideologues and activists, all propagating antiliberal and antiegalitarian ideals. Translations of Counter-Currents' own content, reposted by other groups and websites, extends the reach even farther. Johnson estimated in 2015 that the website consumed 60 to 70 percent of his time.[19] These exertions have reaped dividends. In one typical month in 2017 (November), Counter-Currents received 206,887 unique visitors who made 369,476 visits and viewed 1,447,593 pages of content.[20] Whether such figures indicate that Johnson's metapolitics is meeting with increased receptivity is impossible to say, though anecdotally he claims the "movement" is increasingly attracting younger, smarter, adherents. "I'm just finding less and less opposition to our sorts of ideas when they're spoken," he states.[21]

Counter-Currents also publishes "Books Against Time." To date, Johnson has published forty such books, often serving as editor, including anthologies of his own voluminous metapolitical commentaries on political events and issues of the day, most of which originally featured on the Counter-Currents website: *Confessions of a Reluctant Hater* (2010, 2016); *Truth, Justice, & a Nice White Country* (2015); *In Defense of Prejudice* (2017). His *New Right vs. Old Right* (2013) collects a series of important "foundational" essays while *You Asked for It* (2017) features twelve interviews on a range of topics, which, in aggregate, make a "compelling case for White Nationalism." Johnson also edits *North American New Right*, a print journal modeled on *Tyr*, designed to highlight the "best work" emanating from this milieu.[22]

Through Counter-Currents, Johnson endeavors to provide an educative focus for his readership, believing that in order to inculcate the correct intellectual foundations, "today's White Nationalist movement might work best on the model of a Montessori school, not a Hitler Youth rally."[23] He has also explored numerous ways to extend Counter-Currents' countercultural outreach, including an online radio station that enables listeners to download podcasts of shows (widely disseminated through social media).[24]

Johnson intended for Counter-Currents to become a financially self-supporting node in a wider "integrated network" promoting white nationalist and European New Right ideas, and thereby actively building the counterculture. PayPal's digital deplatforming of Counter-Currents following Heather Heyer's murder at the Unite the Right demonstration in Charlottesville in August 2017 jeopardized these efforts, causing a cash crunch for Counter-Currents, severely disrupting fund-raising and book sales. Recognizing the extent to which "white advocacy" had become dependent upon the very system it abhors, Johnson has since advocated "an integrated electronic ethnostate offering everything from domain registration to webhosting to DDoS [Distributed Denial of Service] protection to mailing list management—all controlled by our movement."[25]

Inspirations

Johnson's ideological inspirations are undoubtedly myriad. Several deserve closer inspection, however. The first embodies almost everything the European New Right rejected: for example, Savitri Devi, an "esoteric Hitlerite" whose view of Nazism was quasi-religious.[26] "Probably you couldn't really imagine anyone more militant than her," observed a fellow ideologue, explaining in part Savitri Devi's transgressive appeal to a younger generation of activists.[27] Johnson learned of Savitri Devi in 2000, after receiving a copy of her *Impeachment of Man* (1959), as well as Nicholas Goodrick-Clarke's scholarly biography, *Hitler's Priestess*. Having initially regarded her as "one of history's great eccentrics," Johnson became increasingly receptive to her ideas: "she made an eccentric out of me too." He came to revere Savitri Devi as a "remarkable individual who has changed my life in countless ways" though by this juncture Johnson was already broadly sympathetic to National Socialism, Indo-European paganism, and the Traditionalist cyclical conception of history.[28]

Using the pen name R. G. Fowler, Johnson created "The Savitri Devi Archive," an online portal dedicated to this "Woman against Time," in order to make her work more easily accessible.[29] Having once aspired to be her biographer, Johnson settled instead for republishing her key works.[30] This enthusiasm for Savitri Devi's work remains undimmed. Counter-Currents republished a centennial edition of her devotional poems to Adolf Hitler titled, tellingly, *Forever and Ever* (2012) in addition to a new edition of her seminal book, *The Lighting and the Sun* (1958), which deified the deceased Führer as an avatar of the Hindu God Vishnu.[31]

Johnson's researches into Savitri Devi's life led him, in 2000, to William Pierce, leader of the National Alliance, who had published her work in *National Socialist World* in the late 1960s. Although repelled by Pierce's novel *The Turner Diaries*, which he argues represent an impediment to serious policy formation, Johnson found himself listening to Pierce's American Dissident Voices broadcasts, from which he learned the relevance of applying white nationalist ideas to contemporary politics, transforming the nature of his own thinking that hitherto had taken place on a "rather rarefied intellectual plane." His political analysis also "particularly benefited" from reading Pierce's anti-Semitic pamphlet, *Who Rules America?* When they met in 2001, Pierce told Johnson that while abandoning academia had been painful—he had a PhD in physics—nothing compared to the freedom of speaking the "truth" as he saw it. "If

Pierce had never said those words, I may never have founded Counter-Currents," Johnson states. "In that sense, at least, I am a follower of William Pierce."[32]

A final inspiration was Jonathan Bowden, formerly cultural officer of the British National Party, whose influence highlights the transnational nature of the contemporary metapolitical milieu. Johnson met Bowden in Atlanta in 2009, having invited him to speak at a private gathering for *TOQ* writers and supporters. Bowden, whom Johnson describes as "one of the funniest, most brilliant, and most intellectually stimulating people I have ever known,"[33] supported Counter-Currents from the outset, contributing thirty-five original articles to its website, plus eight reviews of his own work under a pen name. Bowden, noted for his oratory, also addressed a 2012 gathering organized by Johnson in San Francisco shortly before his death. Johnson dedicated the first volume of *North American New Right* to his late colleague. Several collections of Bowden's writings and speeches followed: *Pulp Fascism* (2013), effectively a memorial, dealt with the right-wing themes its author detected in comics, graphic novels, and popular literature; *Western Civilization Bites Back* (2014) and *Extremists: Studies in Metapolitics* (2017) collected his speeches on a range of metapolitical themes. For Johnson, Bowden combined "mind" and "fist"—a personification of the Nietzschean warrior poet: the "cultured thug."[34]

Bowden was also the "master of ceremonies" for the London Forum, an important transnational hub for metapolitical activists across the world. Johnson addressed several meetings.[35] Seeking to emulate the success of these meetings, Johnson exported the forum model back across the Atlantic, establishing the New York Forum and the Northwest Forum (in Seattle) in 2016, with an Atlanta Forum emerging in 2017, all predicated upon the idea of "stimulating thought, creativity, networking, and solidarity."[36]

Key issues and key ideas

Johnson styles his politics "New Rightist" because he rejects the methods, though not the political model, theoretical frameworks, or indeed leaders of the "old right": Fascism and National Socialism.[37] He fuses this with the European New Right paradigm, privileging metapolitics and the struggle for cultural hegemony. Rather than trying to position Counter-Currents as being "beyond Left and Right"' vis-à-vis earlier Third Position initiatives, Johnson freely concedes that its roots are "objectively on the

Right, especially when you talk about what was the Right at the time of the French Revolution," when elitist, racist, and antiegalitarian ideals were common currency. Emphasizing these illiberal values as being normative before 1789 enables Johnson to claim that, in reality, "we just represent the center, the core values of European civilization."[38]

Johnson also highlights Traditionalism as a driving force. Though Counter-Currents' "guiding principles" derive from the French Traditionalist thinker René Guénon's *The Crisis of the Modern World* (1927), one of the writers who "most influenced" Johnson's metapolitical outlook is Julius Evola. Counter-Currents hosts a plethora of Evola's writings as an educational introduction for the uninitiated.[39]

The influence of both thinkers is discernible in Counter-Currents' mission statement, which proclaims that "History is cyclical" and, as such, civilization has descended from the "Golden Age" into a "Dark Age" in which "decadence reigns and all natural and healthy values are inverted." However, within this Dark Age, there are "counter-currents"—remnants of the past Golden Age "that sustain the world and serve as seeds of the Golden Age to come." Living according to the principles of the Golden Age, in the nadir of its antithesis, is not "futile," however. "Indeed, those who do so play an important role in the passage of the Ages," a process which Counter-Currents aims to accelerate "by promoting knowledge of its deficiencies in the light of Tradition." To this end Counter-Currents seeks to perpetuate "essential ideas and texts" that will help bring about the advent of a new Golden Age.[40] By keeping alive these "counter-currents" Johnson seeks to establish a new cultural and intellectual hegemony, one that he believes radiates from these "eternal" foundations, which will engender "the highest impersonal idealism" and therefore ensure the maintenance of core values "over generations of struggle" leading to the (re)establishment of "a White Republic or Republics in North America."[41]

Johnson's reference to multiple "republics" reflects his belief in ethnoplurality—that all races and ethnicities, including various white ethnicities, should have their own homelands. He rejects its antithesis: "Grandiose Nationalism"—supranational geopolitical visions that homogenize *all* whites into a white imperium. Given the history of empire and colonialism, Johnson dismisses this stance as a "morally retarded attitude." He also objects to such ideological confabulations, believing that they will simply replicate the problems of globalization including a tendency toward political unification, which exacerbates tensions between "European peoples," rather than decreasing them, thereby serving to undermine "real" ethnonationalism.[42] Johnson rejects the nostalgia for the Confederacy that is common among white nationalists on similar grounds. Slavery "is just capitalism at its worst" and therefore "I can't really pine for the South. If I lived in the South, frankly I would have been a White populist revolutionary who would be burning down the big houses."[43]

Johnson's illiberal vision for a white ethnostate hinges on his self-definition as both an "elitist and a populist," a position that grants a role "for certain elements of democracy" within the white polity—an idea of the mixed constitution derived from Aristotle's *Politics* in which aristocratic and democratic elements coexist, counterbalancing one another. "We need to reinfuse modernity with certain things that are treated as archaic," Johnson argues, "and that means identity politics, an aristocratic ethos, a warrior ethos, and things that have been bred out of us by consumerism and bourgeois modernity." This fusion of modernity with archaic values and social forms (within a white ethnostate) appears influenced by Frank Herbert's science fiction novel *Dune* just as much as by political tracts like Guillaume Faye's *Archeofuturism*.[44] This vision of "Classical Republicanism," based upon the sacralization of identity and order, represents the crux of Johnson's idealized "organic society," which he concedes to be "somewhat fascistic." Racially communitarian, future organic societies would enshrine the principle of the common good—the injection of biology into politics—judging all endeavors according to whether they facilitate the continued transmission of white genes and culture, "the things that we have created and valued" that, first, must be restored and then propagated if the white race is to survive in perpetuity.[45]

This, Johnson argues, is impossible within the present system, because it is led by a "rotating elite" of "plutocrats" (Republicans) and "pathological altruists" (Democrats), whose rule leads only to "white extinction," both biologically and culturally.[46] Democracy itself mitigates against racial survival since it "shrinks time horizons," making grand strategies, let alone civilizational or racial goals, impossible to achieve.[47]

Though not immune from imagining racially apocalyptic scenarios—Johnson perceives that unchecked immigration and birth rates will racially despoil the planet, reducing it to a "blackened cinder in space"[48]—he eschews the violent revolutionary strategies of figures like William Pierce, whose genocidal fantasies hinged upon a racially purgative "Day of the Rope" as a means of realizing the White Republic. While believing that a return to segregation and white supremacy would be "improvements," he argues instead that the only viable long-term solution is absolute racial separation, granting African American citizens their own homeland in the South. The main problem facing white nationalists, Johnson argues, emanates from the 1965 Immigration and Nationality Act, which transformed the United States' racial demography within fifty years. The resultant diversity, he claims, is in fact "ethnic cleansing."[49] By way of contrast, the years before 1965, before mass immigration and civil rights, represents a historical idyll, "when American workers were doing the best, when America was sending a man to the moon, when our cities were clean and vibrant in a good way."[50]

To restore racial hegemony, the United States must "decolonize" through a "well-planned, orderly, and humane process of ethnic cleansing." This need not necessarily entail violence, Johnson argues, though this is "morally justified" as an act of racial self-defense.[51] The first step to white racial "rectification" requires the immediate end of nonwhite immigration and the deportation of illegal residents; restricting access to welfare and education would ensure others "deport themselves." Making the case for mass, forced population transfer, Johnson claims that since globalization forces people to relocate for jobs, there can be no real objection to uprooting people for a goal greater "than just the whims of the market and the private interests of capitalists." Even if it took another fifty years to return to the status quo ante, he states the psychological benefit to white Americans, knowing that racial suicide was to be averted, would be immediate and immeasurable, restoring optimism, and economic innovation, reversing declining demographic trends, and returning the white race back to the path of "godhood."[52]

This stance explains in part Johnson's support for Donald Trump. He argued, prior to Trump's election, that his candidacy represented "an immense opportunity" for white nationalism because, although Trump's views were not coterminous with their own, "we want some of the policies that he wants." Trump's economic protectionist, anti-immigration platform, from building the wall to the "Muslim ban," represent measures that, Johnson believes, will slow white demographic decline, "giving us a few extra decades before we are a minority in our homeland."' Trump is not the "last chance" for whites "but he is the last chance for the United States of America," he argues.[53]

Johnson dismissed claims of an actual relationship between the Alt Right and Trump, characterizing this as simply a "one-way man-crush."[54] Sanguine about its success, he observes that although its memes altered mainstream political discourse, the Alt Right failed to leverage policy. Nonetheless, Trump's victory and its accompanying political polarization has created a climate conducive to racial salvation: "Henceforth, the choice will be between nationalism/populism and globalism/elitism. . . . We understand the real significance of Trump's election, perhaps better than Trump himself. This is white America's revolt against demographic Armageddon."[55]

"North American New Right" or "European New Right"?

Johnson's preoccupation with "race" marks a key point of departure from European New Right thought. White "diaspora communities," he argues, characterize the United States. These lack the racial homogeneity allegedly provided by the "real, living ethnically defined nations and sub-nations" that comprise Europe. Thus, the North American New Right had to emphasize another commonality: "biological race."[56] European New Right thinkers, by comparison, consciously rejected biological racism as "an erroneous doctrine, one rooted in time."[57] Underscoring this difference, de Benoist explained to Jared Taylor's *American Renaissance*:

> If I compare you and me, the first difference is that I am aware of race and of the importance of race, but I do not give to it the excessive importance that you do. For me it is a factor, but only one among others.[58]

Johnson intimates that this shift was possible only because European New Right thinkers could fall back upon the concept of a "European" national identity, an option closed to white nationalists in the United States. Counter-Currents, in contrast, gains intellectual succor from long-standing currents of racist and eugenicist thought, from Madison Grant and Lothrop Stoddard on. Johnson's own conceptual frame owes much to Wilmot Robertson (Humphrey Ireland's pen name) editor of *Instauration*, whose books *The Dispossessed Majority* (1972) and *The Ethnostate* (1992), both sold by Counter-Currents, make an explicit case for white ethnostates.[59] It also highlights that despite imbibing the European New Right's antiliberal, elitist, and metapolitical orientation, insofar as race is concerned, Johnson's ideological framework retains its roots in the old Right, as much as the new.

For many right-wing groups, Islam now represents the chief threat. For Johnson, however, the Clash of Civilizations narrative is a misnomer because "we are not fighting for Christendom, which is now more non-white than white. We are fighting for the white race, regardless of religion." Race, *not* religion, is paramount in his thinking because although "Islamic barbarism" provides a useful political foil, since "without Islam, it would be possible for many Europeans to believe that a multiracial, multicultural society might actually work," it is not white nationalism's principal enemy.[60]

Since time immemorial, Johnson argues, the Jews have represented the real existential threat to white racial survival, a titanic, cosmic, struggle cleaving the world in two betwixt "the seed of Abraham and the rest of humanity." This stance on the "Jewish Question" reflects a second fundamental point of fracture with European New Right thought, which publicly eschews anti-Semitism. Johnson views this distinction as resulting from European theorists being at liberty to discuss numerous issues, "in effect by proxy, by just being anti-American, to put it crudely." Living within the belly of the beast, however—Johnson construes the United States as "the citadel of Jewish power in the world"—"we have to name the problem and deal with it explicitly."[61] He regards white nationalism therefore as being, of necessity, "inescapably anti-Semitic."[62] Johnson's interpretation perhaps leans toward self-justification here. The European New Right's opposition to American neoliberal economic and cultural hegemony is not reducible to a proxy for his own anti-Semitic position.

For Johnson, the Jewish Question is a metapolitical question. In seeking to reconfigure the political terrain upon which white racial nationalist arguments are presented, one of Johnson's primary inspirations was Irminsul's Racial Nationalist Library, an online resource founded in 1999 by Irmin Vinson (a pen name). This website, together with Vinson's essays for Pierce's *National Vanguard*, "played an important role in my education as a White Nationalist," he writes.[63] Johnson published a collection of Vinson's articles arguing that the Holocaust represents "the Jewish collective memory of World War Two" and "we who are not Jews are in effect thinking about our past with someone else's memory, seeing both the past and its implications for the present through Jewish eyes rather than through our own."[64]

Vinson's book fulminates against "Holocaustomania," arguing that this represents a "political weapon" used by the Jews to delegitimize and stigmatize "Eurocentrism and White racial cohesion.... Holocaust commemoration racializes Jews and deracializes Whites; it strengthens them and weakens us."[65] Johnson agrees, arguing that Holocaust memorialization represents emotive extortion. "There will never be another holocaust. Get it through your heads.... I'm so fucking sick of this whining and emotional blackmail from the most powerful people on the planet," he states.[66]

While considering historical "revisionism" a legitimate activity for white nationalists, Johnson also regards it as an unnecessary appendage to their political project. Even if the "standard account" were true, he argues, "it would still not imply that there was anything wrong with White Nationalism and the goal of (or [sic]) breaking Jewish power over our destiny and physically separating whites and Jews."[67] Physical segregation is Johnson's ultimate solution to the Jewish Question: to expel *all* Jews to Israel. "We have to stop letting them have it both ways," he contends, "basically you need to go to Israel or we're going to freeze you out of our society."[68]

Following Vinson's argument that Hitler is "less a model to be followed than an avalanche of propaganda we must dig ourselves out from under,"[69] Johnson also rejects the strategy of manufacturing an apologetic "antiracist" stance. In confronting the "burden" of Hitler, Johnson acknowledges that while Hitler represents "the problem" for white nationalists, he also represents "the solution" because his actions were "in self-defense against Jewish aggression—the same Jewish aggression that we are suffering today in a much intensified form."

> Blaming Hitler is just another form of blaming ourselves for our ongoing racial decline. It deflects attention from the real culprits—white traitors and aliens—and replaces righteous anger at our enemies with demoralizing self-reproach and self-doubt. Anger motivates action. Self-reproach promotes passivity. So our march to oblivion continues uninterrupted.[70]

The battle for cultural hegemony

Counter-Currents also provides Johnson with a platform for cultural struggle. Western philosophical, theological, literary, and artistic traditions are regularly discussed in order to "point in the direction we want to go," in contradistinction to the "commercial melting pot" of contemporary societies. Indeed, for Johnson, the very act of creating culture requires "negating materialism."[71] Johnson further proselytizes for elitist notions of "high" culture through studies of right-wing literary modernists, including *Artists of the Right: Resisting Decadence* (2012) and *More Artists of the Right* (2017) by Kerry Bolton. "We hope that if we hold these people up as exemplars we can create a tradition where people might want to imitate them," Johnson notes.[72] To this end, Johnson seeks to serve as a "culture creator"—publishing novels by authors like Ward Kendall and Andy Nowiki and volumes of poetry by Leo Yankevich and Juleigh Howard-Hobson.

Johnson attaches no less importance to leveraging "low" culture, penning several volumes using the pen name Trevor Lynch, which meditate upon the white nationalist ideas and ideals he perceives as prevalent in mainstream cinema as well as analyzing them from this perspective too.[73] "I think that film is the most powerful intellectual tool for creating a world view," Johnson notes.[74] Thus by engaging with popular film, reinterpreting and inverting its meaning, Johnson engages in a form of asymmetric countercultural warfare against liberal society, leveraging its cultural produce against it. To this end, Johnson has published several such works. These include James O'Meara's *The Eldritch Evola . . . and Others: Traditionalist Meditations on Literature, Art and Culture* (2014), a Traditionalist take on the fiction of H. P. Lovecraft and Mickey Spillane, among others, and *End of an Era: Mad Men and the Ordeal of Civility* (2015), discussing this popular television show from a "race realist" and Traditionalist perspective. Jef Costello's *The Importance of James Bond and Other Essays* (2017) meanwhile explores "Traditionalist, New Right, and masculinist themes" in the James Bond films and a range of other movies, television shows, books, opera, art and advertising.

Individual components of Johnson's broader politics have invited lively contestation, perhaps none more so than pronouncing that homosexuality was "beside the point" with regards white nationalism, and that homophobia itself was a product of Judeo-Christianity. "Queer-bashers are in the grip of Jewry without even knowing it. White Nationalism requires that we de-Jew our thinking, but many White Nationalists have no idea of just what a radical change in outlook that requires."[75] His publication of *The Homo and the Negro* (2013) by James O'Meara, an openly gay extreme right-wing activist, elicited further hostility.[76]

Despite being on friendly terms with figures like Jack Donovan, Johnson has become increasingly critical of the "manosphere," which, he argues, "morally corrupts men,"[77] since their ethos, alongside those of other sundry other misogynists and rape advocates, "is no more compatible with the healthy sexual order we want to create than the feminism they oppose." In comparison, while defending heterosexuality as normative, Johnson argues, "as long as homosexuals uphold healthy norms and have something positive to contribute, they can and do make our movement stronger, *if we stop worrying about it.*"[78]

Reception

Counter-Currents was positively received by most white nationalist ideologues, including Tomislav Sunić, the Croatian author who lauded Johnson as "the most prominent intellectual and activist of the cultural and metapolitical school of thought . . . in the USA."[79] Anti-Semitic intellectuals like Kevin MacDonald, the current editor of *TOQ*, have been similarly effusive, penning endorsements for his books. Johnson's personal insistence upon "punching right" as a means of evolving white nationalist ideas has not always been received with equanimity, however, particularly with regards his analysis of the Alt Right.[80]

Johnson has been particularly critical of Richard Spencer, the Alt-Right luminary who coined the term. Following Trump's election in November 2016, Spencer proclaimed, during the course of a speech, "Hail Trump, hail our people, hail victory!" Some audience members gave Nazi salutes in response. This "damaged the Alt-Right brand—perhaps irreparably—by associating it with Nazism," argued Johnson after footage of the event emerged. The irony of some of Johnson's own ideological proclivities aside, Spencer's speech certainly polarized Alt Right and "Alt-Lite" factions, which was, as Johnson noted, diametrically opposed to what the "brand" was supposed to do, which was to allow people to flirt with a host of "dissident Rightist ideas" without embracing stigmatizing labels like "white nationalism" or "national socialism."[81] More recently, Johnson has also been embroiled in a war of words with fellow metapolitical publisher Arktos Media surrounding his allegations of malfeasance and their counter claims of his alleged complicity in an attempted takeover of Arktos.[82]

Conclusion

Counter-Currents continues to pursue its metapolitical approach to advancing white nationalism, gaining it a wide audience in North America and Europe. Johnson's political and ideological significance as a thinker and ideologue is perhaps best located in his fusion of European New Right ideas with more classic variants of American white racism—in effect, repackaging European metapolitical ideas and countercultural strategy for a US audience. In this regard, Counter-Currents acts as an important clearing-house for such ideological experimentation and syncretization. The "North American New Right" often appears intellectually contradictory, purporting to embrace European New Right thought while simultaneously embracing its antithesis: biological racism, conspiratorial anti-Semitism, and indeed the more cultic dimensions of National Socialism. Johnson argues, however, that this seemingly inherent incompatibility is in fact a strength: "We need this diversity, because our goal is to foster versions of White Nationalism that appeal to all existing white constituencies. We can speak to multitudes because we contain multitudes."[83] Therefore, Johnson's ability to assimilate, articulate, synthesize, and critique this broad range of white nationalist positions, to popularize and intellectualize them, combined with his commitment to cultural struggle through the rearticulation of "high"' and "low" culture in support of such propositions, places him in the vanguard of a new generation of white nationalist intellectuals—even though his sympathy for National Socialism and overt anti-Semitism sets him apart from many of them.

Notes

1. Greg Johnson, ed., *North American New Right* (San Francisco: Counter-Currents 2012), 1:1.
2. Greg Johnson, "Counter-Currents/*North American New Right* Newsletter: May 2013," accessed December 14, 2017, http://www.counter-currents.com/2013/06/counter-currents-nanr-newsletter-may-2013.
3. Greg Johnson, "*Between Two Lampshades*: Michael Enoch Interviews Greg Johnson, Part 1," accessed December 14, 2017. https://www.counter-currents.com/2015/06/between-two-lampshades-1/.
4. Greg Johnson, "Heidegger's *Black Notebooks*: The Diaries of a Dissident National Socialist," accessed December 14, 2017. https://www.counter-currents.com/2014/03/heideggers-black-notebooks/.

5. Greg Johnson. "Heidegger Did Nothing Wrong," accessed December 14, 2017, https://www.counter-currents.com/2016/01/heidegger-did-nothing-wrong/.
6. Johnson, "*Between Two Lampshades.*"
7. "PSR Faculty Profiles," accessed December 14, 2017, http://web.archive.org/web/20030715010656/http://psr.edu/page.cfm?l=250 for academic profile.
8. Johnson translated Alain de Benoist's *On Being a Pagan* (2004), published by Ultra, which also publishes *Tyr*, named after the Germanic sky god. Johnson subsequently published books by Colin Cleary one of *Tyr's* founding editors.
9. Johnson, "*Between Two Lampshades.*"
10. Greg Johnson, "Greg Johnson Interviewed by Laura Raim about the Alt Right (Transcript)," accessed December 14, 2017, https://www.counter-currents.com/2016/09/greg-johnson-interviewed-by-laura-raim-about-the-alt-right-transcript/.
11. Greg Johnson, "The Shadow of Trump: Interview with *Il Primato Nazionale*," accessed December 14, 2017, https://www.counter-currents.com/2016/11/interview-with-il-primato-nazionale/.
12. Michael Polignano, "Genes May Determine Racial Attributes," accessed December 14, 2017, http://www.students.emory.edu/WHEEL/Archive/00_Oct06/editorial1.html; Polignano subsequently argued that refusal to take one's "own side" in an ethnic conflict prefaces racial dispossession and extinction. Michael J. Polignano, *Taking Our Own Side* (San Francisco: Counter Currents, 2010), 108–144.
13. Greg Johnson, "comment #239," posted August 29, 2011, accessed December 14, 2017, https://majorityrights.com/weblog/comments/elitism_secrecy_deception_the_way_to_save_white_america/.
14. Polignano was managing editor/webmaster from 2010 to 2013, returning as webzine editor/webmaster in 2017.
15. Counter-Currents Radio, "Greg Johnson interviews Richard Spencer on Radixjournal.com," accessed December 14, 2017, http://www.counter-currents.com/2014/01/greg-johnson-interviews-richard-spencer-on-radixjournal-com/.
16. Greg Johnson, "Tom Sunić Interviews Greg Johnson," accessed December 14, 2017, https://www.counter-currents.com/2015/10/tom-sunic-interviews-greg-johnson/.
17. Ted Sallis, *Review of Jonathan Bowden's Pulp Fascism*, accessed December 14, 2017, http://www.counter-currents.com/2013/07/jonathan-bowdens-pulp-fascism.
18. Jonathan Bowden, *Western Civilization Bites Back*, ed. Greg Johnson (San Francisco: Counter-Currents 2014).
19. Johnson, "Tom Sunić Interviews Greg Johnson."
20. Greg Johnson, "Counter-Currents/*North American New Right* Newsletter: September to November 2017," accessed December 14, 2017, https://www.counter-currents.com/2017/12/counter-currents-nanr-newsletter-september-to-november-2017/.

21. Jesse Singal, "Undercover with the Alt-Right," *New York Times*, accessed December 14, 2017, https://www.nytimes.com/2017/09/19/opinion/alt-right-white-supremacy-undercover.html.
22. Johnson, "Tom Sunić Interviews Greg Johnson."
23. Greg Johnson, "Metapolitics and Occult Warfare, Part 4," accessed December 14, 2017, http://www.counter-currents.com/2012/12/metapolitics-andoccult-warfare-part-4/.
24. Greg Johnson, "The Counter-Currents Radio Network," accessed December 14, 2017, http://www.counter-currents.com/2012/09/the-counter-currents-radio-network/.
25. Greg Johnson, Counter-Currents/*North American New Right* Newsletter: April to August, 2017, accessed December 14, 2017, https://www.counter-currents.com/2017/09/counter-current-nanr-newsletter-april-to-august-2017/.
26. Nicholas Goodrick-Clarke, *Hitler's Priestess: Savitri Devi, the Hindu-Aryan Myth, and neo-Nazism* (New York: NYU Press, 1998).
27. Troy Southgate, ed., *Jonathan Bowden: The Speeches* (London: Black Front Press, 2012), 23–45.
28. Mourning the Ancient, "Savitri Devi: The Woman against Time—Looking Back with R. G. Fowler," accessed December 14, 2017, hhtp://www.mourningtheancient.com/savitri. *Impeachment of Man* was more readily available after its 1991 republication by the Noontide Press, which Johnson sells through Counter-Currents.
29. "The Savitri Devi Archive," accessed December 14, 2017., https://www.savitridevi.org/. Johnson dedicated *Truth, Justice, and a Nice White Country* (2016) to Beryl Cheetham, Savitri Devi's close friend, who assisted him with his research.
30. "Fowler" reprinted *Defiance* (2007) and *Gold in the Furnace* (2006), originally published in 1951 and 1952 respectively.
31. Johnson also published two editions of *And Time Rolls On: The Savitri Devi Interviews* (2005, 2012) and *A Warning to the Hindus* and *The Non-Hindu Indians and Indian Unity* (2013), originally published in 1940. Calcutta, B.K. Brahmachari, Hindu Mission.
32. Greg Johnson, *In Defense of Prejudice* (Counter-Currents: San Francisco 2017), 241–244.
33. Ibid., 238.
34. Jonathan Bowden, *Pulp Fascism: Right-Wing Themes in Comics, Graphic Novels, and Popular Literature*, ed. Greg Johnson (Counter-Currents: San Francisco 2012), v.
35. Graham Macklin, "The 'Cultic Milieu' of Britain's 'New Right': Metapolitical 'Fascism' in Contemporary Britain," in *Cultures of Post-War British Fascism*, ed. Nigel Copsey and John E. Richardson (Abingdon: Routledge, 2015), 177–201, for an overview.

36. Johnson, "The Shadow of Trump: Interview with *Il Primato Nazionale*." These forums built upon a series of Francis Parker Yockey memorial dinners and "annual weekend retreats" which Counter-Currents had been running since 2010.
37. Greg Johnson, "New Right vs. Old Right," accessed December 14, 2017, https://www.counter-currents.com/2012/05/new-right-vs-old-right/.
38. Johnson, "Tom Sunić Interviews Greg Johnson."
39. Greg Johnson, "Remembering Julius Evola: May 19, 1898–June 11, 1974," accessed December 27, 2017, http://www.counter-currents.com/2013/05/remembering-julius-evola-2/.
40. "About Counter-Currents Publishing and *North American New Right*," accessed December 14, 2017, https://www.counter-currents.com/about/.
41. Greg Johnson, "Metapolitics and Occult Warfare, Part 4" and Michael O'Meara, *Towards the White Republic* (San Francisco: Counter-Currents, 2010), 1–21.
42. Johnson, "Greg Johnson Interviewed by Laura Raim" and Greg Johnson, "Grandiose Nationalism," accessed December 14, 2017, https://www.counter-currents.com/2015/02/grandiose-nationalism/.
43. Greg Johnson, "Robert Stark Interviews Greg Johnson on Populism, Elitism, and Economics," accessed December 14, 2017, https://www.counter-currents.com/2015/07/robert-stark-interviews-greg-johnson-on-populism-elitism-and-economics/.
44. Johnson, "*Between Two Lampshades*."
45. Johnson, "Greg Johnson Interviewed by Laura Raim."
46. Greg Johnson, "White Extinction," accessed December 14, 2017, https://www.counter-currents.com/2014/02/white-extinction/ .
47. Johnson, "Greg Johnson Interviewed by Laura Raim."
48. Greg Johnson, "'Set Aside Your Humility and Lead:' Ruuben Kaalep Interviews Greg Johnson," accessed December 14, 2017, https://www.counter-currents.com/2015/10/set-aside-your-humility/, accessed December 14, 2017.
49. Greg Johnson, "White Nationalism is Inevitable," accessed December 14, 2017, https://www.counter-currents.com/2017/05/white-nationalism-is-inevitable/.
50. Johnson, "Greg Johnson Interviewed by Laura Raim."
51. Greg Johnson, "The Slow Cleanse," accessed December 14, 2017, https://www.counter-currents.com/2014/06/the-slow-cleanse/.
52. Johnson, "Greg Interviewed by Laura Raim."
53. Johnson, "The Shadow of Trump: Interview with *Il Primato Nazionale*." Acknowledging Trump as a "civic nationalist" and "pragmatic centrist," Johnson nonetheless found much to admire. Nepotism is reinterpreted as evidence that Trump "thinks dynastically." Skating over the fact that much of his fortune was inherited, the activities Trump derives his wealth from—Trump "builds things, and he builds things that last a long, long time"—stands, for Johnson,

as a counterpoint to the Hungarian Jewish billionaire George Soros, whose self-made wealth derives from financial speculation. See Johnson, "Greg Johnson Interviewed by Laura Raim." Johnson's judgment *In Defense of Prejudice*, 99, that, compared to "evil" Hillary Clinton, Trump "will govern as a centrist, a reconciler, and a peace-maker," appears questionable.

54. Greg Johnson, "Trump, Hillary, and the Alt Right," accessed December 14, 2017, https://www.counter-currents.com/2016/08/trump-hillary-and-the-alt-right/.
55. Greg Johnson, "November 9, 2016," accessed December 14, 2017, https://www.counter-currents.com/2016/11/november-9-2016/.
56. Johnson, "Tom Sunić Interviews Greg Johnson."
57. Tamir Bar-On, *Rethinking the French New Right: Alternatives to Modernity* (Abingdon: Routledge, 2013), 175.
58. American Renaissance, "We Are at the End of Something—A Conversation with Alain de Benoist," accessed December 14, 2017, https://www.amren.com/features/2013/11/we-are-at-the-end-of-something/.
59. Greg Johnson, "*Recommended Reading*: Six Essential Works on White Nationalism," accessed December 14, 2017, https://www.counter-currents.com/2016/04/six-essential-works-on-white-nationalism/.
60. Greg Johnson, "The Muslim Problem," accessed December 14, 2017, https://www.counter-currents.com/2015/01/the-muslim-problem/.
61. Johnson, "Tom Sunić Interviews Greg Johnson."
62. Greg Johnson, "Vanguardism, Vantardism, and Mainstreaming," accessed December 14, 2017, https://www.counter-currents.com/2014/10/vanguardism-vantardism-and-mainstreaming/.
63. Irmin Vinson, *Some Thoughts on Hitler and Other Essays* (San Francisco: Counter-Currents 2012), v.
64. Ibid., viii.
65. Ibid., 43, 51, and 54.
66. Johnson, "*Between Two Lampshades*."
67. Greg Johnson, "Dealing with the Holocaust," accessed December 14, 2017, http://www.theoccidentalobserver.net/2012/07/20/dealing-with-the-holocaust/. Predictably, this argument alienated diehard revisionists and deniers, see Carolyn Yeager, "Nationalism and the Holocaust: A Reply to Johnson," accessed December 14, 2017, https://carolynyeager.net/nationalism-and-holocaust-reply-johnson.
68. Singal, "Undercover with the Alt-Right."
69. Vinson, *Some Thought of Hitler*, 6.
70. Greg Johnson, "The Burden of Hitler, 2013," accessed December 14, 2017, https://www.counter-currents.com/2013/04/the-burden-of-hitler-2013/.
71. Johnson, "Greg Johnson Interviewed by Laura Raim."

72. Counter-Currents Radio, "*Podcast no. 14*—Interview with Charles Krafft, Part 1," accessed December 14, 2017, http://www.counter-currents.com/2012/04/interview-with-charles-krafft-part-1/.
73. *Trevor Lynch's White Nationalist Guide to the Movies*, ed. Greg Johnson (San Francisco: Counter-Currents 2012).
74. Johnson, "Tom Sunić Interviews Greg Johnson."
75. Greg Johnson, "Homosexuality and White Nationalism," accessed December 14, 2017, http://www.counter-currents.com/2010/10/homosexuality-and-white-nationalism/.
76. Greg Johnson, "Gay Panic on the Alt Right," accessed December 14, 2017. https://www.counter-currents.com/2016/03/gay-panic-on-the-alt-right/.
77. Greg Johnson, "Does the Manosphere Morally Corrupt Men?" accessed December 14, 2017, https://www.counter-currents.com/2015/02/does-the-manosphere-morally-corrupt-men.
78. Greg Johnson, "Gay Panic on the Alt Right."
79. Voice of Reason, "The Sunic Journal: Dr. Greg Johnson on the New Right," accessed December 14, 2017, http://reasonradionetwork.com/20110809/the-sunic-journal-dr-greg-johnson-on-the-new-right.
80. Greg Johnson, "Punching Right," accessed December 14, 2017, https://www.counter-currents.com/2016/12/punching-right/.
81. Greg Johnson, "The Alt Right: Obituary for a Brand?" accessed December 14, 2017, https://www.counter-currents.com/2016/11/the-alt-right-obituary-for-a-brand/.
82. Arktos, "The Attacks on Arktos," last accessed December 14, 2017, https://altright.com/2017/06/17/the-attacks-on-arktos/; "Boatsinker," "Greg Johnson, Daniel Friberg and What Happened before Scandza Forum," accessed December 14, 2017, https://forum.therightstuff.biz/topic/48716/greg-johnson-daniel-friberg-and-what-happened-before-scandza-forum?page=1 and Greg Johnson; "Reply to Daniel Friberg," accessed December 14, 2017, https://www.counter-currents.com/2017/06/reply-to-daniel-friberg/.
83. Johnson, "New Right vs. Old Right."

14

Richard B. Spencer and the Alt Right

Tamir Bar-On

BORN IN BOSTON in 1978, Richard Bertrand Spencer is the president of the National Policy Institute,[1] a "white nationalist" think tank founded by William Regnery II, the multimillionaire who also funded the Charles Martel Society, the publisher of the *Occidental Quarterly*.[2] In a 2015 YouTube video titled "Who Are We?" Spencer notes that people are reasserting their identities, and he asks peoples of white European extraction to return to their ancestral identities, to end their attachment to liberal multiculturalism (a "fate worse than death,") to become "seekers" rather than "wanderers" of the "rootless" internationalist and cosmopolitan variety.[3] Spencer also points out that man does not live for "freedom" (which, he insists, equals "shopping" in liberal societies), but rather "for a homeland, a people and its future." Finally, he also asks a primordial question in respect of identity: "Are we ready to become who we are?" For Spencer, white Americans must define themselves as white Europeans as well as promote a politics of white racial solidarity.

In this video, we can see the contours of Spencer's Alt Right worldview: use of the internet as a main vehicle for provoking both conservatives and liberals with politically incorrect language and ideas; a rejection of liberal multiculturalism; a disdain for capitalism because of its tendency to homogenize diverse peoples and cultures; support for political communities wedded to white, European identities; a challenge to "heroic," white, and European elites to create a revolution in mentalities and values (i.e., a right-wing metapolitical struggle) against multiculturalism and immigration; and a desire to create white, homogeneous ethnostates ("homelands") on both sides of the Atlantic. Greg Johnson has suggested that these ethnostates could be erected in "European colonial societies" such as the US, Canada, Australia, New Zealand, and even Uruguay and Argentina.[4]

For Spencer, white homelands are rejected by liberals and conservatives alike, thus suggesting that the Alt Right is as much about hatred for all established and "cosmopolitan" elites as for the traditional liberal Left "enemies." Moreover, Spencer believes that the racialist and anti-Semitic agendas of the Old Right can be attained through metapolitical, legal, and nonviolent methods. In this sense, Spencer's Alt Right is heavily indebted to the French New Right's metapolitical framework, although Spencer is more openly racialist and anti-Semitic compared to the French New Right's leader Alain de Benoist. Thus, the Alt Right aims to unite different elements of the Right from white nationalists and racists to conservatives and others beyond the radical Right, which seek to stem the tide of liberal multiculturalism, advance the interests of the white race through concrete measures such as halting nonwhite immigration, and end "Jewish influence" in politics.

A few weeks after the 2016 presidential election, at a National Policy Institute conference, Spencer declared: "Hail Trump, hail our people, hail victory!"[5] while some of his supporters gave the Nazi salute. Spencer brushed off the incident as a moment of "irony" or exuberance, yet he also called Donald Trump's presidential election win "the victory of will," echoing Leni Riefenstahl's *Triumph of the Will* (1935), a Nazi propaganda film.[6] The desire to break political taboos about Fascism, Nazism, anti-Semitism, and issues of white racial identity also informs the *Weltanschauung* of Spencer and the Alt Right. So, for example, whereas whites historically engaged in ethnic solidarity through colonialist practices, the creation of the Ku Klux Klan (KKK) or apartheid in South Africa, Spencer endorses Jared Taylor's argument that today's whites lack ethnic solidarity and that "nonwhite ethnic solidarity is an entrenched part of the political landscape."[7]

Spencer has been dubbed a "neo-Nazi," "white supremacist," and "ethnic nationalist." The Southern Poverty Law Center called him "a suit-and-tie version of the white supremacists of old, a kind of professional racist in khakis."[8] Spencer, however, denies that he is a white supremacist, fascist, or neo-Nazi because he neither supports the use of extraparliamentary violence or colonialism, nor does he want to impose his societal model on other peoples.[9] Like Johnson and Taylor, Spencer believes that white racial consciousness and political solidarity can be attained without violence, continuing the French New Right's "right-wing Gramscianism," which was promoted by de Benoist and Guillaume Faye.[10]

Spencer has argued that whites are victims of cultural "dispossession" in their own lands because of orthodoxies such as racial equality and multiculturalism. He has called Western immigration and refugee policies a "proxy war" against white Europeans. He has also advocated "peaceful ethnic cleansing" and longs for the erection of "a new society, an ethno-state that would be a gathering point for all Europeans. It would be a new society based on very different ideals than, say, the Declaration of Independence."[11] In short, Spencer's Alt Right is not merely conservative. In their desire to smash liberalism, administrative equality, multiculturalism, and capitalism, as well as create ethnically homogeneous "homelands," Spencer's Alt Right is indeed revolutionary. This point is corroborated by George Hawley, author of *Making Sense of the Alt-Right*, who argues that, unlike mainstream conservatives, the Alt Right conceives of the immigration issue through a racial lens based on a core defense of white identity; rejects two sacred American values, namely, equality and liberty; and wants to, at minimum, end mass immigration to the US.

Spencer is self-described as an "identitarian."[12] The identitarian movement has French and European origins and advocates rights for members of specific European ethnocultural groups. Some of their thinkers include Fabrice Robert and Markus Willinger. Spencer claims to be the inventor of the term "Alt Right,"[13] a term that has also been welcomed by Daniel Friberg, Greg Johnson, Jack Donovan, and Taylor. In a *Radix* interview, Spencer noted that he coined the term "alternative Right" in 2008 in order to differentiate himself from "mainstream American conservatism" and pass down European "ancestral traditions" to new generations.[14] Paul Gottfried argues that both he and Spencer jointly created the Alt Right term.[15] For Spencer, as one can read in the "Alt-Right manifesto,"[16] those "ancestral traditions" are racial preference for white Europeans and anti-Semitism—both decidedly Old Right staples.

Despite his anti-Semitic and pro-Nazi comments, Spencer's key intellectual influences are largely those thinkers concerned with winning the "cultural war" against egalitarianism, liberal democracy, capitalism, socialism, and multiculturalism: the German philosopher Friedrich Nietzsche, French New Right intellectuals such as de Benoist and Faye, Conservative Revolution theorists such as Carl Schmitt, Ernst Jünger, and

Martin Heidegger, European theorists like Julius Evola, Francis Parker Yockey, and Alexander Dugin, and a collection of US right-wingers with a penchant for race-driven politics or anti-Semitism, including Sam Francis, Jared Taylor, and Kevin B. MacDonald. In contrast to parliamentary politics and extraparliamentary violence, Spencer's focus on the cultural realm makes his thought far more threatening for the system and highlights the important evolution of the radical Right on both sides of the Atlantic. That is, the radical Right understands that in an antifascist, antiracist, and anticolonial epoch, conspicuous displays of violence, support for colonialism, or overtly racist language are not acceptable. As Spencer stated, "We have to look good" because few would want to join a movement that is "crazed or ugly or vicious or just stupid."[17]

Life and context

Spencer is "an icon for white supremacists"[18] and a controversial star on the university lecture circuit. Yet his path to mass media stardom was not predictable. He neither suffered materially nor did he have major life crises. He is the son of Rand Spencer (an ophthalmologist) and Sherry Spencer (née Dickenhorst), an heiress to cotton farms in Louisiana. He grew up in Preston Hollow in Dallas, Texas. In high school, he was not intellectually brilliant, yet he did mature intellectually. In 2001, he received a BA in English Literature and Music from the University of Virginia. By 2003, he gained an MA in the Humanities from the University of Chicago. From the summer of 2005 into 2006, he was at the Vienna International Summer University, thus cementing his links to European culture, identity, and history—key Spencerian themes. From 2005 to 2007, he was a PhD student at Duke University in Modern European intellectual history. He joined the Duke Conservative Union, where he met Stephen Miller, later Donald Trump's senior policy advisor. Spencer's former website claims that he did not complete his PhD at Duke in order "to pursue a life of thought-crime," thus suggesting that universities are laboratories for dogmatic thought.

In 2007, Spencer was the assistant editor at the mainstream conservative magazine the *American Conservative*. He was allegedly fired from it because his views were considered extremist. From 2008 to 2009, he was the executive editor of *Taki's Magazine*, a libertarian online politics and culture magazine published by the Greek paleoconservative journalist and socialite Taki Theodoracopulos.

By 2010, Spencer had charted his own intellectual direction. He mocked both established political parties in the US, especially the Republican establishment. In March 2010, he founded AlternativeRight.com, a website which he edited until 2012. In 2011, he became owner and executive director of Washington Summit Publishers. In that same year, he also became president and director of the National Policy Institute. In 2012, he founded *Radix Journal* as a publication of Washington Summit Publishers. Contributors have included white nationalist thinkers such as Kevin MacDonald, Alex Kurtagić, and Samuel T. Francis. He also hosts a weekly podcast called Vanguard Radio. In short, Spencer has focused on using various media outlets to disseminate his views to ordinary people in an accessible manner.

In 2014, Spencer was deported from Budapest, Hungary, after trying to organize the National Policy Institute conference, ironically as Hungary then had one of the most nationalist regimes in Europe under President Victor Orbán,[19] and Spencer's ultranationalist, anti-immigrant, and antirefugee views dovetail with Orbán's.

On January 15, 2017 (Martin Luther King Jr.'s birthday), Spencer launched AltRight.com, a key website for Alt Right supporters. The date was not selected accidentally. If Martin Luther King is the symbol of racial equality, liberal multiculturalism, and desegregation, Spencer is the voice for racial inequality, white nationalism, and segregated white ethnostates. A key contributor on AltRight.com is Jared Taylor, the author of the seminal white nationalist tract *White Identity: Racial Consciousness in the 20th Century*.

It should also be mentioned that Spencer is married to Nina Kouprianova, who has translated numerous books written by Alexander Dugin.[20] Those books have been published by Spencer's Washington Summit Publishers.

Work and thought

Spencer is more known for his YouTube videos, tweets, television and newspaper interviews, and university speaking engagements than for any substantive body of intellectual work. In this respect, he differs from de Benoist, the intellectual leader of the French New Right, who won the prestigious Académie française prize in 1978 for his *Seen from the Right* (*Vu de droite*).[21] What defines Spencer is not his writings but his oratorical skills and his ability to use social media to communicate messages of racial solidarity and white, nationalist identity to larger and mainstream audiences.

Spencer is author of the "Alt-Right manifesto," discussed in more detail later. His other major work is an edited volume titled *The Uprooting of European Identity* (2016).[22] The book's blurb states: "The White man lives in a world his race once dominated and in which Black and Brown are now colonizers, in which European heritage is being taken away piece by piece: cultural heroes, literature, popular icons, identity ultimately, everything." In addition, the work sees whites as victims of multiculturalism and cultural dispossession, and insists that "non-whites are vengeful and intent on destroying white identity." Here he is echoing Alt Right thinkers who call liberal multiculturalism "genocidal"—a term used by Greg Johnson to claim that he is more interested in the contemporary "white genocide" than the Holocaust.[23] A key contributor to the volume is Kevin MacDonald, author of the anti-Semitic *The Culture of Critique: An Evolutionary Analysis of Jewish Involvement in Twentieth-Century Intellectual and Political Movements*. MacDonald's work informs Spencer's view that Jews are not part of the white race; they are instead a dangerous group apart from Euro-American societies, and promote liberal and socialist multiculturalism in order to destroy rooted, white, and European identities. Unlike Johnson, Taylor does not have particular animus toward Jews as long as they let whites create their own homelands.

Spencer also contributed a foreword, "What is the American Right?", to Gottfried's *The Great Purge: The Deformation of the Conservative Movement*.[24] In this piece, he suggests that the mainstream Right in the US is today defined by five characteristics: free-market capitalism, generic Christianity, staunch support for the US military, unambiguous support for the State of Israel, and a values-based conception of American identity, which is universal rather than ethnically based.[25] Spencer himself rejects most of these positions for a more revolutionary politics. He rejects the capitalist model; he is a cultural atheist rather than Christian (echoing the French New Right's paganism);[26] he supports the US military but criticizes its morally tinged interventionism abroad;[27] he is not a staunch supporter of Israel (Israel is a rich country and some US wars are supposedly used to advance Israeli rather than American national interests);[28] and he supports an explicitly ethnic conception of American identity, rejects immigration and refugees, and calls for white ethnostates.[29]

Spencer is known for his numerous speaking engagements, especially to university audiences. These lectures are designed to cultivate an image of a Right that is intellectual, a champion of free speech against political correctness, and to push his agenda in settings seen to be friendly toward the liberal Left and multiculturalism. Spencer was thus invited to Vanderbilt University in 2010 and to Providence College in 2011 by Youth for Western Civilization. His speaking engagements at universities have been fiercely protested and sometimes denied on public safety grounds, including at Texas A&M University and Michigan State University in 2016. He also speaks to more right-wing audiences such as Hans-Hermann Hoppe's Property and Freedom Society, Taylor's American Renaissance conference, and Gottfried's H. L. Mencken Club.

Spencer greeted the inauguration of Donald Trump with optimism. Trump's antiestablishment tone, his anti-immigrant, anti-Mexican rhetoric, his populist economics, and his breaking of the boundaries of political correctness pleased Spencer. Spencer even attended the inauguration of the new US president. As he was giving an interview there, he was punched in the face.

As has been said, Spencer gained greatest fame for his "Alt-Right manifesto," discussed later in this chapter. He also attained notoriety from the violent Unite the Right rally in Charlottesville, Virginia, in 2017. While the rally sought to protest the removal of a statue of Confederate General Robert E. Lee, it tragically saw a white nationalist violently drive over and kill a liberal counterprotester. Spencer condemned the use of violence on his Twitter account. The protesters included a collection of right-wingers: white supremacists, white nationalists, neo-Confederates, neo-Nazis, and various militia movements. A number of marchers chanted racist and anti-Semitic slogans such as "Jews will not replace us," some carried semiautomatic rifles, swastikas, Confederate flags, and anti-Muslim banners. There were also pro-Trump banners: those supporters would have been pleased when Trump blamed the Charlottesville "violence on all sides." Spencer could also claim that "Trump has never denounced the Alt-Right. Nor will he."[30]

Intellectual inspiration

Visitors to Spencer's principal website, AltRight.com, were at one point greeted by a picture of Julius Evola. Founded in 2017, AltRight.com states that it includes "the best writers and analysts from the Alt-Right, in North America, Europe, and around the world." The media partners of AltRight.com include right-wing websites such as *Arktos* (Daniel Friberg),

Radix Journal (Richard Spencer), and *Red Ice* (Henrik Palmgren). Its key European editor is Friberg himself.

Spencer's AltRight.com notes that "The Alt Right draws its inspiration from a variety of schools of thought: the European New Right, Radical Traditionalism, German Conservative Revolutionaries, Paleoconservatism, Human Bio-Diversity and other racialist thinkers." The historian of fascism Roger Griffin would have described this ideological syncretism as "mazeway resynthesis" in which "old and new ideological and ritual elements—some of which would previously have been incongruous or incompatible—are forged through 'ludic recombination' into a totalizing worldview."[31] The specific thinkers that inspire Spencer's Alt Right include French New Right thinkers de Benoist, Faye, Dominique Venner, Dugin, the English nationalist Jonathan Bowden, and "race realism" and white nationalist thinkers from the US such as Samuel Francis and MacDonald, Taylor, and Richard Lynn.

Like the French New Right, Spencer is a fan of the German thinkers Nietzsche and Schmitt. Like de Benoist, he sees Nietzsche as the prophet of the decline of Western civilization, the supporter of elitist antiegalitarianism, and the critic of the "weak" and egalitarian Judeo-Christian values which produced the egalitarian "sicknesses" associated with liberalism, socialism, feminism, and multiculturalism. Spencer sees in Schmitt the champion of friend and enemy as the crucial definition of the political, in contrast to liberals searching for an "end of history" devoid of friends and enemies. In Schmitt, Spencer sees a thinker who hated parliamentary debate and democracy, a supporter of a state that was decisive and violent, and a champion of the ultranationalist cause. "Politics is inherently brutal" and "the state is crystallized violence,"[32] insists Spencer, echoing Schmitt. Spencer also cites other Conservative Revolution thinkers, including Oswald Spengler and Ernst Jünger. In addition, Spencer is influenced by more overt fascists such as Evola, Yukio Mishima, and Francis Parker Yockey. With both the fascists and Conservative Revolution thinkers, Spencer plays a clever double game: openly rejecting violence but simultaneously legitimizing thinkers that promote violence, racism, anti-Semitism, and the rejection of liberal, parliamentary politics.

Four other thinkers are significant for Spencer's intellectual evolution: Jack Donovan, creator of "male tribalism"; Wilmot Robertson, author of *The Dispossessed Majority* (which influenced Spencer's notion that white Europeans who built the US are in decline and hence the decline of the US); the political philosopher Leo Strauss (a fierce critic of liberal democracy and the "crisis of the West"); and Paul Gottfried (in particular, *After Liberalism* and *Multiculturalism and the Politics of Guilt*).

The "Alt-Right Manifesto"

Spencer's major work is his "Alt-Right manifesto," also known as "What It Means To Be Alt-Right: A metapolitical manifesto for the Alt-Right movement" or "The Charlottesville Statement." It was released on August 11, 2017, just before the tragic events in Charlottesville, Virginia.

The "Alt-Right manifesto" is an attempt by Spencer to create a broad white nationalist movement and influence the masses of white Americans wedded to liberal or socialist multiculturalism. It clearly mimics the right-wing manifesto written in 1999 by de Benoist and Charles Champetier.[33] Spencer himself likens it to the manifestos of the conservative and New Left movements of the early 1960s, *The Sharon Statement* (1960) and *The Port Huron Statement* (1962).[34] Spencer's own manifesto consists of twenty points.[35] In suggesting that the manifesto is "metapolitical," Spencer borrows from the cultural struggle of the French New Right. Spencer, like the French New Right, believes that the radical Right must be more Gramscian—winning hearts and minds, changing vocabulary, and bringing issues of race, "Jewish influence," immigration, multiculturalism, ethnic consciousness, and white political solidarity to the center of American political life.

The first point of the manifesto is about race:

> Race is real. Race matters. Race is the foundation of identity. White is shorthand for a worldwide constellation of peoples, each of which is derived from the Indo-European race, often called Aryan. "European" refers to a core stock—Celtic, Germanic, Hellenic, Latin, Nordic, and Slavic—from which related cultures and a shared civilization sprang.

It is significant that *race* is the first point of the manifesto, because for Spencer the US should be a race-based ethnic state devoid of non-Europeans, nonwhites, blacks, and Jews. Whereas historically many white nationalists might have excluded Latin and Slavic peoples from the US, Spencer calls for the unity of all whites on both sides of the Atlantic. Guillaume Faye similarly calls for the unity of white Europeans of different stock.[36] Or, as Spencer puts it in another piece, "Our dream is a new society, an ethno-state that would be a gathering point for all Europeans. It would be a new society based on very different ideals than, say, the Declaration of Independence."[37] How this would be attained is never precisely sketched out by Spencer and the Alt Right, argues George Hawley.

Race is central for Spencer because both the mainstream political parties (Democrats and Republicans), he argues, deny the centrality of race, push for open borders that dilute the sanctity of the white race, and promote a multiculturalism that is a homogenizer of white peoples and ultimately all peoples. "As long as whites continue to avoid and deny their own racial identity, at a time when almost every other racial and ethnic category is rediscovering and asserting its own, whites will have no chance to resist their dispossession,"[38] stated Spencer, echoing Wilmot Robertson.

It is also significant that the notion of race is thoroughly discredited, especially in the West. Spencer thus uses race in order to attack politically correct liberal-Left discourses, which negate the importance of race in politics and human history. He wants to create racial ethnic states globally, which borrows from the New Right's global "cultural ethnopluralism."[39] These ethnostates are seen in a positive light—forces against a "one-world civilization," globalization, multiculturalism, and homogenizing capitalism—all "destroyers" of peoples.[40] Alternative elites like Spencer must lead the drive toward white ethnostates, which Spencer notes in point three of the manifesto. In point two of the manifesto, Spencer writes:

> Jews are an ethno-religious people distinct from Europeans. At various times, they have existed within European societies, without being of them. The preservation of their identity as Jews was and is contingent on resistance to assimilation, sometimes expressed as hostility towards their hosts. "Judeo-Christian values" might be a quaint political slogan, but it is a distortion of the historical and metaphysical reality of both Jews and Europeans.

Here Spencer breaks one of the major taboos of post–World War Two politics: anti-Semitism. Fascism and Nazism were discredited for their racism, imperialism, violence, totalitarianism, and virulent anti-Semitism. The Final Solution demonstrated the genocidal thrust of Nazism and its biological anti-Semitism. Spencer also repeats what Nazis and some others (including Evola) have said about the Jews: that they are a distinctive people compared to Europeans, and hence cannot be Europeans; that they maintain their identity and refuse to assimilate into their host societies;

and that they are hostile to whites or Europeans as they allegedly support internationalist ideologies such as liberalism and socialism and promote capitalism—all "antinational" and "traitorous" forces.

Spencer further advances the notion that the concept of Judeo-Christian values is "a distortion of the historical and metaphysical reality of both Jews and Europeans" and suggests that Jews imposed the egalitarian Judeo-Christian tradition on Europeans. What Europeans really want is elitist, hierarchical, and homogeneous societies, a point repeatedly made by de Benoist.[41] Like whites, Jews should have their own ethnostate (Israel). In one interview for an Israeli television station, Spencer shockingly called himself a Zionist.[42] Despite his anti-Semitism, Spencer also supports a "sort of white Zionism," that would inspire "dispossessed" whites with the dream of such a homeland in a way that Zionism helped push for the establishment of Israel.[43] Finally, Spencer holds that Jews should not be part of the body politic because they are a different race—a position Taylor rejects.

In point three, "ethnostate," Spencer demonstrates the power of the Alt Right to create its own vocabulary on its own terms. "Alt Right" and "ethnostate" are terms used first by Spencer, then picked up by the mainstream media and spread to the public at large—part of the Alt Right's metapolitical war against the liberal-Left elites and establishment. In point three, Spencer writes: "Nations must secure their existence and uniqueness and promote their own development and flourishing. The state is an existential entity, and, at its best, a physical manifestation of a people's being, order, and will to survive. Racially or ethnically defined states are legitimate and necessary."

If we dissect these lines, it follows that whites in both Europe and America need racially and ethnically homogeneous states. Each nation must be racially defined and this alone will allow it to develop and flourish. Multicultural states are doomed to fail because of their racial mixing and are thus illegitimate. Unlike ethnic nationalism, civic nationalism is illegitimate because it focuses on political values that unite rather than racial unity. Finally, there will eventually be a larger, white ethnic racial state.

In point four of the manifesto, "Metapolitics," Spencer states maintains that the Alt Right "wages a situational and ideological war on those deconstructing European history and identity. The decrepit values of Woodstock and Wall Street mean nothing to us." Here Spencer and the Alt Right want to differentiate themselves from Fascism, Nazism, and neo-Fascist political violence and terrorism. Yet, while Spencer condemned the killing of a liberal counterprotester at Charlottesville, he also marched with the KKK and neo-Nazis. When Spencer says that the "decrepit values of Woodstock and Wall Street mean nothing to us," he sounds like de Benoist, who rejects the liberal-Left hedonism of the Woodstock (New Left) generation and the procapitalist Anglo-American New Right.[44] Like the French New Right, Spencer supports a Right that is revolutionary, antiliberal, and anticapitalist.

If points one and three are not clear enough, in point five Spencer calls for a "White America": "Other races inhabited the continent and were often set in conflict or subservience to Whites. Whites alone defined America as a European society and political order." Historically, white nationalists like the KKK demonized Roman Catholics and valorized Protestants. As whites see a world of changing geopolitical power (with the rise of nonwhite powers), demographic change, and immigration and refugee movements, they now need unity. Spencer especially negates African American and Jewish influences in the US, while grudgingly accepting Roman Catholic influences. He advances the notion that nonwhites and non-Protestants had no role in the foundation of the US, that whites defined the US, and that the US is really "a European social and political order." The Canadian philosopher George Grant might have reminded Spencer that Canada and the US include indigenous peoples and that North Americans (outside Mexico) are "Europeans who are not Europeans."[45]

In point six, "Europe," Spencer writes: "Europe is our common home, and our ancestors' bone and blood lie in its soil." For Spencer, Europe means the "blood and soil" of the ancestors, a discredited notion used by Old Right thinkers from the French ultranationalist Charles Maurras to Adolf Hitler. He further holds that white Europeans must unite around the world, and that the refugee crisis, immigration, and uncontrolled borders, are threats to white identity—"an invasion, a war without bullets." This argument has been made by right-wing terrorists such as Anders Behring Breivik, by New Right thinkers such as Faye or de Benoist, and by nationalist parties from the French National Front to the Austrian Freedom Party. Finally, he holds that given open borders and immigration and refugee policies, the Islamization of Europe and North America are possible, echoing Bat Ye'or's "Eurabia."

In point ten, "Foreign Affairs," Spencer writes:

The foreign policies of European states (including immigration, diplomacy, and war) should be based on the safeguarding of its peoples—and not be beholden to special or foreign interests, nor to corporate profit motives, nor to the chimeras of globalism, humanitarianism, or the End of History. Insofar as "chauvinism" means attempting to transform non-Europeans into Europeans, we are not "Western chauvinists."

Spencer thus questions the way most conservatives support Israel, as highlighted in his piece in Gottfried's edited volume *The Great Purge*.[46] Spencer's foreign policy positions consists of a rejection of "end of history" liberalism where the US attempts to convert all states to liberalism, even at gunpoint; a rejection of chauvinistic, Old Right colonialism; and opposition to alleged "Jewish" and "foreign" influences in US foreign policy, a point highlighted by realist thinkers such as Stephen Walt and John Mearsheimer in their book *The Israel Lobby and U.S. Foreign Policy* (2006). He argues that if its foreign policy is determined by "foreign" lobbies or corporate interests, the US is not de facto a sovereign state. The foreign policy of the US must protect white Europeans.

In point fourteen, "The Left," Spencer states: "Leftism is an ideology of death and must be confronted and defeated." The Left's liberalism, socialism, egalitarianism, and multiculturalism must be superseded.

In points fifteen and sixteen, Spencer's echoes the French New Right's antiglobalization and anticapitalist agendas as dangers to all rooted cultures and peoples: "Economic freedom is not an end in itself. All economic policies should serve the people of the nation; the interests of businessmen and global merchants should never take precedence over the well-being of workers, families, and the natural world," and "Globalization threatens not just Europeans but every unique identity on Earth."

In point eighteen, Spencer blames the New Left generation of "the 68ers" for their "childish narcissism," their inability to pass on the legacy of European civilization to their children, and hence argues that "they bear responsibility for today's lamentable state of affairs." De Benoist also blames the 1968 generation for their liberal-Left values, but also praises them for their attention to the importance of gaining ideological hegemony in the mass media and civil society.[47] In this respect, point nineteen, "Education," notes that modern education "has become corrupted past the point of recognition" and it "serves leftist ideologues, loan financiers, and a new class of administrators far more than it serves students and parents." Rather than children "indoctrinated in liberal dogma," Spencer's elitism is clear: "higher education" can only be "appropriate for a cognitive elite dedicated to truth."

What is striking about the manifesto is its focus on the metapolitical as a prelude to a revolutionary, postliberal, and racial order; its intellectual borrowing from the French New Right; and its distinctive focus on homogeneous European identities. Only points eleven and twelve of the manifesto, on free speech and the right to bear arms, are distinctively American.

Conclusion

Spencer understands the power of slowly winning hearts and minds. Although he would suggest that many Americans are liberal and that the media and universities are largely liberal-Left, race cuts across class lines, and white ethnic politics has more support than one might imagine. The Trump phenomenon is an example. It will take time, but winning key elites and convincing the public may lead to the reordering of the political landscape away from liberal multiculturalism toward white racial politics. If elites do not see the coming storm and fail to see the growing white racial consciousness in the US, a revolution of values may divide the masses and elites. Cultural power, insisted de Benoist, will eventually threaten the apparatus of the state.[48] An example of this cultural strategy is the election of Donald Trump, whom Spencer sees as a guardian of white identity because of his vociferously anti-immigrant, anti-Mexican rhetoric.

The revolution longed for by Spencer's Alt Right would require the defeat of egalitarianism, liberalism, multiculturalism, and immigration—a project that requires root and branch changes in mentalities within the cultural and political systems. First, more of the public needs to support race politics, anti-immigrant politics, anti-Jewish politics, and the building of the white ethnic states. Elites are responsible for "deconstructing European history and identity," insists Spencer—for making whites feel ashamed of racial consciousness, anti-immigrant politics, the history of slavery, or even Confederate monuments and symbols.

Spencer's "ideological war" with the establishment led him to even defend the ideals (if not the actions) of the white-supremacist terrorist Dylann Roof, who in 2015 killed nine black churchgoers in Charleston, South Carolina. Spencer, like Taylor, admitted that Roof had "legitimate concerns in his manifesto" since the latter "seriously pondered the implications of race on American society."[49]

Spencer is the leading communicator of the Alt Right message rather than its leading intellectual. What the Alt Right wants was neatly summarized by Greg Johnson: the implementation of Old Right ideals but through new right tactics and strategy.[50] As the "Alt-Right manifesto" showed, Spencer's obsession with race and Jews repeats central Old Right ideals. The rejection of violence, genocide, colonialism, and totalitarianism, and the focus on metapolitics, and global cultural ethnopluralism, are New Right tactics. Spencer's intellectual influences are both Old Right—including numerous fascists—and New Right.

Spencer's metapolitical strategy is a long way from even gaining cultural power, and even farther away from implementing its ideal of homogeneous, white ethnostates. It has won over neither the masses nor the elites of the US. Spencer is not clear on how he will get the Alt Right from his critique of the status quo toward a hierarchical, postliberal, and racial political order. Yet, if we think back to the "Alt-Right manifesto" and rallies like Charlottesville, one aim is to intimidate Jews, blacks, Mexicans, and other minorities to leave the US. Referenda on immigration or multiculturalism could conceivably promote the democratic and legal exclusion of nonwhites. Spencer may also hope that elites in power like Trump will shut the door for nonwhites to enter the US and thus "make America great again." Although his suggestion that Israel is an ethnostate is incorrect, it does suggest that a small white homeland can begin in a few states and then spread to other parts of the US. The Zionist dream was improbable but eventually attained. Similarly, white ethnonationalism is unlikely in the US today as the country prides itself on racial equality, but it is not impossible that one day it might be reached. At minimum, Spencer and the Alt Right seek to end mass immigration and gain acceptance of white identity as a normal element of mainstream politics in the US, insists George Hawley.

It is clear that Spencer has found his niche as the Alt Right provocateur and media spokesman. The mass media are lining up to interview him, and university students are listening to his message. He is the vanguard of an alternative elite that will supposedly defeat liberal multiculturalism and turn the US into white ethnostates. In order to be successful, he will need to convert his predominantly online and anonymous Alt Right into a more organized white nationalist movement, which rubs shoulders with leading political elites in Washington and makes inroads with the masses of white Americans.

Notes

1. "The National Policy Institute," Facebook page, accessed October 14, 2017, https://www.facebook.com/TheNationalPolicyInstitute/.
2. George Hawley, *Making Sense of the Alt-Right* (New York: Columbia University Press, 2017), 58–59; "William H. Regnery II," Southern Poverty Law Center (SPLC), accessed October 30, 2017, https://www.splcenter.org/fighting-hate/extremist-files/individual/william-h-regnery-ii.
3. "Who Are We?" National Policy Institute/Radix, December 12, 2015, accessed October 15, 2017, https://www.youtube.com/watch?v=3rnRPhEwELo.
4. Greg Johnson, *New Right versus Old Right* (San Francisco: Counter-Currents, 2013), xv.
5. "'Hail Trump!': Richard Spencer Speech Excerpts," *Atlantic*, November 21, 2016, accessed October 15, 2017, https://www.youtube.com/watch?v=1o6-bi3jlxk.
6. Joseph Goldstein, "Alt-Right Exults in Donald Trump's Election with a Salute: 'Heil Victory,'" *New York Times*, November 20, 2016.
7. Jared Taylor, *White Identity: Racial Consciousness in the 21st Century* (San Bernardino: New Century Books, 2011), xiv.
8. "Richard Bertrand Spencer," SPLC, accessed October 13, 2015, https://www.splcenter.org/fighting-hate/extremist-files/individual/richard-bertrand-spencer-0.
9. "White Nationalist Richard Spencer Talks to Al Jazeera," *Al-Jazeera*, December 9, 2016, accessed October 15, 2017, http://www.aljazeera.com/news/2016/12/white-nationalist-richard-spencer-talks-al-jazeera-161209184916999.html.
10. Tamir Bar-On, *Rethinking the French New Right: Alternatives to Modernity* (Abingdon: Routledge, 2013), 22–26; Tamir Bar-On, *Where Have All the Fascists Gone?* (Aldershot: Ashgate, 2007), 5.
11. "Richard Bertrand Spencer," SPLC.
12. Max Ehrenfreund, "What the Alt-Right Really Wants, According to a Professor Writing a Book about Them," *Washington Post*, November 21, 2016.
13. Richard Spencer, "The Conservative Write," *Taki's Magazine*, August 6, 2008.
14. *Radix Journal*, AltRight.com, accessed October 1, 2017, https://altright.com/author/radix/.
15. Jacob Siegel, "The Alt-Right's Jewish Godfather," *Tablet*, November 29, 2016, accessed October 15, 2017, http://www.tabletmag.com/jewish-news-and-politics/218712/spencer-gottfried-alt-right.
16. Richard B. Spencer, "What It Means To Be Alt-Right," AltRight.com, August 11, 2017, accessed October 1, 2017, https://altright.com/2017/08/11/what-it-means-to-be-alt-right/.
17. Lauren M. Fox, "The Hatemonger Next Door," *Salon.com*, September 29, 2013, accessed October 15, 2017, https://www.salon.com/2013/09/29/the_hatemonger_next_door/.

18. Graeme Wood, "His Kampf," *Atlantic*, June 2017, October 11, 2017, https://www.theatlantic.com/magazine/archive/2017/06/his-kampf/524505/.
19. Cas Mudde, *On Extremism and Democracy in Europe* (New York: Routledge, 2016), chap. 7.
20. Masha Gessen, *The Future Is History: How Totalitarianism Reclaimed Russia* (New York: Riverhead Books, 2017), 482; Anton Shekhovtsov, *Russia and the Western Far Right: Tango Noir* (New York: Routledge, 2018).
21. Alain de Benoist, *Vu de droite: anthologie critique des idées contemporaines* (Paris: Copernic, 1979).
22. Richard B. Spencer, ed., *The Uprooting of European Identity* (Arlington, VA: Washington Summit Publishers, 2016).
23. Johnson, *New Right versus Old Right*, 95.
24. Richard B. Spencer, "What Is the American Right?" in *The Great Purge: The Deformation of the Conservative Movement*, eds. Paul Gottfried and Richard Spencer (Arlington, VA: Washington Summit Publishers, 2015), ix–xviii.
25. Spencer, "What Is the American Right?," x–xi.
26. Alain de Benoist, *Comment peut-on être païen?* (Paris: Albin Michel, 1981).
27. Alexander Griffing, "Donald Trump Receiving Criticism from Alt-Right Leaders after Israel, Saudi Arabia Visits," *Ha'aretz*, May 25, 2017, accessed October 15, 2017, https://www.haaretz.com/us-news/1.791559.
28. Ibid.
29. Daniel Lombroso and Yoni Appelbaum, "'Hail Trump!': White Nationalists Salute the President-Elect," *Atlantic*, November 21, 2016.
30. Richard B. Spencer, "#ArizonaTrumpRally," Twitter, August 22, 2017, accessed October 30, 2017, https://twitter.com/RichardBSpencer/status/900181906704171013?ref_src=twsrc%5Etfw&ref_url=http%3A%2F%2Fthehill.com%2Fblogs%2Fblog-briefing-room%2Fnews%2F347586-richard-spencer-trump-has-never-denounced-the-alt-right.
31. Roger Griffin, "Foreword: Another Face? Another Mazeway?" in Tamir Bar-On, *Where Have All the Fascists Gone?*, xiii.
32. Wood, "His Kampf."
33. Alain de Benoist and Charles Champetier, "Manifesto of the French New Right in the Year 2000," accessed October 15, 2017, https://neweuropeanconservative.files.wordpress.com/2012/10/manifesto-of-the-french-new-right1.pdf.
34. Spencer, "What It Means To Be Alt-Right."
35. Hereafter I quote the manifesto from Spencer, "What It Means To Be Alt-Right."
36. Guillaume Faye, *Archeofuturism: European Visions of the Post-Catastrophic Age* (Arktos Media, 2010).
37. "Richard Bertrand Spencer," SPLC.
38. Ibid.
39. Martin Lee, *The Beast Reawakens* (Toronto: Little, Brown, 1997), 168–183.
40. Guillaume Faye, *Le Système à tuer les peoples* (Paris: Copernic, 1981).

41. Alain de Benoist, *Vu de droite*, 19, 25.
42. Sam Kestenbaum, "Richard Spencer Touts Himself as 'White Zionist' in Israeli Interview," *Fast Forward*, August 17, 2017, accessed October 15, 2017, http://forward.com/fast-forward/380235/richard-spencer-touts-himself-as-white-zionist-in-israeli-interview/.
43. Ibid.
44. Alain de Benoist, "Confronting Globalization," *Telos* 108 (Summer 1996): 117–137.
45. George Grant, *Technology and Empire* (Concord, Ontario: Anansi, 1969).
46. Spencer, "What Is the American Right?"
47. GRECE, *Le Mai 68 de la nouvelle droite* (Paris: Labyrinthe, 1998).
48. Alain de Benoist, *Les Idées à l'endroit* (Paris: Broché, 1979).
49. Joel A. Brown, "Dylann Roof, the Radicalization of the Alt-Right, and Ritualized Racial Violence," *Sightings*, January 12, 2017, accessed October 13, 2017, https://divinity.uchicago.edu/sightings/dylann-roof-radicalization-alt-right-and-ritualized-racial-violence.
50. Johnson, *New Right versus Old Right*, 5.

15

Jack Donovan and Male Tribalism

Matthew N. Lyons

ON OCTOBER 31, 2015, a powerfully built man addressed the annual conference of a little-known white nationalist organization, Richard B. Spencer's National Policy Institute. Wearing a close-fitting T-shirt instead of the jacket and tie worn by most attendees, Jack Donovan urged his audience to reject "universal morality," which, he told them, "makes men weak, leaves them lost, confused, dependent, helpless." White European men, he said, had simply been putting their own people first when they conquered, killed, or enslaved people all around the world. "They basically did the same things other people have done in every other human society all throughout history. *They were just fucking good at it,*" Donovan shouted to applause. "If white men, if any men, want to be free, want to be strong, want to say yes to life again, they're going to have to abandon universalist morality and liberate their tribal minds."[1]

Donovan's "Tribal Mind" speech embodied several of the themes and tensions that have helped to make him one of the American Right's most innovative and distinctive thinkers. He is a skilled writer and speaker who has a knack for expressing deeply controversial ideas in simple and compelling terms. He believes that human equality is a lie, violence is necessary, and exclusionary groups are the only real basis for a workable system of ethics. He has a history of seeking common ground with white nationalists, but he is actually not one of them: in Donovan's ideology race is ultimately secondary to gender, and he is concerned with how not only white men, but "any men," can be free and strong.

The "Tribal Mind" speech also highlighted Donovan's political use of his own body. Here, as in many online photographs, Donovan's physique advertised the masculine strength and power he idealizes, in a way that carried both class and sexual tensions. In a gathering that sought to present white nationalists as clean-cut professionals (not boots-and-suspenders skinheads or camouflage-wearing survivalists), Donovan looked like a lumberjack or stevedore, and while he is very much an intellectual (and an artist), he has in fact supported himself largely through physical labor. At the same time, showing off his body was also an implicit reminder that Donovan was an openly homosexual man speaking to a movement that has traditionally reviled homosexuality, and that his vision of masculinity encompasses sexual relationships between "manly men" even as it rejects and vilifies gay culture.

Implicitly, Donovan's "Tribal Mind" speech offered many core elements of his chief contribution to right-wing thought: the doctrine of male tribalism, a form of male supremacist ideology that centers on the comradeship of fighters and departs from established patriarchal doctrines, notably that of the Christian Right. Male tribalism is distinct from, but complementary to, white nationalism, and Donovan's years of collaborating with white nationalists have helped them to forge a multifaceted supremacist ideology.[2]

Writings and Activities

Jack Donovan was born in 1974 and grew up in rural Pennsylvania. He has also lived in New York City and California, and for the past several years has lived in or near Portland, Oregon.[3] He has worked at a variety of jobs, from go-go dancer to truck driver to tattoo artist. His first book, *Androphilia: A Manifesto*, was published in 2006 under the pen name Jack Malebranche. Three years later, he coauthored *Blood Brotherhood and Other Rites of Male Alliance* with Nathan F. Miller. Since then, he has self-published three books under the Dissonant Hum imprint: *The Way of Men* (2012), *A Sky Without Eagles* (2014), and *Becoming a Barbarian* (2016). Donovan has also put out numerous articles about masculinity and related topics, either on his own Jack Donovan website, or on other right-wing sites. *The Way of Men*, arguably his most important and systematic work, has been translated into French, Portuguese, and German.[4]

Since 2006, Donovan has been involved in various organizations and movements. As of 2007 he was a priest of the Church of Satan, which he described as "very much a do-it-yourself religion when it comes to personal ethics," but resigned from the church in 2009.[5] He has had a limited connection with the "manosphere," an antifeminist online subculture, which has fostered ideas about masculinity that are related to his own. From 2010 to 2017, Donovan was an active participant in the Alt Right. Since 2015, he has been a member of the Wolves of Vinland, a Virginia-based neopagan group that embodies many of his male tribalist principles, and he founded a Pacific Northwest branch of the organization.[6]

Core Ideas of Male Tribalism

Donovan began to develop a philosophy of male bonding in his first book, *Androphilia*. Here he defines and celebrates a specific form of male homosexuality. "I do not simply prefer to have sex with male bodies. I am attracted socially, sexually and conceptually to adult men and adult masculinity. . . . I am attracted to the expression of MAN as an archetype."[7] In *Androphilia*, Donovan rejects the label "gay," criticizes gay culture for promoting effeminacy among homosexual men and for allying with feminism, and argues that homosexual men should be held to the same gender expectations as heterosexual men. Donovan also rejected same-sex marriage on the grounds that society has an interest in promoting traditional nuclear families. He regards the union between two men as something fundamentally different from marriage. This led him to coauthor the book *Blood Brotherhood*, which draws on blood-bonding rituals from different cultures as a basis for formalizing homosexual relationships between men.

From these beginnings, Donovan expanded his scope to address male bonding as a fundamental basis for male identity and society as a whole. "The Way of Men," Donovan argues in the book of that title, "is the way of the gang." "For most of their time on this planet, men have organized in small survival bands, set against a hostile environment, competing for women and resources with other bands of men."[8] These gangs, he claims, have provided the security that makes all human culture and civilization possible. They are also the social framework that men need to realize their true selves. Donovan's gangs foster and depend on the "tactical virtues" of strength, courage, mastery, and honor, which together form his definition of masculinity.[9] Gang life centers on fighting, hierarchy, and drawing the perimeter against outsiders ("separating *us* from *them*"). Homosexuality creates problems within gangs mainly if it correlates with submissiveness or effeminacy, which weaken the gang's collective survival capacity. Patriarchy, he argues, is the natural and rightful state of human affairs because it is rooted in this primeval survival scenario where women are a prize that male gangs fight over.

Donovan sees a basic tension between the wildness and violence of gang life and the restraint and orderliness that civilization requires: civilization benefits men through technological and cultural advances, but it also saps their primal masculinity—their strength, courage, mastery, and honor. For most of human history, he says, men have fashioned workable compromises between the two, but with societal changes over the past century that has become less and less possible. Today, "globalist civilization requires the abandonment of the gang narrative, of *us* against *them*. It requires the abandonment of human scale identity groups for 'one world tribe.'"[10] This attack on masculinity is being led by "feminists, elite bureaucrats, and wealthy men," who "all have something to gain for themselves by pitching widespread male passivity. The way of the gang disrupts stable systems, threatens the business interests (and social status) of the wealthy, and creates danger and uncertainty for women."[11] With the help of globalist elites, feminists have supposedly dismantled patriarchy and put women in a dominant role. "For the first time in history, at least on this scale, women wield the ax of the state over men." Women have "control over virtually all aspects of reproduction," and "a mere whisper from a woman can place a man in shackles and force him to either confess or prove that he is innocent of even the pettiest charges." Faced with the bumper-sticker slogan, "Feminism is the radical notion that women are human beings," Donovan retorts that this should be rewritten as "Feminism is the radical notion that men should do whatever women say, so that women can do whatever the hell they want."[12]

To counteract the decline of masculinity, Donovan advocates a latter-day tribal order that he calls "The Brotherhood." Like his imagined primeval gang experience, The Brotherhood consists of small, closely knit bands of men, all of whom affirm a sacred oath of loyalty to each other against the outside world. A man's position is based on "hierarchy through meritocracy," not inherited wealth or status. The Brotherhood would not be limited to any one economic or political model. It might be run as a democracy or it might have a king, "as long as he had to start at the bottom and demonstrate his worth—and the next king did too." All men would be expected to train and serve as warriors, and only warriors would have a political voice. Women would not be "permitted to rule or take part in the political life of The Brotherhood, though women have always and will always influence their husbands."[13]

In keeping with his rejection of "universalist morality," Donovan does not advocate The Brotherhood as a dream for everybody. "I don't believe that people with different interests who live far away from each other should have to agree on a way of living, and I believe that forcing them to accept a foreign or unwanted way of life is tyranny ... the world is better and far more interesting if there are many cultures with different values and ideals."[14] At the same time, he does regard the reassertion of traditional masculinity and male power as an ideal that cuts across ethnicities and cultures:

> For instance, I am not a Native American, but I have been in contact with a Native American activist who read *The Way of Men* and contacted me to tell me about his brotherhood. I could never belong to that tribe, but I wish him great success in his efforts to promote virility among his tribesmen.[15]

Male Tribalism in ideological context

Donovan's male tribalism builds on several basic premises that are standard across most right-wing movements: that gender roles are natural and immutable; that men as a group should hold power over women; and that women's main roles should be to bear and raise children, and to provide men with support, care, and sexual satisfaction. Yet Donovan's gender politics differ sharply from those of the Christian Right, which has been at the forefront of patriarchal initiatives in the US for several decades. Donovan's reliance on evolutionary psychology contrasts with the Christian Right, which justifies male dominance as obedience to God's law, and the "androphilia" he celebrates would be anathema to Christian Rightists, who have made open homosexuality a major political target.

Christian Right ideology emphasizes an idealized model of the "traditional" family, where women obey their fathers and husbands, who in turn provide them with security, economic support, and love. Although women are firmly subordinated to male authority, they are offered a sense of meaning as housewives and mothers. By contrast, Donovan's vision of The Brotherhood makes the family itself peripheral, thereby devaluing women's roles even more. As the white nationalist Jef Costello has noted, Donovan reverses the conventional idea that men hunt and fight to protect and provide for their families, arguing instead that women exist to bring men into the world, and the family exists because it makes idealized male gang life possible.[16]

In addition, sections of the Christian Right have appropriated elements of feminist politics in the service of the movement's patriarchal agenda, claiming, for example, that abortion "exploits women" or that federal support for childcare is wrong because it limits women's choices, as well as encouraging women to become politically active, speak publicly, and even take on leadership roles. Donovan, on the other hand, is completely uninterested in speaking to women's concerns or recruiting women to be politically active.

Tracing Donovan's intellectual influences can be difficult. He uses few footnotes yet refers to a wide range of other writers, ranging from classical authors such as Aristotle and Livy to modern leftists such as Noam Chomsky and bell hooks [Gloria Jean Watkins]. *Androphilia* cites some other right-wing homosexual male writers such as Andrew Sullivan and Yukio Mishima. *The Way of Men* draws on the work of various authors who have called for reasserting traditional masculinity, such as Harvey C. Mansfield and James Bowman. Here and in his essay "No Man's Land," Donovan also draws on advocates of evolutionary psychology such as Lionel Tiger and Derek Freeman. Parts of *Becoming a Barbarian*, Donovan's most recent book, draw heavily on Norse mythology, presumably reflecting his new membership in the Wolves of Vinland, which practices a form of Odinism. Yet Donovan reworks and synthesizes these eclectic elements in new and original ways.

Some of Donovan's ideas, such as his emphasis on male bonding and his belief that violence offers a kind of spiritual fulfillment, echo Conservative Revolutionaries such as Ernst Jünger, whose work he has reviewed sympathetically.[17] Some of Donovan's ideas, such as his rejection of universalist morality in favor of tribalist loyalties, may be influenced by European New Right authors such as Alain de Benoist. Yet their critiques of universalism differ, at least in emphasis: while de Benoist argues that universalism is wrong because different cultures answer "essential questions" differently, Donovan's main critique is that it is smarter and more natural for men of all cultures to apply different ethical approaches to group members and outsiders.[18] And aside from favorable comments about Guillaume Faye's *Archaeofuturism*, Donovan does not cite European New Rightists.[19]

In broader terms, Donovan's male tribalism resonates strongly with themes found in classical fascism—meaning the broad political category that in the 1920s–1940s encompassed movements in many countries—of violent male camaraderie at odds with "bourgeois" family life, glorification of the masculine body, exclusion of women, and sometimes even homoeroticism. F. T. Marinetti's 1909 "Futurist Manifesto" prefigured some of these themes: "We want to glorify war—the only cure for the world—militarism, patriotism, the destructive gesture of the anarchists, the beautiful ideas which kill, and contempt for woman."[20] Early fascism took the intense, trauma-laced bonds that World War I veterans had formed in the trenches and transferred them into street-fighting formations such as the Italian *squadristi* and German storm troopers. And while fascism in power murderously suppressed homosexuality, the movement celebrated manliness and spiritual ties between men in ways that were sometimes homoerotic, with Ernst Röhm's Brownshirts the most famous example.

Donovan alluded to these resonances in a 2013 essay in which he embraced the term "anarcho-fascism." Donovan highlighted connections between male tribalist principles and the original fascist symbol, the *fasces*, a bundle of wooden rods that stands for strength and unity. Rejecting the common belief that fascism equals a totalitarian state or top-down bureaucratic rule, he identified the *fasces* with the "bottom-up idea" of "a unified male collective. . . . True tribal unity can't be imposed from above. It's an organic phenomenon. Profound unity comes from men bound together by a red ribbon of blood." The ax at the center of the *fasces* represented "a threat of violence . . . a warning, a promise of retaliation" that men could still take up a century later. "The modern, effeminate, bourgeois 'First World' states can no longer produce new honor cultures. New, pure warrior-gangs can only rise in anarchic opposition to the corrupt, feminist, anti-tribal, degraded institutions of the established order. . . . Ur-fascism is the source of honor culture and authentic patriarchal tradition."[21]

Broader social critique and vision of change

While Donovan's critique of US society centers on gender, it also includes several other common right-wing themes. Like many rightists, Donovan criticizes "globalism," meaning a project spearheaded by elites in recent decades to weaken borders in pursuit of profit and power. Globalism's emphasis on trade, he argues, has helped enshrine universalism (an effeminate form of ethics with roots in classical philosophy) as ideologically dominant.[22] He denounces "the progressive state" for pursuing policies—such as globalism, multiculturalism, and militarism—that serve only economic and political elites and those loyal to them.

The US in Donovan's view has a fundamentally broken system, under which "the rulers and toadies" safeguard their own status by keeping most people "separate, emasculated, weak, dependent, faithless, fearful and 'non-violent.'" He believes the US is on the road to become "a failed state—a state where no one believes in the system, where the government is just another shakedown gang, where no one confuses the law with justice."[23] To him this is a hopeful scenario: "In a failed state, we go back to Wild West rules, and America becomes a place for men again—a land full of promise and possibility that rewards daring and ingenuity, a place where men can restart the world."[24]

This forecast affects Donovan's ideas about how to bring about the society he wants. Instead of conventional forms of political activism such as public demonstrations, electoral campaigns, or even armed struggle against the progressive state, his strategy for change is for men to "build the kinds of resilient communities and networks of skilled people that can survive the collapse and preserve [their] identities after the Fall."[25] Donovan calls on men to forge small groups and build trust through shared activities such as hunting, martial arts, and sports. He also urges people to sever their "emotional connection" to the state and stop looking to it for help and direction.[26]

Reception and political involvement

Donovan's innovative thought and prolific output have enhanced his visibility and helped him to engage with several interrelated political networks.

Manosphere

Donovan is sometimes seen as part of the manosphere, an online subculture of men who believe that women hold too much power, and who advocate various strategies to reassert male dominance, ranging from vilifying feminists, to changing divorce and domestic violence laws, to sexual predation. Like Donovan, many manospherians invoke evolutionary psychology to bolster claims that traditional gender roles are inherent in human nature, and many of them emphasize male bonding as a key part of reasserting men's power. Donovan has written favorably that "The manosphere is an outer realm where male tribalism rules. . . . [It] is not about what women want, or about making sure men and women are equal. The manosphere is about men writing about who men are and what they want, without supervision."[27] For a time he was a regular contributor to the *Spearhead*, an antifeminist online journal founded by W. F. Price that operated from 2009 to 2014. Since then, however, his involvement in manosphere discussions and activities has been more limited. For example, he had little or no involvement in Gamergate, a major campaign launched by manosphere activists in 2014 to harass and vilify women who worked in, or were critical of sexism in, the video game industry.[28] In addition, Donovan's name does not appear in searches of several leading manosphere websites and blogs.[29]

Homophobia is widespread within the manosphere, and this has affected Donovan's reception there, although not necessarily in the way one would expect. For example, influential manospherian Daryush Valizadeh ("Roosh V"), who is staunchly antigay, commented after reading *The Way of Men*, "Ironic that a gay man wrote one of the manliest books I've ever read." Another prominent manosphere figure, Paul Elam, has contended that Donovan has become "obsessed" with proving that he is manly as a result of being homosexual in a culture that does not regard him as a real man. "Lighten up, Jack. *You're gay*. Just accept it. You don't have to be heterosexual, or an over compensating asshole, to be a man."[30]

Alt Right

Donovan's involvement with the Alt Right has been more extensive and important. Donovan wrote for Spencer's original *AlternativeRight.com* online journal, which operated from 2010 to 2012. He has written for several other Alt Right publications, such as Spencer's later online journal *Radix*, Jared Taylor's *American Renaissance*, and Greg Johnson's Counter-Currents; and has spoken at both National Policy Institute and American Renaissance conferences. Alt Rightists have been important supporters of his work for years; in the acknowledgments for *The Way of Men*, for example, Donovan thanks several of them, including Spencer, Johnson, Scott Locklin of *AlternativeRight.com*, and Jef Costello of Counter-Currents.[31]

Donovan has contributed to an ideological shift within the Alt Right toward more misogynistic politics. In its early years, the Alt Right encompassed a range of viewpoints on gender. Several writers argued that women's political participation was valuable and important, and some expressed concern that women were underrepresented in Alt Right circles.

Andrew Yeoman declared bluntly in *AlternativeRight.com* that sexual harassment and other sexist behavior by men in the movement were driving women away: "We need women's help, now more than ever," yet "nothing says 'you are not important to us' [more] than sexualizing women in the movement."[32]

Within a few years, however, such quasi-feminist sentiments had disappeared from the Alt Right, replaced by claims that women were unsuited by nature to political activism, and that "it's not that women should be unwelcome [in the Alt Right], it's that they're unimportant," as Matt Forney put it.[33] This shift partly reflected an influx of manospherians into the Alt Right since about 2014, as antifeminist activists such as Forney and Andrew Auernheimer ("weev") embraced white nationalism. Yet the change built directly on gender politics that Jack Donovan had been advocating within the Alt Right for years.

Donovan's sexuality has made him a focal point for controversy within the Alt Right. One outraged blogger asked in 2012, "How on Earth [does] a nationalist site that purports to defend traditional, white interests end up promoting the views of out-of-the-closet homosexuals?" In 2015 Andrew Anglin of the *Daily Stormer* urged people to boycott the National Policy Institute conference when he learned that Donovan would be speaking.[34]

Many Alt Rightists, however, have actively defended the inclusion of homosexual men in the movement. In 2010, Counter-Currents republished a 2002 article by Greg Johnson, which argued that white nationalists should not allow themselves to be divided over sexuality, homophobia was a Jewish invention, and "the bonded male group, the *Männerbund* . . . is the foundation of all higher forms of civilization, particularly Aryan civilizations." These themes have been further elaborated by a Counter-Currents author, James O'Meara, who is both a white nationalist and openly homosexual. Donovan's participation in the movement has also been treated respectfully even by those who emphasize "traditional" values, such as the Christian-identified Brad Griffin of the *Occidental Dissent* blog and Matthew Heimbach of the Traditionalist Worker Party.[35] Donovan's involvement in the Alt Right made it easier for the flamboyantly gay rightwinger Milo Yiannopoulos to carve out a role as an ambassador between the Alt Right and mainstream conservatism.

Questions of his sexuality aside, some of Donovan's other views set him apart from the majority of Alt Rightists. While most enthusiastically supported Donald Trump's 2016 presidential campaign, Donovan did not. He argued that a President Trump would simply mask the system's fatal flaws and that a Hillary Clinton presidency would be preferable, because it would "drive home the reality that white men are no longer in charge... and that [the United States] is no longer their country and never will be again."[36]

Donovan was also unusual in that his politics center on gender, not race. He is sympathetic to many white nationalist aims and considers it "heroic" to challenge "the deeply entrenched anti-white bias of multiculturalist orthodoxies."[37] Yet he also declared that "I am not a White Nationalist because I don't think people are worth saving just because they're white. . . . Most white people suck. *What else have you got?*" In broader terms, "a tribal community has to have a lot more going for it than race. . . . Race alone isn't enough to unite a people."[38]

Despite these criticisms, Donovan aided white nationalists for years by associating with them visibly and publicly. As Greg Johnson of Counter-Currents wrote in a public reply to Donovan's "Why I Am Not a White Nationalist":

> You are a valuable ally precisely because you never claimed to be a White Nationalist, but you still stuck up publicly for White Nationalists, wrote for our publications, and spoke at our events. Having people who are not White Nationalists openly associate with us gives us social validation and builds bridges to the mainstream.[39]

However, in August 2017 Donovan posted an update to "Why I Am Not a White Nationalist," in which he repudiated the Alt Right and declared that he would no longer allow white nationalists to publish or use his work. Although the vast majority of Alt Rightists had identified with white nationalism for several years, Donovan criticized a recent manifesto by Richard Spencer for proclaiming the Alt Right to be a white nationalist movement, and the recent "Unite the Right" rally in Charlottesville (at which an antifascist protester was killed) for bringing Alt Rightists together with neo-Nazis and Ku Klux Klansmen, "people who actively despise me and my friends."[40]

Wolves of Vinland

Donovan joined the Wolves of Vinland after a 2014 visit to their Virginia camp.[41] Founded in or around 2006 by the brothers Paul and Mattias Waggener, the Wolves draws on Norse and Germanic paganism, Julius

Evola's Traditionalism, the manosphere, motorcycle gangs, and powerlifting and mixed martial arts. There are three chapters in North America (including the Pacific Northwest branch that Donovan founded), with a larger feeder organization known as Operation Werewolf active in several European countries as well as the US.

The Wolves is often labeled white nationalist, a description that Donovan rejects.[42] Members of the Wolves often sport symbols, such as the Black Sun and the Wolfsangel, that have been extensively (but not exclusively) used by white nationalist groups, and Operation Werewolf shares its name with the Nazi underground military organization set up in 1944–45 to operate behind Allied lines. The Wolves also rallied behind one member who was imprisoned for burning down a black church. A number of Alt Right groups have viewed the Wolves as a kindred organization representing principles similar to their own. But unlike most of the Alt Right, the Wolves of Vinland is primarily a physical membership organization, and it also differs from the predominantly white-collar Alt Right in that most of its membership appears to be working class.[43]

The Wolves of Vinland embodies many aspects of male tribalism, although it initially took shape without reference to Donovan's work. Paul Waggener has commented that when he first read *The Way of Men*, he "kind of looked around [and thought], 'Man, has this guy been following us or what?'" Donovan's work helped the group clarify and define its philosophy, so that developing Donovan's "four pillars of masculinity . . . strength, courage, mastery, and honor," became "the core of what we do."[44] The Wolves of Vinland celebrates male bonding and violence in ways that are literally ritualistic, using animal sacrifices and holding fights between members to test their manliness.[45] There is a strong emphasis on tribalism in the sense of being culturally separate from the outside world. And although Waggener says that they "look for equality between sexes," men and women are seen as having sharply different roles, with men firmly at the center.[46] Members of the Wolves, Donovan included, also emphasize the aesthetics of masculinity, using social media extensively to show off their muscular bodies, weapons, and tattoos.[47]

Like Donovan, the Wolves criticizes current-day society not only for shaking up traditional gender roles but also for moving toward a "corporate monoculture" that "mediates all activity through television, through the internet" and "creates hollow people . . . who have no sense of community . . . roots, [or] tribe." Again like Donovan, its approach to bringing about the kind of society it wants is simply to build it—to forge relationships and ways of living that embody their principles. This involves some efforts to make its communities economically and financially self-reliant. The Wolves has little or no interest in political activism in the conventional sense.[48]

Conclusion

Through his writings, his organizational activities, and most recently his aggressive use of his own physical image, Jack Donovan has contributed an important strand to right-wing politics. His doctrine of male tribalism evokes powerful themes of violence and community, of embracing and overcoming danger, of reaffirming manhood and restoring it to dominance. Male tribalism offers a critique of the status quo and a vision of the future that is just as sweeping and systematic as the Christian Right's gender ideology, and that is complementary to white nationalism but not dependent on it.

Donovan's work is part of a long-term rightist backlash against the rise of feminism. In the past, many rightists accommodated elements of feminist politics within a patriarchal framework to help them mobilize women, but Donovan, the Alt Right, and the manosphere embody a recent, harsher trend to vilify women's political agency or exclude them altogether. This has been coupled with moves among some rightist networks to accept or even welcome homosexual men, and to emphasize secular and pagan ideologies over Christianity. All of these trends echo elements of classical fascism, and they illustrate the capacity of the Right's new thinkers to rework old political themes in creative ways.

Notes

1. Jack Donovan, "The Tribal Mind" (video), speech at National Policy Institute Conference, October 31, 2015, YouTube, https://www.youtube.com/watch?v=TNrsXtQWRJM.
2. Some passages in this chapter appear in different form in *Insurgent Supremacists: The U. S. Far Right's Challenge to State and Empire* (Oakland, CA: PM Press, 2018); "Ctrl-Alt-Delete: The Origins and Ideology of the Alternative Right," Political Research Associates, January 20, 2017, http://www.politicalresearch.org/2017/01/20/ctrl-alt-delete-report-on-the-alternative-right/#sthash.59B4l69h.1JRopEJI.dpbs; or "Jack Donovan on Men: A Masculine Tribalism for the Far Right," *Three*

Way Fight (blog), November 23, 2015, http://threewayfight.blogspot.com/2015/11/jack-donovan-on-men-masculine-tribalism.html.
3. "About Jack Donovan," Jack Donovan (website), archived May 10, 2011, https://web.archive.org/web/20110510212918/http://www.jack-donovan.com:80/axis/bio/.
4. See bibliography for a list of Donovan's books.
5. Chip Smith, "The First Rule of Androphilia: An Interview with Jack Malebranche," *The Hoover Hog*, January 2009.
6. Jack Donovan, "A Time for Wolves," Jack Donovan, June 14, 2014, http://www.jack-donovan.com/axis/2014/06/a-time-for-wolves/; "The Wolves of Vinland: A Fascist Countercultural 'Tribe' in the Pacific Northwest," Rose City Antifa, November 7, 2016, http://rosecityantifa.org/articles/the-wolves-of-vinland-a-fascist-countercultural-tribe-in-the-pacific-northwest/.
7. Smith, "First Rule of Androphilia."
8. Jack Donovan, *The Way of Men* (Milwaukie, OR: Dissonant Hum, 2012), 3.
9. Ibid., 19.
10. Ibid., 139.
11. Ibid., 138.
12. Jack Donovan, "No Man's Land: Masculinity Maligned, Reimagined," Jack Donovan, 2011, http://www.jack-donovan.com/axis/no-mans-land/.
13. Jack Donovan, "The Brotherhood," *A Sky Without Eagles* (Milwaukie, OR: Dissonant Hum, 2014), 153–167; quotations are from pages 161, 162, and 158.
14. Ibid., 156.
15. Ibid., 166–167.
16. Jef Costello, review of *A Sky Without Eagles* by Jack Donovan, Counter-Currents, July 2014, http://www.counter-currents.com/2014/07/jack-donovans-a-sky-without-eagles/.
17. Jack Donovan, "A Tribe Among the Trees: Ernst Jünger's *The Forest Passage*," Counter-Currents, June 30, 2014, https://www.counter-currents.com/2014/06/a-tribe-among-the-trees/.
18. Alain de Benoist and Charles Champetier, "Manifesto of the French New Right in Year 2000," New European Conservative (website), undated, https://neweuropeanconservative.files.wordpress.com/2012/10/manifesto-of-the-french-new-right1.pdf; Donovan, "The Moral Gear Shift," in *Becoming a Barbarian*.
19. Jack Donovan, "Paleofuturism for the Man; Archeofuturism for the People," Counter-Currents, November 2013, https://www.counter-currents.com/2013/11/paleofuturism-for-the-man-archeofuturism-for-the-people/.
20. F. T. Marinetti, "The Futurist Manifesto" (1909), in *Three Intellectuals in Politics*, by James Joll (New York: Pantheon Books, 1960), 182.

21. Jack Donovan, "Anarcho-Fascism," Jack Donovan, March 3, 2013, archived March 31, 2017, at https://web.archive.org/web/20170331060008/http://www.jack-donovan.com/axis/2013/03/anarcho-fascism/.
22. Jack Donovan, "The Empire of Nothing" and "The Mother of Exiles," in *Becoming a Barbarian*.
23. Jack Donovan, "Becoming the New Barbarians," *Radix*, December 23, 2013, archived February 9, 2014, at https://web.archive.org/web/20140209144417/http://www.radixjournal.com/journal/becoming-the-new-barbarians.
24. Jack Donovan, "The Bright Side of Illegal Immigration," Jack Donovan, November 13, 2012, archived November 15, 2012, at https://web.archive.org/web/20121115235941/http://www.jack-donovan.com:80/axis/2012/11/the-bright-side-of-illegal-immigration/.
25. Donovan, "Becoming the New Barbarians."
26. Donovan, *Way of Men*, 165, 158.
27. Jack Donovan, "Long Live the Manosphere," Jack Donovan, September 9, 2012, archived June 17, 2013, at https://web.archive.org/web/20130617174230/http://www.jack-donovan.com/axis/2012/09/long-live-the-manosphere/.
28. On Gamergate, see Amanda Marcotte, "Gaming Misogyny Gets Infinite Lives," *Daily Beast*, August 22, 2014, http://www.thedailybeast.com/gaming-misogyny-gets-infinite-lives-zoe-quinn-virtual-rape-and-sexism; Stephen Totilo, "Another Woman in Gaming Flees Home Following Death Threats," Kotaku, October 11, 2014, http://kotaku.com/another-woman-in-gaming-flees-home-following-death-thre-1645280338.
29. Keyword searches for "Jack Donovan" performed on The Anti-Feminist (http://theantifeminist.com), Chateau Heartiste (https://heartiste.wordpress.com/), *The Counter-Feminist* (http://counterfem.blogspot.com/), and Vox Popoli (http://voxday.blogspot.com/) returned no results.
30. Roosh V [Daryush Valizadeh], Comment on "Jack Donovan" thread, Roosh V Forum, November 16, 2012, https://www.rooshvforum.com/thread-17870.html; Paul Elam, "What the Fuck is Wrong with Jack Donovan?" A Voice for Men, January 20, 2011, https://www.avoiceformen.com/miscellaneous/what-the-fuck-is-wrong-with-jack-donovan/.
31. Donovan, *Way of Men*, 169–170.
32. Quoted in Matthew N. Lyons, "AlternativeRight.com: Paleoconservatism for the 21st Century," *Three Way Fight*, September 10, 2010, http://threewayfight.blogspot.com/2010/09/alternativerightcom-paleoconservatism.html.
33. Matt Parrott, "Where the White Women At," Traditionalist Worker Party (website), April 13, 2015, https://www.tradworker.org/2015/04/where-the-white-women-at/; Danielle Paquette, "The Alt-Right Isn't Only about White Supremacy. It's about White Male Supremacy." *Chicago Tribune*, November 25, 2016, https://www.washingtonpost.com/news/wonk/wp/2016/11/25/

the-alt-right-isnt-just-about-white-supremacy-its-about-white-male-supremacy/?utm_term=.273dff8917cb.

34. "Pseudomen in White Nationalism," *West's Darkest Hour* (blog), March 26, 2012, https://chechar.wordpress.com/2012/03/26/pseudo-men-in-white-nationalism/; Ari Feldman, "Can The 'Alt-Right' Distance Itself from Neo-Nazis?" *Forward*, August 31, 2016, http://forward.com/news/national/348366/can-the-alt-right-distance-itself-from-neo-nazis/.

35. Greg Johnson, "Homosexuality and White Nationalism," Counter-Currents, October 2010, https://www.counter-currents.com/2010/10/homosexuality-and-white-nationalism/; "The Homo & the Negro: Masculinist Meditations on Politics and Popular Culture, by James O'Meara" (book notice), Counter-Currents, 2012, https://www.counter-currents.com/the-homo-and-the-negro/; "A Chorus of Violence: Jack Donovan and the Organizing Power of Male Supremacy," Southern Poverty Law Center, March 27, 2017, https://www.splcenter.org/hatewatch/2017/03/27/chorus-violence-jack-donovan-and-organizing-power-male-supremacy; Hunter Wallace [Brad Griffin], "Review: 2014 American Renaissance Conference," Occidental Dissent, April 28, 2014, http://www.occidentaldissent.com/2014/04/28/review-2014-american-renaissance-conference/.

36. Jack Donovan, "No One Will Ever Make America Great Again." Jack Donovan, July 7, 2016, http://www.jack-donovan.com/axis/2016/07/no-one-will-ever-make-america-great-again/; on the Alt right's responses to Donald Trump, see Lyons, "Ctrl-Alt-Delete."

37. Jack Donovan, "Mighty White," Jack Donovan, December 18, 2011, http://www.jack-donovan.com/axis/2011/12/mighty-white/.

38. Jack Donovan, "Why I Am Not a White Nationalist," Jack Donovan, May 31, 2017 (updated August 19, 2017), https://www.jack-donovan.com/axis/2017/05/why-i-am-not-a-white-nationalist/.

39. Greg Johnson, "A Reply to Jack Donovan," Counter-Currents, June 2017, https://www.counter-currents.com/2017/06/a-reply-to-jack-donovan/.

40. Donovan, "Why I Am Not a White Nationalist"; Richard Spencer, "What It Means To Be Alt-Right," AltRight.com, August 11, 2017, https://altright.com/2017/08/11/what-it-means-to-be-alt-right/.

41. Donovan, "Time for Wolves."

42. Maureen O'Connor, "The Philosophical Fascists of the Gay Alt-Right," *The Cut*, April 30, 2017, https://www.thecut.com/2017/04/jack-donovan-philosophical-fascists-of-the-gay-alt-right.html.

43. "The Wolves of Vinland."

44. "Greg Johnson Interviews Paul Waggener," Counter-Currents, February 2016, https://www.counter-currents.com/2016/02/greg-johnson-interviews-paul-waggener-2/.

45. Donovan, "Time for Wolves."

46. "Greg Johnson Interviews Paul Waggener."
47. "Wolves of Vinland." See also the Operation Werewolf website at http://www.operationwerewolf.com/ and the Jack Donovan website at http://www.jack-donovan.com/axis/, as well as Jack Donovan's author page on Facebook at https://www.facebook.com/author.jack.donovan/.
48. "Greg Johnson interviews Paul Waggener."

16

Daniel Friberg and Metapolitics in Action

Benjamin Teitelbaum

DANIEL FRIBERG SPENT most of his early career as a background figure in European white nationalism. If you study an anti-immigrant political party, militant organization, think tank, retail outlet, or festival in 1990s and early 2000s Sweden you are likely to find his hand in it, and projects for which he was centrally responsible later became mainstays for radical rightists throughout the globe. Then, as Brexit and the rise of Donald Trump focused global media attention on the Right, Friberg emerged as one of its international faces. His name began appearing in North American and European white nationalist media like Counter-Currents and *American Renaissance*, and he was profiled in mainstream outlets in his native Sweden as well as in international publications like *International Business Times, Buzzfeed*, and the *Wall Street Journal*. The coverage came not because of any sensational act or statement on his part, but instead due to his slow-moving, steady, and effective efforts to promote antiliberal culture and intellectualism. He had assembled a media, literature, and music empire whose expansion seemed exponential, always with the goal of cultivating a new generation of rightists with tools to challenge the Left at the level of ideas. The content of those ideas varied throughout Friberg's career and across his initiatives: for him it is method, rather than ideology, that matters most.

And it has been a particular type of method, one called "metapolitics." The method figured into the activism of many Western antiliberals during the early twenty-first century, and for that reason it has been mentioned frequently throughout this book. Defined by Guillaume Faye as the "social diffusion of ideas and cultural values for the sake of provoking profound, long-term, political transformation,"[1] metapolitical campaigning diverges from standard activist dualisms of party politics versus militancy. It is based on the assumption that meaningful political change originates in education, media, and creative expression; parliamentary or revolutionary initiatives succeed only when they build upon existing cultural sympathies forged in those arenas. Though rooted in the thinking of neo-Marxist Antonio Gramsci, metapolitics as a theorized concept entered the radical Right via the French New Right.[2] Daniel Friberg, however, emerged as its foremost strategist and implementer.

This chapter traces Friberg's life, thought, and activism. It investigates a plurality of initiatives and projects rather than a single opus. Metapolitical activism typically strives to saturate multiple discursive arenas, subcultures, and expressive forms with its radical message, and, following that logic, Friberg's work cannot be justifiably localized to any one format or product. I trace in broadly chronological order his creation of magazines and newspapers; literature and music production firms; online communities; blog and media portals; annual seminars and festivals; online encyclopedias; and his own authored literature. To help make sense of these projects and to gain a broader view of their trajectory and significance, I highlight those instances where Friberg describes his broader strategy. Seldom have those statements come in formal settings: as he told me once, "metapolitics works best when people don't know you're shaping the way they think."[3] Instead, I find this material in interviews he held with journalists and colleagues, as well as with me. And we have spoken often. I have followed Friberg's career since I began conducting ethnographic research on Nordic nationalists in 2010, and have come to know and enjoy him personally—and this despite major differences between us.[4] I have dined, drunk, and lived with him. Such contact can be corrupting; it may make it less likely that I provide a dispassionate account of the person, if not the career. But it also provides me uncommon access to his criticisms and reflections, which in turn add a dialogic element to my account—a feature I welcome as a contrast with the often reflexively monophonic nature of commentary on the radical Right.

Although this chapter discusses the actions of an individual, Friberg's story is in embryo that of the Western radical Right at the turn of the twenty-first century. In his journey we find the transition away from a cultural model based on skinheadism, the strengthening of digital activism, the diffusion of French New Right concepts and methods, and the emergence of a new topography in which activists organize themselves based more on medium, forum, and tactic than ideology. But in order to understand Friberg's career and how it relates to the broader radical Right, we must first explore the practice of metapolitics and the ways it has been conceived and implemented as activism.

Metapolitics

The emergence of metapolitics as a named, self-conscious practice within the radical Right relied on a particular assessment of postwar social and political history in the West. Liberalism, according to French New Right thinkers like Alain de Benoist and Guillaume Faye, was so entrenched in Western society that its values persisted regardless of whether ostensibly liberal or antiliberal forces controlled government. After the fall of Fascism and Nazism, values like liberty and equality were no longer thought of as the ideology of a peculiar political cause. Instead, they were understood as transcendent common sense: their power was hegemonic. And just as Gramsci blamed culture for having made communist revolution an impossibility in 1930s Italy, so too did the New Right seek to counteract the dominance of liberal values in the West through cultural campaigning—through metapolitics—with the hope of forging a new consensus and political common denominator to work from.

There was little clarity from the New Right as to what counted as "culture" in this scheme.[5] The approach was embraced nonetheless by activists throughout the early-twenty-first-century radical Right, from the proto Alt Right blogger and producer Greg Johnson, to the semimilitant Vigrid party in Norway, to the populist Sweden Democrats.[6] Based on their and others' actions, the "culture" that is the target of metapolitics appears broad, consisting in educational platforms and media as well as expressive genres like film, literature, art, theater, and music.

The intended purpose of metapolitics, too, varies. Such campaigning can seek either to infiltrate or replicate dominant cultural forms and forums. It may, for example, strive to alter the curricula of public schools, or create a parallel educational system saturated with radical values. While the first approach attempts to shape thinking within a broader population, the second aims to build a parallel population of zealots. Crucially, society at large is not always the target arena for metapolitical campaigning, as activists may also train their efforts on transforming the profile of a marginal group. In the case of the radical Right, the latter often concerns efforts to reform antiliberal, anti-immigrant activism and movements.

While most activists have restricted their metapolitical campaigning to one of these forums or objectives, one figure made it his business to pursue them all.

Daniel Friberg

Daniel Friberg is perpetually late and impeccably dapper. He drinks and smokes hard, but always keeps his cool, moving and talking slowly with the deepest of voices. Since 2014 he has lived in Budapest, Hungary, and spends most of his days roving between the city's bars and cafés with his business partners, dining almost always with hands shuffling between a cell phone, laptop, beer, and cigarettes. And he is friendly, at least toward me. He was a notorious brawler during his youth and was tried in court for hate speech and, later, for threatening a former business associate with a gun.[7] That reputation may have insured his survival. A former member of a militant National Socialist organization told me that he and his associates once considered attacking Friberg, but refrained because they regarded him as too dangerous a target.

His career—like that of most marginal political actors—has been contentious, creating enemies out of potential allies, and vice versa, at every turn. If one constant in Friberg's story is interpersonal conflict, however, so too is his leveraging of metapolitics to shape the activism of friend and foe alike. He was born 1978 in the western Swedish city of Gothenburg to a family he describes as relatively affluent, educated, and leftist. Encounters with a more multiethnic population in middle school (*högstadiet*) convinced him to break away from that foundation, and at that young age he entered the dominant anti-immigrant scene in Sweden: white-power skinheadism. He shaved his head, donned combat boots and a bomber jacket, and started attending concerts organized by local Gothenburg white-power music promoters. The close-cropped cut would be short-lived for Friberg. He recalls having quickly soured on the subculture, and came to lament the fact that its stigmatizing boorishness and brutalism had seized the nationalist cause. He recalls:

> When I grew more politically conscious as a teenager, my first impression was that mass immigration was harmful to Sweden. And

my second impression was that the reaction toward mass immigration was essentially worthless. And I saw it as my opportunity to steer the movement in another direction, to steer all that energy toward constructive ends. I wanted it to go in a more intellectual direction, and away from everything I found problematic, everything from skinhead subculture, to Third Reich nostalgia, to primitive white power music, and so on.[8]

It is worth noting that Friberg nonetheless aligned ideologically with the more radical members of that scene. He was what was Swedes referred to as an "ethnonationalist"—a nationalist who fights for racial and ethnic purity, as opposed to "cultural nationalists" who claim to fight only for cultural homogeneity while disavowing interest in race. Friberg's criticism of other nationalists thus dealt with style, expression, and lifestyle rather than agenda.

As part of his effort to transform anti-immigrant activism in his home society, Friberg would use metapolitical tactics before he had a name for them. His first political activism came in middle school when he handed out leaflets for the nationalist Sweden Democrats (Sverigedemokraterna) party. Shortly thereafter—and armed with a new laser printer—he began making his own anti-immigrant propaganda to post around his school. But his efforts accelerated when he founded Alternative Media in 1997, a project conceived both to propagate to the populace at large and to provide nationalists in Sweden with literature other than the scene's mainstays of white-power music fanzines. He began by producing the newspaper *Framtid* (*Future*), spending his entire savings as a nineteen-year-old to print 21,000 copies, and sent them to all graduating high-school students in Stockholm in Gothenburg.[9] The initiative provided few immediate results, but it profiled Friberg within nationalist circles as a bold media campaigner. The following year he joined the editorial staff of the newspaper *Folktribunen* (*People's Tribune*), which served as the main media outlet for the newly established Swedish Resistance Movement (Svenska motståndsrörelsen, today the largest militant National Socialist organization in the Nordic countries). He and his closest team of collaborators quickly exited the Resistance Movement as it was radicalizing, however, and initiated a project more expressly in line with his original reformist goals.

The Nordic League

In 2001 Friberg cofounded Nordiska förlaget (Nordic Press) with the twin aims of providing nationalists new "education" and "inspiration." According to their debut website, translating—initially into Swedish—and marketing books would fulfill the first goal, while music distribution served the second.[10] Friberg would make a vital contribution to the organization's musical offerings. His agency Alternative Media initiated the three-CD, acoustic singer/songwriter project Svensk ungdom (Swedish Youth). The project aspired to break with trends inside of white nationalist music making, which since the 1980s had been consumed by skinhead punk and metal. In contrast with that status quo, it featured subdued ballads and reigned-in language. Svensk ungdom passed from Alternative Media to Nordiska förlaget, and the first release in the series, *Frihetssånger* (*Freedom Songs*), remains one of the most popular nationalist albums in the Nordic countries today. But Nordiska förlaget's starkest contrast with the nationalist status quo centered on book production. By sponsoring new texts, making translations, or marketing existing offerings, Nordiska förlaget became the first major source for literature in the anti-immigrant, white nationalist scene. Thanks to them, nationalist concerts and festivals at the turn of the twenty-first century began to feature, not only T-shirts and music recordings but now books—most of them with a semiacademic character.

Friberg was injecting—if nothing else—an aesthetic for intellectualism into anti-immigrant activism that would mature as the years went by. Meanwhile, he would continue to produce smaller newspapers and magazines with the goal of allowing radical rightists to disconnect from the mainstream media. His 2003 tabloid *Folkets nyheter* (*People's News*), for example, promoted itself with the statement: "By subscribing to *Folkets nyheter*, you will no longer need to read the established papers, no longer need to support them financially, no longer need to read between the lines to keep yourself updated as to what is happening around the world."[11]

It sounded a lot like a campaign of metapolitics trained on cultivating a parallel society. But Friberg had been operating on instinct up until this point, following his own impressions of how one ought to build a stronger opposition to liberalism. That all changed the following year when he first came into contact with the writings of French New Right intellectuals. He recalls:

DF: It was this translation of the *Nouvelle Droite* [New Right] manifesto that I read. It was online, written in English. And there I had this "aha" experience. Thought it was totally brilliant, and wondered why these ideas weren't better known.

BT: What was so good about them?

DF: It was the logical construction, the intellectual caliber—it was on a totally different level that I was used to reading, texts from the right, that is. It was the best I had ever read in the radical Right milieu. . . . It was radical, but appropriately so. It dismissed egalitarianism, for example. That is a core feature of today's left-wing liberal society—it is that it was so encompassing and well-argued.[12]

The French New Right's call for an ostensibly nonchauvinistic ethnic separatism appealed to Friberg as a morally defensible and thereby politically formidable alternative to white-power jingoism. Likewise, the school's methodological imperative to metapolitics motivated him to expand his own campaign—giving it a name and intellectual cachet to defend the approach from naysayers.

Changes to Friberg's activism came in swift succession. That same year, in 2004, his team of partners established Nordiska förbundet (the Nordic League)—an umbrella entity that would contain the Press—in a declaration of their ambition to create a more comprehensive output. It also sought to profile itself as more self-consciously metapolitical, writing on their debut website:

> Both parliamentarian efforts and the physical struggle must be seen as smaller parts or complements to a much broader ethnic and political pursuit. We need a wide-ranging, and long-term approach, a long-term Nordic survival strategy. We need a strategy that moves forward and reinforces our positions in many different areas, that deals constructively with the here and now, but that, at the same time, has its sights on the horizon—that has its sights set on our own Nordic, vital, and viable society. . . . And the first and vital step in every survival strategy is education, to grow and spread knowledge, to grow and spread inspiration.[13]

Rejecting democracy and militancy, Nordiska förbundet embraced a strategy advancing their cause in "many different areas," which is to say, to message in multiple arenas of social behavior and communication. The goal was to forge an intellectual foundation for political mobilization. In metapolitical practice, this would come to mean both refining the behavior and thinking of current activists, as well as evangelizing to new audiences previously turned off by nationalism's crude forms.

If a turn toward the French New Right was apparent in Nordiska förbundet's branding, so too was it registering in their merchandise. Friberg and Nordiska förbundet cofounder Lennart Berg were pushing to include more and more texts from the French intellectual school and associated radical Traditionalists like Julius Evola and René Guénon in their production while also striving to rid themselves more thoroughly of white-power skinheadism. They met resistance, both from the wider population of nationalists in Sweden at the time, and from old-guard members of Nordiska förbundet itself (first and foremost cofounder and white-power music connoisseur Peter Melander). Friberg recalls being dismissive of such complaints and regards them today as by-products of nationalism's depravity at the time:

> Their reactions were like, "What is this stuff that I can't really understand? It must be harmful in some way, because it makes us feel inadequate since we don't understand it, so this must be resisted. It is some kind of ideological deviance!" They saw it as a threat. Because it was more intellectual, or because it was—in their eyes—more liberal or because it was a departure from what they saw as a more radical nationalism. But that isn't true. It is instead an idea that is being expressed in a way that attracts groups other than those who existed in the Swedish nationalist milieu at the time. And of course these old groups experienced this as a threat since they were not the main target of these new texts, and they weren't capable of understanding it, really.[14]

Openness to French New Right and Traditionalist thought became, for Friberg, a sort of litmus test, a measure by which foot soldiers of a stale and dying radical Right were separated from the vanguards of his new ideal.

Friberg gradually emerged as the foremost figurehead of Nordiska förbundet during the following years as other leaders quit, were sidelined, or were chased out. In parallel, Nordiska förbundet slowly centered itself on French New Right and Traditionalist ideology—often under the heading "identitarianism"—and amassed a greater and greater number of affiliated projects that would outlive Nordiska förbundet itself. In

July 2006, leaders established the Swedish-language blog portal *Motpol*, featuring writers who were often ultraconservatives steeped in identitarian thinking, but who had little background in white-power skinheadism. That same year, Nordiska förbundet created the Wikipedia-styled online encyclopedia Metapedia. In an interview in *Folkets nyheter*, Friberg (writing under the pen name Martin Brandt) described the motivation behind the project, framing the initiative as part of an effort to advance a "cultural war" (*kulturkamp*):

> A few friends and I were discussing how important it is for the nationalist culture war to be able to present our own interpretations of concepts, phenomena, and historic events for a broader public. It is especially important these days, since many concepts have been distorted and lost their original meaning, which you can see as an outcome of our political opponents' successful culture contestation.... Just look at how the Frankfurt School and their ideological heirs have succeeded in stigmatizing what were once completely natural values, by introducing concepts like ... "xenophobia," "homophobia," and so on.[15]

The expression "cultural war" is here a substitute for the term "metapolitics." Metapedia would strive to replicate the educational function of Wikipedia, allowing those on the radical Right to craft their own resources for interpreting concepts and phenomena. It would also have an infiltrating function by blending more seamlessly into online search results. At the same time that Nordiska förbundet used Metapedia to penetrate the digital media and education landscape, they were also working to craft an alternative to online social networking. In 2007, the organization opened *Nordic*—an online community page marketing itself as a "portal for Nordic identity, culture, and tradition." Users created accounts with names and often profile images and thereby gained access to online games, radio, and discussion threads ranging on topics from politics to homework assistance and second-hand shopping. It aimed, in other words, to allow users to disconnect from sites like Myspace and satisfy all of their online social needs in an ideologically friendly environment.

Both Metapedia and Nordic strove to expand beyond the Swedish context. The online social networking sites were mostly in Swedish, but they were marketed to and occasionally included threads for other Scandinavian language-users. The online encyclopedia, though originating with a

Swedish page, began expanding to other languages immediately—first to Danish, then German and English. And while Metapedia and Nordic appealed to the cultural mainstream, Nordiska förbundet continued to advance its highbrow intellectual campaign as well. In 2009, it established an annual seminar series called Identitarian Ideas/Identitär Idé.

That same year, in what seemed a retrospective or mere formality at that point, Nordiska förbundet posted its declaration of a metapolitical agenda. A statement on their website coauthored by Friberg concludes:

> To forge a metapolitical avant garde—and thereby an essential complement to every political initiative—is Nordiska förbundet's mission. We see metapolitics as a multidimensional, flexible, and dynamic force with potential to capture the essence of key issues and expose perspectives that undermine and deconstruct the politically correct malaise and the guilt that today burdens the Nordic peoples.
> But metapolitics isn't only about undermining and deconstructing. It creates, encourages, inspires, and exposes. In total, our metapolitics strives to set an identitarian movement in motion, a cause growing in strength both through our own channels as well as those of the partially censored channels of the establishment. A cause that, when it has reached a critical mass, will determine its own path to fundamentally transform today's shackling public space and prepare the way for a Nordic cultural and folk renaissance—the rebirth of a new Nordic golden age.[16]

It was a good time to make such a declaration. By 2009, Nordiska förbundet's metapolitical campaigning seemed ascendant. Projects like *Motpol* and identitarian Ideas were satisfying the aims of crafting a more refined space and ideal for the radical Right cause. And if they provided intellectual depth, Nordiska förbundet's other initiatives were achieving remarkable breadth. Metapedia quickly spread throughout Europe and North America, expanding its pages from Swedish, Danish, English, and German to include Spanish, French, Hungarian, Romanian, Estonian, Croatian, Slovenian, Greek, Czech, Portuguese, Norwegian, and Dutch. Combined, these pages produced nearly three hundred thousand articles.[17] The social networking site Nordic likewise grew rapidly, reaching twenty thousand registered users from throughout Sweden, Norway, and Denmark by the same time, and serving as the main online hub for nationalist activists of various kinds, from populist party politicians to terrorist Anders Behring Breivik.

Arktos

The curse of the postwar radical Right—infighting—would be the death of Nordiska förbundet. Simmering conflicts over ideology led to purges, and clandestine saboteurs even managed to cause the organization significant financial losses. These developments, combined with the heavy cost of buying the rights for the Nordiska förlaget's signature translation—*Culture of Critique* by Kevin MacDonald—made for a dire economic situation. Friberg assumed sole ownership of Nordiska förbundet in 2009, and that same year he ceased its operations while allowing Metapedia, Nordic, and *Motpol* to continue. "It was all just as well," Friberg told me, thinking back. Nordiska förlaget in particular had been born too close to the old white-power skinhead scene, in his mind, and it revealed those roots in its shrunken, but ever-present body of products celebrating Nazism and decadent youth subculture. "I wanted to have a fresh start that was more in line with the project I envisioned from the beginning with Nordiska förbundet," an initiative that was radical, but intelligent, welcoming, respectable, and innovative. He wanted something with the ideological profile of his blog portal *Motpol*—something grounded in the French New Right and Traditionalist perspective—but a publishing house, something with a wider reach to complement the spread of *Metapedia* internationally.[18]

In October 2009 Friberg sat at a meeting in Aarhus, Denmark, together with a Norwegian politician and two Danes to establish the publishing house Arktos, which became a reality in 2010. Absorbing both the inventory of Nordiska förlaget and the Danish company Integral Traditions Publishing, Arktos would emerge as the foremost producer of English-language Traditionalist and New Right literature, featuring authors like Evola, de Benoist, and Faye, as well as international authors like Alexander Dugin, and Paul Gottfried. Various figures from the Scandinavian radical Right would enter and exit Arktos throughout the following years, but Friberg assumed the role of CEO and served as its organizational pillar along with American John Morgan as chief editor.

By multiple measures, the venture succeeded. The publishing house appears to have become the largest retailer of radical Right literature in the world during the 2010s, attracting a large (though somewhat artificially inflated) social media following in the process. Arktos would also assume the role as hub for Friberg's other projects in much the same way that Nordiska förlaget did before, but operating internationally beyond the Nordic region and in English. It became the sponsor of the annual identitarian Ideas seminar that, by 2013, was becoming a major international gathering for antiliberal philosophers, politicians, and political commentators.

The metapolitical impact of these efforts registered internally within the radical Right in Northern Europe. As I have noted elsewhere,[19] one can see an iconography of books and other emblems of learnedness surfacing in radical Nordic nationalists' self-depictions in online social media at this time, with individual activists choosing to take profile photos of themselves standing in libraries or in front of packed bookshelves. Friberg's desire for a new standard for social capital within the radical Right seemed to have spread. Likewise, writing, both for blogs as well as for book-length publications, grew as an insider practice even among younger generations of activists. And identitarian Ideas became the main annual meeting place for intellectually ambitious participants in various types of rightist organizations. This marks a major lifestyle change, replacing an old anti-immigrant activist prototype based in skinheadism, music production, and decadence with one of academic refinement and orderliness.

The Alt Right and Internationalization

Despite his successes, however, Friberg's goal was not only to reform existing activist circles or to cater exclusively to those aspiring to a cultural elitism. He wanted access to the international online media market—one that, if not low-brow per se, was at least accustomed to commentary in bite-sized formats suited to distribution in social media. To pursue these ends alongside his other initiatives, Friberg and his partners established RightOn.net in early 2015. The outlet featured articles by a handful of authors, video commentary streaming through YouTube, and two semiweekly podcasts—one by the American Matt Forney, and the other by Friberg along with John Morgan and the Swedish white nationalist Jonas De Geer.[20]

RightOn.net's slogan, "Putting the Action in Reactionary,"[21] revealed a nascent Zeitgeist shift coming to all of Friberg's projects that year, one whereby the defensive, recuperative pose of his early metapolitics was giving way to a new one, on the offensive. On a *Motpol* blog post in July 2015, Friberg issued a call seeking distance from the principle of "riding the tiger," the strategy Evola described for post–World War II antiliberals in the West whereby activism could only consist in remaining conspicuous and avoiding explicit proselytizing and conflict while waiting for the tiger of modernity to run its course and wither of old age. That final stage of modernity, Friberg thought, had come, and nonintervention and withdrawal were no longer survival tactics for the rightist dissident; they were cowardice squandering opportunity. Such opportunity, the sign of fatigue from the tiger of modernity, showed itself in the electoral victories of European populist parties, in the strength of Vladimir Putin's antiliberalism, in the nascent campaign of Donald Trump, and in general dismay in Europe relating to the 2015 refugee crisis. Friberg wrote:

> Even if "riding the tiger," to use Evola's terms, was once a healthy and necessary strategy during the latter half of the past century, it isn't any more. Europe is bleeding, but the tiger—liberal modernity—is dying as well. It is time to climb off and strangle it while a European civilization still exists.[22]

"Strangolare la tigre" (strangle the tiger) became a brief rallying cry in Right social media thereafter. Just what strangling the tiger meant—what transitioning away from secretive activism entailed—the article didn't clarify. But for Friberg, the statement seemed a declaration of his ongoing move into public discourse. If careful, subversive metapolitical strategy involved concealing one's identity and its association with radical politics, Friberg would now break that dogma in what was for him unprecedented fashion.

In 2015 he published his first book, *The Real Right Returns* (*Högern kommer tillbaka*). The impetus for this book was his conviction that the regime of liberalism in the West that had previously made open resistance suicidal was losing its hegemonic position, and that an explicit radical Right could now enter the public space without fear of devastating repression. A sort of handbook premised on that very account of history, the text outlines strategies for activists to conduct politics in public while counteracting the challenges of the liberal establishment. Publishing a book under his own name was for him an unprecedented move, and so too was his speech in 2015 at the eighth identitarian Ideas conference[23]— the background figure and organizer was becoming a public personality. That same year, he began giving interviews in rightist media like *Europa Terra Nostra*, Red Ice Radio, and Greg Johnson's Counter-Currents. But notoriety and new metapolitical opportunity awaited Friberg as he began to seize on a new transnational movement, about to reap unprecedented rewards.

In January 2017, in anticipation of the ninth identitarian Ideas conference to be held the following month, Friberg entered into a partnership together with Richard Spencer and his National Policy Institute, and the Swede Henrik Palmgren and his media outlet Red Ice Creations, to form the Alt-Right Corporation. This initiative, coming on the heels of Brexit and the American presidential election the previous year, was conceived as a flagship effort to unify major players in the transatlantic white-identity movement. It centered on the formation of a website, AltRight.com, which in many ways replicated the format of Friberg's previous platform RightOn.net, but which now harnessed the media reach and—in the context of Far-Right activism—exceptional production quality of Palmgren's Red Ice Creations, as well as Spencer's celebrity.[24]

Aligning with the Alt Right at a pseudo-administrative level was in keeping with many aspects of Friberg's past activism. The American movement had grown in part from some his own initiatives: to the extent that it channeled ideals of the French New Right, that intellectual engagement relied on the distribution of English translations of thinkers like de Benoist and Faye—many of which spread through Friberg's publishing companies. Indeed, Spencer credited Arktos with having increased intellectually inclined white nationalist Americans' access to the French New Right and identitarianism.[25] Likewise, the world of anonymous bloggers, Twitter users, meme crafters, and YouTube video producers that make up the Alt Right rank-and-file trafficked in references to ideas channeled in Friberg's publications, be they the Archeofuturism of Faye or the antimodernism of Evola.[26] But the Alt Right also represented resounding affirmation of rightist metapolitics more broadly. Mainstream political commentators had credited the American movement in part for Donald Trump's landmark election to the US presidency in 2016. Such narratives endorse a standard metapolitical script: first cultural interventions transformed public conversations, then political behavior (in form of voting) shifted. The Alt Right at once offered Friberg recognition of the spread of his initiatives as well as the opportunity to carry his brand of activism to a wider population.

Conclusion

Though his career eventually gained an international scope, Friberg's most tangible metapolitical achievements are to be seen in his home political milieu. While white-power skinhead subculture lives on in Central and Eastern Europe, it is all but dead in Scandinavia. Brandishing swastikas and screaming "Sieg heil!" in public just seems so 1990s today. There are multiple reasons for the subculture's downfall, but Friberg can take credit for having replaced it with something: being a good nationalist in the region now entails—much in line with his early wishes—fluency in a body of radical Right intellectual thought and aspiration toward personas of erudition and professionalism. This development was enabled directly by his metapolitical initiatives, Nordiska förbundet in particular.

Friberg's international impact is less easily measured. It is difficult to gage the success of his efforts to expand the circle of white nationalist sympathizers. How many individuals throughout Europe and North America were converted to the cause by stumbling across Metapedia articles online? Only dubious answers await such questions, we can be certain that Friberg's efforts shaped and strengthened the global exposure of a select radical rightist intelligentsia, and in this respect his influence abroad resembles that in Scandinavia. Not only have his publishing houses been the avenues through which Alt-Right activists accessed the French New Right and radical Traditionalism, but the same presses as well as his various lecture series bolstered the international profile of writers like MacDonald, Gottfried, and Dugin. Those efforts helped craft what today appears a new intellectual canon in the global radical Right, and Friberg's publicizing talents meant that his projects became the forums and supplied the language for activists to engage with a celebrate that body of thought. White nationalist Twitter trolls traffic in French New Right or tradionalist-inspired hashtags like #archeofuturism and #kaliyuga, while party politicians like Gábor Vona of the Hungarian party Jobbik pen the foreword for Arktos's Evola texts.[27] And coming out of the watershed year 2016 with all its political triumphs for the international radical Right, Friberg remained convinced that his method remained essential—that Western society had not, in fact, passed to a state wherein cultural activism could be replaced wholesale with political initiatives. "Metapolitics is always necessary. Always," he told me. "Some people see Trump as the end goal, but I don't, and we still have a lot to do."[28]

Notes

1. Guillaume Faye, *Why We Fight: Manifesto of the European Resistance* (London: Arktos Media, 2011), 190.
2. Tamir Bar-On, *Where Have All the Fascists Gone* (Abingdon: Ashgate, 2007); Bar-On, *Rethinking the French New Right: Alternatives to Modernity* (Abingdon: Routledge, 2013).
3. Daniel Friberg, personal communication with author, June 6, 2014.
4. For more on my research practices and methodology, see Benjamin R. Teitelbaum, *Lions of the North: Sounds of the New Nordic Radical Nationalism* (New York: Oxford University Press, 2017).
5. Michael O'Meara's attempt at an explanation in *New Culture, New Right: Anti-Liberalism in Postmodern Europe* (London: Arktos Media, 2013) can hardly be seen as changing that.
6. Teitelbaum, *Lions of the North*.
7. Mathias Wåg, "Nationell kulturkamp—Från vit maktmusik till metapolitik," in *Det vita fältet: Samtida forskning om högerextremism*, ed. Mats Deland, Fredrik Hertzberg, and Thomas Hvitfeldt (Uppsala: University of Uppsala Department of History, 2010), 97–125.
8. Daniel Friberg, interview with author, November 6, 2017.
9. "Daniel Friberg—Return of the Real Right: Metapolitics and Rising Opposition." Accessed November 5, 2017, https://www.youtube.com/watch?v=xPgO6kb381U&t=2757s.
10. Nordiska förlaget, "Folkbildning och inspiration."
11. "Folkets Nyheter." Accessed July 11, 2012, http://sv.metapedia.org/wiki/Folkets_Nyheter.
12. Daniel Friberg, interview with author, June 6, 2014.
13. Accessed June 2, 2014, http://web.archive.org/web/20050308025324/http://www.nordiskaforbundet.se/forbundet.asp.
14. Daniel Friberg, interview with author, June 6, 2014.
15. Martin Brandt, "Metapedia," *People's News*, no. 10, 2006, July 25, 2015.
16. "Behovet av en metapolitisk strategi." Accessed November 8, 2017, http://web.archive.org/web/20090513005038/http://www.nordiskaforbundet.se:80/artikel.asp?aID=109.
17. Accessed November 8, 2017, http://www.metapedia.org.
18. Daniel Friberg, interview with author, June 6, 2014.
19. Teitelbaum, *Lions of the North*, 57–58.
20. These podcasts built on and replaced an initiative from the previous year on *Motpol*. From 2014 to 2015 Friberg, along with Swedes Patrik Ehn and Eva Johansson, produced four Swedish-language shows, uploaded to YouTube.
21. "Who We Are." Accessed October 30, 2017, https://web.archive.org/web/20160310115756/https://www.righton.net/who-we-are/.

22. Friberg, "Låt äventyret börja [Let the Adventure Begin]," *Motpol*, July 25, 2015. https://motpol.nu/danielfriberg/2015/07/25/lat-aventyret-borja/.
23. "The Migrant Invasion: Victory or Valhalla—Speech by Daniel Friberg @ Identitarian Ideas VII (2015)." Accessed October 31, 2017, https://www.youtube.com/watch?v=PdcMOclSVJM.
24. Friberg, for his part, was also acting almost unilaterally on behalf of Arktos in this merger. Just as the Alt Right corporation was being formed, he broke with his Arktos partner John Morgan, replacing Morgan as editor in chief with Jason Reza Jorjani. Friberg also joined forces with another collaborator, a former Sweden Democrat named Christoffer Dulny, to forge a largely independent, Swedish-language branch of the Alt Right initiative titled the Nordic Alt Right.
25. "#20—The Odyssey of Richard Spencer." Accessed November 20, 2017, https://www.youtube.com/watch?v=zVG8C_9qyTc&t=1364s.
26. Famous fashwave music producers "Xurious," for example, even wrote tribute pieces to Arktos's publications. See "Xurious—Right Wing Youth." Accessed November 20, 2017, https://www.youtube.com/watch?v=1tcEDIFg9Ik.
27. Evola, *Handbook for Right-Wing Youth* (London: Arktos Media, 2017).
28. Daniel Friberg, interview with author, November 6, 2017.

Select Bibliographies

GENERAL WORKS

Ashbee, Edward. "Politics of Paleoconservatism." *Society* 37, no. 3 (March 2000): 75–84.

Bar-On, Tamir. *Rethinking the French New Right: Alternatives to Modernity*. Abingdon: Routledge, 2013.

Bar-On, Tamir. *Where Have All the Fascists Gone?* Abingdon: Ashgate, 2007.

Camus, Jean-Yves, and Nicolas Lebourg. *Far Right Politics in Europe*. Translated by Jane Marie Todd. Cambridge, MA: Harvard University Press, 2017.

Duranton-Crabol, Anne-Marie. *Visages de la Nouvelle droite: le GRECE et son histoire*. Paris: Presses de Sciences Po, 1988.

Durham, Martin. *The Christian Right, the Far Right, and the Boundaries of American Conservatism*. Manchester: Manchester University Press, 2000.

Francis, Samuel T. *Revolution from the Middle*. Raleigh, NC: Middle American Press, 1997.

Gregor, A. James. *The Search for Neofascism: The Use and Abuse of Social Science*. New York: Cambridge University Press, 2006.

Hartman, Andrew. *A War for the Soul of America: A History of the Culture Wars*. Chicago: University of Chicago Press, 2015.

Hawley, George. *Making Sense of the Alt-Right*. New York: Columbia University Press, 2017.

Hawley, George. *Right-Wing Critics of American Conservatism*. Lawrence: University Press of Kansas, 2017.

Hemmer, Nicole. *Messengers of the Right: Conservative Media and the Transformation of American Politics*. Philadelphia: University of Pennsylvania Press, 2016.

Johnson, Greg. "Homosexuality and White Nationalism." Counter-Currents, October 4, 2010. http://www.counter-currents.com/2010/10/homosexuality-and-white-nationalism/.

Lyons, Matthew N. "AlternativeRight.com: Paleoconservatism for the 21st Century." *Three Way Fight* (blog), September 10, 2010. http://threewayfight.blogspot.com/2010/09/alternativerightcom-paleoconservatism.html.

Lyons, Matthew N. "Ctrl-Alt-Delete: The Origins and Ideology of the Alternative Right." Political Research Associates, January 20, 2017. http://www.politicalresearch.org/2017/01/20/ctrl-alt-delete-report-on-the-alternative-right/#sthash.59B4l69h.1JRopEJI.dpbs.

Lyons, Matthew N. *Insurgent Supremacists: The U.S. Far Right's Challenge to State and Empire*. Oakland, CA: PM Press, 2018.

Merkel, Peter H., and Leonard Weinberg, eds. *The Revival of Right Wing Extremism in the Nineties*. London: Frank Cass, 1997.

Murphy, David T. *The Heroic Earth: Geopolitical Thought in Weimar Germany, 1918–1933*. Kent, OH: Kent State University Press, 1997.

Murphy, Paul. *The Rebuke of History: The Southern Agrarians and American Conservative Thought*. Chapel Hill: University of North Carolina Press, 2001.

Nash, George. *The Conservative Intellectual Movement in America Since 1945*. Wilmington, DE: ISI Books, 2006.

Raimondo, Justin. *Reclaiming the American Right: The Lost Legacy of the Conservative Movement*. Wilmington, DE: ISI Books, 2008.

Sedgwick, Mark. *Against the Modern World: Traditionalism and the Secret Intellectual History of the Twentieth Century*. New York: Oxford University Press, 2004.

Stanley, Timothy. *The Crusader: The Life and Tumultuous Times of Pat Buchanan*. New York: Thomas Dunne Books, 2012.

Teitelbaum, Benjamin R. *Lions of the North: Sounds of the New Nordic Radical Nationalism*. New York: Oxford University Press, 2017.

Taguieff, Pierre-André. *Sur la Nouvelle Droite: Jalons d'une analyse critique*. Paris: Descartes et Cie, 1994.

Taguieff, Pierre-André. *The Force of Prejudice: On Racism and its Doubles*. Minneapolis: University of Minnesota Press, 2001. Originally published as *La Force du préjugé: Essai sur le racisme et ses doubles*. Paris, La Découverte, 1988.

Zeskind, Leonard. *Blood and Politics: The History of the White Nationalist Movement from the Margins to the Mainstream*. New York: Farrar, Straus and Giroux, 2009.

1. OSWALD SPENGLER

By Spengler

Man and Technics. Translated by Charles Francis Atkinson. New York: Alfred A. Knopf, 1932. Originally published as *Der Mensch und die Technik*. Munich: C. H. Beck, 1931.

Neubau des deutschen Reiches. Munich: C. H. Beck, 1924.

Politische Pflichten der deutschen Jugend. Munich: C. H. Beck, 1924.

Politische Schriften. Munich: C. H. Beck, 1932.

Prussianism and Socialism. Translated by Charles Francis Atkinson. New York: Alfred A. Knopf, 1922. Originally published as *Preußentum und Sozialismus*. Munich: C. H. Beck, 1919.

The Decline of the West. Outlines of a Morphology of World History. Translated by Charles Francis Atkinson. New York: Alfred A. Knopf, 1927. Originally published as *Der Untergang des Abendlandes: Umrisse einer Morphologie der Weltgeschichte*. Vol. 1: Vienna: Braumüller, 1918. Rev. ed. Munich, 1923; vol. 2: Munich: C. H. Beck, 1922.

The Hour of Decision. Translated by Charles Francis Atkinson. New York: Alfred A. Knopf, 1934. Originally published as *Jahre der Entscheidung*. Munich: C. H. Beck, 1933.

About Spengler

De Winde, Arne, S. Fabré, S. Maes, and B. Philipsen, eds. *Tektonik der Systeme: Neulektüren von Oswald Spengler*. Heidelberg: Synchron, 2016.

Demandt, Alexander. *Untergänge des Abendlandes: Studien zu Oswald Spengler*. Cologne: Böhlau, 2017.

Demandt, Alexander, and John Farrenkopf, eds. *Der Fall Spengler: Eine kritische Bilanz*. Cologne: Böhlau, 1994.

Engels, David, Max Otte, and Michael Thöndl, eds. *Der lange Schatten Oswald Spenglers: 100 Jahre Untergang des Abendlandes*. Waltrop: Manuscriptum, 2018.

Fink, Sebastian, and Robert Rollinger, eds. *Oswald Spenglers Kulturmorphologie—eine multiperspektivische Annäherung*. Berlin: Springer, 2018.

Gasimov, Zaur, and C. A. Lemke Duque, eds. *Oswald Spengler als europäisches Phänomen*. Göttingen: Vandenhoeck and Ruprecht, 2013.

Guerri, Maurizio, and Markus Ophälders, eds. *Oswald Spengler: Tramonto e metamorfosi dell'Occidente*. Milan: Mimesis, 2004.

Koktanek. Anton M., ed. *Spengler Studien: Festgabe für M. Schröter zum 85. Geburtstag*. Munich: C. H. Beck, 1965.

Ludz, Peter Chr., ed. *Spengler heute: Sechs Essays mit einem Vorwort von Hermann Lübbe*. Munich: C. H. Beck, 1980.

Merlio, Gilbert, and Daniel Meyer, eds. *Spengler ohne Ende*. Frankfurt a.M.: Peter Lang, 2014.

2. ERNST JÜNGER

By Jünger

Eumeswil. Translated by Johannes Neugroschel. New York: Telos Press, 2015. Originally published as *Eumeswil*. Stuttgart: Klett-Cotta, 1977.

On the Marble Cliffs, Translated by George Stein. New York: Penguin, 1984. Originally published as *Auf den Marmorklippen*. Berlin: Ziegler, 1939. Rev. ed. Tübingen: Reichl, 1949.

Siebzig Verweht 1–4. Stuttgart: Klett-Cotta, 1998.

Storm of Steel. Translated by Michael Hofmann. New York: Penguin, 2004. Originally published as *In Stahlgewittern*. NP: NP, 1920.

Strahlungen. Stuttgart: Klett-Cotta, 1998.
The Adventurous Heart: Figures and Capriccios. Translated by Thomas Friese. Candor, NY: Telos Press, 2012. Originally published as *Das Abenteurliche Herz; Aufzeichnungen bei Tag und Nacht.* Berlin: Frundsberg, 1929. Rev. ed., Hanseatische Verlagsanstalt, Hamburg, 1938.
The Forest Passage. Translated by Thomas Friese. New York: Telos Press, 2013. Originally published as *Der Waldgang.* Frankfurt am Main: Klostermann, 1951.
The Worker. Translated by Bogdan Costea and Laurence Paul Hemming. Evanston, IL: Northwestern University Press, 2017. Originally published as *Der Arbeiter.* Hamburg: Hanseatische Verlaganstalt, 1932.

About Jünger

Amos, Thomas. *Ernst Jünger.* Hamburg: Rowohlt, 2011.
Bullock, Marcus. *The Violent Eye: Ernst Jünger's Visions and Revisions on the European Right.* Detroit: Wayne State University Press, 1992.
Kiesel, Helmuth. *Ernst Jünger: die Biographie.* Munich: Siedler, 2007.
Loose, Gerhard. *Ernst Jünger: Gestalt und Werk.* Frankfurt: Klostermann, 1957.
Meyer, Martin. *Ernst Jünger.* Munich: Hanser, 1990.
Mitchell, Allan. *The Devil's Captain: Ernst Jünger in Nazi Paris, 1941–1944.* New York: Berghahn, 2011.
Neaman, Elliot. *A Dubious Past: Ernst Jünger and the Politics of Literature after Nazism.* Berkeley: University of California Press, 1999.
Nevin, Thomas. *Ernst Jünger and Germany: Into the Abyss 1914–1945.* Durham, NC: Duke University Press, 1996.
Noack, Paul. *Ernst Jünger: eine Biographie.* Berlin: Fest, 1998.
Schwilk, Heimo. *Ernst Jünger: Ein Jahrhundertleben.* Munich: Piper, 2007.

3. CARL SCHMITT
By Schmitt

Carl Schmitt/Ernst Rudolf Huber: Briefwechsel 1926–1981. Mit ergänzenden Materialien. Edited by Ewald Grothe. Berlin: Duncker & Humblot, 2014.
Constitutional Theory. Translated by Jeffrey Seitzer. Durham, NC: Duke University Press, 2007. Originally published as *Verfassungslehre.* Munich: Duncker & Humblot, 1928.
Frieden oder Pazifismus? Arbeiten zum Völkerrecht und zur internationalen Politik. Edited by Günter Maschke. Berlin: Duncker & Humblot, 2005.
Glossarium: Aufzeichnungen aus den Jahren 1947 bis 1958. Edited by Gerd Giesler and Martin Tielke. Berlin: Duncker & Humblot, 2015.
Political Theology: Four Capters on the Concept of Sovereignty. Translated by George Schwab. Cambridge, MA: MIT Press, 1985; Originally published in 1922 as

Politische Theologie: Vier Kapitel zur Lehre von der Souveränität. Berlin: Duncker & Humblot, 1979.

Staat, Großraum, Nomos: Arbeiten aus den Jahren 1916–1969. Edited by Günter Maschke. Berlin: Duncker & Humblot, 1995.

Tagebücher 1930 bis 1934. Edited by Wolfgang Schuller. Berlin: Akademie-Verlag, 2010.

The Concept of the Political. Translated by. George Schwab. Chicago: University of Chicago Press, 1996. Originally published in 1932 as *Der Begriff des Politischen.* Berlin: Duncker & Humblot, 1963.

The Crisis of Parliamentary Democracy. Translated by Ellen Kennedy. Cambridge, MA: MIT Press, 1985. Originally published in 1923 as *Die geistesgeschichtliche Lage des heutigen Parlamentarismus.* Munich: Duncker & Humblot, 1926.

The Leviathan in the State Theory of Thomas Hobbes: Meaning and Failure of a Political Symbol. Translated by George Schwab and Erna Hilfstein. Westport: Greenwood Press, 1996. Originally published as *Der Leviathan in der Staatslehre des Thomas Hobbes: Sinn und Fehlschlag eines Symbols.* Hamburg: Hanseatische Verlagsanstalt, 1938.

The Nomos of the Earth in the International Law of the "Jus Publicum Europaeum." Translated by. Gary L. Ulmen. New York: Telos Press, 2003. Originally published as *Der Nomos der Erde im Völkerrecht des Jus Publicum Europaeum.* Cologne: Greven-Verlag, 1950.

Theory of the Partisan: Immediate Commentary on the Concept of the Political. Translated by Gary L. Ulmen. New York: Telos Press, 2007. Originally published as *Theorie des Partisanen: Zwischenbemerkung zum Begriff des Politischen.* Berlin: Duncker & Humblot, 1963.

Verfassungsrechtliche Aufsätze aus den Jahren 1924–1954: Materialien zu einer Verfassungslehre. Berlin: Duncker & Humblot, 1958.

About Schmitt

Balakrishnan, Gopal. *The Enemy: An Intellectual Portrait of Carl Schmitt.* New York: Verso, 2000.

Bendersky, Joseph H. *Carl Schmitt: Theorist for the Reich.* Princeton, NJ: Princeton University Press, 1983.

Hofmann, Hasso. *Legitimität gegen Legalität: Der Weg der politischen Philosophie Carl Schmitts.* Berlin: Duncker & Humblot, 2002.

Krockow, Christian von. *Die Entscheidung. Eine Untersuchung über Ernst Jünger, Carl Schmitt und Martin Heidegger.* Stuttgart: Ferdinand Enke, 1958.

McCormick, John P. *Carl Schmitt's Critique of Liberalism Against Politics as Technology.* Cambridge: Cambridge University Press, 1997.

Mehring, Reinhard, ed. *Carl Schmitt, Der Begriff des Politischen: Ein kooperativer Kommentar.* Berlin: Akademie-Verlag, 2003.

Mehring, Reinhard. *Carl Schmitt: A Biography.* Cambridge: Polity, 2014. Originally published as *Carl Schmitt: Aufstieg und Fall: Eine Biographie.* Munich: Beck-Verlag, 2009.
Mehring, Reinhard. *Carl Schmitt: Denker im Widerstreit: Werk—Wirkung—Aktualität.* Freiburg: Alber-Verlag, 2017.
Meierheinrich, Jens, and Oliver Simons, eds. *The Oxford Handbook of Carl Schmitt.* Oxford: Oxford University Press, 2016.
Quaritsch, Helmut. *Positionen und Begriffe Carl Schmitts.* Berlin: Duncker & Humblot, 1989.

4. JULIUS EVOLA
By Evola

A Traditionalist Confronts Fascism: Selected Essays. Translated by E. Christian Kopff. London: Arktos, 2015.
Fascism Viewed from the Right. Translated by E. Christian Kopff. London: Arktos, 2013. Originally published as *Il fascismo visto dalla destra: Note sul III Reich.* NP: Giovanni Volpe editore, 1979.
Men Among the Ruins: Postwar Reflections of a Radical Traditionalist. Translated by Guido Stucco. Rochester, VT: Inner Traditions, 2002. Originally published as *Gli uomini e le rovine.* Rome: Edizioni dell'Ascia, 1953.
Revolt Against the Modern World. Translated by Guido Stucco. Rochester, VT: Inner Traditions, 1995. Originally published as *Rivolta contro il mondo moderno.* Milan: Ulrico Hoepli, 1934.
Ride the Tiger: A Survival Manual for the Aristocrats of the Soul. Translated by Joscelyn Godwin and Constance Fontana. Rochester, VT: Inner Traditions, 2003. Originally published as *Cavalcare la tigre.* Milan: All'Insegna del Pesce d'Oro, 1961.
The Path of Cinnabar: An Intellectual Autobiography of Julius Evola. Translated by Sergio Knipe. London: Integral Tradition Publishing, 2009. Originally published as *Il cammino del cinabro.* Milan: All'Insegna del Pesce d'Oro, 1963.

About Evola

Benoist, Alain de. "Julius Evola, Radical Reactionary and Committed Metaphysician: A Critical Analysis of the Political Thought of Julius Evola," PDF, available https://s3-eu-west-1.amazonaws.com/alaindebenoist/pdf/julius_evola_radical_reactionary.pdf. Originally published as "Julius Evola, reazionario radicale e metafisico impegnato." In *Gli Uomini e le Rovine e Orientamenti*, edited by Julius Evola. Rome: Edizioni Mediterranee, 2002, 19–54.
Cassata, Francesco. *A destra del fascismo: Profilo politico di Julius Evola.* Turin: Bollati Boringhieri, 2003.
Furlong, Paul. *Social and Political Thought of Julius Evola.* London: Routledge, 2011.

Hansen, H. T. [pseud. of H. T. Hakl]. "Julius Evola's Political Endeavors." In *Men Among the Ruins*, edited by Julius Evola. Rochester, VT: Inner Traditions, 2002, 1–106.

Hansen, H. T. [pseud. of H. T. Hakl]. *Julius Evola et la Révolution Conservatrice Allemande*. Montreuil-sous-Bois: Les Deux Étendards, 2002.

Turris, Gianfranco de. *Elogio e difesa di Julius Evola: Il Barone e i terroristi*. Rome: Edizioni Mediterranee, 1997.

5. ALAIN DE BENOIST

By de Benoist

Beyond Human Rights: Defending freedoms. NP: Arktos, 2011. Originally published as *Au-delà des droits de l'homme: pour défendre les libertés*. Paris: Krisis, 2004.

Comment peut-on être païen? Paris: Albin Michel, 1981.

Critiques-Théoriques. Lausanne: L'Âge d'Homme, 2003.

Le moment populiste. Paris: éditions Pierre-Guillaume de Roux, 2017.

Les Idées à l'endroit. Paris: Libres-Hallier, 1978.

Mémoire vive/Entretiens avec François Bousquet. Paris: Éditions de Fallois, 2012.

Nous et les autres: problématique de l'identité. Paris: Krisis, 2007.

View from the Right. vol.1, *Heritage and Foundations*. NP: Arktos, 2017. Originally published as *Vu de droite. Anthologie critique des idées contemporaines*. Paris: Copernic, 1977.

[With Charles Champetier]. *Manifesto for a European Renaissance*. NP: Arktos, 2012. Originally published as *Manifeste pour une renaissance européenne: À la découverte du GRECE. Son histoire, ses idées, son organization*. Paris: GRECE, 2000.

About de Benoist

Alain de Benoist Bibliographie 1960–2010, Paris: Les amis d'Alain de Benoist, 2009.

Germinario, Francesco. "Tra tradizione e innovazione della cultura di destra. Note in margine ad alcuni aspetti del pensiero politico di Alain de Benoist." In *Il Presente e la storia* 50 (December 1996): 67–83.

Gottfried, Paul. "Alain de Benoist's Anti-Americanism." *Telos* (December 21, 1993): 127–133.

Griffin, Roger. "Between Metapolitics and Apoliteia: The Nouvelle Droite's Strategy for Conserving the Fascist Vision in the 'Interregnum.'" *Modern and Contemporary France* 8, no. 1 (2000): 35–53.

Schobert, Alfred. "Alain de Benoists Vorstellungen von europäischer Identität." In *Mythos Identität. Fiktion mit Folgen*, edited by Alfred Schobert and Siegfried Jäger. Münster: Unrast, 2004, 31–61.

Sheehan, Thomas. "Myth and Violence: The Fascism of Julius Evola and Alain de Benoist." *Social Research* 48, no. 1 (1981): 45–73.

6. GUILLAUME FAYE

By Faye

Archeofuturism 2.0. Translated by Ann Sterzinger. London: Arktos Media, 2016. Originally published as *L'Archéofuturisme V2.0: nouvelles cataclysmiques.* Chevaigné: Le Lore, 2012.

Archeofuturism: European Visions of Post-catastrophtic Age. Translated by Sergio Knipe. London: Arktos Media, 2010. Originally published as *L'Archéofuturisme.* Paris: L'Æncre, 1998.

Convergences of Catastrophes. Translated by E. Christian Kopff. London: Arktos Media, 2012. Originally published as Corvus, Guillaume, *La Convergence des catastrophes.* Paris: Diffusion International Éditions, 2004.

Le Système à tuer les peuples. Paris: Copernic, 1981.

Les Nouveaux enjeux idéologiques. Paris: Le Labyrinthe, 1985.

Sex and Deviance. London: Arktos Media, 2014. Originally published as *Sexe et dévoiement.* Chevaigné: Le Lore, 2011.

The Colonization of Europe. Translated by Roger Adwan. London: Arktos Media, 2016. Originally published as *La Colonisation de l'Europe: discours vrai sur l'immigration et l'Islam.* Paris: L'Æncre, 2000.

Understanding Islam. Translated by Roger Adwan. London: Arktos Media, 2017. Originally published as *Comprendre l'islam.* Paris: Tatamis, 2015.

Why We Fight:. Manifesto of European Resistance. Translated by Michael O'Meara. London: Arktos Media, 2011. Originally published as *Pourquoi nous combattons: manifeste de la résistance européenne.* Paris: L'Æncre, 2001.

About Faye

François, Stéphane. *La Modernité en procès: Éléments d'un refus du monde moderne.* Valenciennes: Presses Universitaires de Valenciennes, 2013.

François, Stéphane. *Les Néo-paganismes et la Nouvelle Droite (1980–2006). Pour une autre approche.* Milan: Archè, 2008.

François, Stéphane, and Nicolas Lebourg. *Histoire de la haine identitaire: Mutations et diffusions de l'altérophobie.* Valenciennes: Presses Universitaires de Valenciennes, 2016.

Lebourg Nicolas. *Le Monde vu depuis la plus extrême droite: Du fascisme au nationalisme-révolutionnaire.* Perpignan: Presses Universitaires de Perpignan, 2010.

7. PAUL GOTTFRIED

By Gottfried

After Liberalism: Mass Democracy in the Managerial State. Princeton, NJ: Princeton University Press, 1999.

Carl Schmitt: Politics and Theory. New York: Greenwood Press, 1990.

Conservatism in America: Making Sense of the American Right. New York: Palgrave, 2007.
Encounters: My Life with Nixon, Marcuse, and Other Friends and Teachers. Wilmington, DE: Intercollegiate Studies Institute Books, 2009.
Fascism: The Career of a Concept. DeKalb: Northern Illinois University Press, 2017.
Leo Strauss and the Conservative Movement in America: A Critical Appraisal. New York: Cambridge University Press, 2012.
Multiculturalism and the Politics of Guilt: Toward a Secular Theocracy. Columbia: University of Missouri Press, 2002.
Revisions and Dissents: Essays. DeKalb: Northern Illinois University Press, 2017.
The Search for Historical Meaning: Hegel and the Postwar American Right. DeKalb: Northern Illinois University Press, 1986.
The Strange Death of Marxism: the European Left in the New Millennium. Columbia: University of Missouri Press, 2005.

About Gottfried

Bartee, Seth. "Imagination Movers: The Construction of Conservative Counter-Narratives in Reaction to Consensus Liberalism." PhD diss., Virginia Polytechnic Institute and State University, 2014.
Scotchie, Joseph, ed. *The Paleoconservatives: New Voices of the Old Right.* New Brunswick, NJ: Transaction Publishers, 1999.
Trepanier, Lee, ed. "A Symposium on Paul Gottfried's Conservatism in America: Making Sense of the American Right." Special issue, *Political Science Reviewer* 40 (2016).

8. PATRICK J. BUCHANAN
By Buchanan

Right from the Beginning. Washington, DC: Regnery Gateway, 1990.
The Death of the West: How Dying Populations and Immigrant Invasions Imperil Our Country and Civilization. New York: Thomas Dunne Books, 2001.
1992 Republican National Convention Speech. Patrick J. Buchanan—Official Website, August 17, 2017. http://buchanan.org/blog/1992-republican-national-convention-speech-148.

About Buchanan

Alberta, Tim. "The Ideas Made It, But I Didn't." *Politico Magazine,* May/June 2017. http://www.politico.com/magazine/story/2017/04/22/pat-buchanan-trump-president-history-profile-215042.
Durham, Martin. "On American Conservatism and Kim Phillips-Fein's Survey of the Field." *Journal of American History* 98 (2011): 756–759.

Edsall, Thomas B. "White Working Chaos." *New York Times*, June 25, 2012. https://campaignstops.blogs.nytimes.com/2012/06/25/white-working-chaos/?_r=0.

Glazer, Nathan. "The Enmity Within." *New York Times*, September 27, 1992. http://www.nytimes.com/books/00/07/16/specials/buckley-anti.html.

Goldberg, Jonah. "Killing Whitey." *National Review*, February 25, 2002. http://www.nationalreview.com/article/205150/killing-whitey-jonah-goldberg.

Green, Joshua. *Devil's Bargain: Steve Bannon, Donald Trump, and the Storming of the Presidency*. New York: Penguin Press, 2017.

MacGillis, Rick. "Rick Santorum, Closet Populist?" *New Republic*, December 29. 2011. https://newrepublic.com/article/99017/the-other-huckabee-santorum-connection.

Newsweek. "Is Pat Buchanan Anti-Semitic?" *Newsweek*, December 22, 1991. http://www.newsweek.com/pat-buchanan-anti-semitic-201176.

9. JARED TAYLOR

By Taylor

"A Conversation with Arthur Jensen." *American Renaissance*, September 1992. https://www.amren.com/archives/back-issues/september-1992/.

"Diversity Destroys Trust." *American Renaissance*, September 2007. https://www.amren.com/archives/back-issues/september-2007/.

"Homogeneity: The Japanese Know How to Run a Country." *American Renaissance* August, 2007. https://www.amren.com/archives/back-issues/august-2007/.

"How Can We Solve the Race Problem?" *American Renaissance*, September 26, 2017. https://www.amren.com/videos/2017/09/can-solve-race-problem/.

"Is a Multiracial Nation Possible?" *American Renaissance*, February 1992. https://www.amren.com/archives/back-issues/february-1992/.

Paved with Good Intentions. New York: Carol and Graf, 1992.

Shadows of the Rising Sun. New York: William Morrow and Company, 1983.

"Sowing the Seeds of Destruction: Gunnar Myrdal's Assault on America." *American Renaissance*, April 1996. https://www.amren.com/archives/back-issues/april-1996/.

White Identity: Racial Consciousness in the 21st Century. Oakton, VA: New Century Foundation, 2011.

"Who Speaks for Us." *American Renaissance*, November 1990. https://www.amren.com/archives/back-issues/novmber-1990.

About Taylor

Anti-Defamation League. "Jared Taylor: Academic Racist." www.adl.org, February 13, 2014.

Beauchamp, Zack. "A Leading White Nationalist Says It Plainly: Trump's Victory Was about White Identity." www.vox.com, November 21, 2016.
Southern Poverty Law Center. "Mainstream Scholars Attend Racist Conference Hosted by Jewish Astrophysicist," *Hatewatch*, March 18, 2009.
Swain, Carol M. *The New White Nationalism in America: Its Challenge to Integration.* New York: Cambridge University Press, 2002.
Swain, Carol M., and Russ Nieli. *Contemporary Voices of White Nationalism in America.* New York: Cambridge University Press, 2003.
Tilove, Jonathan. "White Nationalists Conference Ponders Whether Jews and Nazis Can Get Along." *Forward*, March 3, 2006.
Zeskind, Leonard. *Blood and Politics: The History of the White Nationalist Movement from the Margins to the Mainstream.* New York: Farrar, Straus and Giroux, 2009.

10. ALEXANDER DUGIN
By Dugin

Eurasian Mission: An Introduction to Neo-Eurasianism. Edited by John B. Morgan. Budapest: Arktos Media, 2014.
Foundations of Geopolitics: The Geopolitical Future of Russia. NP: NP, 2017. Originally published as *Osnovy geopolitiki: Geopoliticheskoe budushchee Rossii.* Moscow: Arktogeia, 1997.
Martin Heidegger: The Philosophy of Another Beginning. Translated by Nina Kouprianova. Whitefish, MT: Washington Summit Publishers, 2014. Originally published as *Martin Khaidegger: filosofiia drugogo nachala.* Moscow: Akademicheskii proekt, 2010.
Martin Khaidegger: vozmozhnost' russkoi filosofii. Moscow: Akademicheskii proekt, 2011.
Misterii Evrazii. Moscow: Arktogeia, 1996.
Tampliery proletariata: Natsional-bol'shevizm i initsiatsiia. Moscow: Arktogeia, 1997.
The Fourth Political Theory. Translated by Mark Sleboda and Michael Millerman. Budapest: Arktos Media, 2012. Originally published as *Chetvertaia politicheskaia teoriia.* Moscow: Amfora, 2009.
Znaki velikogo norda. Moscow: Veche, 2008.

About Dugin

Clover, Charles. *Black Wind, White Snow: The Rise of Russia's New Nationalism.* New Haven, CT: Yale University Press, 2016.
Dunlop, John B. "Aleksandr Dugin's 'Neo-Eurasian' Textbook and Dmitrii Trenin's Ambivalent Response." *Harvard Ukrainian Studies* 25, no. 1–2 (2001): 91–127.

Laruelle, Marlene, ed. *Eurasianism and European Far Right: Reshaping the Europe-Russia Relationship.* Lanham, MD: Lexington, 2015.

Laruelle, Marlene. *Russian Eurasianism: An Ideology of Empire.* Washington, DC: Woodrow Wilson Press, 2008.

Shekhovtsov, Anton. "Aleksandr Dugin's New Eurasianism: The New Right à la russe." *Religion Compass* 3–4: (2009): 697–716.

Shekhovtsov, Anton. *Russia and the Western Far Right: Tango Noir.* London: Routledge, 2017.

Shekhovstov, Anton. "The Palingenetic Thrust of Russian Neo-Eurasianism: Ideas of Rebirth in Aleksandr Dugin's Worldview." *Totalitarian Movements and Political Religions* 9, no. 4 (2008): 491–506.

Umland, Andreas. "Aleksandr Dugin's Transformation from a Lunatic Fringe Figure into a Mainstream Political Publicist, 1980–1998: A Case Study in the Rise of Late and Post-Soviet Russian Fascism." *Journal of Eurasian Studies* 1 (2010): 144–152.

Umland, Andreas. "Classification, Julius Evola and the Nature of Dugin's Ideology." *Erwägen, Wissen, Ethik* 16, no. 4 (2005): 566–569.

Umland, Andreas, and Anton Shekhovtsov. "Is Dugin a Traditionalist? 'Neo-Eurasianism' and Perennial Philosophy." *Russian Review* 68 (October 2009): 662–78.

11. BAT YE'OR
By Bat Ye'or

Eurabia: The Euro-Arab Axis. Madison, NJ: Fairleigh Dickinson Press, 2005.

Europe, Globalization and the Coming of the Universal Caliphate. Madison, NJ: Fairleigh Dickinson University Press, 2011.

The Decline of Eastern Christianity: From Islam to Dhimmitude: Seventh to Twentieth Century. Madison, NJ: Fairleigh Dickinson Press, 1998.

About Bat Ye'or

Aydin, Cemil. *The Idea of The Muslim World.* Cambridge, MA: Harvard University Press, 2017.

Bangstad, Sindre. *Anders Breivik and the Rise of Islamophobia.* London: Zed Books, 2014.

Griffith, Sydney H. Review of Bat Ye'or, *The Decline of Eastern Christianity: From Jihad to Dhimmitude: Seventh to Twentieth Century. International Journal of Middle East Studies* 30, no. 4 (1998): 619–621.

Sedgwick, Mark, "The Origins and Growth of the Eurabia Narrative." Undated and incomplete draft manuscript provided to the author.

Zia-Ebrahimi, Reza. "When The Elders of Zion Relocated in Eurabia: Conspiratorial Racialization in Antisemitism and Islamophobia." *Patterns of Prejudice* 52, no. 4 (2018): 314–337.

12. MENCIUS MOLDBUG
By Moldbug

"A Gentle Introduction to Unqualified Reservations," Kindle edition, Unqualified Reservations, 2015.
"An Open Letter to Open-Minded Progressives," Kindle edition, Unqualified Reservations, 2015.
"How Dawkins Got Pwned," Kindle edition, Unqualified Reservations, 2015.
"Moldbug on Carlyle," Kindle edition, Unqualified Reservations, 2015.
Unqualified Reservations (blog). http://unqualified-reservations.blogspot.com.

About Moldbug

Borsook, Paulina. *Cyberselfish: A Critical Romp through the Terribly Libertarian Culture of High Tech*. New York: PublicAffairs, 2000.
Nagle, Angela. *Kill All Normies: The Online Culture Wars from Tumblr and 4chan to the Alt-Right and Trump*. Washington: Zero Books, 2017.

13. GREG JOHNSON
By Johnson

Confessions of a Reluctant Hater. Revised and expanded. San Francisco: Counter-Currents, 2016.
In Defense of Prejudice. San Francisco: Counter-Currents, 2017.
New Right vs. Old Right. San Francisco: Counter-Currents, 2013.
North American New Right. Edited by Greg Johnson. 2 vols. San Francisco: Counter-Currents, 2012–2017.
Truth, Justice, and a Nice White Country. San Francisco: Counter-Currents, 2015.
You Asked for It: Selected Interviews. Vol. 1. San Francisco: Counter-Currents, 2017.
[as Trevor Lynch]. *Son of Trevor Lynch's White Nationalist Guide to the Movies*. Edited by Greg Johnson. San Francisco: Counter-Currents, 2015.
[as Trevor Lynch]. *Trevor Lynch's White Nationalist Guide to the Movies*. Edited by Greg Johnson. San Francisco: Counter-Currents, 2012.

About Johnson

See works on the Alt Right in the general section.

14. RICHARD B. SPENCER
By Spencer

The Uprooting of European Identity, edited by Richard Spencer. Arlington, VA: Washington Summit Publishers, 2016.

"What Is the American Right?" In *The Great Purge: The Deformation of the Conservative Movement*, edited by Paul Gottfried and Richard Spencer. Arlington, VA: Washington Summit Publishers, 2015.

"What It Means to be Alt-Right," AltRight.com, August 11, 2017. https://altright.com/2017/08/11/what-it-means-to-be-alt-right/.

About Spencer

Champetier, Charles, and Alain De Benoist. "Manifesto of the French New Right in the Year 2000." https://neweuropeanconservative.files.wordpress.com/2012/10/manifesto-of-the-french-new-right1.pdf.

Hedges, Chris. *American Fascists: The Christian Right and the War on America*. New York: Free Press, 2006.

Johnson, Greg. *New Right versus Old Right*. San Francisco: Counter-Currents, 2013.

Siegel, Jacob. "The Alt-Right's Jewish Godfather." *Tablet*, November 29, 2016. http://www.tabletmag.com/jewish-news-and-politics/218712/spencer-gottfried-alt-right.

Taylor, Jared. *White Identity: Racial Consciousness in the 21st Century*. Oakton, VA: New Century Foundation, 2011.

Wood, Graeme. "His Kampf," *Atlantic*, June 2017. https://www.theatlantic.com/magazine/archive/2017/06/his-kampf/524505/.

15. JACK DONOVAN

By Donovan

"A Time for Wolves." Jack Donovan (website), June 14, 2014. http://www.jack-donovan.com/axis/2014/06/a-time-for-wolves/.

"Anarcho-Fascism." Jack Donovan, March 3, 2013. http://www.jack-donovan.com/axis/2013/03/anarcho-fascism/.

"Becoming the New Barbarians." *Radix*, December 23, 2013. http://www.radixjournal.com/journal/becoming-the-new-barbarians.

Becoming a Barbarian. Milwaukie, OR: Dissonant Hum: 2016.

"No Man's Land: Masculinity Maligned, Reimagined." Jack Donovan, 2011. http://www.jack-donovan.com/axis/no-mans-land/.

Sky Without Eagles: Selected Essays and Speeches 2010–2014. Milwaukie, OR: Dissonant Hum, 2014.

The Way of Men. Milwaukie, OR: Dissonant Hum: 2012.

[As Malebranche, Jack]. *Androphilia: A Manifesto: Rejecting the Gay Identity, Reclaiming Masculinity*. Baltimore: Scapegoat Publishing, 2006. Republished in an expanded edition as *Androphilia: Rejecting the Gay Identity, Reclaiming Masculinity* by Jack Donovan. Milwaukie, OR: Dissonant Hum: 2012.

[With Miller, Nathan F.]. *Blood Brotherhood and Other Rites of Male Alliance: A Survey for Androphiles*. Portland, OR: Jack Donovan, 2009.

"Why I Am Not a White Nationalist." Jack Donovan, May 31, 2017. https://www.jackdonovan.com/axis/2017/05/why-i-am-not-a-white-nationalist/.

About Donovan

Johnson, Greg. "Greg Johnson Interviews Paul Waggener." Counter-Currents, February 2016. https://www.counter-currents.com/2016/02/greg-johnson-interviews-paul-waggener-2/.
"The Wolves of Vinland: a Fascist Countercultural 'Tribe' in the Pacific Northwest." Rose City Antifa, November 7, 2016. http://rosecityantifa.org/articles/the-wolves-of-vinland-a-fascist-countercultural-tribe-in-the-pacific-northwest/.

16. DANIEL FRIBERG
By Friberg

"Låt äventyret börja." *Motpol*, July 25, 2015. https://motpol.nu/danielfriberg/2015/07/25/lat-aventyret-borja/.
Metapedia. http://www.metapedia.org.
Nordiska förbundet. http://web.archive.org/web/20090513005038/http://www.nordiskaforbundet.se:80/artikel.asp?aID=109.
Nordiska förlaget. http://web.archive.org/web/20040810070901/http://www.nordiskaforlaget.se/info/.
The Real Right Returns. London: Arktos Media, 2015.
RightOn. https://web.archive.org/web/20161114164300/https://www.righton.net/.
[As Brandt, Martin]. "Metapedia." *People's News*, no. 10, 2006.

About Friberg

Wåg, Mathias. "Nationell kulturkamp—Från vit maktmusik till metapolitik [National Culture War—From White Power Music to Meta-Politics]." In *Det vita fältet: Samtida forskning om högerextremism*, edited by Mats Deland, Fredrik Hertzberg, and Thomas Hvitfeldt. Uppsala: University of Uppsala Department of History, 2010: 97–125.

Important to Friberg

MacDonald, Kevin. *The Culture of Critique: An Evolutionary Analysis of Jewish Involvement in Twentieth-Century Intellectual and Political Movements*. Westport, CT: Praeger, 1998.
O'Meara, Michael. *New Culture, New Right: Anti-Liberalism in Postmodern Europe*. London: Arktos Media, 2013.

Index

1848 revolution, 42
1969 student revolution, 83

Abellio, Raymond, 76
abortion, 130–31, 133, 247
absolute individual, 57
Abstract Art, by Julius Evola, 57
Academy of Philosophy and Letters, 112
Adinolfi, Gabriel, 98
Adorno, Theodor, 15, 111
AfD, 85, 150
Afghan War, 192
African American homeland, 211
African Americans
   and Greg Johnson, 212
   and Jared Taylor, 139, 140,
      144–47, 149–50
   and Mencius Moldbug, 194
   and Richard B. Spencer, 229, 232,
      235, 238
   terrorist attacks against in
      Charleston, SC, 237
Africans, 142–43, 148
After Liberalism, by Paul Gottfried,
   110, 232
Agamben, Georgio, 50
Agnew, Spiro, 122
Agrarian, Southern. *See* Southern
   Agrarian

Ahnenerbe, 63, 159
AIDS, 130
Ain Soph, 66
Aleanza Nazionale, 85
Alexander the Great, 10
Algerian War, 74, 79, 177
Ali, Ayaan Hirsi, 170
Alien Nation, by Peter Brimelow, 131
Allerseelen, 66
Almirante, Giorgio, 85
Alt Right, 225–38
   and Alain de Benoist, 73
   and Alexander Dugin, 165, 167
   and Daniel Friberg, 261, 270–73
   and Greg Johnson, 212–13, 217
   and Guillaume Faye, 97, 98
   and Jack Donovan, 226, 250–52,
      253, 254
   and Jared Taylor, 151
   and Mencius Moldbug, 187, 195, 199
   origin of term, 217, 226
   and Patrick J. Buchanan, 133
   and Paul Gottfried, 113, 116
Alt-Right Corporation, 272
Alt-Right Manifesto, 229, 232–37
AltRight.com, 228, 230–31, 272
Alternativ für Deutschland, 85, 150
Alternative Media, 263, 264
AlternativeRight.com, 228, 250, 251

Althusius, Johannes, 77
American Civil War, 148–49, 196
American Conservative, The, 125, 227
American Enterprise Institute, 115
American Independence Party, 122
American Indians. *See* Native Americans
American Renaissance, 138–39
   and Alain de Benoist, 213
   and Daniel Friberg, 259
   and evolutionary biology, 142
   and Guillaume Faye, 98
   and Jack Donovan, 250
   Jared Taylor in, 144, 146, 148, 149, 150
   and Jews, 143–44
   and Richard B. Spencer, 230
   and Samuel Francis, 150
   and white identity, 129, 131
Anarch, the, 34, 81–82
anarchism, 44, 45, 248
anarcho-fascism, 248
Androphilia, by Jack Donovan, 243, 244, 247
Anglin, Andrew, 251
animals, 63, 142, 253
Anthroposophy, 54
anti-Americanism
   of Alain de Benoist, 76, 86
   of Alexander Dugin, 159, 160, 162, 167
   of Guillaume Faye, 86, 92, 95, 96, 99
anti-Christianity
   of Alain de Benoist, 74, 78, 79, 82, 84
   of European Right, 30
   of Greg Johnson, 206, 216
   of Guillaume Faye, 95
   of Julius Evola, 55, 60
   of Louis Rougier, 79
   of Richard B. Spencer, 229, 231, 233
anti-Semitism
   and Alexander Dugin, 162
   of Carl Schmitt, 36, 38, 39, 41, 45
   in Charlottesville, 230
   and Donald Trump, 134
   of Ernst Jünger, 26, 29
   and Greg Johnson, 205, 214
   of Henry Coston, 75
   and Jared Taylor, 143–44
   of Joe Sobran, 129
   of Julius Evola, 63–64, 65
   of Kevin MacDonald, 217, 229
   of North American New Right, 218, 227
   and Patrick J. Buchanan, 132, 134
   rejected by Alain de Benoist, 74
   rejected by Mencius Moldbug, 196
   rejected by European New Right, 214
   and Richard B. Spencer, 225, 226, 231, 233–34
   of William Pierce, 208
antidemocratic positions. *See* democracy
antifeminism, 195, 244, 250, 251
antimodernism. *See* archaism; modernity; nonmodernism
antiprogressives, 187–89, 197, 199. *See also* progress, belief in
apocalypticism
   of Alexander Dugin, 161
   of Bat Ye'or, 178
   of Carl Schmitt, 36, 37, 44, 45
   of Greg Johnson, 211
Apoliteia, 65
Arab Spring, 127
Arab world, and Europe, 96, 177
Arabs
   and Alain de Benoist, 91
   civilization of, as understood by Oswald Spengler, 7, 8, 9, 10, 11
   and Guillaume Faye, 92, 95, 96, 99
   See also Bat Ye'or
archaism, 94, 211

Archeofuturism 2.0, by Guillaume
  Faye, 98
Archeofuturism of Guillaume Faye,
  91, 94, 98
  and Daniel Friberg, 272
  and Greg Johnson, 211
  and Jack Donovan, 247
Ardeyev, Vladimir, 98
Ardrey, Robert, 92
Aristotle, 211
Arktos, 269–70
  as Alt.Right partner, 230
  and Counter-Currents, 206
  engaged in controversy with Greg
    Johnson, 217
  and Gábor Vona, 273
  impact in North America, 272
  publish Paul Gottfried, 114
  publish translations of Evola, 66
  publish translations of Guillaume
    Faye, 98
  publish translations of French New
    Right, 206
arms, right to bear, 237
art
  appreciated by Carl Schmitt, 42
  early Christian, 10
  and James O'Meara and Greg
    Johnson, 216
  and Julius Evola, 57
  and metapolitics, 261
  modern, 37
  of surrealists and expressionists, 25
Aryanism, 6, 159, 161, 232, 251. *See
  also* race
Asians
  immigration by, 96
  interest organizations for, 139
  superiority of, 142–43, 145, 148
Association for World Education, 172
Atlantic, The, 199
Atlanticism, 162

Auernheimer, Andrew, 251
Augier, Marc, 79
Austrian School, 190–91
Austro-Marxists, 77
Authoritarianism
  and Carl Schmitt, 39, 41,
    43–44, 48, 51
  and Ernst Jünger, 26
  and Guillaume Faye, 95, 97
  and Mencius Moldbug, 187, 188, 191,
    195, 197
  nineteenth-century, 74
  and Paul Gottfried, 111–12
Avalon, Arthur, 64
Ayaan Hirsi Ali, 170

Bachofen, Jakob, 60
Bacon, Francis, 8
Bagby, Philip, 14
Balkan Wars, 174, 175
Ball, Hugo, 49
Ballas, Eleftherios, 98
Bannon, Steve, xxv, 187, 199
Bardèche, Maurice, 98
Bat Ye'or, 170–79
  and apocalypticism, 178
  and Christianity, 173–74, 176,
    177, 178–79
  and civilization, 173, 177, 178
  and globalization, 170
  and Islam, 170–79
  and Israel, 172, 173, 174, 177–78
  and Richard B. Spencer, 235
  and totalitarianism, 178
battle, 24, 44, 45–46, 58.
  See also heroism; virility;
  warrior
Baudrillard, Jean, 85
Bauer, Otto, 77
Bawer, Bruce, 170
Becoming a Barbarian, by
  Jack Donovan, 243, 247

Beliën, Paul, 175
Bell Curve, The, by Richard Herrnstein and Charles Murray, 131
bell hooks, 247
Benjamin, Walter, 49
Benn, Gottfried, 61, 62
Bennett, William, 106–07
Benoist, Alain de, 73–86
   accused of Fascism, 75, 77
   Alexander Dugin and, 155, 159, 165
   and anti-Americanism, 76, 86
   and anti-Christianity, 74, 78, 79, 82, 84
   and Antonio Gramsci, 74, 86
   and capitalism, 75–77
   and civilization, 76, 79
   and class, 74, 77, 81
   on communism, 79, 84, 85
   and Conservative Revolution, 73–74, 81
   on culture, 81, 83, 84, 86
   and democracy, 75, 76, 80
   dispute with Guillaume Faye, 76, 93–94, 99
   on Europe, 78, 83, 84, 86
   and globalization, 75, 76, 78, 86
   Greg Johnson and, 205, 206
   Guillaume Faye second to, 91
   and identity, 73, 77–79
   on immigration, 78, 83
   inspires Alexander Dugin and Alt Right, 73
   and Islam, 76, 78
   and Jack Donovan, 247
   and Jared Taylor, 213
   and Jews, 74, 78
   on Marxism, 75, 77
   Mencius Moldbug compared to, 188
   and metapolitics, 74, 76, 85
   on multiculturalism, 85, 86
   and neopaganism, 76, 79, 82
   published by Arktos, 269, 272
   and Robert Spencer, 225, 226, 228, 231, 234–36, 237
   and socialism, 77, 81
   on race and ethnicity, 77–79, 83
   on the state, 77, 82–83
   views on Liberalism, 261
   and white supremacism, 79, 82, 85
Berg, Lennart, 266
Berlusconi, Silvio, 85
Bhagavad Gita, 58
birthrate. *See* demography
black Americans. *See* African Americans
Black Death, the, 128
Black Notebooks, by Heidegger, 205
Black Power, 194
black. *See* African American
blogging
   by Anders Behring Breivik, 175
   anonymous, 272
   by Brad Griffin, 251
   by Daniel Friberg, 260–61, 267, 269–70
   by Edward S. May, 175
   by Fjordman, 170
   by Glenn Reynolds, 190
   by Mencius Moldbug, 187, 188–89, 191, 192–94, 198–99
   by Richard B. Spencer, 113
blood and soil, 26, 235
Blood Axis, 66
Blood Brotherhood, by Jack Donovan and Nathan F. Miller, 243
Blot, Yvan, 83
Blumenberg, Hans, 49
Böckenförde, Ernst-Wolfgang, 49
Bolton, Kerry, 216
Bond, James, 216
Books Against Time, 207
Boot, Max, 116
Bosnian War, 174–75
Bostom, Andrew, 175

Bouchet, Christian, 165
Boudon, Raymond, 85
bourgeois society, 3, 62
bourgeois state, 33, 38, 39, 43, 48
Bowden, Jonathan, 209, 231
Bowman, James, 247
Bradford, Mel, 104, 106–07
Brahmin, 59, 189, 195
Breitbart, 187, 199
Breivik, Anders Behring, 170–71, 175, 235, 269
Breton, André, 25
Brexit, 259, 272
Brimelow, Peter, 112–13, 131
British National Party, 209
Brix, Helle Merete, 175
Brotherhood, the, 245–46
Brownshirts, 248
Bryan, William Jennings, 114
Buber, Martin, 77
Buchanan, Patrick J., 121–34
   and anti-Semitism, 132, 134
   and Catholicism, 121, 130, 133
   and civilization, 131–32
   and the counterculture, 128, 130
   and culture, 124, 128
   and democracy, 127, 128
   on demography, 123, 128–29
   on ethnicity, 126, 129
   and feminism and gender, 128, 130, 130, 133
   on global elites, 126, 132
   and globalization, 126, 130
   and identity, 126, 127, 129
   and immigration, 122–23, 129, 131, 132, 134
   and Israel, 127, 132, 134
   on Marxism, 128, 130
   and the neoconservatives, 124–27, 131
   and paleoconservatism, 121, 125–27, 129–31
   and Paul Gottfried, 113
   on race, 125, 126, 129–30, 131
   and the Republican Party, 121, 122–25, 127, 130, 131–34
   and the state, 121–22, 125, 132
   and white identity, 127, 129, 131
   and white nationalism, 131–32
Buckley, Joshua, 205
Buckley, William F., Jr., 110, 112–13, 115, 125, 131, 151
Buddhism, 56, 161
Budgen, Sebastien, 85
Building the German Empire Anew, by Oswald Spengler, 4, 5
Burkeanism, 109, 113–14
Burnham, James, 126, 191–92
Bush, George H. W., 104, 123
Bush, George W., 103, 104, 112, 124, 127

Cacciari, Massimo, 85
Calhoun, John C., 149
Campbell, Joseph, 66
capitalism
   and Alain de Benoist, 75–77
   and Alexander Dugin, 159
   in the Alt-Right Manifesto, 236
   and Greg Johnson, 211, 212
   and Julius Evola, 66
   and Marine Le Pen, 86
   and Oswald Spengler, 6, 14
   and Patrick J. Buchanan, 126
   and Richard B. Spencer, 224, 226, 229, 233–34, 235
   and Samuel T. Francis, 130
Carlyle, Thomas, 191–92, 197
Carter, Jimmy, 106
Carvalho, Olavo de, 165
caste, 58–60, 161. *See also* class
Cathedral, the, 193–98
Catholicism
   accepted by Richard B. Spencer, 235
   of Carl Schmitt, 37, 43, 46, 62
   and Mussolini, 58

Catholicism (*cont.*)
   of Patrick J. Buchanan, 121, 130, 133
   rejected by Julius Evola, 55, 60, 62
   rejected by KKK, 235
Catholics
   and Alain de Benoist, 82, 85
   and Charles Maurras, 86
   and Guillaume Faye, 94, 98
   opposed to fascism, 174
Center for Conservative Research, 157
Chambers, Whittaker, 115
Champetier, Charles, 232
Charles Martel Society, 205, 224
Charlottesville, 207, 230, 232, 235, 238, 252
Charlottesville Statement, 232
Chomsky, Noam, 247
Christian Broadcasting Network, 123
Christian Coalition, 123
Christian Democratic Party, German, 32
Christian Right, 130–31, 133, 243, 246–47
Christianity
   and Bat Ye'or, 173–74, 176, 177, 178–79
   and Carl Schmitt, 37, 42, 43, 44–45
   decline of, 126, 128
   and Ernst Jünger, 30, 30–31
   and Oswald Spengler, 10, 11, 12
   and Paul Gottfried, 102
   See also anti-Christianity; Catholicism; evangelicals; Protestants
Chronicles, 124, 125
Church of Satan, 243
Civil Rights Act, 102, 146
civil rights movement, 114, 147, 212
civil rights programs, 194
Civil War, American, 148–49, 196
Civil War, Lebanese, 173, 174
Civil War, Russian, 161
Civilization
   and Alain de Benoist, 76, 79
   and Alexander Dugin, 160–61
   and Bat Ye'or, 173, 177, 178
   and Conservative Revolution, 25
   and Daniel Friberg, 271
   and Ernst Jünger, 24, 32
   and Greg Johnson, 209, 211, 214
   and Guillaume Faye, 95–98
   and Jack Donovan, 244, 245, 251
   and Jared Taylor, 138, 142
   and Julius Evola, 59
   and Mencius Moldbug, 191, 199
   for Oswald Spengler, 3–4, 6–8, 10–11, 16
   and Patrick J. Buchanan, 131–32
   and Paul Gottfried, 102, 109
   and Richard B. Spencer, 231, 232, 233, 236
Clash of Civilizations, 214
class
   and Alain de Benoist, 74, 77, 81
   and Jack Donovan, 243, 253
   and Jared Taylor, 144
   and Mencius Moldbug, 194, 200
   and Patrick J. Buchanan, 132
   and Paul Gottfried, 110–11
   and Richard B. Spencer, 237
   See also elites
climate
   change, 97, 194 (*see also* ecology)
   impact of, 142
Clinton, Bill, 124, 130
Clinton, Hilary, 130, 189, 252
Cocteau, Jean, 27
Codreanu, Corneliu, 62
Cold War, 79
   impact on Italian politics, 65
   impact on reception of Oswald Spengler, 4, 15
   impact on US politics, 122
colonialism
   and Greg Johnson, 210
   and Richard B. Spencer, 225, 227, 236, 238
   Western, 179

Colonization of Europe, The, by
    Guillaume Faye, 76, 94, 98
Commentary, 115
communism
    and Alain de Benoist, 79, 84, 85
    and Alexander Dugin, 161
    American Christian opposition
        to, 174
    and Antonio Gramsci, 261
    fall of, 32, 85–86
    and Mencius Moldbug, 199–200
    and the *National Review,* 125–26
    and neoconservatives, 103
    and Paul Gottfried, 103–04
Communist Party
    French, 85
    Russian, 86, 157
Concept of the Political, The, by Carl
    Schmitt, 38, 45, 46–47, 49
Confederacy. *See* neo-Confederates
Confederate statues, 116, 230, 237. *See
    also* neo-Confederates
Confessions of a Reluctant Hater, by Greg
    Johnson, 207
Congdon, Lee, 114
Conservatism in America, by Paul
    Gottfried, 112
Conservative Century, The, by Gregory
    Schneider, 116
*Conservative Intellectual Movement
    in America, The,* by George
    Nash, 108–09
Conservative Millenarians, by Paul
    Gottfried, 107
Conservative Mind, The, by Russell
    Kirk, 102
Conservative Movement, The, by
    Paul Gottfried and Thomas
    Fleming, 109
Conservative Revolution
    Alain de Benoist and, 73, 81
    Alexander Dugin and, 155–56, 159,
        160–61, 162, 167

Carl Schmitt as part of, 39, 44, 48
defined by Armin Mohler, 24–25
Edgar Jung as part of, 41
Ernst Jünger as part of, 24
Guillaume Faye and, 91, 92
Jack Donovan and, 247
Julius Evola meets, 62
Oswald Spengler as part of, 15
Richard B. Spencer and, 226, 231
Constitutional Theory of Carl
    Schmitt, 38
Convergence of Catastrophes, The,
    by Guillaume Faye, 98
cosmopolitan elites. *See*
    elites: cosmopolitan
cosmopolitanism, 78, 137, 188.
    See also universalism
Costello, Jef, 216, 246–47, 250
Coston, Henry, 74
Counter-Currents, 206–10, 213,
    215–16, 217–18
    and Daniel Friberg, 259
    and Greg Johnson, 143, 204
    and Guillaume Faye, 98
    and Jack Donovan, 250, 251
counter-Enlightenment, 31
Counter-jihadism, 170–71, 173,
    175–76
Counter-Reformation, 10
counterculture
    and Alexander Dugin, 156, 158,
        163, 164
    and the Democratic
        Party, 104
    and Greg Johnson, 207, 216, 218
    and Guillaume Faye, 91–92
    and neoconservatism, 114
    and Patrick J. Buchanan, 128, 130
    and *Telos,* 109–10
counterrevolution
    and Carl Schmidt, 36, 42, 43, 44
    and Guillaume Faye, 94
Croce, Benedetto, 54

Culture
  and Alain de Benoist, 81, 83, 84, 86
  and Alexander Dugin, 159, 162
  and Antonio Gramsci, 261
  and Daniel Friberg, 267, 269
  and Ernst Jünger, 32, 34
  and Greg Johnson, 211, 216
  and Guillaume Faye, 96
  and Jack Donovan, 244, 246–48, 250
  and Jared Taylor, 140, 141
  and Julius Evola, 60–61, 66
  and Mencius Moldbug, 193, 194
  and Oswald Spengler, 8–12, 14–15
  and Patrick J. Buchanan, 124, 128
  and Paul Gottfried, 106, 107, 115
  and Richard B. Spencer, 224, 232, 236
  See also ethnicity; *Volk*; civilization

D'Annunzio, Gabriele, 55
d'Orcival, François, 79
da Silva, Vicente Ferreira, 166
Dadaism, 57
Daily Stormer, 251
Danilevskii, Nikolai, 160
Darwinianism, 25, 78, 96, 149
  social, 25, 78, 96, 149
  See also evolution
Däubler, Theodor, 37–38, 44
de Benoist, Alain. *See* Benoist, Alain de
de Carvalho, Olavo, 165
De Geer, Jonas, 270
de Lesquen, Henry, 83
de Turris, Gianfranco, 65
Death of the West, The, by Patrick J. Buchanan, 127–29, 131
Debord, Guy, 92
decline, 60. *See also* Europe: decline of
Decline of Eastern Christianity, The, by Bat Ye'or and David G. Littman, 176, 178

Decline of the West by Oswald Spengler, 3, 5–6, 7, 12–14
Decter, Midge, 104
Defoe, Daniel, 198
Deleuze, Gilles, 92
Delphi, oath of, 93
demagoguery, 6, 34, 63. *See also* populism
Demidov, Ivan, 164
democracy
  and Alain de Benoist, 75, 76, 80
  and Carl Schmitt, 42, 43, 44, 48, 49
  and Daniel Friberg, 265
  and Ernst Jünger, 24, 25, 31
  and founding of US, 106
  and Greg Johnson, 206, 211
  and Guillaume Faye, 96
  and Hans-Herman Hoppe, 191
  and Jack Donovan, 245
  and Julius Evola, 55, 61, 62;
  and Mencius Moldbug, 187–88, 191–93, 195–96, 199, 200
  and neoconservatives, 127
  and Oswald Spengler, 6, 13, 14, 16
  and Patrick J. Buchanan, 127, 128
  and Paul Gottfried, 110, 111, 112, 114, 115
  and Robert B. Spencer, 226, 231, 232
Democracy, by Hans-Herman Hoppe, 191
Democratic Party, the
  allegedly supported by William Bennett, 106
  duopoly with Republicans, 124
  ignores race, 233
  neoconservatives break with, 104, 127
  Paul Gottfried likens conservatives to, 103
  Republicans win votes from, 132
  supported by immigrants, 129
demography
  and Greg Johnson, 211–13
  and Guillaume Faye, 96–97

and Jared Taylor, 140, 141, 145,
    149, 150–51
and Mussolini, 62
and Patrick J. Buchanan, 123, 128–29
and Richard B. Spencer, 235
Deneen, Patrick, 113
Deng Xiaoping, 195
Derrida, Jacques, 50
Devi, Savitri, 208
Dhimmi, The, by Bat Ye'or, 176
dhimmitude, 173, 178
Dickson, Sam, 150
dictatorship
    and Carl Schmitt, 38–39,
        42–44, 48, 51
    and Ernst Jünger, 27
    and Guillaume Faye, 97
    and Mencius Moldbug, 200
    and Oswald Spengler, 6
    See also monarchy
digital media. *See* blogging; internet
Dobrenkov, Vladimir, 157
Donoso Cortés, Juan, 42, 44, 62
Donovan, Jack, 242–54
    and the Alt Right, 226, 250–52,
        253, 254
    and civilization, 244, 245, 251
    and class, 243, 253
    and Counter-Currents, 250, 251
    and culture, 244, 246–48, 250
    and Donald Trump, 251–52
    and Fascism, 247–48, 254
    and feminism, 244, 245, 247, 248,
        249, 250, 251, 254
    and gender, 242–46, 254
    on global elites, 245, 248–49
    and Greg Johnson, 217
    and hierarchies, 244, 245–46
    on homosexuality, 243–44, 246–48,
        250, 251, 254
    and identity, 244–45, 267, 271–272
    on masculinity, 242–48, 253

and multiculturalism, 249, 252
and National Socialism, 252, 253
and neopaganism, 244, 252, 254
on progress, 248–49
on race, 242, 252
and Richard B. Spencer, 231
and the state, 245, 248–49
and violence, 242, 243, 245, 248, 254
and white nationalism, 242, 243, 252
drugs, 31, 56
Dugin, Alexander, 155–67
    and the Alt Right, 165, 167
    and anti-Americanism, 159, 160,
        162, 167
    and civilization, 160–61
    and the Conservative
        Revolution, 155–56, 159, 160–61,
        162, 167
    and the counterculture, 156, 158,
        163, 164
    and culture, 159, 162
    and Daniel Friberg, 269, 273
    on Fascism, 159, 160–61
    and Guénonian Traditionalism, 155,
        156, 159, 163, 165, 166, 167
    and Islam, 157, 162, 165
    and liberalism, 157, 160–62
    and modernity, 161–62
    and National Socialism, 159, 160, 161
    and Richard B. Spencer, 227, 228, 231
    and totalitarianism, 160, 161
    and violence, 158, 162, 179
    and white nationalism, 162
    and white supremacism, 162, 165
Duke, David, 124, 133, 144
Dune, 211
Dzhemal, Geidar, 155

Eckhart, Meister, 56–57
Eco, Umberto, 67
ecology, 4, 75, 97, 142, 159.
    See also climate change

education, 212, 236–37, 260, 261, 264–65, 267
  bilingual, 141
Eichberg, Henning, 75
Eisler, Fritz, 37–38
Elam, Paul, 250
Eldritch Evola, The, by James O'Meara, 216
Éléments, 73, 78, 82, 85, 92
Eliade, Mircea, 62, 64
elites
  cosmopolitan, 34, 162, 224, 225
  global
    for Alain de Benoist, 86
    for Greg Johnson, 213
    for Jack Donovan, 245, 248–49
    for Patrick J. Buchanan, 126, 132
    for Paul Gottfried, 110, 111
Emanations, by Ernst Jünger, 28
Encounters, by Paul Gottfried, 104, 105
equality; and Jack Donovan, 242
Essays on Magical Idealism, by Julius Evola, 56, 58
ether, 56
ethnic cleansing, 212, 226
ethnicity
  for Alain de Benoist, 77–79, 83
  for Daniel Friberg, 262, 263, 265
  European, 84, 96
  for Greg Johnson, 210–12, 213
  for Guillaume Faye, 92–93, 96, 98
  for Jack Donovan, 246
  for Jared Taylor, 139–41, 142–44, 148–50
  for Patrick J. Buchanan, 126, 129
  for Richard B. Spencer, 225–26, 229, 232–34, 237
  See also *Volk*
ethnonationalism, in Sweden, 263
ethnopluralism, 238
ethnoplurality, 210
ethnostate, 225, 233, 234

eugenics, 79, 82, 96, 149, 213
Eurabia, 170, 177–78
Eurabia, by Bat Ye'or, 170, 176
Eurasian Party, 157
Eurasian Union of Youth, 158
Eurasianism
  of Alexander Dugin, 159, 160, 161, 166
  interwar, 159–60
Eurasianist Movement, International, 157
Eurasianists, 85, 157, 165
Euro-Arab Dialogue, 170, 177
Europa Terra Nostra, 271
Europe-Action, 74, 79
Europe, Globalization, and the Coming Universal Caliphate, by Bat Ye'or, 170, 176
Europe
  in the Alt-Right Manifesto, 235
  and the Arab world, 96, 177
  centralized, 79
  decline of, 32, 33, 34, 79, 83, 97, 128
  defense of, 95, 96
  federal, 77, 79
  feudalism in, 109
  German-dominated, possible, 4, 14, 41
  immigration into
    for Alain de Benoist, 78, 83, 84, 86
    for Guillaume Faye, 94–95, 96
    for Richard B. Spencer, 226
  inspires Burkean conservatives, 113
  Muslim control of, 170–71, 173–74, 177–78
  opposed to monotheism, 84
  pagan, 78, 79, 96, 208
  postwar, for Ernst Jünger, 29–30
  and Russia, 160, 162, 167
  and the United States
    for Guillaume Faye, 95, 96, 97
    for Patrick J. Buchanan, 128
    for Richard B. Spencer, 236

See also ethnicity: European;
    identity: European;
    nationalism: European
European Committee for the
    Coordination of Friendship
    Associations with the Muslim
    World, 177
European Economic Community, 177.
    See also European Union
European heritage of United States.
    See United States: European
    heritage of
European IQs, 142–43
European Liberation Front, 165
European Union, 16, 170, 177, 178.
    See also European Economic
    Community
Eurosiberia, 97
evangelicals, 102, 103, 114, 130, 133
Evola, Julius, 54–67
    and Alain de Benoist, 76
    for Alexander Dugin, 86, 156, 159,
        161–62, 166–67
    and anti-Semitism, 63–64, 65
    and Catholicism, 55, 60, 62
    compared to Mencius Moldbug, 188
    and culture, 60–61, 66
    for Daniel Friberg, 266, 270–71
    and democracy, 55, 61, 62
    and Fascism, 61, 62, 64, 65
    for Gábor Vona, 273
    and gender, 55, 60, 65
    for Greg Johnson, 205, 210, 216
    for Guillaume Faye, 91, 94
    influence on Nordiska
        förbundet, 266
    for Jack Donovan, 252–53
    and the Jews, 55, 63–64
    and Judaism, 55, 64–64
    meets Carl Schmitt, 44
    and modernity, 59–61, 63–64
    and neopaganism, 58, 61, 62
    as part of Conservative
        Revolution, 24
    published by Arktos, 269
    on race, 63–64
    for Richard B. Spencer, 227, 230,
        231, 233
evolution
    of civilizations, 7
    of cultures, 9, 11
    of the eye, 5
    human, 4, 8
    of identities, 78
    See also Darwinianism; decline
evolutionary biology, 142
evolutionary genetics, 142
evolutionary psychology, 142, 249
Existentialism, 46–47, 49, 79

Fallaci, Oriana, 176, 177
family
    and Alain de Benoist, 77
    and Jack Donovan, 246–47
    and Jared Taylor, 144–45
    and Patrick J. Buchanan, 128
Fascism
    Alain de Benoist
        accused of, 75, 77
        views on, 85
    Alexander Dugin on, 159, 160–61
    as context for Carl Schmitt, 48–49
    Ernst Jünger accused of, 24, 26
    Greg Johnson on, 209, 211
    Jack Donovan on, 247–48, 254
    and Julius Evola, 61, 62, 64, 65
    Lyndon Johnson accused
        of, 105–05
    Mencius Moldbug on, 196
    Oswald Spengler on, 6
    Richard B. Spencer on, 31,
        225, 233–34
    See also anarcho-fascism
Faurisson, Robert, 98

Faye, Guillaume, 91–99
  and Alain de Benoist, 76, 93–94, 99
  and the Alt Right, 97, 98
  and anti-Americanism, 86, 92, 95, 96, 99
  and authoritarianism, 95, 97
  and civilization, 95–98
  and Conservative Revolution, 91, 92
  and the counterculture, 91–92
  and Daniel Friberg, 260
  on demography, 96–97
  on ethnicity, 92–93, 96, 98
  and Europe, 94–95, 96
  and Greg Johnson, 206, 211
  on homosexuality, 93, 95
  and identity, 92–93, 94–95, 96–97
  and immigration, 76, 92–93, 96
  and Islam, 76, 91, 92, 96–98, 99
  and Israel, 95, 96, 98
  and Jack Donovan, 247
  and Jared Taylor, 150–51
  and Jews, 94, 98
  leaves GRECE, 93
  and liberalism, 92, 96
  and modernity, 91, 94–95
  and National Socialism, 92, 93
  and neopaganism, 93–96
  on race, 95, 96
  and Richard B. Spencer, 226, 231, 232, 235
  on Zionism, 95, 98
Federalist Papers, 147
Feminism
  for Jack Donovan, 244, 245, 247, 248, 249, 250, 251, 254
  for Mencius Moldbug, 195, 200, 217
  for Patrick J. Buchanan, 128, 130
  for Richard B. Spencer, 231
  See also gender
Ferguson, Niall, 170, 177
Fichte, Johann Gottlieb, 57
film, 216
Fitzhugh, George, 149
Fjordman, 170, 175
Fleming, Thomas, 109, 125
Folkets nyheter, 264, 267
Folktribunen, 263
Foreign Legion, French, 23–24
foreign policy
  in the Alt-Right Manifesto, 235–36
  American, 103–04, 105, 123
  European, 235
  German, 46
Forney, Matt, 251, 270
Fortuyn, Pim, 175
Foucault, 155
Foundations of Geopolitics, The, by Alexander Dugin, 156–57, 162–63
Fourth Political Theory, by Alexander Dugin, 161
Framtid, 263
Francis, Samuel T., 129–30, 131, 150, 227, 228, 231
Frank, Hans, 40
Frankfurt School, 15, 93, 95, 105, 111, 128, 267
free speech, 230, 237
Freedom Party, Austrian, 150, 235
Freeman, Derek, 247
Freemasonry, 58, 64, 74, 156, 162
Fremskrittspartiet, 171
French Foreign Legion, 23–24
French Revolution, 25, 31, 42, 44, 60, 76, 210
Freson, Pierre, 97
Freund, Julien, 92
Friberg, Daniel, 259–73
  and the Alt Right, 261, 270–73
  and AltRight.com, 230–31
  and *American Renaissance*, 259
  and blogging, 260–61, 267, 269–70
  and civilization, 271
  and Counter-Currents, 259
  and culture, 267, 269

and democracy, 265
and Donald Trump, 271–73
on ethnicity, 262, 263, 265
and Guénonian Traditionalism, 266, 269, 273
and identitarianism, 266–68, 272
and immigration, 262–63
and liberalism, 259, 264–66, 270–71
and metapolitics, 259–73
and modernity, 271, 272
and National Socialism, 261, 269
and populism, 268–69
on race, 263
and white identity, 272
and white nationalism, 259, 264, 273
Frick, Wilhelm, 40
Futurism, 56–57, 248
futurism of Mencius Moldbug, 188–89, 190, 197

Gabriel, Brigitte, 175
Gaffney, Frank, 175
Gamergate, 250
gangs, 244–45
Gates of Vienna, 175
Gauchet, Marcel, 85
Gaullism, 74, 82, 83–84
gay culture, 243, 244. See also homosexuality
gay rights, 104, 130, 162
Gehlen, Arnold, 32, 92
Gemayael, Bashir, 171
gender
  and Alain de Benoist, 77
  and Carl Schmitt, 45
  and Jack Donovan, 242–46, 254
  and Julius Evola, 55, 60, 65
  and Mencius Moldbug, 197
  and Patrick J. Buchanan, 128, 130
  See also battle; feminism; heroism; homosexuality; masculinity; virility; warrior
genocide, 174, 229, 238. See also Holocaust
Gentile, Giovanni, 54
geopolitics of Alexander Dugin, 160
Germanic myth, 252
Giscard d'Estaing, Valéry, 80, 83
global elites. See elites: global
globalization
  for Alain de Benoist, 75, 76, 78, 86
  in the Alt-Right Manifesto, 236
  for Bat Ye'or, 170
  for Chantal Mouffe, 50
  for Ernst Jünger, 34
  for Greg Johnson, 210, 212
  for Patrick J. Buchanan, 126, 130
  for Richard B. Spencer, 233
God
  for Alain de Benoist, 80
  for Carl Schmitt, 44–45
  death of, 80
  for Jared Taylor, 137–38, 149
  for Julius Evola, 56–57, 58, 59, 60, 65
godhood, 212
Goebbels, Josef, 29
Goethe Prize, 33
Goethe, Johann Wolfgang von, 7
Goldberg, Jonah, 131
Golden Dawn, 165
Goldwater, Barry, 103, 106, 122
Golovin, Yevgenii, 155, 156
Gordian Knot, The, by Ernst Jünger, 31
Göring, Hermann, 40
Gottfried, Paul, 102–16
  and the Alt Right, 113, 116
  and authoritarianism, 111–12
  and civilization, 102, 109
  and class, 110–11
  and communism, 103–04
  and culture, 106, 107, 115
  and Daniel Friberg, 269, 273
  and democracy, 110, 111, 112, 114, 115
  on global elites, 110, 111

Gottfried, Paul (*cont.*)
   and identity, 103, 110
   and Israel, 104, 105
   and Jack Donovan, 231
   and the Jews, 104–05
   and liberalism, 110, 111–12, 114, 232
   and libertarianism, 108, 109
   on Marxism, 107, 111–12
   and modernity, 110–11, 116
   and multiculturalism, 110, 111, 232
   and National Socialism, 109
   and the neoconservatives, 102–08, 114–15
   and origin of "Alt Right," 226
   and paleoconservatism, 102, 109–13, 115–16
   and Patrick J. Buchanan, 125
   and the Republican Party, 102, 105–06, 109–10, 114, 116
   and Richard B. Spencer, 229, 230
   and the state, 111, 112
Gramsci, Antonio
   and Alain de Benoist, 74, 86
   Alexander Dugin compared to, 155
   cited by Mencius Moldbug, 193
   cited by Patrick J. Buchanan, 128
   and Richard B. Spencer, 226, 232
   as source of metapolitics, 260, 261
Grant, George, 235
Grant, Madison, 149, 213
Great Betrayal, The, by Patrick J. Buchanan, 127
Great Purge, The, by Paul Gottfried and Richard Spencer, 114, 236
GRECE
   and Alain de Benoist, 75–76, 78–80, 82–83, 84, 86
   and Guillaume Faye, 91, 92–94, 97–99
   and Robert Steuckers, 165
Griffin, Brad, 251
Griotteray, Alain, 83

Grjebine, André, 85
Group of Ur, 58–59, 62
Groupement de recherche et d'études pour la civilisation européenne. *See* GRECE
Guénon, René
   and Alain de Benoist, 76, 86
   and Alexander Dugin, 156, 159, 165, 166–67
   and Daniel Friberg, 266
   and Greg Johnson, 210
   and Guillaume Faye, 94
   and Julius Evola, 59
Gulf War, 127, 132. *See also* Iraq War
Günther, Hans, 83

H. L. Mencken Club, 108, 112–14, 116, 230
Habermas, Jürgen, 36, 50, 92, 99
Hagelin, John, 124
Hamas, 127
Harper, William, 149
Hart, Michael, 144
Hartz, Louis, 109
Haudry, Jean, 94
Haushofer, Karl, 165–66
Hedegaard, Lars, 175
Hegel
   and Carl Schmitt, 42, 47
   and Guillaume Faye, 92
   and Oswald Spengler, 8
   and Paul Gottfried, 108
Heimbach, Matthew, 165, 251
Heinlein, Robert, 190
Heliopolis, by Ernst Jünger, 30
Heraclitus, 5
Herbert, Frank, 211
Herder, 11
Heritage Foundation, the, 115
heroism
   for Alain de Benoist, 81
   for Ernst Jünger, 32

for Jack Donovan, 252
for Julius Evola, 60
for Nietzsche, 12
for Richard B. Spencer, 225
See also warriors
Herrnstein, Richard, 131
Hesse, Hermann, 3, 14
Heyer, Heather, 207
Hezbollah, 127
hierarchies
  for Jack Donovan, 244, 245–46
  for Jared Taylor, 139, 141
  for Mencius Moldbug, 187, 189, 195, 197
  of paganism, 79
  for Patrick J. Buchanan, 125
  of races, 75, 83
  for Richard B. Spencer, 233, 238
  in Traditionalism, 59–60, 61
  See also class; elites
Himmelfarb, Gertrude, 104
Himmler, Heinrich, 29, 63
Hinduism, 58, 60, 208
Hirsi Ali, Ayaan, 170
Hispanic interest organizations, 139
Hispanic migration, 127, 129, 148
Hitler, Adolf
  compared to Abraham Lincoln, 106
  meets Julius Evola, 64
  meets Oswald Spengler, 6
  offers Ernst Jünger seat in Reichstag, 26
  and Savitri Devi, 208
  See also National Socialism
Hobbes, Thomas, 42, 44–45, 47, 49
Hobbits, 66
Hoffman, Albert, 31
Hoffman, Hasso, 49
Holocaust
  and Ernst Jünger, 29
  and Greg Johnson, 229
  and Irmin Vinson, 214, 215
  and Leo Strauss, 109

Holocaust denial, 98, 132, 205
Holocaustomania, 215
homelands. *See* ethnostates
homophobia, 216, 248, 250, 251, 267.
  See also homosexuality
homosexuality
  Alain de Benoist on, 93
  Alexander Dugin on, 162
  Greg Johnson on, 216–17
  Guillaume Faye on, 93, 95
  Jack Donovan on, 243–44, 246–48, 250, 251, 254
  James O'Meara on, 216–17
  Mencius Moldbug on, 197
  neoconservatives on, 104
  Patrick J. Buchanan on, 130, 133
honor, 81, 244, 245, 248, 253
Hoppe, Hans-Hermann, 191, 230
Horizons of the Spirit, by Julius Evola, 64
Howard-Hobson, Juleigh, 216
Huckabee, Mike, 132
human nature, 138, 146, 147, 195, 249, 251
Human Rights' Service, 171
Hupin Georges, 75
Hyperborea, 60, 159, 161
hypermodernity, 95

Ibn Warraq, 175
Ideas Have Consequences, by Richard Weaver, 102
Identitarian Ideas seminar, 270, 271, 272
Identitarianism
  and Alain de Benoist, 73
  and Alexander Dugin, 159
  and Daniel Friberg, 266–68, 272
  and Jared Taylor, 138–41, 143, 150
  and Mencius Moldbug, 199
  and Patrick J. Buchanan, 127
  and Richard B. Spencer, 226

identity
  and Alain de Benoist, 73, 77–79
  and Carl Schmitt, 36, 46–48
  ethnic (*see* ethnicity)
  European, 73, 79, 93, 213, 224, 229 (*see also* nationalism: European; ethnicity: European)
  and Greg Johnson, 211, 213
  and Guillaume Faye, 92–93, 94–95, 96–97
  and Jack Donovan, 244–45, 267, 271–72
  and Jared Taylor, 139–41, 143, 144, 146, 150
  and Patrick J. Buchanan, 126, 127, 129
  and Paul Gottfried, 103, 110
  and Richard B. Spencer, 225–27, 228–29, 232–36, 237–38
immigration
  and Alain de Benoist, 78, 83
  and Daniel Friberg, 262–63
  and Greg Johnson, 211–12
  and Guillaume Faye, 76, 92–93, 96
  and Jared Taylor, 140–41, 149
  and Patrick J. Buchanan, 122–23, 129, 131, 132, 134
  and Progress Party (Norway), 171
  and Richard B. Spencer, 224–26, 229, 232, 235–36, 237–38
In Defense of Prejudice, by Greg Johnson, 207
Individualism, 78, 86, 128
Indo-European
  race and peoples, 82, 84, 208, 232 (*see also* Aryanism)
  tradition, 162
Inner Traditions, 66
Integral Traditionalism. *See* Traditionalism, Guénonian
Integral Traditions Publishing, 269

International Eurasianist Movement, 157
International Free Press Society, 175
internet, 188–89, 190, 194
  and Daniel Friberg, 260–61, 270, 271
  and Jack Donovan, 253
  and Mencius Moldbug, 198, 200
  and Richard B. Spencer, 224
  See also blogging
IQ and race, 131, 142–44, 194
Iran-Contra scandal, 123
Iraq War, 103, 112, 127, 132, 192
Ireland, Humphrey, 213
Irving, David, 205
Islam
  and Alain de Benoist, 76, 78
  and Alexander Dugin, 157, 162, 165
  and Bat Ye'or, 170–79
  and Charlottesville, 230
  and Greg Johnson, 212, 214
  and Guillaume Faye, 76, 91, 92, 96–98, 99
  and Oswald Spengler, 9, 11, 12
  and Patrick J. Buchanan, 128
  and Richard B. Spencer, 235
Islam and Dhimmitude, by Bat Ye'or, 176
Islamization, in the Alt-Right Manifesto, 235
Israel
  and Alexander Dugin, 162
  in the Alt-Right Manifesto, 237
  and Bat Ye'or, 172, 173, 174, 177–78
  and David Littman, 172
  and Greg Johnson, 215
  and Guillaume Faye, 95, 96, 98
  and Patrick J. Buchanan, 127, 132, 134
  and Paul Gottfried, 104, 105
  and Richard B. Spencer, 229, 234, 236, 238
  See also Zionism
Ivanov, Anatoly, 98
Izborsky Club, 163

Jaffa, Harry, 106–07
Japan, and Jared Taylor, 137, 140, 141–42, 148, 150
Jaspers, Karl, 30
Jaulin, Robert, 92
Jay, John, 147
Jefferson, Thomas, 146
Jensen, Arthur, 148
Jensen, Peder Are Nøstvold (Fjordman), 170, 175
Jews of Egypt, The, by Bat Ye'or, 176
Jews
   and Alain de Benoist, 74, 78
   and Alexander Dugin, 162
   in the Alt-Right Manifesto, 232, 233–34, 235
   and Carl Schmitt, 38, 41, 42, 49–50
   in Egypt, 171–72, 176
   and Ernst Jünger, 26, 29
   in Europe, 174
   and Greg Johnson, 204–05, 214–16, 251
   and Guillaume Faye, 94, 98
   intelligence of, 143–44
   and Jared Taylor, 143–44
   and Julius Evola, 55, 63–64
   in Israel, 174
   and Kevin MacDonald, 229
   in Morocco, 172
   as neoconservatives, 103, 106
   and Otto Weininger, 64
   and Patrick J. Buchanan, 132
   and Paul Gottfried, 104–05
   and Pierre Vial, 78
   and Richard B. Spencer, 225, 235–38
   See also anti-Semitism; Judaism
jihad, 170, 177–179.
   See also Counter-jihadism
Jihad Watch, 175
Joachim of Fiore, 8
Jobbik, 165
John Birch Society, 125–26
Johnson, Greg, 204–18
   and apocalypticism, 211
   and Counter-Currents, 143, 204
   and Daniel Friberg, 271
   and Guénonian Traditionalism, 204, 205, 208, 210, 216
   and immigration, 211–12
   and Jack Donovan, 250, 251, 252
   and the Jews, 204–05, 214–16, 251
   and liberalism, 204, 206, 210, 211, 216
   and metapolitics, 204, 207, 209
   and modernity, 204, 211, 216
   and Richard B. Spencer, 225, 226, 238
   and white nationalism, 204–05, 207–08, 211–16, 217, 218
Johnson, Lyndon, 127
Jones, Alex, 165
Judaism
   for Alexander Dugin, 162
   for Carl Schmitt, 42, 49–50
   for Guillaume Faye, 98
   for Julius Evola, 55, 64–64
   of Mencius Moldbug, 189
   for Oswald Spengler, 12
   of Paul Gottfried, 104
   See also anti-Semitism; Jews
Judeo-Christian
   civilization, 173, 177
   concept, 173–74, 234
   culture, 83
   values, 130, 231, 233
Julliard, Jacques, 85
Jung, Carl, 30
Junge Freiheit, 75, 85
Jünger, Ernst, 22–34
   accused of Fascism, 24, 26
   and Alain de Benoist, 73, 81
   and Alexander Dugin, 159, 161
   and anti-Semitism, 26, 29
   and Carl Schmitt, 39–40, 44

Jünger, Ernst (*cont.*)
    and Christianity, 30, 30–31
    and civilization, 24, 32
    and culture, 32, 34
    and democracy, 24, 25, 31
    and the First World War, 22, 23–24
    on German nationalism, 22, 24–26, 30, 33–34
    in and on the Second World War, 27–28, 29–30, 32, 34
    and Jack Donovan, 247
    and the Jews, 26, 29
    and Julius Evola, 62, 64
    and modernity, 22, 29, 31, 33–34
    and National Socialism, 22, 25–27, 29, 30, 32–33
    and pessimism, 26, 34
    and postwar Europe, 29–30
    and Richard B. Spencer, 226–27, 231
    and the state, 25, 31, 33, 34
    on technology, 31, 34
    and totalitarianism, 27, 31
    and violence, 24, 28, 33

Kabbalah, 64
Kahn, Jean-François, 85
Kalb, James, 114
kali-yuga, 60, 273
Karadžić, Radovan, 174
Kendall, Ward, 216
Kendall, Wilmoore, 106
King, Martin Luther, 228
Kirchheimer, Otto, 49
Kirk, Russell, 102, 103, 104, 106, 113–14, 115
Kissinger, Henry, 15
Klu Klux Klan (KKK), 124, 132, 225, 235, 252
Kohl, Helmut, 32–33
Korovin, Valerii, 158
Koselleck, Reinhart, 49
Kouprianova, Nina, 228
Krauthammer, Charles, 116
Krebs, Pierre, 98
Kremlin, the, 157–58, 163–64
Krisis, 73, 75, 85
Kristol, Bill, 116
Kristol, Irving, 104
kshatriya, 58, 59
Kuhn, Helmut, 49
Kurtagić, Alex, 228

La Torre, 62
Lasch, Christopher
    and Alain de Benoist, 75
    and Guillaume Faye, 92
    and Paul Gottfried, 105, 107, 110, 111, 116
Laurent, Jean-Pierre, 85
law, natural, 37
Le Gallou, Jean-Yves, 74, 83
Le Guin, Ursula, 190
Le Pen, Marine, 86
Lebanese Civil War, 173, 174
Lefebvre, Henri, 92
Lega Nord, 165
Leitkultur, 86
Leo Strauss and the Conservative Movement in America, by Paul Gottfried, 115
Leontiev, Konstantin, 160
Leontiev, Mikhail, 164
lesbian rights, 130
Lesquen, Henry de, 83
Leviathan, 28, 31, 41, 45
Leviathan in the State Theory of Thomas Hobbes, The, by Carl Schmitt, 45
Lévy, Bernard-Henri, 84
Lewis, Bernard, 173, 176
liberalism
    abandoned by Christopher Lasch, 116
    abandoned by *Telos*, 109–10
    allegedly promoted by Jews, 229
    challenged by McCarthy, 122

critiqued by Mencius Moldbug,
    190, 193
favored by Ernst-Wolfgang
    Böckenförde, 49
of Lyndon Johnson, 107
Martin Luther King as symbol of, 228
of Mencius Moldbug, 189
opposed by Alexander Dugin,
    157, 160–62
opposed by Ernst Jünger, 25
promoted by US, 127, 128
rejected by Alt Right, 226, 229
rejected by Carl Schmitt, 36, 39, 42,
    43, 47–48, 50–51
rejected by Conservative Revolution,
    39, 48, 160–61
rejected by Daniel Friberg, 259,
    264–66, 270–71
rejected by French New Right, 73
rejected by Greg Johnson, 204, 206,
    210, 211, 216
rejected by Guillaume Faye, 92, 96
rejected by Jared Taylor,
    137–38, 144–45
rejected by Juan Donoso
    Cortés, 42, 62
rejected by Leo Strauss, 231–32
rejected by Paul Gottfried, 110, 111–12,
    114, 232
rejected by Richard B. Spencer, 224–
    26, 229, 231, 233, 235–37
rejected by Steve Bannon, 199
rejected by Vladimir Putin, 271
of Weimar, 24
welcoming migration, 140–41
See also neoliberalism
liberals, opposing Alain de
    Benoist, 82, 84
libertarianism
    and Alain de Benoist, 83
    and Greg Johnson, 204
    and Jared Taylor, 144, 145
    and Mencius Moldbug, 187, 188,
        189–93, 196–97, 200
    and Patrick J. Buchanan, 125
    and Paul Gottfried, 108, 109
    and Richard B. Spencer, 227.
    (*See also* paleolibertarianism)
Liberty Lobby, 126
Limonov, Eduard, 156
Lincoln, Abraham, 106–07, 146–47
Little Lexicon of the European Partisan,
    by Guillaume Faye, 97
Littman, David G., 172–73, 176
Littman, Gisèle. *See* Bat Ye'or
Livy, 247
Llopart, José Antonio, 165
Locchi, Giorgio, 92
Locklin, Scott, and Jack Donovan, 250
Louis Napoleon, 25
Lovecraft, H. P., 14, 216
Löwith, Karl, 49
Lowry, Rich, 116
Lozko, Galina, 98
LSD, 31
Lübbe, Hermann, 49
Lynn, Richard, 142

Mabire, Jean, 76, 79, 94
MacDonald, Kevin
    and Daniel Friberg, 269, 273
    and Greg Johnson, 217
    and Jared Taylor, 143
    and Richard B. Spencer, 227, 228,
        229, 231
Machiavelli, 47, 191
Maffesoli, Michel, 92, 94
magic
    and Ernst Jünger, 23, 25
    and Julius Evola, 56, 57–58, 66
magic culture, 9, 11
magical idealism, 57
Malaud, Philippe, 83
Malofeev, Konstantin, 158, 164

Mamleev, Yuri, 155, 156
Man as Power of Julius Evola, 58
managerial class, 126
managerial state, 110, 111
Manent, Pierre, 85
Manji, Irshad, 170
Mann, Thomas, 3, 11, 14, 24
manosphere, 132, 217, 243–44, 249–51, 253, 254
Mansfield, Harvey C., 247
Marble Cliffs, The, by Ernst Jünger, 26–27
Marcel, Gabriel, 64
Marcuse, Herbert, 66, 105, 116
Marinetti, Filippo Tommaso, 56, 91, 248
marriage, 128, 130, 133, 144–45, 146, 197, 244
Marxism trilogy, by Paul Gottfried, 110–112
Marxism
    approved by Alain de Benoist, 77
    Austro-Marxists, 77
    and Carl Schmitt, 49
    debate with Alain de Benoist, 85
    discussed by Paul Gottfried, 107, 111–12
    dominant in France, 73
    and neoconservatism, 103, 105, 114–15
    opposed by Alain de Benoist, 75
    opposed in Italy, 54
    as seen by Alexander Dugin, 160
    as seen by Patrick J. Buchanan, 128, 130
    See also Austro-Marxists; neo-Marxism; post-Marxism
masculinity
    of Carl Schmitt, 45
    for Greg Johnson, 216
    for Jack Donovan, 242–48, 253
    for Julius Evola, 55, 60
    See also gender
Masonry, 58, 64, 74, 156, 162

Matrix, The, 194–95
Maurras, Charles, 235
May, Edward S., 175
McCain, John, 124
McCarthyism, 122
Meister Eckhart, 56–57
Melander, Peter, 266
Men Among the Ruins, by Julius Evola, 61
Mencius Moldbug. *See* Moldbug, Mencius
Mencken, H. L., 114. *See also* H. L. Mencken Club
Metapedia, 267–68, 269
Metaphysics of Sex, The, by Julius Evola, 65
metapolitics
    and Alain de Benoist, 74, 76, 85
    in the Alt-Right Manifesto, 234–35
    and Daniel Friberg, 259–73
    and Greg Johnson, 204, 207, 209
    and Guillaume Faye, 93
    and Mencius Moldbug, 200
    and Richard B. Spencer, 224–25, 238
Mexico
    and Donald Trump, 230
    and Jared Taylor, 148
    and Oswald Spengler, 7, 9
    and Patrick J. Buchanan, 129
    and Richard B. Spencer, 235, 237, 238
Meyer, Eduard, 7, 13
Meyer, Frank, 106
Meyrink, Gustav, 64
Michels, Robert, 191
Michelstaedter, Carlo, 55
Mila, Ernesto, 98
Miller, Henry, 14
Miller, Nathan F., 243
Miller, Stephen, 227
Mises, Ludwig von, 190–92, 197
Mishima, Yukio, 231, 247
Mitterand, François, 3

Modern Age, 107
modernity
  and Alain de Benoist, 79
  and Alexander Dugin, 161–62
  and Carl Schmitt, 44, 47
  and Daniel Friberg, 271, 272
  for Ernst Jünger, 22, 29, 31, 33–34
  and Greg Johnson, 204, 211, 216
  and Guillaume Faye, 91, 94–95
  and Julius Evola, 59–61, 63–64
  and Paul Gottfried, 110–11, 116
  See also postmodernity
Moeller van den Bruck, Arthur, 44, 81, 161
Mohler, Armin, 24, 30, 73
Molau, Andras, 98
Moldbug, Mencius, 187–200
  and the Alt Right, 187, 195, 199
  and authoritarianism, 187, 188, 191, 195, 197
  and blogging, 187, 188–89, 191, 192–94, 198–99
  and civilization, 191, 199
  and class, 194, 200
  and communism, 199–200
  and culture, 193, 194
  and democracy, 187–88, 191–93, 195–96, 199, 200
  and feminism, 195, 200, 217
  and hierarchies, 187, 189, 195, 197
  and liberalism, 189, 190, 193
  and libertarianism, 187, 188, 189–93, 196–97, 200
  and National Socialism, 193–94, 196, 198
  on progress, 188, 193, 197–99
  on race, 194, 197, 199
  and the state, 192, 193, 195, 197, 198
  and violence, 192, 194, 196, 197
  and white nationalism, 196, 199
Molnar, Thomas, 103

monarchy
  and Alain de Benoist, 82, 94
  and Hans-Herman Hoppe, 191
  and Julius Evola, 61
  and Mencius Moldbug, 189, 191, 197
Monnerot, Jules, 92
Morgan, John, 269, 270
Mosca, Gaetano, 191
Mossad, 172
Motpol, 267, 268, 269, 270
Mouffe, Chantal, 50
mountains, 56, 64
Movimento Sociale Italiano, 85
Moynihan, Daniel Patrick, 144–45
multiculturalism
  and Alain de Benoist, 85, 86
  and Greg Johnson, 214
  and Guillaume Faye, 95
  and Jack Donovan, 249, 252
  and Jared Taylor, 141
  and Paul Gottfried, 110, 111, 232
  and Richard B. Spencer, 224–26, 228–34, 236, 237–38
  See also liberalism; universalism
Multiculturalism and the Politics of Guilt, by Paul Gottfried, 110, 111, 232
multiracialism. *See* race
Murray, Charles, 131
music
  and Daniel Friberg, 259, 260–63, 264, 266, 270
  and Julius Evola, 66
Muslim Ban, 171, 212
Muslim Brotherhood, 127
Muslims. *See* Islam
Mussolini, Benito
  admires Oswald Spengler, 6
  admires work of Julius Evola, 63
  meets Julius Evola, 64
  targeted by Group of Ur, 58
  See also Fascism
Mutti, Claudio, 159, 165

Myrdal, Gunnar, 111, 149
Myspace, 267

Napoleon, 10
narcotics, 31, 56
Nash, George, 105–06, 108–09
National Bolshevik Party, 156, 164
National Endowment for the Arts, 130
National Endowment for the Humanities, 106
National Front, French, 75, 83, 86, 150, 235
National Policy Institute, 224, 225, 228
   and Daniel Friberg, 272
   and Jack Donovan, 242, 250, 251
   and Paul Gottfried, 113
National Review
   and Patrick J. Buchanan, 125, 129, 131–32
   and Paul Gottfried, 106, 110, 113, 115–16
National Socialism
   and Alain de Benoist, 83
   and Alexander Dugin, 159, 160, 161
   and Carl Schmitt, 39–41, 48, 50
   and Conservative Revolution, 161
   and Daniel Friberg, 261, 269
   and Ernst Jünger, 22, 25–27, 29, 30, 32–33
   and Greg Johnson, 205, 208, 209, 216, 217, 218
   and Guillaume Faye, 92, 93
   and Jack Donovan, 252, 253
   and Jared Taylor, 138
   and Julius Evola, 63
   and Mencius Moldbug, 193–94, 196, 198
   and Oswald Spengler, 4, 6, 14, 16
   and Patrick J. Buchanan, 132
   and Paul Gottfried, 109
   and Richard B. Spencer, 225, 226, 233, 234, 235, 252
   and Yevgenii Golovin, 156
   See also National Socialism, modern

National Socialism, modern, 262, 263. See also Neo-Nazism
National Socialist World, 208
nationalism, 50, 161, 196, 213
   American, 122, 127, 132
   Arab, 172
   German
      and Carl Schmitt, 36–37, 39–40, 46–48, 50
      and Ernst Jünger, 22, 24–26, 30, 33–34
      and Julius Evola, 63
   English, 231
   European, 75, 79, 92, 95, 259
      and Alain de Benoist, 85
   French, 74, 75, 76, 79, 92, 93, 235
   Italian, 57, 61
   Mexican, 129
   Norwegian, 171
   Palestinian, 174
   Russian, 86, 155, 157–58, 164
   Serbian, 171, 174
   Swedish, 262, 266
   See also Identity: European; white nationalism
nationhood, bases of, 140
Native Americans, interest organizations for, 139
natural law, 37
Natural Right and History, by Leo Strauss, 102
nature, 29, 56, 97. See also human nature
Nazi Party. See National Socialism
Nazism. See National Socialism
NCS, The, by Guillaume Faye, 97
Negro Family, The, by Daniel Patrick Moynihan, 144
neo-Confederates, 112–13, 126, 196, 230. See also Confederate statues; South, American

neo-fascism
  Alain de Benoist accused of, 77, 84
  of Giorgio Almirante's Movimento Sociale Italiano, 85
  not attractive, 79
  Richard B. Spencer appeals to, 238
  See also Fascism
neo-Marxism, 260
Neo-Nazism
  Alain de Benoist alleged to be, 75, 82
  at Charlottesville, 252
  and Guillaume Faye, 98
  and Mencius Moldbug, 199–200
  and Milo Yiannopoulos, 199–200
  and Richard B. Spencer, 225, 226, 230, 235, 236
  See also National Socialism, modern
neoconservatives
  and Greg Johnson, 204
  and Patrick J. Buchanan, 124–27, 131
  and Paul Gottfried, 102–08, 114–15
neoliberalism, 214
neopaganism
  and Alan de Benoist, 76, 79, 82
  echoed by Richard B. Spencer, 209
  and Ernst Jünger, 30
  and Greg Johnson, 208
  and Guillaume Faye, 93, 94–95, 96
  and Jack Donovan, 244, 252–53, 254
  and Joshua Buckley, 205
  and Julius Evola, 58, 61, 62
  of *Tyr*, 205
Neoplatonism, 30
Neoreaction, 187, 188
Neue Rechte, 75
New Consumer Society, The, by Guillaume Faye, 97
New Deal, 102, 108, 114, 122, 125, 196
New Ideological Issues, by Guillaume Faye, 97
New Jewish Question, The, by Guillaume Gaye, 94, 98

New Left
  and Alain de Benoist, 75
  in the Alt-Right Manifesto, 232, 235, 236
  and Christopher Lasch, 107
  and the Democratic Party, 104
  and Guillaume Faye, 99
New Right vs. Old Right, by Greg Johnson, 207
Niemöller, Martin, 30
Nietzsche Archive, 6
Nietzsche, Friedrich
  and Alain de Benoist, 80, 83
  and Ernst Jünger, 23, 25
  and Greg Johnson, 209
  and Guillaume Faye, 92, 94
  and Julius Evola, 55
  and Oswald Spengler, 7, 12, 16
  and Richard B. Spencer, 226, 231
Nixon, Richard, 122, 123
Nomos of the Earth, The, by Carl Schmitt, 48
Non-Conformists, 73
nonmodernism, 94
Nordic culture, 267–68
Nordic god-men, 60
Nordic League, 264–69, 270
Nordicism, 76
Nordiska förbundet. *See* Nordic League
Nordiska förlaget, 264, 269
Norse myth, 247, 252
North American New Right, 207
Nøstvold Jensen, Peder Are (Fjordman), 170, 175
Nouvelle école, 73, 92
Novalis, 57
Nowiki, Andy, 216
Nyborg, Helmuth, 142

O'Meara, James, 216, 251
oath of Delphi, 93
Obama, Barack, 192

Occidental Dissent, 251
Occidental Quarterly, The, 143, 205–06, 209, 217, 224
Odinism, 247
Operation Werewolf, 253
Orbaum, Sam, 177
Orcival, François d', 79
organic society, 211
Orientations, by Julius Evola, 61
Ortega y Gasset, José, 13
Orthodox Judaism, 64
Orthodoxy (Christian), 158, 160, 164, 165, 166, 169
Orwell, George, 193

Pagan Imperialism, by Julius Evola, 58, 61, 62
paganism. *See* neopaganism
paleoconservatism
   and Greg Johnson, 204
   and Patrick J. Buchanan, 121, 125–27, 129–31
   and Paul Gottfried, 102, 109–13, 115–16
   and Richard B. Spencer, 227, 231
   and Taki Theodoracopulos, 227
paleolibertarianism, 126, 132
Palin, Sarah, 133
Palmgren, Henrik, 231, 272
Pamyat, 85
Papen, Chancellor Franz von, 39, 40, 41
Papini, Giovanni, 56
Pareto, Vilfredo, 191
Passing of the Great Race, The, by Madison Grant, 149
Path of Cinnabar, The, by Julius Evola, 54
patriarchy, 243–48, 254
Paved with Good Intentions, by Jared Taylor, 144–46
PayPal, 207
Peace, The, by Ernst Jünger, 30
perennialism, 59, 76, 85

Perot, Ross, 124, 133
pessimism
   for Alain de Benoist, 81
   for Carl Schmitt, 45, 47
   for Ernst Jünger, 26, 34
   for Julius Evola, 65
   for Oswald Spengler, 12–13, 14–15
   for Patrick J. Buchanan, 133
   See also apocalypticism
Phenomenology of the Absolute Individual, by Julius Evola, 57
Philadelphia Society, the, 115
Phillips, Melanie, 170
Piccone, Paul, 75, 99, 105, 110, 116
Pierce, William, 208–09, 211, 214
Pinochet, Augusto, 197
Pipes, Daniel, 175
Plato, 42, 57, 61
Plavšić, Biljana, 174
Podhoretz, Norman, 104, 115
Polignano, Michael J., 206
Political Duties of German Youth, by Oswald Spengler, 4, 5
Political Theology, by Carl Schmitt, 37, 38, 43–44, 46, 49, 50
Political Theology II, by Carl Schmitt, 49
Poniatowski, Michel, 83
populism
   and American electorate, 122, 132
   of Christopher Lasch, 107, 110
   of Daniel Friberg, 268–69
   distinct from Burkeanism, 109
   of Donald Trump, 230
   draws new attention to *The Decline of the West*, 15
   electoral victories of, 271
   Fascists as, 61
   favored by Kremlin, 167
   of Greg Johnson, 211
   increases relevance of work of Carl Schmitt, 51
   of Jared Taylor, 150

of Marine Le Pen, 86
of McCarthyism, 122
of Mencius Moldbug, 199
of Patrick J. Buchanan, 121
of Paul Gottfried, 112
of Paul Piccone, 110
of Pim Fortuyn, 176
of Rick Santorum and Mike Huckabee, 133
of Sarah Palin, 133
of Sweden Democrats, 261
See also demagoguery
post-Marxism, 191, 193, 260
postmodernity, 75, 77, 80, 91, 108, 205
power
    for Carl Schmitt, 42, 43, 45
    for Guillaume Faye, 99
    for Julius Evola, 56–58, 60, 61
    male, 246, 249
    for Mencius Moldbug, 195, 196–98
    of the National Socialists, 40
    of Oswald Spengler's Cultures, 10
    of the state, 34, 146
    Will to Power, 80
Preston, Keith, 114
Preve, Costanzo, 75
Price, W. F., 250
programmer culture, 189–90
Progress Party (of Norway), 171
progress, belief in
    of all American political parties, 110
    of American Jewish conservatives, 105, 115
    of American Left and liberals, 103, 109, 111, 122
    challenged by Oswald Spengler, 33
    criticized by Jack Donovan, 248–49
    criticized by Mencius Moldbug, 188, 193, 197–99
    evangelical, 114
    hegemony of, 191–93, 195–96, 197–98
    impact of First World War on, 25
    opposed to traditionalism, 111
    questioned by Alain de Benoist, 81
    progressive elites, 187, 193, 196.
        See also progress, belief in: of American Left and liberals
Progressives, 75
Prokhanov, Alexander, 156, 163, 164
Prussianism and Socialism, by Oswald Spengler, 4, 5, 13
Public Interest, 115
Putin, Vladimir, 163–64, 271
Pythagoreanism, 58

Quesada, Ernesto, 13

race
    and Alain de Benoist, 77–78
    and Alexander Dugin, 162
    in the Alt-Right Manifesto, 232–33
    as an alternative to nation in the Americas, 213
    American electorate, 122
    and Daniel Friberg, 263
    and Ernst Jünger, 26
    and Greg Johnson, 206, 210–13, 213–16
    and Guillaume Faye, 95, 96
    and H. L. Mencken Club, 113
    and IQ, 131, 142–44, 194
    and Jack Donovan, 242, 252
    and Jared Taylor, 137–51
    and Julius Evola, 63–64
    and Mencius Moldbug, 194, 197, 199
    and Michael Hart, 144
    and Oswald Spengler, 4, 6, 14
    and Patrick J. Buchanan, 125, 126, 129–30, 131
    and Paul Gottfried, 113
    and Richard B. Spencer, 224–29, 231–38
    See also white identity; white nationalism; white supremacism

race realism, 144, 146, 216, 231
racial consciousness, white, 226
Racial Nationalist Library, 98
racial theory. See race
racism
    alleged of Alain de Benoist, 75, 82–83
    Guillaume Faye charged with, 94
    See also race
Radix Journal, 228, 230–31, 250
Rand, Ayn, 204
Ravello, Enrique, 98
Reagan, Ronald, 80, 103–06, 108, 123
Real Right Returns, The, by Daniel Friberg, 271
Red Ice, 230–31
Red Ice Creations, 272
Red Ice Radio, 271
red pill, the, 194–95
Reform Party, the, 124
Reghini, Arturo, 58, 59
Regnery William, 114, 224
Reich, Third. See National Socialism
Renaissance, 60
Renner, Karl, 77
Republican Party, the
    and Greg Johnson, 211
    and Mencius Moldbug, 196
    and Patrick J. Buchanan, 121, 122–25, 127, 130, 131–34
    and Paul Gottfried, 102, 105–06, 109–10, 114, 116
    and Richard B. Spencer, 228, 233
    duopoly with Democrats, 124
Resistance, French, 83
Revolt Against the Modern World, by Julius Evola, 59–61
revolution, aesthetic, 37
Revolution. See under name of
revolutions, nature of, 74
Reynolds, Glenn, 190
Rhodesia, 79

Ride the Tiger, by Julius Evola, 65, 270–72
riding the tiger, 270–71
Right from the Beginning, by Patrick Buchanan, 121
RightOn.net, 270
Rimbaud, Arthur, 55
Rising Tide of Color, The, by Lothrop Stoddard, 149
Robert, Fabrice, 226
Robertson, Pat, 123
Robertson, Wilmot, 213, 231, 233
Rodionov, Igor, 156
Röhm, Ernst, 248
Rollet, Maurice, 76
Roman Catholicism. See Catholicism
Roof, Dylann, 237
Roosevelt, Franklin, 121, 196
Roosh V, 250
Rosenberg, Alfred, 26
Rostand, Jean, 79
Rothbard, Murray, 190–92
Rougier, Louis, 79
Rushton, J. Philippe, 142
Russia
    and Alain de Benoist, 85–86
    and Alexander Dugin, 155–67
    culture of, for Oswald Spengler, 9
    and Europe, 160, 162, 167
    and Guillaume Faye, 97, 98
    in Second World War, 28
    and socialism, 14–15
Russian Civil War, 161
Ryn, Claes, 112

sacrifice, animal, 253
Santorum, Rick, 133
Sartre, Jean-Paul, 79
Satan, Church of, 243
Schelling, Friedrich Wilhelm Joseph (von), 57
Schiller, 11

Schleicher, Canceller Kurt von, 39, 41
Schmitt, Carl, 36–51
   and Alexander Dugin, 159
   and anti-Semitism, 36, 38, 39, 41, 45
   and apocalypticism, 36, 37, 44, 45
   and authoritarianism, 39, 41, 43–44, 48, 51
   and Christianity, 37, 42, 43, 44–45, 46, 62
   as Conservative Revolutionary, 24–25
   and democracy, 42, 43, 44, 48, 49
   on dictatorship, 38–39, 42–44, 48, 51
   and Ernst Jünger, 30, 32
   and the First World War, 37–38
   on German nationalism, 36–37, 39–40, 46–48, 50
   and Guillaume Faye, 92, 99
   and identity, 36, 46–48
   and Judaism, 42, 49–50
   and Julius Evola, 62
   and liberalism, 36, 39, 42, 43, 47–48, 50–51
   and modernity, 44, 47
   and National Socialism, 39–41, 48, 50
   as part of Conservative Revolution, 39, 44, 48
   and pessimism, 45, 47
   and Richard B. Spencer, 226–27, 231
   and the Jews, 38, 41, 42, 49–50
   and the Second World War, 41
   and the state, 36, 38–44, 46–49, 51
   used by Alain de Benoist, 78
   and the Weimar Republic, 36, 39, 42–43, 46
Schneider, Gregory, 116
Schuon, Frithjof, 165
science fiction, 66, 190, 192, 211
Scott Fitzgerald, Francis, 14
Scruton, Roger, 175
Search for Historical Meaning, The, by Paul Gottfried, 108, 109
Seeckt, Hans von, 5

Seen from the Right, by Alain de Benoist, 80
Seleznev, Gennadii, 157, 164
Seneca, 7, 12
Sex and Character, by Julius Evola, 55
Sex and Deviance, by Guillaume Faye, 95, 98
Sex and Ideology, by Guillaume Faye, 95
sex, Guillaume Faye on, 95, 97, 98
sexual
   harassment, 250, 251
   predation, 249
sexuality, 55, 65, 95, 97, 243, 246. See also homosexuality
Shadows of the Rising Sun, by Jared Taylor, 141
Sheehan, Thomas, 205
Sherman, Alfred, 174
Siegel, Jacob, 113
Silicon Valley, 189–90
Simmel, Georg, 92
Six-Day War, 105
skinheads, 260, 263, 270
Sky Without Eagles, A, by Jack Donovan, 243
slavery, 211
Sobran, Joe, 129
social Darwinianism, 25, 78, 96, 149. See also evolution
Social Democratic Party, Prussian, 39
social democrats, French, 84, 85
socialism
   and Alain de Benoist, 77, 81
   and Ernst Jünger, 33
   and Greg Johnson, 205
   and Oswald Spengler, 4, 5, 13, 14
   and Richard B. Spencer, 226, 229, 231, 232, 234, 236
Socialist Party, in Italy, 62
society, bourgeois, 3, 62
Sombart, Werner, 63
Sorel, Georges, 81

South Africa, 225
South America, 48, 66, 143
South, of United States
   and Greg Johnson, 211, 212
   and Jared Taylor, 146, 148–50
   and Mencius Moldbug, 196
   and Patrick J. Buchanan, 122, 125–26, 129, 132
   and Paul Gottfried, 103, 106, 116
   See also neo-Confederates
Southern Agrarians, 102
southern hemisphere, 97
Spearhead, 250
Spencer, Herbert, 92
Spencer, Richard B., 224–38
   on African Americans, 229, 232, 235, 238
   and anti-Christianity, 229, 231, 233
   and anti-Semitism, 225, 226, 231, 233–34
   and Antonio Gramsci, 226, 232
   and capitalism, 224, 226, 229, 233–34, 235
   and civilization, 231, 232, 233, 236
   and Conservative Revolution, 226, 231
   and culture, 224, 232, 236
   and Daniel Frieberg, 272
   and Donald Trump, 217, 225, 230, 237, 238
   on ethnicity, 225–26, 229, 232–34, 237
   on Fascism, 225, 231, 233–34
   and Greg Johnson, 217
   and Guénonian Traditionalism, 231, 251, 252–53
   and hierarchies, 233, 238
   and identity, 225–27, 228–29, 232–36, 237–38
   and immigration, 224–26, 229, 232, 235–36, 237–38
   and Israel, 229, 234, 236, 238
   and Jack Donovan, 242, 250, 252
   and the Jews, 225, 235–38
   and liberalism, 224–26, 229, 231, 233, 235–37
   and metapolitics, 224–25, 238
   and multiculturalism, 224–26, 228–34, 236, 237–38
   and National Socialism, 225, 226, 233, 234, 235, 252
   and paleoconservatism, 227, 231
   and Paul Gottfried, 113, 114, 116
   on race, 224–29, 231–38
   on the Republican Party, 228, 233
   and socialism, 226, 229, 231, 232, 234, 236
   and the state, 231, 234, 236, 237
   and totalitarianism, 233, 238
   and violence, 225–27, 231, 234, 238
   and white identity, 224–26, 228–29, 235, 238
   and white nationalism, 224, 225, 228, 231, 232
   and white supremacism, 225, 227
Spencer, Robert, 170, 175, 176
Spengler, Oswald, 3–17
   and Alain de Benoist, 81
   and capitalism, 6, 14
   and Christianity, 10, 11, 12
   and civilization, 3–4, 6–8, 10–11, 16
   and culture, 8–12, 14–15
   and democracy, 6, 13, 14, 16
   ignored by Carl Schmitt, 44
   and Islam, 9, 11, 12
   and National Socialism, 4, 6, 14, 16
   as part of Conservative Revolution, 24
   and pessimism, 12–13, 14–15
   on race, 4, 6, 14
   and Richard B. Spencer, 231
   and socialism, 4, 5, 13, 14
   on technology, 3, 6, 10
   translated by Julius Evola but not important to him, 62, 64
   and the Weimar Republic, 14, 16

Spillane, Mickey, 216
Srinivasan, Balaji, 200
Stahlgewittern. See *Storm of Steel*
Stahlhelm, 24
Star Wars, 66
State of Exception of Carl Schmitt, 37, 40, 41, 43, 44, 45
State of Normality of Carl Schmitt, 37, 40, 43, 45, 49
state, the
   and Alain de Benoist, 77, 82–83
   and Alexander Dugin, 160
   and Carl Schmitt, 36, 38–44, 46–49, 51
   and Ernst Jünger, 25, 31, 33, 34
   and H. L. Mencken, 114
   for Jack Donovan, 245, 248–49
   and Jared Taylor, 150
   and Julius Evola, 61
   managerial, 110, 111
   for Mencius Moldbug, 192, 193, 195, 197, 198
   Patrick J. Buchanan, 121–22, 125, 132
   and Paul Gottfried, 111, 112
   and Richard B. Spencer, 231, 234, 236, 237
Stauffenberg Plot, 27
Stauffenberg, Schenk zu, 30
Stepanov, Vladimir, 155–56
Steuckers, Robert, 75, 97, 165
Steyn, Mark, 170, 175
Stoddard, Lothrop, 149, 213
Stoicism, 12, 65
Storhaug, Hege, 171
Storm of Steel by Ernst Jünger, 23
Strange Death of Marxism, The, by Paul Gottfried, 110, 111
Strasser, Otto, 165
strategy of tension, 65
Strauss, Leo
   criticizes Carl Schmitt, 49
   and Greg Johnson, 204

   and Paul Gottfried, 102, 108, 109, 115
   and Richard B. Spencer, 231–32
   See also Straussians
Straussians, 108, 115
Stülpnagel, Carl Heinrich von, 27
Stülpnagel, Otto von, 27
Suez War, 172
Sullivan, Andrew, 247
Sunić, Tomislav, 217
Surkov, Vladislav, 164
surrealism, 25
Suzuki, D. T., 64
Svensk ungdom, 264
Sweden Democrats, 261, 263
Swedish Resistance Movement, 263
SYRIZA, 165
System to Kill the Peoples, The, by Guillaume Faye, 97

Taft, Robert, 125
Taguieff, Pierre-André, 78, 83, 84
Taki's Magazine, 227
Tantrism, 58
Tao Te Ching, 58
Taoism, 58
Tarchi, Marco, 66, 75
Taubes, Jakob, 49
Taylor, Jared, 137–51
   on African Americans, 139, 140, 144–47, 149–50
   and *American Renaissance*, 144, 146, 148, 149, 150
   and anti-Semitism, 143–44
   and civilization, 138, 142
   contributes to AltRight.com, 228
   and culture, 140, 141
   on demography, 140, 141, 145, 149, 150–51
   on ethnicity, 139–41, 142–44, 148–50
   and hierarchies, 139, 141
   and identitarianism, 138–41, 143, 150
   and identity, 139–41, 143, 144, 146, 150

Taylor, Jared (cont.)
　and immigration, 140–41, 149
　and Jack Donovan, 250
　and the Jews, 143–44
　on Jews, 229
　and liberalism, 137–38, 144–45
　and libertarianism, 144, 145
　on race, 137–51
　and Richard B. Spencer, 225–26, 227, 231, 234, 237
　welcomes term "Alt Right," 226
　and white identity, 138–41, 143, 150–51, 228
tech culture, 189–90
technology
　Alain de Benoist on, 81
　Carl Schmitt on, 38
　Ernst Jünger on, 31, 34
　Julius Evola on, 59
　Mencius Moldbug on, 200
　Oswald Spengler on, 3, 6, 10
Telos, 75, 99, 105, 107, 109
terrorism, 64–65, 170–71, 173–74, 178, 234–35, 237, 253
Thatcher, Margaret, 80
Theodoracopulos, Taki, 227
Theory of the Absolute Individual, by Julius Evola, 57
Theory of the Partisan, by Carl Schmitt, 46
Theosophy, 54
Thiel, Peter, 200
Third Reich. *See* National Socialism
Thiriart, Jean, 79, 165
thought control, 187
Thule, 159, 161
Tiger, Lionel, 247
tiger, riding the, 65, 270–72
Tillenon, Yann-Ber, 98
Tjiel, Peter, 187
Tolkien, J.R. R., 66
Tönnies, Ferdinand, 92

Torigian, Michael, 99
Total Mobilization, The, by Ernst Jünger, 26, 30
totalitarianism
　and Alexander Dugin, 160, 161
　and Bat Ye'or, 178
　and Carl Schmitt, 41
　and Ernst Jünger, 27, 31
　and Jack Donovan, 248
　and Julius Evola, 61
　and Richard B. Spencer, 233, 238
Toynbee, Arnold, 8, 14
traditionalism, Catholic, 82, 94, 98
Traditionalism, Guénonian
　and Alexander Dugin, 155, 156, 159, 163, 165, 166, 167
　and Daniel Friberg, 266, 269, 273
　and Greg Johnson, 204, 205, 208, 210, 216
　and Richard B. Spencer, 231, 251, 252–53
　See also Evola, Julius; Guénon, René
traditionalism, Kirkian and Agrarian
　and Jared Taylor, 149
　and Paul Gottfried, 102–103, 104, 105, 106–09, 111, 114
Traditionalist Worker Party, 251
transcendence
　and Carl Schmitt, 44
　and Julius Evola, 54–61, 63, 65, 67
transcendental meditation, 124
transcendental pragmatics, 43
tribalism; of Jack Donovan, 242, 244–48, 253, 254
Trifkovic, Srdja, 174
Trotha, Thilo von, 26
Truman, Harry, 147, 148
Trump, Donald
　compared to Patrick J. Buchanan, 133–34
　and Daniel Friberg, 271–73
　differs from Mencius Moldbug, 199

endorsed by Jared Taylor, 141
hailed by Richard B. Spencer, 217, 225, 230, 237, 238
and the Muslim Ban, 171
not supported by Jack Donovan, 251–52
phenomenon, 237
and the Reform Party, 124
sounds neoreactionary notes, 199
supported by Alexander Dugin, 162
supported by Greg Johnson, 212–13
themes in White House of, 187, 200
Truth, Justice, & a Nice White Country, by Greg Johnson, 207
Tulaev, Pavel, 98
Tyr, 205, 207
Tzara, Tristan, 57

UKIP, British, 150
Ukraine, 157–58, 161–62, 164
Ungern-Sternberg, Baron von, 161
Unite the Right, 207, 230, 252
United Nations Commission on Human Rights, 172
United Nations, 126
United States
  and Europe
    for Alain de Benoist, 83, 84, 86
    for Guillaume Faye, 95, 96, 97
    for Patrick J. Buchanan, 128
    for Richard B. Spencer, 236
  European heritage of
    for Greg Johnson, 210
    for Jared Taylor, 150
    for Patrick J. Buchanan, 126, 131–32
    for Richard B. Spencer, 224–25, 226, 229, 231, 235
  See also anti-Americanism
universal morality
  rejected by Jack Donovan, 242, 247
universalism
  and Alain de Benoist, 82, 247
  and Carl Schmitt, 47, 50, 140–41
  and Guillaume Faye, 93
  and Jack Donovan, 242, 246–48
  and Mencius Moldbug, 193, 194
Unqualified Reservations, blog by Mencius Moldbug, 188, 192–94, 198–99, 200
Untergang des Abendlandes. See *Decline of the West*
Uprooting of European Identity, The, by Richard B. Spencer, 228
Ur, Group of, 58–59, 62

Valizadeh, Daryush, 250
Vanguard Radio, 228
Venner, Dominique, 73, 79, 231
Vial, Pierre, 76, 93, 94, 98
Vico, Giambattista, 8
Vietnam War, 103, 104–05
Vigrid Party, 261
Vinson, Irmin, 214
violence
  and Alain de Benoist, 81
  and Alexander Dugin, 158, 162, 179
  and Carl Schmitt, 45
  domestic, 249
  and Ernst Jünger, 24, 28, 33
  and Greg Johnson, 211, 212
  and Italian Fascism, 61
  and Jack Donovan, 242, 243, 245, 248, 254
  and Julius Evola, 58
  and Mencius Moldbug, 192, 194, 196, 197
  in postwar Italy, 65
  and Richard B. Spencer, 225–27, 231, 234, 238
  and the Wolves of Vinland, 253
virility, 10, 55, 246
Vishnu, 208
vitalism, 7, 9
Vlaams Belang, 150

Voegelin, Eric, 103
Volk, 25. *See also* ethnicity
völkish ideology
    Alain de Benoist accused of, 76
    and Alexander Dugin, 155–56, 159, 161, 165, 167
    and Guillaume Faye, 94
    of Herman Wirth, 63
    of some members of GRECE, 78
Volksgeist, 8, 11
Volodin, Viacheslav, 164
Voloshin, Alexander, 164
von Mises, Ludwig, 190–92, 197
von Papen, Chancellor Franz, 39, 40, 41
von Schleicher, Canceller Kurt, 39, 41
Von Thronstahl, 66

Wadlow, René, 172
Waggener, Paul and Mattias, 252
Wallace, George, 122–23
war
    Alexander Dugin on, 161–62
    between North and South, 60
    cultural, 226, 267
    Guillaume Faye on, 96
    Jack Donovan on, 248
    in Middle East, 229
    regime during, 38, 45, 47–48
    See also under name of war;
    See also heroism; jihad
war crimes, 41, 132
Warren, David, 130
warriors
    Alain de Benoist on, 81
    Alexander Dugin on, 161
    Greg Johnson on, 21, 209
    Jack Donovan on, 245, 248
    Julius Evola on, 58, 59, 63
    See also battle; heroism; virility
Washington Summit Publishers, 228
Way of Men, The, by Jack Donovan, 243, 247, 250, 253

We and the Others, by Alain de Benoist, 77
Weaver, Richard, 102, 103
web, world-wide. *See* internet
Weber, Max, 36, 38, 42, 44, 155
Weimar Republic
    crises of, 39
    disappoints Oswald Spengler, 16
    discredited by Oswald Spengler, 14
    engagement of veterans in, 24
    lack of sympathy of Carl Schmitt towards, 36, 39, 42–43, 46
Weininger, Otto, 55, 63–64
white America, in the Alt-Right Manifesto, 235
white ethnostate
    of Greg Johnson, 204, 210–11, 213, 225
    of Richard B. Spencer, 225, 228, 229, 233–35, 237–38
white genes, 132, 211
white genocide, 229
white homelands. *See* white ethnostate
White House
    of Donald Trump, 187, 200
    of Gerald Ford, 123
    of Richard Nixon, 122
    of Ronald Reagan, 123
white identity
    and *American Renaissance*, 129
    and Daniel Friberg, 272
    and Donald Trump, 237
    and Jared Taylor, 138–41, 143, 150–51, 228
    and Patrick J. Buchanan, 127, 129, 131
    and Richard B. Spencer, 224–26, 228–29, 235, 238
White Identity, by Jared Taylor, 139, 144
white nationalism
    and Alexander Dugin, 162
    and antifeminism, 251
    at Charlottesville, 230
    and Daniel Friberg, 259, 264, 273

and Donald Trump, 212
  and Greg Johnson, 204–05, 207–08,
    211–16, 217, 218
  and Jack Donovan, 242, 243, 252
  and Jonas De Geer, 270
  and Mencius Moldbug, 196, 199
  and Patrick J. Buchanan, 131–32
  and Paul Gottfried, 113
  and *Radix Journal*, 228
  and Richard B. Spencer, 224, 225,
    228, 231, 232
  of the Wolves of Vinland, 253
white power, 262–63, 265–67, 269, 273
white race, 232, 233
white racial consciousness, 237
White Russians, 161
white supremacism
  and Alain de Benoist, 79, 82, 85
  and Alexander Dugin, 162, 165
  at Charlottesville, 230
  and David Duke, 124
  of Dylann Roof, 237
  and Greg Johnson, 211
  and Guillaume Faye, 98
  and Jared Taylor, 149
  and Richard B. Spencer, 225, 227
  and Southern writers, 149
Why We Fight, by Guillaume Faye, 98
Wiginton, Preston, 165
Wilde, Oscar, 55
Wilders, Geert, 175
Willinger, Markus, 226
Wirth, Herman, 63, 156, 159
Wolves of Vinland, 244, 247, 252–54
Worker, The, by Ernst Jünger, 26, 62
World Union for Progressive Judaism, 172

World War, First
  Carl Schmitt and, 37–38
  Ernst Jünger and, 22, 23–24
  impact of, 25, 32, 81, 248
  Julius Evola and, 56
  Mencius Moldbug on, 196
World War, Second
  Carl Schmitt and, 41
  Ernst Jünger in and on, 27–28,
    29–30, 32, 34
  in France, 83, 92
  impact on reception of Oswald
    Spengler, 4, 13
  impact on Russia, 159
  Mencius Moldbug on, 196
  Patrick J. Buchanan on, 132

Yankevich, Leo, 216
Yarvin, Curtis. *See* Moldbug, Mencius
Yeltsin, Boris, 156
Yeoman, Andrew, 251
Yiannopoulos, Milo, 199, 200, 251
Yockey, Francis Parker, 165, 227, 231
You Asked for It, by Greg Johnson, 207
YouTube, 224, 228, 270, 272
Yuzhinsky Circle, 155–56, 164, 166

Zhirinovsky, Vladimir, 157
Zionism
  as example for the Alt Right, 238
  Greg Johnson on, 204
  Guillaume Faye on, 95, 98
  Paul Gottfried on, 104
  Richard B. Spencer on, 234
Zolo, Danilo, 75
Zyuganov, Genadii, 157